MAGNIFICENT MISSOURIAN

MAGNIFICENT
MISSOURIAN

The Life of Thomas Hart Benton

BY ELBERT B. SMITH

1958

J. B. LIPPINCOTT COMPANY

PHILADELPHIA · NEW YORK

To the memory of Effie C. Huffaker, scholar, gentlewoman, and peerless teacher of the very young, this book is dedicated in love and gratitude.

ACKNOWLEDGEMENTS

MY DEBTS GO BACK twenty years to Jessie Heron and Verton Queener of Maryville College, who labored valiantly against heavy resistance, and continue through a chain of gifted teachers at the University of Chicago. To Professors Avery Craven, William T. Hutchinson, and Walter Johnson I owe much of my general approach to the period. Professor Craven in particular first stimulated my interest in Benton and opened my eyes to the richness and universal significance of ante-bellum American history. He has read the manuscript with a critical eye, and his generosity, kindness, and encouragement have gone far beyond the possibility of repayment. My former colleague David Behen listened long and patiently, and occasionally defied my runaway metaphors at the risk of being trampled.

Less directly, former colleagues Pauline Botty, Clarence Gould, Stephen Fulkerson, Elizabeth Sterenberg, and Vern Bullough have contributed encouragement and assistance in varying degrees. Librarians too numerous for mention have treated and served me as an honored guest, but James Pirie, Dorothy Forney, and Elmer Rogers deserve special mention for their success in providing me with rare items via the inter-library loan procedure.

And finally, if personal contentment adds to creativity, Jean and the noisy five, Randy, Stevie, Amy, Scotty, and Bobby, have done most of all.

ELBERT B. SMITH

Iowa State College

FOREWORD

In APRIL, 1858, the citizens of the sovereign state of Missouri were moved by a universal topic of conversation. Thomas Hart Benton was coming home for the last time. This huge, domineering man, with his inexhaustible energy, indomitable will, and savage temper, had overshadowed their political lives from the noisy, brawling, boastful days of his younger manhood down through the final hours when he had stamped among them with the angry yet majestic tread of an old buffalo. But now he was dead, and friend and foe alike paused to measure the significance of his passing.

For thirty-eight years he had stood in plain view above them all when Americans looked in the direction of Missouri, but for the last eight of those years the Old Bison had often walked in lonely solitude, rejected by those whom he had tried to serve best. For two dozen years in the United States Senate he had enjoyed unprecedented popularity and political power among his fellow Missourians. He had moved from one furious political conflict to another, often leading and always supporting the national policies most in tune with the needs and emotions of the numerous and raucous devotees of frontier democracy in a democratic age. But then he had had a vision and had become a prophet, and his power had vanished in the fire of his determination to turn a nation away from catastrophe. His people,

7

and at times even his family, had not understood this and, when his prophecies conflicted with their emotions and ambitions, had rejected him.

Thomas Hart Benton in the year 1820 had seen a future America stretching from ocean to ocean, extending its culture and influence to the shores of the Celestial Kingdom itself. No one saw the size, power, and world significance of the America-to-be earlier or more clearly, and he never lost this vision. By 1843, however, he saw a shadow blurring his dream. In the great political issues of that year he foresaw an America torn by the pangs of conscience and bitterness of sacrifice in an unjust war against Mexico. He looked further and saw a nation divided by sectional struggles over the spoils of this war which, if unchecked by the voices of reason, could lead only to disunion, civil war, and tragedy. The Mexican War came, and its aftermath was all that he had feared. He was ill-prepared by temperament and experience to play the role of peacemaker, but if he lacked skill and finesse for the task, there was no shortage of devotion, courage, and dedication. If the tone of his voice was not always the tone of reason, the words he spoke usually were like brief glimmerings of clear sky on a day filled with thunderclouds. His tragedy was the tragedy of America, and his story is in many ways the story of America in the days leading to its greatest sorrow.

CONTENTS

MAGNIFICENT MISSOURIAN

CHAPTER I

———————————

THE CRADLE

THE YEAR 1782 was important in the annals of a young nation struggling for birth. For all practical purposes the Revolutionary War had ended, but the American peace delegation was still striving desperately to avoid a betrayal by French allies who wished to see the Ohio River and the Allegheny Mountains become the boundaries of the new America. The issue for a time was in doubt, but by the year's end, the vast western land claims of Jesse Benton and many like him were at least reasonably safe from the threat of British or Spanish control. This point marked also the beginning of a period of economic depression and political chaos, but within a decade the young republic would be tottering back toward stability on the weak but growing legs of the new Constitution. The year saw also the birth of three men who would achieve fame defending the soon-to-be Constitution, each according to his own understanding and in his own way. Daniel Webster of New England arrived in January. In the Carolinas, John C. Calhoun and Thomas Hart Benton were born during the same week in March. Henry Clay of Kentucky was already five years old.

Thomas Hart Benton, son of Jesse and grandson of Samuel, was born near the village of Hillsboro, in the North Carolina piedmont. His parents were living on a small plantation near the little Eno River, and were rather typical members of the self-made aristocracy so often generated by the fluid structure of society and the broad opportunities of frontier colonial America.

Indeed, perhaps no American colony ever offered more equality of opportunity for those armed with the ambition and ability to become unequal than did the rough, turbulent, and democratic society which was eighteenth century North Carolina. Other colonies were richer in the prizes offered, but none offered a better chance for a fair start in the race. And few men have been better equipped to thrive in such an environment than one Samuel Benton, who came on the scene by way of Virginia at some point before the middle of the century. Intelligent, acquisitive, not overly scrupulous, and bursting with energy and imagination, Samuel fought his way through ups and downs to a position of wealth and influence, leaving a trail of outraged enemies in his wake.

Granville County, Samuel's theater of operations, was governed by the local justices of the peace, who not only exercised wide judicial powers and duties, but also controlled the sheriff, the clerk of the court, the local militia, and the vestrymen. At a price, they regulated every legal phase of colonial life, and this power was self-perpetuating, because the governor usually appointed justices only upon the recommendation of the justices already serving. The sheriff was almost always selected from among the justices, and this office offered additional rewards, such as the opportunity to steal public funds and manipulate elections either by influence or the miscounting of votes.

By 1752, if his opponents can be believed, Samuel Benton was a justice well aware of the perquisites of his office. In 1756 he declined reappointment because of the disability involved in serving a jail sentence for debt, but by 1760, he was not only restored as a justice, but had become also a member of the provincial assembly in an election which raised widespread doubts as to the sheriff's ability to count accurately. By 1764 he was also serving as clerk of the court and register of deeds, and in his spare time was cultivating a large and rich plantation which carried the dignified name of Oxford and possessed a library famed throughout the area. Neighbors believed Samuel to be a graduate of Oxford University, but there is no evidence to sup-

port this pretension. In the same year Samuel introduced a bill
to divide Granville County and establish a new county seat in
his own section. He himself emerged as head of the commission
for creating the new county, and by a strange coincidence the
county seat was located on his own plantation at Oxford. Holding the more important county offices, Samuel directed the
county from his own private courthouse. An angry spokesman
for the radical reform movement known as the Regulation
claimed that Benton charged exorbitant fees without authority
and then offered poor men the privilege of paying their fees by
performing common labor on his own plantation.[1]

Samuel survived the Regulation, however, and died peace-
fully in 1770, leaving his wife and three sons well established
with a wealthy estate. Jesse, the eldest son, was named execu-
tor, but the greater share of the land and slaves went to Samuel,
Jr. Jesse was honored by a special gift of the old man's case of
pistols and ten pounds to buy a sword.

If Jesse Benton did not carry on the local dynasty built by his
aggressive father, he left more friends and fewer enemies. His
administration of the few offices he held occasioned little comment, and he pursued the legal profession with diligence and
considerable success. In politics and personal life he remained
the quiet conservative. When the Regulators went on the
march again, he joined the "Redressors," and helped oppose
this democratic threat to the welfare of all good men of property and stability.

In one respect Jesse Benton was a man of vision and daring.
When the Transylvania Company bought the great tract of
Tennessee and Kentucky wilderness known as the Watauga
Purchase, Jesse was one of the original partners. In March,
1775, a little band of adventurers met the Cherokee Indian
leaders in a wild mountain retreat for a business deal, and for
two thousand pounds Jesse and his friends bought much of
what later became Tennessee and Kentucky. By 1788 Jesse
held claims to some twenty-four thousand acres, most of it in
Tennessee. Unfortunately the legality of the claims was precarious, and despite Jesse's efforts and sacrifices, his heirs were
finally able to take possession of only a small portion of the
tracts. This remnant, however, provided the foundation for

his family's later position of wealth and leadership in Middle Tennessee.

When the Revolution came to North Carolina, the essentially conservative Jesse remained neutral until July, 1781, when he was elected to the state assembly. There he served on a committee for raising a patriot militia and opposed a bill to protect creditors against debtors by adjusting debts in proportion to the depreciation of the continental currency. The ghost of old Samuel may have been disturbed considerably. By the fall of 1781 Jesse was finally in active service with the patriots. Tory bands had been plundering the countryside, and Jesse joined a party of volunteers who marched out to find their camp and report its whereabouts to the army of General Butler. This led to the final destruction of the North Carolina Tories.[2]

Meanwhile, Jesse had accepted the responsibilities of marriage and a thriving family, and as a husband and father he stands out most clearly as a man of sensitivity and depth of spirit.[3] His choice of a bride was fortunate. Ann Gooch Benton was a beautiful and intelligent young woman with iron in her soul. She was destined to endure tragedy and hardship undaunted and finish a long and active life many decades later in St. Louis, managing her own property and answering the requests of her sons for business advice and information to the end. Called Nancy by her husband, Ann was the only child of James Gooch, younger brother of Sir William Gooch, who had a distinguished career as royal governor of Virginia. Orphaned in early childhood, she was brought to North Carolina by her uncle, Thomas Hart, who was a friend of both Samuel and Jesse Benton. Thomas Hart was wealthy and prominent, a political leader, a colonel in the Revolutionary army, and a landowner and speculator of remarkable success.

The first two children of Jesse and Nancy Benton were daughters. The third was a son, and it was only natural that he be given the proud name of his mother's guardian. Little Thomas was followed in rapid succession by Jesse, Jr., Nancy, Samuel, Nathaniel, and Susannah. These, with the older sisters, Peggy and Polly, were a gay and happy group. Their mother was warm and affectionate, and seemingly gifted with boundless energy, as she managed her extensive household and found time to teach and amuse the children between tasks.

The security and prestige of this happy but expensive tribe rested on a frail support. Looking to the future, Jesse Benton had mortgaged his immediate property heavily to increase his new landholdings and clear the titles to the great stretches of western lands which could pay dividends only in the future. Although a large landholder, with 1,408 acres in North Carolina in addition to his enormous western claims, Jesse was constantly harassed by the need for money. He bought a larger family plantation on an installment basis from Thomas Hart, and, although Hart was lenient, the payments were a constant problem. He also served as county clerk and practiced law with some success, but even these additional sources of income did not bring security.[4]

Finally came the terrible moment when Jesse knew beyond doubt that his days were numbered by tuberculosis. As the disease slowly pulled him down he made one last effort. In the winter of 1790 he sent an agent to survey ten thousand acres in western Tennessee near the present site of Memphis, with instructions to relocate the claims if they conflicted with prior claims of others, and the surveyor returned in the fall to report a successful mission. By the end of the winter of 1790-91, Jesse Benton was dead, and the multitude of little Bentons had lost a kind father and faithful guardian.

Life had been a happy lark for robust, active little Thomas Benton until the death of his father, but this event brought the first realities of heartbreak and responsibility. He never forgot the day when his grief-stricken mother placed his hand on that of his baby sister and softly announced that he must now be head of the family. For several days he was inconsolable, but time and the skillful counsel of a kindly chaplain finally eased the shock. The eight-year-old boy understood that the past could not be restored and that the future would include responsibility as well as play.[5]

For the widow Benton needed all the help and comfort available. Striving valiantly to the end, Jesse had nonetheless fallen in the midst of the battle, and his large estate carried an enormous burden of debt. The thirty-two-year-old Nancy was determined not only to meet her obligations, but also to rear her

eight children in the style which they deserved. She was resolved also to stay in the beautiful country of her happy years,
despite the possible lure of her western landholdings. The sale
of a considerable amount of property, the renting of mills on
one of the plantations, and the generosity of her guardian,
Thomas Hart, made her objectives possible, but the process involved endless anxiety and hard work. Thomas Hart, himself
one of her major creditors, accepted her bond on two occasions,
and when debts required the sale of still more of the estate in
1792, he bought it to hold in trust for her and the children.[6]
Perhaps young Thomas Benton in these years acquired the be-
ginnings of his lifetime distrust of banks and any related credit
institutions tending to encourage debt.

Working endlessly at supporting her large brood, Nancy
Benton still found time to continue in the role of devoted
mother. She taught her children a respect for learning and
sought to impress upon them her own profound religious faith
and moral principles. A devout Episcopalian, she strongly opposed tobacco, liquor, and gambling, and Thomas remained a
puritan in these respects throughout his life. Nancy was particularly attentive in the training of her eldest son. Jesse had
left a library excellent for its day, and by the time Thomas was
ten, she had launched him upon a program of reading in such
tomes as Plutarch's *Lives,* the records of British state trials, and
British history in general. In old age he would still recall his
intense sorrow, anger, and excitement, as he lived with the
tyrants, victims, and heroes of British history. In addition to
his home training, the boy attended school in Hillsboro, where
he was taught by Richard Sanford, a young New England immigrant who later served many years in Congress.[7]

Thus, during the childhood years following the death of his
father, young Thomas Benton continued to live the pleasant
life of a fairly privileged young aristocrat. In addition to slaves
for doing the work and the advantages of family position and
education, he and his brothers had dogs, guns, horses, and great
stretches of untamed field and forest in which to use them. By
the age of sixteen, he was rapidly acquiring the physical
strength and endurance which later would be unique even

among the more rugged specimens of a frontier America noted
for the brawn of its citizens.

This carefree existence, however, was probably never completely free from the knowledge of his mother's problems, and
Thomas must have felt a strong sense of responsibility as he left
home in January, 1798, to enroll at the University of North
Carolina. The university was only four years old, and had a
student body of forty, many of them the sons of wealthier tide-
water families. The curriculum included Latin and various
Latin classics, the Greek Testament, algebra, astronomy, trig-
onometry, arithmetic, geography, Millot's *Elements of History,*
Paley's *Moral Philosophy,* and Blair's *Lectures.* In addition to
classroom education, much of the university life revolved about
the two literary societies, the Philanthropic Society and the
Dialectical Society. Everyone joined one or the other, and their
meetings included declamations, delivery of original composi-
tions, and debates on various subjects.

At this stage of his life, the sixteen-year-old Thomas apparently felt qualified and obligated to enforce the public morals.
When John Lytle, a small boy attending the adjacent grammar
school, committed an "act of indiscretion," the newly enrolled
university freshman assumed the duty of threatening punishment. John's older brother, Archibald, also a university student, entered the discussion by calling Benton a "damned
rascal." After an exchange of various threats and uncompli-
mentary titles, Benton produced a loaded pistol, and Archibald
departed in search of a weapon for himself. Fortunately, a professor managed to disarm Benton before his adversary returned,
and a possible tragedy was averted. Young Thomas later assured a faculty investigation that he had not intended to kill
Archibald, but only to wound him. If Benton appeared in this
affair to be something of a bully, little John Lytle's alleged
misconduct was not specified, and Thomas was at least equally
prepared to do battle with big brother Archibald. Life as the
only "man" in a large family including five younger children
probably increased both his feelings of self-importance and his
sense of responsibility in matters of discipline. Another small
boy named John Duncan Toomer long remembered Benton as
a kind friend and protector, and the young man's standing

with fellow students apparently did not suffer from the Lytle affair. Accepting the incident as just another example of boyish exuberance, the university faculty inflicted no punishment.[8]

Meanwhile, the aggressive young Benton joined the Philanthropic Society and entered its deliberations with gusto. By February 12 the "Phi" was debating Benton's question: "whether is it most conducive to public Utility that the power of disposing of posts under the Government should be vested in the President or legislative body?" Two weeks later he and two fellow students opened the debate on "Wheather has the French revolution been attended with beneficial effects with regard to mankind in general." This question was decided in the negative. At each of the two following weekly meetings he again opened the discussion of "wheather ought Americans to wish success to the French or British." At one meeting Benton was fined five cents for an "irregularity." Politics apparently began to lose its glamor, because on March 12 they agreed that the topic for the following week would be "Wheather is a murderer or the seducer of an innocent maid the most worthy of destestation." [9]

Unfortunately, however, the academic career of young Thomas Hart Benton came to an inglorious end before he was privileged to debate the relative merits of murderers and seducers.

His mother apparently did not supply him with sufficient funds to keep pace with the gay and free spending of his three roommates, who carefully noted his frugal habits and constant lack of cash. The proud boy was caught in the struggle between high social position and inadequate means for meeting its demands. Academic bills came due, but he waited in vain for the money from home needed for paying them, and he was probably unwilling to complain to a mother already bearing heavy responsibilities.

The historian, unhappily, does not create his own characters, and must often seek understanding from the sparsest of facts. On March 19, 1799, Thomas Benton was expelled by unanimous vote from the Philanthropic Society and therewith the university, and his confession as related in the deposition of his roommates remains the uncontradicted explanation for his disgrace.[10] Locked in Benton's trunk was a purse given him for safekeeping by roommate Fleming Saunders, and one night Thomas simply unlocked the trunk and took nine dollars from the purse. When Saunders asked for the purse and discovered the loss, Benton feigned surprise, and the matter was not pressed. Shortly afterward, he took a pocketbook with eight dollars from the coat of roommate William Cherry during the night, and at some point took eighteen dollars from roommate Marmaduke Baker. When Benton was finally reported to be carrying a new and rare Federal one dollar bill similar to the one lost by Cherry, the roommates confronted him with their suspicions, searched him, and forced a verbal confession of all three thefts. Two days after his expulsion, he was questioned also by one Thomas King, and admitted further that he had had a key made to fit King's trunk and had stolen from him also.

While the only record of these events is the testimony of Saunders, Cherry, Baker, and King, the truth of the essential charge cannot be doubted. The boy who had sought a pistol contest with Archibald Lytle, who would later repel an armed attacker with well-aimed stones, and would on two occasions exchange shots with adversaries at point-blank range, would never have submitted so tamely to such humiliation if inflicted unjustly. No one could have made a false charge of this nature against Thomas Hart Benton without either paying with his life or shooting Benton in self-defense.

Benton's young friend, John Duncan Toomer, recalled many years later that Benton had sadly confided to him that because money expected from home to pay his college dues had not arrived, he had taken money from a roommate, hoping to replace it before the theft could be discovered. Having been charged, he had confessed and must now go home in disgrace.[11] The only support for the truth of this explanation lies in the fact that Benton was highly intelligent, and the actions described in the testimony of his roommates were almost incredibly stupid for one attempting to perpetrate a deliberate theft without detection. The money of Saunders was locked in a trunk to which Benton alone had a key. That he could have expected Saunders to accept such a loss without suspicion is possible, but most unlikely, and the succeeding thefts so close upon the first were equally lacking in precaution. This line of reasoning must be approached with caution, however, because the argument that only stupid people commit stupid deeds is an obvious historical absurdity.

The impact of this miserable experience on the proud, sensitive soul of an ambitious, imaginative seventeen-year-old is beyond question. The following years would be characterized by the most scrupulous honesty in his public life and by ambitions almost compulsive in nature. For many years, any reflection upon his honor was ground for an immediate challenge to a duel, and he compensated for the loss of a college career by becoming one of the best educated men of his time. Tradition at the University of North Carolina has it that when he was preparing to ride away amid the jeers of his fellow students, he turned for a final word and shouted, "I am leaving here now, but damn you, you will hear from me again." Twenty-eight years later, the Philanthropic Society of the University of North Carolina passed a resoultion that "Thos. H. Benton be readmitted a member of our Society" and that "a certificate stating the same, signed by the President and Sec.ᵗ be transmitted to Mr. Benton." In 1832, some four years after this reinstatement, Senator Thomas Hart Benton wrote the society a friendly letter promising a contribution of twenty dollars.[12]

The sternness or compassion or both with which Nancy Benton greeted the downfall of her favorite son can only be guessed. She may have felt a partial responsibility and been goaded to take greater risks and make heavier personal sacrifice for his welfare. Within two years, she resolved to take the family to the wilderness holdings left by Jesse's adventurous speculations, and this decision may well have resulted from her son's disgrace. She shared his ambitions, and they both surely knew that a future career in North Carolina might be stifled in its infancy by this early blot on his reputation. America was big in 1800, and life could begin anew elsewhere, free, at least temporarily, from the errors of the past. Nancy had always loved the beautiful Eno Valley. Leaving the scenes of her happiest years was not easy, but in 1801 she and her big, nineteen-year-old son loaded the family and a handful of slaves into the wagons for the long, long trek to Middle Tennessee.

CHAPTER II

———·✦———

THE LAWYER

THE LITTLE CARAVAN of children and slaves which Nancy and Thomas Benton led across the towering green mountains probably traveled through Tennessee over a dusty road choked with fellow immigrants. Tennessee was a frontier literally catapulting toward civilization, and the rich limestone soils of the Nashville area were attracting settlers by the thousands.

The Bentons finally settled on a homestead of 2,560 acres on the West Harpeth River, which was apparently all they could prove of the twenty thousand acres in Tennessee originally claimed by Jesse. Their new home was twenty-five miles south of Nashville, bordering lands left to the Indians in recent peace settlements after long and bitter warfare. The widow Benton had lived a fairly sheltered life in North Carolina, and the countless Indians swarming about the household of young children made her new situation difficult. More people were required, and she met the need by establishing a little colony. She offered leases without rent for seven years and moderate rents thereafter, and the area was soon populated. A handful of cabins, a rude log schoolhouse, a rough meetinghouse, and some roads and mills composed the new village of Benton Town, and the wilderness was on its way to civilization. The Bentons built themselves a two-story house partly of stone, which, though not luxurious, contrasted sharply with the average frontiersman's

floorless cabin. Their relatively large landholdings and a handful of slaves clearly distinguished them as members of the
emerging frontier aristocracy.

Young Thomas worked hard at managing the family estate,
but farming had little appeal for him. Far more important was
the need to continue the education which had been so rudely
and painfully interrupted, and he must now teach himself. In
later years he remembered that history and geography were his
"light reading," while national, civil, and common law constituted his studies.[1]

Though farming provided a living, the aspiring young student of self-taught law could not appreciate the insecurities and
disappointments always present in this noble profession. The
year after the Bentons arrived in Tennessee, the cotton crop
was magnificent, but at market time the port of New Orleans
had been closed, and the crop could not be sold. The next year,
another splendid cotton crop was nursed up to the point of har-
vest, only to be destroyed by a premature frost. This was
enough. Young Thomas Hart Benton threw his plow into a
corner and announced that he would follow a profession less
subject to the whims of luck and nature.

In 1804, the large, self-assured young man deserted the plantation and went off to teach school in a small settlement called
Duck River. This was to be a period of learning as well as
teaching, and he decided to sell some land for money to buy
lawbooks. Fortunately, however, there was a friend who believed in the young man's future. Nicholas Hardeman, a Franklin merchant, offered to buy the books and wait for payment
until the newly appointed schoolteacher could earn the money.
The process of self-education, the problems involved in this
brief venture, and the young teacher's sense of humor were recorded in a letter to his merchant creditor:

I am now at Duck River, where I shall remain for the winter.
Those books I spoke of when with you, I request you will now
send me. They are Mittot's General History; Legar's Fred on
William; Cooke's Voyages; Goldsmith's Natural History; Gray's
Fables and Sheridan's Dictionary. Further, I want you to send
me an almanac, not a last year's one, a pen knife, best double
bladed, a comb to straighten out my hair with, a pair of black

cotton stockings, half a dozen quires of common writing paper, and one pair of strong coarse shoes, any size.

In an idle hour, to prevent the evaporation of Peter's industry, I would be glad if you get him to transcribe my account, and when he has finished, I desire that Peter will remind you from time to time of sending it to me, as a knowledge of its amount will interest me in the regulation of my financial concerns. I am, dearest sirs, more thine than mine own.

Many years later, Senator Benton expressed his gratitude to the Hardeman family by refusing payment for some important legal services.[2]

Perseverance was finally rewarded. Hugh Lawson White, John Overton, and George Campbell, superior court justices all famous in Tennessee history, granted Thomas Benton a license to practice law, and on July 15, 1806, he was admitted to the bar. Middle Tennessee was filled with litigants quarreling over a wide variety of subjects, ranging from land claims to outright robberies, with homicide never far distant, and the young attorney was soon busy. He was only twenty-four years old, but he had the physical size and aggressive courage which were often more essential to the frontier lawyer than mere legal ability and experience, and such distinguished elder colleagues as Andrew Jackson, James Robertson, Judge McNairy, and Major Thomas Hardeman, gave him friendship and aid.

The swiftly moving years of early manhood were pleasant and exciting for Thomas Benton, but there were also days of tragedy and difficulty. He loved his family dearly, and the younger sisters usually looked to him as the father whom they had lost. By the spring of 1807 the dreaded family curse, tuberculosis, had struck again, and Peggy and Nancy were dead.

In the midst of this grief other ghosts appeared. Patrick Campbell sued the Bentons for eight thousand dollars, charging that twenty-four years earlier Jesse had bound himself along with John Rice to pay Campbell five hundred pounds if Rice did not provide Campbell one thousand acres or fine him five thousand acres elsewhere. The case was tried three times before Campbell finally received a judgment of four thousand dollars, a bitter blow in the light of the Benton family's inability to legalize Jesse's many land claims of the same period. Also near the end of 1807 their benefactor, Colonel Thomas Hart, sued them for past debts, and a sheriff's sale of 1,280 acres of the family property was advertised to settle his claim. Hart may have brought suit only to save the estate from Campbell, with the idea that his prior claims might induce Campbell to settle on a reasonable basis. Regardless, the Bentons lost half their property, Campbell was pacified, and Uncle Thomas Hart remained friendly. Dying in 1810, Hart left them a legacy of 3,200 acres.[3]

*   *   *   *   *   *   *   *

In his twenty-sixth year the young lawyer began a public career, and for the first time became reasonably visible as the logical product of his environment and early experiences. Physically he was large, powerful, and utterly fearless. He had read much, but his learning remained untested, and genuine intellectual ability was still a question. He had known the love and experiences of membership in a large family, suffered heartbreak and adolescent humiliation, and carried heavy responsibilities, but their effects in terms of compassion, understanding, kindness, and patience were as yet unrevealed by any records available to the historian. These would later emerge, but in 1808 the young man's clearest trademarks were aggressiveness, ambition, determination, imagination, and a boundless self-confidence.

Family background and home training had been conservative influences on this son of the Gooches, Harts, and Carolina Bentons, and Thomas had gone to Tennessee in 1801 considering himself a Federalist. Actual experiences, however, had prepared him for an easy change. He thrilled at the magnificent imagination and immense possibilities of the Louisiana Purchase and was compelled to respect the wisdom of Jefferson. Then, the obviously respectable leaders of Tennessee were Jeffersonians whose every move contradicted the Federalist charges of Jacobin radicalism. Dreaming of a political career in Tennessee, Benton could easily recall many valid reasons for having been a Jeffersonian all along. Aristocratic planters in appearance, the heirs of Jesse Benton had been in reality an overburdened family constantly on the make and forever engaged in economic struggle. His own problems had been difficult

enough to create a genuine sympathy for others in the same position, and he had not forgotten his humiliation in North Carolina at the hands of those more privileged than himself. Perhaps
above all, the Jeffersonians were the party of nationalism and
expansion, dedicated to the development of a West abounding
in equality of opportunity, and Thomas was the grandson of
Samuel Benton. If he lacked Samuel's devotion to the great
god Mammon, he still sniffed the same air in frontier Tennessee that his grandfather had found so delectable in colonial
North Carolina. Tennessee was rapidly moving from frontier
to plantation, equality of opportunity was giving way to inequality for those of ability, and Thomas Benton found the
process an exhilarating challenge. His nation was on its way to
greatness, and he would grow with it.

Benton's earliest blow for Jefferson and nationalism came in
1806, when Aaron Burr passed through Nashville, leaving a
trail of confusion and excitement over his intentions. A large
and noisy public gathering at Franklin, Tennessee, left no
doubt as to its attitude. With Benton as secretary, the meeting
passed resolutions of deepest loyalty and praise for the national
Government and highest affection and respect for Thomas Jefferson.

The young attorney's next venture marked the real beginning of his career. Both as lawyer and litigant he had long
shared the ordinary man's frequent irritations with the cum-
bersome and inefficient Tennessee judicial system. A complete
reorganization was needed, and Thomas Hart Benton was
ready to assume the task. Powerful judges and lawyers, backed
by wealthy interests, would defend the system, and Benton was
a struggling novice with only eighteen months' experience at
the bar, but the self-appointed reformer had certain advantages
of his own. His self-confidence was breathtaking, and he was
instinctively acting in step with the increased democracy toward
which Tennessee was moving.

Almost weekly from February through September in 1808,
Benton, writing as "Sir John Oldcastle," a British reformer executed some four centuries earlier, carried on a one-man newspaper war against the judicial system.[4] Justice, he declared, had
become injustice for the common people because of delays,

quibbling over minor legal points, and the unfair organization
of the courts. Untrained county magistrates could easily be
misled by clever lawyers even when sober, yet, "In some of the
back counties the magistrates have no sense even of common
decency; little tin cups of whiskey circulate among them on the
bench, and they get so drunk they are hardly able to keep their
seats—yet these men have the whole body of British and American law spread out before them, and are invested with authority to decide upon it!" Also, declared Sir John, people often
had to endure long and expensive delays after traveling a hundred miles to reach a superior court. Every man should have
justice in the center of his own county, and its denial was a
clear-cut oppression. In citing Sir Edward Coke against the
system, Benton expected "a better issue than . . . Coke experienced, because a different tribunal will judge me; the plain
good sense of the sovereign citizens of the state of Tennessee,
and not the princely wisdom of his majesty James the first."

The young man's bold and brash words were carefully supported with references to older authorities like Coke, Black-
stone, Swift, Tucker, and Hume, and the reformer offered a
constructive program. A single supreme court should sit alter-
nately in Knoxville and Nashville with powers of review over
lower courts. Six judicial circuits should be established with a
court of one judge in each to sit three times a year in each
county composing its district. County courts should be deprived of law jurisdiction except in minor cases and remain free
for their primary duties of county administration. All distinctions between cases in law and cases in equity should be eliminated. The long-deceased professional justice of the peace,
Samuel Benton, would have been shocked by his grandson's
heresy.

Sir John welcomed opposition, sending his "compliments to
those who turn up their noses." He wrote "for those who suffer
by the abuses of the present court system, not for those who
gain fortunes by it." By September Thomas Benton was feeling the power of his twenty-six years: "I defy the combined
talents of the bench and of the bar in the discussion of this subject. I dare them to attack me. I pledge myself to the public to

crush every assailant on the ground with as much ease as a giant
would crush an egg-shell."

The judicial question identified Benton with the people, but
he was no flaming radical. In the Presidential election of 1808
he attacked Monroe fiercely as a friend of the "Atheist Tom
Paine" and a tool of the Jacobins who delivered up American
commerce to French spoliations and tried to involve America in
war with Britain. Monroe, he said, had "fraternized with the
Sans Culotte Bloodhounds so cordially, and entered their mad
projects so enthusiastically, that general Washington was under
the necessity of recalling and disgracing him. . . ." Above all,
said Benton, Napoleon obviously had designs upon America,
and a pro-French President would therefore be dangerous.[5]

The war against the court system made Benton famous overnight. His law practice grew rapidly, and by 1809 he was a
candidate for the state Senate. Attorney Benton had created the
judiciary issue and he was on the right side of it. When the
next legislative session met in Knoxville, Senator Benton was
there to assume a position of leadership.

The Senate's newly arrived judiciary expert immediately became head of a committee to consult with the House on prospective changes in the system, and within two months most of
his recommendations were enacted. Many inefficiencies were
eliminated, and most of the handicaps of the poor man seeking
justice in Tennessee were removed. It was a genuinely remarkable achievement, and the boisterous young Senator could
justly be proud.

The daring young lawmaker also offered a resolution for a
committee to consider granting slaves a fairer trial in cases
where their lives were at stake and to review the laws related to
emancipation of slaves and the regulation of free Negroes. He
hoped to secure the right of trial by jury for slaves, but his colleagues were unconcerned with such matters, and nothing was
done.

The legislature of a thirteen-year-old state dealt with prece-
dent-making issues. One Zebulon Baird, having killed a friend
in a fit of passion, submitted a well-endorsed petition asking for
immediate freedom because of the distressed condition of his
family. Baird was most penitent: "I am astonished at myself,

and loathe myself, and repent before God who delighteth in mercy, and I hope and believe has, for his mercy's sake forgiven my sin, which emboldens me to come in the next place, to cast my case at your feet, praying your honorable body to cast an eye of pity on my distressed circumstance." Benton and six colleagues were not moved to the point of following the divine example cited by Baird and petitioned the legislature to reject the request. It would establish too dangerous a precedent.

Perhaps Benton was busiest and happiest as a member of the Committee on Lands, a subject upon which he was already developing firm convictions. He long remembered Granny White, an elderly widow who had come to Tennessee with two grandchildren and little else. A generous neighbor gave her a fifty-acre plot covering two facing hills. Part of a hill had to be dug out to make room for a house, and her pumpkins had to be propped with sticks to prevent their rolling away, but with this small beginning she and her grandchildren ultimately expanded their holdings and became wealthy. Such happenings and the experiences of his own family convinced Benton at an early age that the rapid settlement of the public lands by hardworking citizens was far more important to America than any revenue to be gained from their sale.

Having lost a fortune because of his father's inadequate land titles, Benton was also highly sympathetic to those who built houses and improved their lands only to find that other men had better titles to the same property. He therefore introduced and promoted successfully a bill giving such settlers either a chance to keep the land or the right to acquire another equal plot from the state.

On the other hand, he was unwilling for persons who innocently settled on the land of others to recover damages for the value of their improvements. Under such a law, said Benton, a rich man with slaves might strip the timber from a tract and then collect damages from the owner for his depredations. He also opposed a request from settlers for preference in their holdings and protection for their improvements in lands not yet acquired from the Indians. The state should not "grant premiums to those who have trampled the laws of the general gov-

ernment under their feet." This devotion to legal right
continued throughout Benton's life.

And finally, the young Senator was already a nationalist. He
served first on a joint committee appointed to "express to the
government of the United States, the sense of this legislature,
relative to the base, unprecedented and unjustifiable conduct
of the British ministry towards this government." These were
fighting words, and Tennessee should not be unprepared. Ammunition was needed, and Benton served as chairman of a committee which recommended that the legislature reimburse
former Governor Sevier seven hundred and fifty dollars for the
purchase of fifteen hundred pounds of gunpowder and authorize Governor Blount to buy three thousand pounds of lead.
The Senate voted to pay for the powder, but refused to buy
the lead.[6]

When the session ended, Senator Benton rode home with
$207.50 plus four hundred miles' travel expenses for a sixty-
seven-day session. He had begun a successful career, the family
fortune would soon be supplemented with the thirty-two-hun-
dred-acre inheritance from Thomas Hart, and his law practice
was still expanding. Life was good.

But the ancient Benton enemy, tuberculosis, was still stalking
its prey. Teen-aged Susannah returned home from a happy
season at a young ladies' boarding school to find herself marked
as the next victim, and soon joined her sisters on the hillside.
The disease played no favorites. Nancy's house slave, Joe, was
carried up the hill next, and then Thomas himself felt the
dreaded symptoms. A constant fever, hacking cough, and terrible thirst cast him into the depths of despair.[7]

Everything seemed at an end for Thomas Benton, but as he
drove himself mercilessly to maintain his law practice and attend family business, a new and shining opportunity to gain
fame ahead of the impending doom suddenly appeared. The
American Congress was dominated by the warhawks from the
West, and these gentlemen were chafing for an excuse to attack
Canada and drive British influence from the continent. They
would soon convince their colleagues that the ships and sailors
of New England and the honor of the young nation must be
defended against the depredations of the British. Taking ad-

vantage of the Napoleonic war, growing rich on the profits of neutral trade, and violently opposed to an American war with Britain or anyone else, the New England merchants and their representatives in Congress might protest with vigor against the solicitude of their fellow Americans, but it would be in vain. Congress might vote the war declaration and adjourn without voting the means to pursue the conflict, but it would not find the sensitive-souled backwoodsmen of Tennessee unprepared.

CHAPTER III

THE SOLDIER

Andrew Jackson was Major General of the Tennessee militia in 1812, and young Thomas Benton was already established as one of the great man's favorites. At their first meeting, Jackson recalled a visit of many years before at the Benton home in North Carolina and invited the young man to visit the Hermitage, Jackson's beautiful plantation home some thirty miles from Franklin. Later, Attorney Benton assisted in the prosecution of Perry Magness, who had killed one of Jackson's close friends. To Jackson's disgust, Magness escaped with a light sentence for manslaughter, but the famous warrior, who did not offer his friendship lightly, had only praise for Benton's efforts.

Thus, in January, 1812, as the clouds of war gathered, the ailing young lawyer was neither shy nor reticent. In a letter to Jackson he offered to recruit a force, freely volunteered his services as aide, and justified the ambition:

> If there should be an expedition to the Canada's I shall make an experiment of my capacity to use the pen as well as the sword. I mean to preserve a journal of the operations of the army; and to give a history of such transactions as are worthy of being remembered. . . . You recognize the principle that to mount the eminence of distinction, the votary for fame must dare everything. I deem it more honorable to fail in honorable efforts than to

make no attempt at all to drag myself from obscurity. I think with Tacitus, that every man should aim at doing something worthy of being written, or at writing something worthy of being done.[1]

When word came that Congress had passed a bill to raise volunteers, the aspiring soldier quickly composed a plan for recruiting three regiments and went galloping off through thirty miles of rain, sleet, hail, and mud to see General Jackson. The General was seated before a great fire with his young adopted son and a lamb between his knees. The child had asked that the pet be rescued from the cold and rain; and Jackson, who could be gentle as well as fierce, had readily complied. The General was impressed with his young friend's ideas.[2]

On March 7, 1812, Jackson issued a call to arms, and on April 29 Thomas Benton was commissioned as captain of a volunteer infantry company. The call to arms was clearly a Benton production. America was to fight "to seek some indemnity for past injuries, some security against future aggressions, by the conquest of all the British dominions upon the continent of north america." As for the joys in all this awaiting the young volunteer, a march to Canada would provide

a military *promenade* into a distant country, a succession of new and interesting objects would perpetually fill and delight his imagination the effect of which would be heightened by the war like appearance, the martial music, and the grand evolutions of an army of fifty thousand men.

To view the stupendous works of nature, exemplified in the falls of Niagara and the cataract of Montmorenci; to tread the consecrated spot on which Wolf and Montgomery fell, would of themselves repay the young soldier for a march across the continent. But why should these inducements be held out to the young men of America? They need them not. Animated as they are by an ambition to rival the exploits of Rome, they will never prefer an inglorious sloth, a supine inactivity to the honorable toil of carrying the republican standard to the heights of abraham.[3]

By the time war was declared on June 18, Benton had been promoted to major. The glorious news of war arrived just in time for the July 4 celebrations throughout the area. Guns boomed, bands played, crowds sang and cheered, and the toasts rang out. At a meeting in Franklin twenty-five toasts "were drank with enthusiasm," including one by Major Benton: "The War against England; Honor and life to its friends: confusion to its enemies." [4]

And if no Englishmen were yet available for warfare in the American South, Major Benton had another idea. Mexico was already fighting its first revolution against Spain, and writing as "Americus," Benton proposed an American expedition to Mexico to insure the triumph of democracy against royalist forces who might become tools of Britian. Two months before the war declaration, Americus insisted that Mexico and its vast resources of gold and silver could not be safe without *"the expulsion of the British from . . . North America!"* Two months later he wanted the United States to send an army to liberate Mexico and also help Mexico take Cuba because:

> The road to the East Indies lies through the Isthmus of Darien. The project of connecting the two seas in the neighborhood of that Isthmus, by the lake of *Nicaraugua* . . . would be revived the moment that Mexico should become independent, or fall into the hands of any great nation. The . . . project, by saving the doubling of Cape Horn, would bring the East Indies *nine thousand miles nearer* to New Orleans and Philadelphia. The rich commerce of the east would then flow by our own doors. The enterprising American merchants would forestall the English in their own trade, and the pillar of British wealth would be sapped at its foundation.[5]

Whether concerned or not with Mexican republicanism or East Indian trade, readers probably enjoyed his imagination, and any reasons for fighting the British were enough to insure the writer's popularity.

When Indians carried out a few sporadic raids, Tennesseeans naturally concluded that the dastardly British were responsible and defined the Indians and the British as a common enemy. Major Benton worked endlessly at recruiting volunteers for an expedition against the Indians, but no action could be taken without Federal authority. For many weeks the little force drilled and talked of glory, while the ambitious officers strained at the leash. Jackson offered his command to the President and promised to be at Quebec in ninety days, but certain jealous Washington officials had not forgotten the General's brief associations with Aaron Burr, long since disgraced and now living in obscurity, and were not anxious to give him an opportunity for fame. The Tennessee volunteers, therefore, sat in Nashville while the efforts of others to take Canada against minor opposition were lost through inept leadership.

Major Benton had already decided to go to Washington and ask for service in Canada when the glorious word finally came that the Tennessee warriors were to march and float down the Mississippi to defend New Orleans against a possible attack. Again Jackson had a flamboyant word for his soldiers. They were

> now to act a part in the honorable contest of securing the rights and liberties of a great and rising Republic. In placing before the volunteers the illustrious actions of their fathers in the war of the revolution, he presumes to hope that they will not prove themselves a degenerate race, nor suffer it to be said, they are unworthy of the blessings which the blood of so many thousand heroes has purchased for them.

Armed with this proclamation, Benton raced up and down the countryside making "ardent addresses . . . stimulating the inherent courage and patriotism of the young men." [6]

In late November the ninety officers of the division met to divide the prospective troops into a regiment of cavalry and two regiments of infantry and to elect their field commanders. Benton was rewarded for his imagination, enthusiasm, and energy by selection as the commanding colonel of the Second Regiment Infantry. He and the other recruiters had done well, and they had drawn from a region equipped with a full reservoir of fighting spirit. Fifteen hundred men were expected, but by the end of muster on a bitter, snowy December day some eighteen hundred men had reported, and on the following day another two hundred determined warriors trudged and rode through the snow to join the cavalcade. Recruits were required to be "hail and sound; free from sore legs, scurvy, scalled heads, ruptures, and other infirmities." It is doubtful that anyone really wishing to go remained behind.[7]

"Americus" had already expressed the thoughts of Thomas
Hart Benton in a poem of November 10, 1812:

> HARK! the wheels of Bellona's fierce chariot of war,
> Resound o'er the land and the main;
> While the groans of the wretched are borne from afar,
> In the harsh notes of anguish and pain.
> 'Tis the voice of the ill-fated sons of the north—
> The wilderness groans with the sound;
> The fierce savage chief leads his warriors forth,
> And with groans and blood strews the ground.
> See each high crested hero, now waving on high,
> An adieu to his home and his friends.
> Reproving the fear, and the heart-rending sigh,
> While his steel-eas'd companions attend.
> Our country! they cry, 'tis her cause we espouse;
> Arous'd by the Clarion of Fame,
> We have sworn, (and to Heaven have ascended our vows)
> To die, or secure her a name.[8]

Jackson gave the volunteers wide latitude in matters of dress,
but the field officers reveled in splendid regalia identical to that
of equal rank in the regular army. Colonel Benton carried the
added distinction of appointment as "first aid" to the General.

On January 7, 1813, Colonel John Coffee and the cavalry
rode away down the Natchez Trace. Next day, as flags waved
and admiring crowds cheered, Colonel Thomas Benton super-
vised the loading of the First Regiment Infantry aboard large
flatboats for the long trip down the Cumberland, Ohio, and
Mississippi rivers. As the boats floated away, Colonel Benton
marched proudly off downstream at the head of his own seven-
hundred-man regiment. His men were to march overland until
enough boats could be commandeered to put them afloat. After
leading them for several miles, the Colonel returned to Nashville and set out downstream with several other officers by boat.

Thomas Hart Benton's cup of happiness was full. He was on
the way to fame in the defense of his nation, and had probably
already begun to suspect that he was not going to die from
tuberculosis after all. In later years he remembered that the
disease was arrested by the vigorous outdoor life of sunshine,
bathing in cold streams, and strenuous exercise involved in the

expedition. Constant exposure to sunshine, daily cold-water baths, and merciless scrubbings with a stiff brush would remain part of his daily routine for the rest of his life. He sent back to the Nashville *Democratic Clarion* a detailed journal of the voyage,[9] and the grandiloquent words and poetic phrases were more than a mere effort to impress his readers. The journal was the work of an imaginative young man bursting with the sheer joy of being alive, to whom every item of nature and moment of adventure carried a meaning and excitement all its own. The chronicles of Tom Sawyer and Huck Finn had not yet been written, but thirty-year-old Tom Benton would have understood and appreciated fully the younger Tom's search for story book adventures on the Mississippi.

As Benton and his fellow officers embarked at midnight:

> The moon had not yet gone down, and her pale beams were glistening upon the surface of the water. The night was intensely cold, but still, and nothing was heard to interrupt the silence that reigned save the hollow mumuring of the water which broke up on the rocky shore.

None of them knew anything about the river or the boat:

> Col. Anderson placed himself at the helm; the other officers stood by him. No one said he was afraid; but the question of Caesar to to the pilot, *Quid times?* repeatedly and involuntarily occurred. Finally, recollecting that they were fatalistic, they gave the boat to the stream; surrendered themselves to their destiny, and went below into the cabin.

Next morning

> the sky was perfectly clear; and the sun, rising without a cloud upon a deep and still river, appeared with uncommon splendor. A more beautiful morning was never seen in autumn. Several stands of colors, of superb workmanship, were playing from the head of different boats, the music was playing; and a number of fine-looking men, in military dresses, were a walking on the tops of the boats. The whole together exhibited a grand spectacle and extremely animated the feelings.

Colonels Benton and Anderson had a trunkful of "choicest military works" to read and study when they were not admiring the picturesque scenery. Also, he reassured the home folks:

Perhaps in so large an assemblage of military men, there never
was seen so small a number of drunkards and gamesters. The
beautiful pocket edition of the Bible . . . found a place in the
baggage of several officers; and the whole detachment emulated
the conduct of their general in paying to religion and its ministers
the highest respect.

At Clarksville, five days and sixty-seven miles downstream,
Colonel Benton waited for his regiment. The army needed
flour; so, the Colonel promptly "sent out the bayonet" to acquire seventy barrels at the high price of eight dollars a barrel
from enterprising merchants hoarding it in hope of an even
higher reward. With boats, however, he was less successful, and
his regiment fell ten days behind Jackson and the others while
enough were being secured. This, the angry Benton informed
the public in his journal, cost the United States twenty thousand dollars, and the fault rested with the quartermasters who
had allowed businessmen to keep boats which should have been
taken. Quartermasters, he argued, should be under the direct
command of the field general instead of being controlled from
Washington. The general should be able to replace or overrule
a delinquent quartermaster on the spot rather than be compelled to carry on long-distance arguments with Washington
over such matters.

On January 23 the journey was resumed. Because of the
"universal ardor to overtake the General," the expedition kept
going despite a fearful storm which caused the boats to run
aground on one occasion. Along the way the Colonel received
and relayed a vivid description of the church services held on
Jackson's boats which had gone before:

the gospel morality of Christ was heard to resound upon the
bosom of a river and upon the spot, where, within the memory of
several present, the Buffalo had come to drink; the Indians to
way-lay the solitary travellers, and the enterprising whiteman
had cautiously crept along, in continual peril of his life.

By nightfall on January 26 the regiment landed at Smith-
land, a little Kentucky town at the junction of the Cumberland
and the Ohio. Bitterly cold weather had been followed by a
thaw, and the Ohio was churning with massive ice floes capable

of smashing a boat to pieces. The local citizenry begged them to wait, but the resolute Colonel, despite his painful anxiety, "as he reflected that upon a word which he was to speak, it might depend whether a multitude of fine men should perish in the ice, or live to see their friends again," ordered the boats into the stream. The command was obeyed promptly, and using long poles spiked with iron to fend off the ice the intrepid boatmen survived the crisis without mishap.

Terrible earthquakes had recently shaken the Mississippi Valley, and even at best the sandbar- and sawyer-filled river was unsafe. Traveling only by day and by moonlight the boats kept in hot pursuit of Jackson, however, and on the evening of February 13 Colonel Thomas Benton and the Second Infantry rendezvoused with their General at Natchez. Colonel Coffee and the cavalry arrived three days later.

The march to glory, however, was halted at Natchez by the orders of Jackson's regular army superior, General James Wilkinson, already in New Orleans gazing upon the exploits of his rival with obvious distaste. Week after week the bored and impatient troops fretted at Natchez, until on March 15 they received the final cruel sting of shattered hopes and gross ingratitude. A brief missive from the Secretary of War ordered the General to dismiss his army immediately and deliver all public property to Wilkinson, adding: "Accept for yourself and the Corps the thanks of the President of the United States." Instead of recognizing the speedy expedition as the only significant military feat of the war to date, the Government had dismissed an army of 2,070 men eight hundred miles from home, without pay or rations, and without transportation or medicine for the sick.

General Wilkinson politely suggested that Jackson encourage his abandoned men to join the regular army in New Orleans, but the raging Jackson and his commanders had no such intention. Wilkinson would not get their fine soldiers by the mere promise of something to eat. Jackson ordered any regular army recruiting officer to be drummed from camp on sight, and in a fiery proclamation announced that he would take the army home on his own means and responsibility. Colonel Thomas Benton shared his General's distaste for Wilkinson and agreed with Jackson's decision, but openly questioned his peerless leader on one point. Wilkinson, he believed, did outrank Jackson legally, and if ordered to fight under Wilkinson he and his regiment would not refuse. Happily this did not become a practical issue, and Benton co-operated fully with Jackson's Herculean effort to keep the troops home.

Jackson acquired twenty days of rations from Wilkinson by "firm" insistence, spent a great deal of his own money, and pledged his credit lavishly. He spent more than a thousand dollars on the sick, and joined his officers and men on foot, while the ailing rode the horses. The army finally completed the long march and filed into Nashville weary, ill, and footsore, but with highest praise for Old Hickory and his "aid." According to the *Clarion*, Colonel Benton "shared every fatigue with the most common soldier, and in no case shunned the mire his men had to wade through."

Mutual achievement and shared persecution generate powerful bonds of friendship, and Benton and Jackson had now experienced both. On the long and painful trek up the Natchez Trace new plans were laid. Both men were eager for action on the Canadian front, and the General's finances were in serious condition. Benton should go to Washington to work for Jackson's financial reimbursement for the expenses of the Natchez expedition and at the same time seek their reassignment to a fighting area.

First, however, there was another matter. Major William B. Lewis, the deputy Quartermaster for the volunteer division in Nashville, had read Benton's "Journal" in the press and did not appreciate its remarks about quartermasters. With Benton at a safe distance, the Major succumbed to his passions and sent the newspaper a prompt and insulting reply. After pointing out that the boats had been contracted before his own appointment, Lewis ridiculed the flowery language of the journal and pictured its writer as a glory-seeking show-off of doubtful courage. He charged also that a private named Hays in Benton's regiment had been handed over without trial to Colonel Anderson for stealing a fowl from Anderson and had been left alone in Indian country where he had not been heard from since. True, said Lewis, he had never walked at the head of his troops for the "sole purpose of being gazetteered," but Colonel Benton must have been amply repaid by his views of the "faintly glimmering beams" of the moon.

The first answer came from Colonel Anderson, who pointed out that Private Hays had been locked in the guardhouse at Fort Massac rather than being abandoned anywhere. Anderson demanded a statement of intentions, which Lewis quickly answered with assurances that his quarrel was only with Benton. Still another Benton supporter pointed out that Colonel Benton had named no names and suggested that no one without a sore conscience could have been insulted.

As Major Lewis pondered this logic, his adversary and the undefeated if untried heroes of Natchez returned from the campaign to parade through Nashville before the admiring home folks. Colonel Benton read the *Clarion,* and Ensign Lyttleton Johnston carried his challenge to Lewis within the hour: "I shall neither give nor take explanations. . . . I lay before you the pistol, the sword, and the dagger: take what you like."

Lewis had a cautious answer. He was busy disposing of public property left by the expedition, and could not indulge himself the luxury of a duel while the public welfare required his attention.

Benton would take no such excuse: "You must fight me sir or you must flinch openly . . . to demand indefinite time now, is to say, that as you attacked me with lies when I was 500 miles to the South, so you will be ready to fight me when I have gone 500 miles to the North."

Lewis still refused to set a date; so Benton denounced him as a "cockaded and gold-laced coward," and distributed their correspondence as a handbill. Lewis, thinking the affair finished, tried a last word. He would fight sometime, and in publishing the leaflet Benton was taking an easy and safe way out. Lewis was not to have the last word, however, as the Colonel now assured him that he would postpone his trip if the Major would name the hour, the day, and the place—any hour, any day, any place. Again Lewis declined to be definite except in his intention not to fight, and announced that "henceforth I shall neither make nor receive any further communications from you."

Duty and fame could wait no longer. Benton now gave the correspondence to the press with a personal statement. He apologized to the "People of Tennessee" for wasting time when the republic needed his services, but honor had required it. And in farewell, "if the chances of war prevent me from returning, suffer me not to be lied out of your friendship by men without honor; without shame . . . who, under the pretext of serving their country, have been laboring to destroy me in my absence! me! whom thousands hold not indemnity for the sacrifices I have made and am still making in support of that country of which I am called the enemy!" [10]

The young warrior rode away to Washington with head and banners high, stopping at the Hermitage for a letter of introduction from Jackson. The General did not waste words: "did I think any thing was necessary to be said on the fitness of Colo. Benton to command it would be here added. his uniform good conduct, his industry and attention to the discipline and police of his regiment speak more for his fitness than words, and a personal acquaintaince with Colo. Benton will soon decide on the capacity of his mind. . . ." [11]

Though still not much of a city, Washington was a far cry from Nashville, and the leaders there included some of the sacred Founding Fathers, but the brash young man from Tennessee was in no way taken aback. He visited President Madison and virtually haunted the War Department where he stubbornly argued Jackson's case in spite of slowness and deliberate delays. Jackson's claims were not only just, he contended, but any mistreatment of Old Hickory might lose Tennessee for the administration in the next election. Secretary of War Armstrong was impressed. They were not assigned to Canada, but Jackson's claims were honored, and Benton was commissioned lieutenant colonel of the Thirty Ninth Infantry Regiment, Regular Army. The regiment would have to be recruited in Tennessee, but Lieutenant Colonel Benton could still ride back to Nashville proud of his successful mission and firm in the hope that glory lay just around the corner.

The Colonel's exuberant spirits, however, were soon dampened. He had expected to bask in the favor of a grateful Andrew Jackson, but en route home learned differently. Back in

Nashville his younger brother, Jesse, and his young friend, Ensign Lyttleton Johnston, had launched a series of events destined to change the course of Thomas Benton's life. Major William Carroll as brigade inspector in Jackson's army had irritated numerous subordinates, and the moment the army disbanded Jesse Benton carried him a duel challenge from Johnston. Carroll, a notoriously poor shot, refused on the ground that Johnston was no gentleman. This was an indirect insult to both Bentons because Johnston had also carried the challenge of Thomas to Major Lewis. Jesse Benton did not lag far behind his brother in aggressiveness. On one occasion he had been assessed twenty dollars damages for assault and battery on a neighbor, and he had published a quick answer to the charges of Lewis against Thomas. Word soon reached Carroll that Jesse was threatening to throw his own high social standing into the fray.

Carroll conferred with Jackson, who rode into Nashville in the unfamiliar role of peacemaker, bearing a note from Carroll to Jesse:

> I presume you are apprized that I would not have anything to do with Mr. Johnston in the way he requested, and your coming forward as his friend, after having this knowledge, makes it probable you have volunteered in his behalf. If so, you can explain to Gen'l Jackson, your object and your wishes, and it will only rest with your self the line of conduct you intend to pursue hereafter as no communications from Johnston will be attended by me.[12]

This communication could not have been interpreted as a peace offering by a sensitive gentleman of old Tennessee, and Jesse did not so regard it. When Jackson assured Jesse that the note did not obligate him to fight Carroll and urged that the matter be dropped, Jesse agreed momentarily, but after conversations with other enemies of Carroll and Jackson decided that the note was an insult which left no alternative but a challenge.

Jesse expected to stand and fire at the usual ten paces, but Carroll, who as the challenged party had the choice of rules, surprised him with a procedure designed to compensate for what Jackson called the Major's "remarkably defective" marksmanship. They would stand back to back only ten feet apart and wheel and fire on the signal. Apparently Jesse was not warned of this in advance, while Carroll, under Jackson's supervision, spent three days practicing the maneuver. According to Carroll, Jackson suggested a distance of fifteen feet, but unable to hit anything practicing at this distance he himself insisted upon the shorter range.[13] To the end of his days, Jackson saw no inconsistency between his assistance to Carroll in a ten-foot duel against Jesse and his personal friendship with Thomas Hart Benton.

Jesse protested, but had no alternative except to finish what he had begun. For him the duel ended in great physical pain and mortal humiliation. He wheeled, fired, missed, and kept wheeling in a squatting position to reduce his target area. Carroll's bullet went through the seat of Jesse's trousers leaving a dangerous wound and a permanently bruised soul. Tennesseans were given a joke which outlasted the practice of dueling.

The brotherly discussion between Thomas and Jesse Benton over the latter's dueling etiquette can only be imagined, but Jesse apparently managed to cast most of the blame upon Jackson. The mere fact of Jackson's participation on the opposing side was enough to lend credence to Jesse's complaints, and the family honor, after all, had to be protected. Thomas Benton remained home, avoiding his erstwhile hero, but did not hesitate to express his opinions.

Personal brawls were a major spectator sport in frontier society, and neither Benton nor Jackson lacked enemies willing to promote trouble. One Andrew Hynes wrote Jackson in reference to Benton that he was "unwilling to believe that any man could be so stamped with ingratitude as to turn traitor to his Patron and to be the reviler of Him, who brought him out of obscurity into fame and consequence in the world. . . . A man who is ungrateful, renounces all moral obligation, and is capable of committing every Species of iniquity." [14]

When such rumors continued to spread, and his late messenger to Washington still did not report, Jackson forced the issue. He wrote Benton a note of ominous calm, inquiring as to the truth of the reports. Hadn't Benton left the Hermitage as a friend? Why had he not come with information? Had he threatened a publication? Had any of his own acts been "inconsistent with the strictest principles of friendship" and if so, how? And finally, had Benton threatened a challenge?

Benton answered with equal frankness. His friendship for Jackson had been proven. Recently, however, he had said certain things of a different nature. It was poor business, he had said, for a man of Jackson's age to conduct a duel about nothing between two young men who had no harm against each other, when he should have been "advising them to reserve their courage for the public enemy." It was mean of Jackson to carry a note from Carroll to Jesse, dictated by Jackson, which left Jesse no honorable alternative to a duel. Jackson might at least have conducted the duel fairly instead of in "a savage, unequal, unfair, and base manner." The short distance and wheeling maneuver had been kept a secret from Jesse while Carroll was practicing it. He knew, Benton wrote, that Jackson would say that Carroll insisted on the procedure, but from "your known influence over Mr. C. you might have managed the affair as you pleased; if not, you were at least a free man, and might have quit him if you did not approve of his course. To this effect, but in language much stronger, I have expressed myself when speaking of this matter." He had appreciated Jackson's friendship, but could not smile assent while Jackson was breaking "the heart of an aged and widowed mother, and hurrying into his grave a young man, a brother, whose life ought to have been preserved for the comfort of his family and the service of his country." And, finally, Jackson had misrepresented him by informing Washington that all of their troops had been unwilling to fight under Wilkinson. This had not been true of his own regiment, and Jackson knew it. He would not challenge Jackson, but the terror of the General's pistols would not seal his lips. He would continue to speak what he believed to be true, neither seeking nor declining a duel.

Jackson was stung to the quick, and had an immediate answer. "It is the character of the man of honor, and particularly of the *soldier* not to quarrel and brawl like the fish woman." Carroll, he avowed, had the right to select the manner of the duel and had acted to minimize Jesse's superior marksmanship. Never before had he heard of a challenger complaining about the mode of fighting, and nothing had been concealed from Jesse "that could with propriety have been made known to him." As Carroll's second, he had assumed the proper duty of working for the safety of his friend. Carroll had chosen the distance, but had the decision been left to him, he too would have advised it. Benton should either admit error or demand satisfaction.[15]

For the next six weeks, busybodies continued to work on both parties, until Jackson announced that by the Eternal he would horsewhip Tom Benton on sight. Finally, on the morning of September 4, Thomas and Jesse Benton arrived in Nashville on business, staying at a hotel not frequented by Jackson, to avoid, in Benton's words, "a possibility of unpleasantness." The word spread quickly, and soon, Jackson, Colonel John Coffee, and Mrs. Jackson's nephew, Stockley Hays, arrived at the Nashville Inn. Both Coffee and Hays were gigantic in size, a fit palace guard for their smaller but more aggressive leader. Each of the Bentons carried two pistols. The Jackson war party was also armed, with Jackson, true to his pledge, carrying a riding whip.

Jackson and Coffee strolled first to the Post Office, passing near the Talbot Hotel, where the Bentons were standing on the walk. Returning the same way, they saw Jesse Benton step from the pavement into the hotel. At this point, Jackson and his party clearly became the aggressors by following Jesse Benton into the hotel. Jesse had disappeared, but Thomas was standing in the doorway of the hall that led to the rear porch. Jackson advanced upon Thomas Benton brandishing the whip: "Now defend yourself, you damned rascal!" Benton reached for his pistols, but Jackson's draw was faster. Looking into the muzzle of Jackson's gun, Thomas Benton slowly retreated, with Jackson following step by step. At this point Jesse stepped through a doorway behind Jackson, raised his pistol, and fired. In the same motion, Jackson fired at Thomas, who fired back twice in return. Jackson fell with his left shoulder shattered and a ball imbedded in his arm. The blast from Jackson's gun had burned a hole in Thomas Benton's coat sleeve. The massive John Coffee blasted away at Thomas, missed, and then attacked with clubbed pistol. Fortunately the carnage was limited by the fact that the later Colt six-shooter had not yet been invented, and the fire-belching smooth-bore pistols in use were notoriously inaccurate as well as relatively useless when once fired. Jackson's friends, however, by now reinforced, almost finished their leader's mission. Coffee and Alexander Donaldson managed to wound Thomas Benton in five places with their daggers. Stockley Hays and Charles Hammond stabbed away at Jesse, and only a large and strong button which broke the blade of Hays' sword cane saved Jesse from being perforated. In a fair exchange of accidents, Jesse pulled the trigger of his remaining pistol with the muzzle against Hays' body, but the charge misfired. Jesse was finally rescued by the aid of James Sumner. Thomas, meanwhile, had fallen backward down a flight of stairs. The attack stopped at this point, probably because of the desperate plight of Jackson. His friends carried the General back to the Nashville Hotel, where he soaked two mattresses with blood. An ordinary man would have died, but iron-willed Andrew Jackson had not yet reached such a decision. Jackson was defeated, however, and Thomas Benton sealed the victory by breaking Jackson's sword across his knee in the public square.

Shooting Nashville's hero was no step on the pathway to fame and fortune. Soon Thomas Benton was "literally in hell." "It is a settled plan to turn out puppy after puppy to bully me," he wrote, "and when I have got into a scrape, to have me killed somehow in the scuffle." Only a decisive duel would bring relief. His alternatives were to kill or be killed, because he would not crouch to Jackson. Major Carroll published a statement of his position, which Benton considered a challenge. He wrote Carroll an immediate acceptance, but Carroll answered that his statements had not been aimed at Benton. Carroll challenged no one, but he would fight if challenged. Here the matter ended.[16]

Thomas Benton had never subscribed to the proverb, "All good things come to him who waits," but was now to suffer from its vindication. As a volunteer colonel he had gnashed his teeth while the opportunities for glory went to the regular army. Becoming a regular lieutenant colonel had required much effort, but now the smile of fortune shifted back to the volunteers. Soon, the incredible Jackson, his arm in a sling, was leading the volunteers south again, this time to well-publicized victories against the marauding Creek Indians. Carroll, Coffee, and other "puppies of the Gen'l" were becoming heroes, while Colonel Benton moped in Nashville, recruiting and training his regiment of regulars, his pleas that the regiment be sent to the Canadian border going unanswered.

Finally, Lieutenant Colonel Benton and his regiment, with one Sam Houston as ensign, were ordered south to join Jackson and the volunteers, and by February, 1814, were in Alabama preparing for the great Battle of Horseshoe Bend. He had trained the regiment, and in the battle their exploits justified his pride, with Sam Houston, in particular, emerging as the battle's greatest hero. But the regiment's bitterly frustrated commander was not with them. On the eve of battle, he was ordered back to recruiting duty in Tennessee, where again he poured out his heart in bitter complaints and fervent pleas for service in action.[17]

By July, he was back with the regiment, near Mobile Bay, begging for authority to pursue the Indians into Florida and occupy their headquarters at Pensacola. On July 12, Benton's regiment was joined by a force of Mississippi volunteers under Lieutenant Colonel George H. Nixon, and by the following day they were only fifty miles from Pensacola. Again on the verge of battle and fame, Benton this time became seriously ill and was forced to return to the main fort. The army under Nixon met the Indians and fought well, but Lieutenant Colonel Benton was absent.

Within a few weeks, a revived but still unhappy Benton led his troops back to Montgomery's Redoubt, above Mobile Bay, under orders to watch the British, who by this time had occupied Pensacola with permission of their belated Spanish allies. Soon Benton was warning General Jackson that the British were about to strike at Mobile Point. An adventurer named Boyles had reported ships sailing from Pensacola to Mobile carrying motley hordes of British, Indians, Negroes, American deserters, and Spaniards. Jackson's confidence in his recent adversary was less than complete. The General replied by warning that Boyles had probably been sent by the British to divert attention from Pensacola. When Benton reported a dozen British men-of-war off Mobile Point, Jackson thought it just a "faint" to save Pensacola.[18]

By this time, Wellington had defeated Napoleon in Europe, and the British were free to turn their full attention to their rambunctious American cousins. Maine was conquered, Washington was sacked, New England was threatening secession. Perhaps the war would still be won or lost in the South, which had not yet managed to copy the bungling, inefficiency, cowardice, and general stupidity of the war effort in other regions. Jackson now planned a full-scale attack upon Pensacola, and again Colonel Benton prepared to serve his nation in its hour of crisis. By September 22 he was on the Bay of Perdido, just west of Pensacola, waiting for the assault to begin. Indecision in Washington delayed the attack, however, and soon the anxious Colonel was back at Fort Montgomery, worried now because the one-year enlistments of his men were expiring and the regiment was being depleted. Jackson finally decided to attack without authority, but he had another assignment for his "favorite" colonel. Benton and six fellow officers were ordered back to Tennessee for further recruiting.

The seven were brokenhearted, and sent an eloquent plea to the Adjutant General: "Finding ourselves unexpectedly ordered upon the recruiting service at a moment when active operations were about to commence, unwilling to be seen creeping home at such a period, desirous of being employed in some way . . . we respectfully request that we may be permitted to serve in the rank of the file. . . ."

Jackson had legitimate reasons for refusing their request, but could not resist the opportunity to indulge in a bit of subtle vindictiveness. Benton had written for the seven, and the Adjutant General answered, but Old Hickory inserted one paragraph in his own handwriting. "Not only the wishes of some, but the publick services would be promoted by the order given." He must heed first his feelings for "the brave and meritorious services of many of the platoon officers . . . that served with him in the last winters campaign." Having a "sincere desire to see these brave officers at the head of their respective commands where fresh laurels await them, and finding that they cannot fill their companies here," the General could not think of "recinding his order." [19]

But the Colonel was unwilling to give up. He would fight in Canada if he had to go alone. He persuaded his regular army superior, Colonel Williams, to order him to Washington, and off he went, carrying a petition from the officers of his regiment begging for action. Before he reached Washington, Andrew Jackson won undying fame at New Orleans, and Thomas Hart Benton in his desperate search for a battle and glory was still moving in the opposite direction. In Washington he waited for still more weeks, until orders finally came for him to proceed to Canada. Before he could leave, the great news arrived. The war had ended, even before Jackson's glorious victory at New Orleans. The republic had been saved, with a minimum of assistance from Lieutenant Colonel Thomas Hart Benton. He had spent the war panting for a battle, expending vast quantities of ink and lung power, and executing his assigned duties with skill and dispatch, but in terms of military reputation had arrived exactly nowhere. His only victory had been over the conflict's greatest hero, General Andrew Jackson, and this was a battle which might easily be renewed.

Should he return to Nashville to face the enmity of the nation's idol, or was there perhaps a more fruitful prospect? Thomas Hart Benton had seen much and forgotten little. A great, rich continent lay beyond the Mississippi. It would ultimately be part of the nation, and some of it would be knocking at the door very soon. The new territory of Missouri was a land of opportunity, and it would need leaders—leaders of intellectual ability as well as physical strength and courage. The blood which had taken old Samuel to North Carolina and had led his father into futile dreams of owning a western empire was stirring in his veins. Thomas Benton made his decision and set a course for the struggling little village of St. Louis.

*   *   *   *   *   *   *

One errand remained, however. In the army he had found a staunch friend in General James Preston of Virginia, and, stopping with the Prestons on his journeys to Washington, had met also the General's niece, Elizabeth McDowell. The road to

Missouri took him back through Virginia. The letters tracing the progress of the many years of long-distance courtship between Thomas Benton and Elizabeth McDowell have apparently been lost, perhaps in the fire which gutted the Benton home in 1856. Privacy must be respected, therefore, even by the historian, who is left only with the basic outlines. Elizabeth McDowell was a fragile, lovely girl of the utmost delicacy and gentleness of spirit. Thomas Benton, usually in search of a battle and probably mixing warlike ferocity with his vast dreams of the national destiny in every other sentence, must have been in 1815 a terrifying suitor. He departed alone for Missouri, and Elizabeth pondered the issue for six more years before his "endless courtship" was finally successful. The distance between Virginia and Missouri may have been fortunate. With all of his fiery and at times almost brutal aggressiveness, Thomas Benton was capable of the most profound tenderness. Letters may have revealed the sunshine, while distance hid the thunderstorms and hurricanes from view. But if this were indeed true, it was known only in the gentle heart of Elizabeth McDowell.

CHAPTER IV

THE MISSOURIAN

ONE PLEASANT Sunday evening in 1815, a tall, powerfully built stranger with four hundred dollars in his pocket and great expectations in his heart crossed the broad Mississippi into St. Louis. He was a lawyer, but his previous experience with the Anglo-Saxon common law would be inadequate in a region still dominated by French and Spanish legal traditions of the Roman law. He was uncommonly well versed in the finer points of the English language, but he must now study law in French, and many of his future clients, and perhaps an occasional judge, would speak only in that language. The obstacles to success at the bar might have appeared formidable to a man of ordinary self-confidence, but the stranger was Thomas Hart Benton, and he could learn and do anything.

St. Louis in 1815 was a town of two thousand people, housed in a conglomeration of log and whitewashed mud houses, broken only by a handful of brick buildings and the high, massive stone walls of the pretentious estate of Auguste Chouteau, the great fur trader. The view from the opposite shore was impressive, with the sun gleaming on the whitewash and the water-front limestone bluff forming something of a natural amphitheater, but as the boat drew nearer, the "beauty at a distance" gave way to "native meanness." Had it been raining, the stranger would have found several streets rendered impassable by the "want of a common footway or drains to carry off the rain-water." But Thomas Hart Benton probably saw neither the beauty nor the meanness of the present. The frontier village on the approaching shore was to be a great city thrusting its roots and branches into a vast continental empire, and he had come to assist in the process. Beyond the roof of the Chouteau mansion, he was already looking at the dim outlines of the Pacific.

St. Louis was a melting pot of French and Spanish, a few Irish and Germans, and an ever-increasing horde of frontier Americans of the older stocks. Loud, boastful, brawling boatmen of the Mike Fink variety; reckless, singing, adventurous Canadian *voyageurs;* loitering Indians of various tribes, wandering aimlessly or marching in full regalia to visit the great "Red-headed White Father," General William Clark; buckskin-clad, sharp-eyed frontier hunters and trappers; solid citizens of stern Calvinist visage; and merry French sophisticates as urbane and gay as any to be found in Paris—all rubbed shoulders in friendship, enmity, distrust, and tolerance in frontier Missouri. Protestants frowned at the gaily-dressed French crowds which stopped at the billiard tables and card games on their way home from church. The French, for their part, believed "that a sullen countenance, and attention to gloomy subjects, a set form of speech, and a stiff behaviour" were "much more indicative of hypocrisy than of religion." Anyone practicing such excessive piety on Sunday would probably cheat and defraud his neighbors during the week.

The newcomer was not long in finding friends. Thomas Benton had lived with frontiersmen, boatmen, and Indians on their own terms. He had also enjoyed the hospitality of the President of the United States, and his strict Protestant upbringing did not prevent an appreciation of the literary and cultural tastes of the sophisticated French. After climbing the rough, steep path up from the water front and taking a look around, he inquired for a boardinghouse. A distinguished-looking old gentleman simply pointed to his own home, and the stranger moved in as an honored guest for his first six weeks in the town. Benton had found a remarkable host. Charles Gratiot, once of Geneva, Switzerland, had served under George

Rogers Clark, and had been among the first to exhort his fellow Frenchmen to cheer when the American flag was raised over Louisiana. A wealthy trader in his own right, Gratiot was married to Victoria Chouteau, of the fur-trading family, and had been the first presiding judge of the Court of Common Pleas, a justice of the peace, and chairman of the city's board of trustees. A historian later called him "better known in New York and Philadelphia than in" St. Louis, and "better known in Paris, London, and Geneva than on this continent." Gratiot was an immediate bridge for Benton into a highly select circle.[1]

And there were people to teach him French, at least one of them highly distinguished. Many of the elder French citizens flatly refused to learn English, and English did not win over French in the streets of St. Louis until after 1820. Others, however, such as the cultured Bishop Du Bourg, the founder of St. Louis University, felt a responsibility to meet the Saxons in their own language. The good Bishop secluded himself for several weeks with the family of an American farmer to learn English in an atmosphere where he would hear no French. The great day finally came when he could announce a sermon in English to be delivered on some occasion of general interest. Thomas Benton never forgot the sermon, which began with the hearty salutation: "My friends: I am right-down glad to see such a smart chance of folks here today." [2] Thomas Benton could teach the Bishop the king's English in a more refined form, and by so doing learned French from an equally able teacher.

Benton's self-confidence was justified. His law practice was an immediate success. Louisiana had been transferred to American jurisdiction under treaty pledges to respect all existing private property arrangements which could be validated. This had left the region a paradise for the lawyer willing to perform laborious legal research and defend his efforts with oratory fiery enough to impress a jury. For all of its frontier crudeness, St. Louis possessed a highly ornate culture among its leading citizens, many of them well versed in literature and the classics. The ability to embellish practical reasoning with a cloak of impressive erudition was a marked legal asset. Benton's close friend, Edward Hempstead, was long considered the ablest

lawyer in the region, but after Hempstead's death in 1817, the
New England missionary, Timothy Flint, wrote that "Colonel
B., well known in another place, has since been supreme at the
bar. He is acute, laboured, florid, rather sophomorical, to use
our word, but a man of strong sense. There flashes 'strange fire'
from his eye, and all that he does 'smells of the lamp!' " [3]

In early 1817 Benton returned to Tennessee for his mother.
Bringing her own small group of slaves, Nancy Ann Gooch
Benton moved west for the last time. Thomas provided her
with a pleasant home, and when his later career required for his
family long periods of residence in Washington, she was undisputed mistress of the St. Louis household. Her younger son,
Samuel, left his motherless brood with her, and again Nancy
took up the task of rearing a family of children, thriving upon
the responsibility until her death in 1838 at the age of almost
eighty. This branch of the family would ultimately produce a
noted educator, a Congressman, and one of America's best
known twentieth century painters. In 1821 the Bentons were
renting a good-sized frame dwelling, but later acquired a large
house on half a city square, with "beautifully improved"
grounds "covered with magnificent forest trees." [4]

Also in 1817, Attorney Benton became a member of the first
board of school trustees. The town had long boasted a number
of apparently excellent private schools, including a Catholic
school for young ladies and a school run by Timothy Flint and
James Sawyer, pledged to "watch over the manners, the morals,
the improvement and happiness of their pupils with undeviat-
ing strictness and fidelity." On January 30, 1817, the territorial
legislature supplemented these by establishing a public school
board. The long document for this purpose promised, among
other things, that there would be no "preference to any religious denomination whatever." Benton's colleagues were
General Clark, William C. Carr, Bernard Pratte, Auguste Chouteau, Alex McNair, and John P. Cabanné, a group of remarkable distinction in early St. Louis history. At their first meeting,
General Clark assumed the chair, while Benton was secretary
pro tem.[5]

The following year found him back in Tennessee, drawn by
the prospect of a treaty between the Government and the

Chickasaw tribes which might validate some of his own ancient claims in the Memphis area. The treaty he considered a "great event for the U. States, as it will carry the warlike population of Ken. and Ten. to the banks of the Mississippi, within ten or twelve days of sail of New Orleans, and will give to that place the means of a prompt and military aid, in comparison of which forts and garrisons will be as nothing." And the Colonel was still no pacifist. If the Seminole War raging between Americans and Indians on the borders of Florida should lead to a war with Spain, he would "deem it an event of the first importance for the human race, as it will by that means lead to the complete emancipation of the *New* from the *old* world."

His land claims were still unsuccessful, and Andrew Jackson was among those holding superior titles. In the following year, however, the successful attorney could feel gratitude to the heavens for much prosperity. The only regret was that four years earlier his funds had not matched his vision. He wrote General Preston:

> If I had brought with me twenty or thirty thousand dollars, I would have been worth today from a quarter to half a million. For I had seen enough of this world to see things as they were, and as they would be. I came among people who would not believe it possible that ground about St. Louis, then selling for thirty dollars an acre, should sell at this day for two thousand; but I did believe, nay knew it, and daily saw splendid fortunes passing in review before me, and falling into the hands of those who look ahead.[6]

And his dreams of the future of his new home had not diminished:

> Our country still presents the finest theatre in America. Our lands are yet cheap, and advance in price while sinking everywhere else. Our towns flourish while so many others are perishing. Our noble rivers are enlivened with commerce; and the tide of emigration flows in upon us with a force and steadiness which should announce to the old states that the power of this continent is gravitating to the borders of the Mississippi. Look back to what we were thirty years ago; see what we are today; tell what we must be in 1830. From that day the west will give the law to the Re-

public; and those who have views beyond that period will plant themselves on the waters of the West. . . .[7]

*   *   *   *   *   *   *

Thomas Hart Benton's career in St. Louis had been successful, but it had not been tranquil. For all of their gentility, the French were no less addicted to settling disputes with the pistol or sword than any other frontiersmen. Success required courage and a steady aim no less than legal skill, and many leaders of early Missouri were adventurers of heroic proportions. Benton's closest friend until 1817, Edward Hempstead, after a classical education from private tutors in New England, had found his way from Connecticut to Vincennes by way of Rhode Island, and had then walked all the way from Vincennes to St. Louis with a bundle on his back. Another friend, Luke Lawless, later a judge, had left Ireland in his teens to escape hanging for revolutionary activity. Reaching France, Lawless was badly wounded while fighting in the army of Napoleon and later rendered lame in a Paris duel. Occasionally not above justifying his name, Lawless was a valuable ally in a quarrel. Benton was also on excellent terms with Colonel John Smith T of St. Genevieve. This worthy gentleman always added a "T" to his name because he was from Tennessee and did not wish to be mistaken for any ordinary John Smith. This error was unlikely. Smith was described by a conservative contemporary as one who killed "most of the men he shot in fair and open duels," and who always stood his trial and was honorably acquitted after killing anyone in a "broil," a perfect gentleman and "as mild a mannered man as ever put a bullet into the human body." [8]

Politics as well as legal disputes were usually pursued with uncommon vigor. After the election for territorial delegate in 1817, the *Missouri Gazette* complained that

> a large shed covered with boat-sails was erected . . . under which was spread tables covered with whiskey, etc., and at which presided the most thoughtless assemblage ever witnessed, armed with daggers, pistols, and clubs, insulting every person whom [sic] they believed would vote for Col. Easton and inducing the inexperienced to drink ardent spirits until they would vote for their candidate. A great number of persons who intended to support

Col. Easton were deterred from appearing at the election, preferring the relinquishment of their right of elective franchise than
to risk the dagger, pistol, or club.

Fighting, stabbing, and cudgeling occurred. The street near
the courthouse door and whiskey tables were so crowded by the
mob that a person, in pushing through the crowd, was in danger
of being assassinated without knowing who did it.

. . . . A lieutenant of the regular army having attacked a
mechanic of this place, a nephew of Governor Clark stabbed him
with a dagger, and afterward begged his pardon, saying "he had
mistaken him for one of Easton's friends." 9

A few hundred yards off the shore of St. Louis lay a small island known as Bloody Island because of the people killed there
in duels, and the record of the island was an index of the sensitivity of frontier honor. One could fall from high status to
disgrace very quickly by submitting to an insult. As late as
1831 Major Thomas Biddle, brother of Nicholas Biddle, and
Representative Spencer Pettis fought at a distance of only five
feet, with Biddle setting the distance because of his nearsightedness and a fear that he would not have an even chance. When
the long-barreled pistols were raised, the muzzles overlapped.
Both men were killed, but they lived long enough to forgive
each other.10

Benton became acquainted with the island all too quickly.
In August, 1816, he served as second for Thomas Hempstead in
a duel with Joshua Barton, with Edward Bates standing by for
Barton. This affray was happier than most, as the participants
missed each other, shook hands, confessed no ill will, and departed, each having conducted himself in "the most proper
and correct and honorable manner." 11

In November, 1816, the fiery attorney found himself involved
in a quarrel with Charles Lucas, an able and attractive young
man with a promising future. The father of Lucas, Judge John
B. C. Lucas, had been among the first commissioners of land
titles sent out by Jefferson in 1805, and had remained to become one of the region's wealthiest and most prominent citizens. Charles Lucas and Benton were on opposite sides of a
court case. According to Lucas, Benton summarized his case by
stating that "the evidence being so and so," the court should

instruct the jury to find accordingly. Lucas answered by stating that there was no such evidence to his remembrance.

Benton countered, "I contradict you, sir."

To which Lucas replied, "I contradict you, sir."

Benton angrily retorted, "If you deny that, you deny the truth."

Lucas stood his ground: "If you assert that, you assert what is not true."

The jury agreed with Lucas, bringing in a verdict which Benton did not challenge with a request for a new trial. Opposing advocates usually express opposite interpretations of courtroom evidence, but Lucas apparently took Benton's first statement as something personal beyond a mere routine defense of his client's interests, and replied with a denial equally personal in tone. The die was cast. Benton sent an immediate challenge, which Lucas answered with both logic and intelligence:

> for such causes as the one you complain of, I would not feel justified in . . . taking your life, or jeopardizing my own.
>
> I will not suffer the free exercise of my rights or performances of my duties at the bar to be with me the subject of private disputes; nor will I allow it to others for doing my duty to my clients. . . .
>
> You complain of my having given you the lie direct, and have as much right to complain of the whole jury, who on their oaths found a verdict in direct contradiction to what you stated to be the evidence.

Here the matter died and should have remained buried.

Nine months later, for some unexplainable reason, Charles Lucas chose to reopen the quarrel. In later years friends of Benton charged that a group led by Judge John B. C. Lucas resented Benton's prominence and were seeking a way to eliminate him from public life. In this version, Charles Lucas was the innocent victim of the schemes of his father and actually drew the assignment of baiting Benton in a lottery. This was probably a gross exaggeration, but according to his own written statement Charles Lucas himself clearly took the next step. When Benton was in the act of casting his ballot in the election of August, 1817, Lucas challenged his right to vote by asking if he had paid his poll tax in time. Lucas could not have expected the man who had sent a duel challenge over a court-room contradiction to accept without answer the implication that he would vote dishonestly. Different people remembered Benton's exact reply differently, but all agreed that it contained the word, "puppy."

Apparently after checking his own memory with that of others, Lucas sent his answer: "Sir: I am informed you applied to me on the day of the election the epithet of 'puppy.' If so I shall expect that satisfaction which is due from one gentleman to another for such an indignity."

The challenge reached Benton in the morning after he had been up all night attending the wake of his dead friend, Edward Hempstead, who had been killed by an accidental fall from his horse. His answer was equally direct: "I accept, but I must go now and bury a dead friend; that is my first duty. After that is discharged I will fight tonight if possible, if not to-morrow at daybreak. I accept your challenge, sir, and Colonel Lawless will write the acceptance and fix the terms for me."

At six A.M. on August 12, the men rowed across to the island, with Joshua Barton as second to Lucas, and Colonel Luke Lawless, late of Napoleon's imperial army, serving his friend Benton. The smooth-bore pistols "not over 11 inches long" were loaded on the premises. The seconds were armed and prepared to shoot either antagonist who fired before giving of the word. The distance was thirty feet, and the men were stripped to their shirts. Both appeared to be cool and confident. They fired al-most simultaneously. Benton received a slight wound on the knee. Blood spurted from the left side of Lucas' throat; a glancing ball had struck the side of his windpipe. Both men were willing to fire again, and Lucas requested a shorter dis-tance, but Barton and the surgeon, Dr. Quarles, felt that this would be unfair. Lucas was in no condition to continue, and was carried in a fainting condition to the boat.

During the next few days, when friends came to see him, Lucas said frankly that in their next meeting he would shorten the distance to make the contest more even. However, he was satisfied with the outcome, and would be willing to forego any further meeting. Benton, on the other hand, was adamant in his demands for another duel, until friends convinced him that nothing could be gained from it and that Lucas was truly repentant. Benton apparently even visited Lucas, and the two men shook hands.

But the troublemakers would not be thwarted so easily. Word soon came that Lucas' friends, and especially the elder Lucas, were charging that Benton had declined to fight again because of his fears of a duel at the shorter distance. Benton was particularly sensitive to this brand of insult, because Jesse's complaints about the shortness of the distance in the duel with Carroll had caused his fight with Jackson, and Jesse's duel was well known in Missouri as well as other places. There were many former Tennesseeans in Missouri, including Lucas' second, Joshua Barton, who had come to St. Louis with his two brothers only a year before Benton. As late as 1824, Andrew Jackson could write a letter about Jesse Benton, "The redoubtable *hero,* of Squoting memory."

The furious Benton waited until Lucas was recovered and then demanded an explanation. Lawless and Barton handled these negotiations, and despite the later claims of both to innocence and high principle, it is doubtful that either did all he could to keep the peace. There were two contradictory versions of what happened, neither of them Benton's, because he never again discussed the affair except to mention it briefly with an expression of deep regret. Both stories agreed that Lawless drew up a statement which Lucas agreed to sign, but Benton rejected as inadequate. Then Lawless drew up a second statement, more "consistent with the honor of both." According to the elder Lucas, Charles accepted and signed this statement also. According to the Benton supporters, Charles was prepared to sign the latter statement, but was forbidden to do so by his father, who had carried on a steady stream of public invective against Benton throughout, usually adding that "Charles thinks so, too." In this version, Benton kept waiting for the note, but Charles finally told Lawless sadly that no note would be forthcoming, and added, "If Benton wants my blood he can have it." Charles Lucas did sign the following statement:

In consequence of reports having reached Colonel Benton of declarations coming from me, respecting the shortness of the distance, at which I intended to bring him at our next meeting, I hereby declare, that I never said anything on that subject, with a view to its becoming public, or its coming to the knowledge of Col. Benton; and that I never said, or insinuated, or caused to be said or insinuated, that Col. Benton was not disposed and ready to meet me at any distance, and at any time whatsoever.

On September 23, Thomas Hart Benton wrote Charles Lucas:

When I released you from your engagement to return to the island, I yielded to a feeling of generosity in my own bosom, and to a sentiment of deference to the judgement of others. From the reports which now fill the country, it would seem that yourself and some of your friends have placed my conduct to very different motives. The object of this is to bring these calumnies to an end, and to give you an opportunity of justifying the great expectation which has been excited. Col. Lawless will receive your terms, and I expect your distance not to exceed nine feet.

The exact reply of Lucas was lost, but Joshua Barton wrote a copy from memory on the following day. Although "conscious that a respectable man in society cannot be found who will say that he ever heard any of the reports" from himself, and thinking it more likely that they were fabricated by Benton's friends than his own, he would allow Benton and his news carriers to gratify their wishes.

The second duel occurred on a hot, humid September morning. Benton was attended by Lawless, Major Pilcher, and Dr. Farrar; Lucas by Joshua Barton, Colonel Clemson, and Dr. Quarles. Colonel Clemson drew the responsibility for giving the signal. The two men were to stand only ten feet apart. Clemson was to ask, "Are you ready?" If neither answered, he was to continue, "Fire, one, two, three!" No firing was to be permitted before "one" or after "three." As they went to the post, Benton suddenly complained about the heat and delayed the proceedings long enough to roll up his sleeves and bathe his face and hands in cold water. While he was still drying, Clemson asked, "Gentlemen, are you ready?"

Benton answered angrily, "Can't you see I'm not ready?" Hurriedly and with his shirt only partially adjusted, Benton went to the post. Clemson, apparently upset by his blunder and Benton's anger, forgot to ask if they were ready and began to count without saying, "Fire." Benton was startled and glanced at Clemson. Lawless, suspecting foul play, raised his gun to shoot Lucas if any unfair advantage should be taken. At the count of two, Lucas leveled his pistol, and Benton raised his own "as quick as lightning" and fired. The guns sounded simultaneously. Benton was unhurt. A ball went through Lucas' right arm and lodged near his heart.

Benton was horror-stricken and rushed to the side of Lucas. According to the elder Lucas, the dying man said, "Colonel Benton, you have persecuted me and murdered me—I do not or cannot forgive you." Then as life was slipping away, he said, "I can forgive you—I do forgive you." Lawless, however, always insisted that Lucas expressed himself as being perfectly satisfied with Benton's conduct and took upon himself full blame for the meeting. Benton, choked with emotion, pressed the dying man's hand and withdrew immediately.[12]

Judge John B. C. Lucas spent the rest of his life trying to prove that Thomas Hart Benton, a superior marksman and experienced duelist, had relentlessly forced this murderous duel upon Charles to rid himself of the young man as a potential political opponent. This accusation, however, was unfair. Charles Lucas had reopened the quarrel and sent the challenge which led to the first duel. Benton was not an experienced duelist— his only duels were with Lucas. While he may have been a better marskman, a duel fought with the pistol muzzles less than three paces apart is a test of luck, and perhaps nerve, rather than skill, and Benton was much the broader target. Indeed, Benton had fired twice at Jackson at point-blank range, yet Jackson's biographers agree uniformly that the bullets which felled Jackson came from Jesse's gun. The final duel with Lucas was unnecessary and unfortunate, but it was the angry decision of a furious-tempered man whose courage had been impugned, and whose family crest already carried one blot of similar nature. The shot which penetrated the "squoting" rear end of Jesse Benton may have contributed materially to the death of Charles Lucas.

Benton regretted the killing of Lucas to the day of his death, and never again consented to fight a duel. On at least two occasions he simply refused to accept notes of challenge, and twice he endured the most virulent insults and ignored invitations to challenge. There were other affrays, but none in which Benton was armed. His last altercation in Missouri occurred in 1819, when one Richard Venables approached him angrily with a pistol. Benton countered with a barrage of well-aimed stones, and Venables fled into a near-by store.[13] Several years later Judge Lucas met Benton at a social function and berated him violently in the most insulting manner possible. Benton stood silent and impassive. Thus ended a phase of a man's development. Thomas Hart Benton had reached maturity.

Another significant if bloodless conflict of Attorney Benton stemmed from his relations with the Bank of St. Louis, chartered by the Missouri territorial legislature in 1817. Benton, Joshua Pilcher, and other stockholders of the bank believed that the cashier was speculating with paper money from Kentucky, Ohio, and Pennsylvania, and disagreed with its paper money policies in general. Charging that the bank could no longer redeem its money with specie, Benton and his followers simply stormed the bank, took the keys, and padlocked the doors. It never reopened. The rebel stockholders were indicted and forced to post bond, but all were acquitted. Later Benton became a stockholder and director of the prosperous Bank of Missouri, with Auguste Chouteau as president. This bank, which held the Far Western funds of the United States Government, unfortunately failed in 1821, leaving the stockholders liable for the Government's loss. Thomas Hart Benton spent most of his life under the shadow of a Federal judgment of approximately seven thousand dollars as his share of this loss. His later conviction that gold and silver were the only real and safe money and his instinctive distrust of banks rested upon a firm foundation of personal experience.[14]

*   *   *   *   *   *   *

Perhaps Benton's most important friendships were with the great explorers, trappers, and fur traders. General William Clark, who with Meriwether Lewis had first pursued the buffalo and Indian trails into the wilderness and on to the great Pacific, was serving in St. Louis as governor of the territory and superintendent of Indian affairs. Clark was related by marriage to the Preston family of Virginia, and Benton found the Clark household congenial and pleasant. Early factional politics in St. Louis tended to divide on the question of friendship or enmity for Clark, and Benton from the beginning was an eager friend. When Clark's trip east in 1818 led to gossip that the Governor was unpopular in St. Louis, Benton answered the rumors by organizing a great public dinner to welcome Clark's return. Clark was more than a mere dreamer. He had seen the great West, and could add fact and substance to the vivid imagination of his younger friend.

Benton had always thrilled to the exploits of Robert Clive in India, and now found the great empire-builder's counterparts in the great Missouri fur traders. Auguste Chouteau, the elder, had founded St. Louis as a trading post in 1764. His brother, Jean Pierre, had established a fort in present-day Oklahoma in 1802, and Jean Pierre's son, Auguste Pierre, just home from a West Point education and a successful career in the army, was already planning further exploits which would lead him to a permanent château in the Oklahoma region. In 1807 Manuel Lisa had taken the first commercial expedition up the Missouri River, leaving Fort Manuel at the junction of the Big Horn and Yellowstone rivers in present-day Montana. In 1812 the Chouteaus and Manuel Lisa had reorganized their company into the new Missouri Fur Company, with a capital of fifty thousand dollars, and this company later gave way to the great alliance between the Chouteaus, Lisa, Bernard Pratte, and John Cabanné of the Missouri Company and John Jacob Astor's American Fur Company. When Astor retired from the fur business in 1834, Pierre Chouteau, Jr., became top man in the American Fur Company as well as one of the nation's greatest financiers.

These intrepid adventurers were rewarded well for their achievements. The Chouteau estate covered an entire city block, and included a beautiful artificial lake which was useful as well as aesthetic, serving as a reservoir for a private gristmill. Residents long remembered the picnics, fishing, bathing, boating, and love-making facilities afforded by the lake's beautiful shore, as well as the excellent meal and flour which fed most of the city. To Thomas Benton, however, the traders were more than self-seeking profit-makers. They were agents of the national destiny, pushing the continent's borders in the direction of Asia. To Benton's imaginative mind the competition between the Missouri Fur Company and the Hudson Bay Company was more than a commercial rivalry. It was the struggle between Clive and the French for India being repeated by different antagonists in a new age and for a new empire. The traders, supported by the stories of missionary priests, complained that every Indian attack was fomented by the British company, and that the joint occupation of Oregon would deliver the road to India to Britain. Thomas Hart Benton saw the traders' problems as national problems, and made their interests his own.[15]

By 1819 Attorney Benton had found a new medium of influence. Until 1815 St. Louis was blessed with only one newspaper, the *Missouri Gazette,* founded by the irascible Joseph Charless in 1808. Charless was a stormy figure, and from the beginning his paper was in violent conflict with Governor Clark and all his friends. Though, strangely enough, their conflicts never reached the pistol stage, the relations of Charless and Benton were particularly bitter. In 1815 a small group with a thousand dollars' capital organized the *Western Journal* to combat the *Gazette.* The *Journal* later became the *Emigrant,* and in 1818 was finally bought by Isaac Henry, Evarist Maury, and Thomas Hart Benton, who changed it to the *St. Louis Enquirer,* with Benton as editor. Benton finally sold his interest to Duff Green in 1826, but not until it had served his purposes well.[16]

The *Enquirer* gave the free-running imagination of Thomas Hart Benton a forum. With logic and his usual fire he began advocating statehood, Federal protection for the Missouri border and for the fur traders, elimination of the Government fur-trading system and incorporation of a private American Fur

Company, the sale of Federally owned lead mine and salt spring resources to private interests, a national road to Washington, post roads to New Orleans and Louisville, and canals between Lake Michigan and the Illinois River and between Lake Superior and the Mississippi. This was a sound capitalistic program for aspiring adventurers ready to develop the country for a price, and Benton had an equal concern for the older gentry whose wealth rested on the old Spanish and French land grants.

The Spanish grants had been both lavish and careless, and in the spirit of *mañana* the survey and full legalization of numerous important claims had never been completed. Judge Lucas as land commissioner had followed rigid standards, while the Federal Government had simply turned its back by reserving the disputed land from sale without either confirming or absolutely denying the rights of the claimants. Editor Benton soon won powerful friends by advocating a liberal spirit and full confirmation of all questionable claims involving reasonable evidence.[17]

And when the United States and Britain agreed in 1818 to occupy Oregon jointly, and the Florida treaty of 1819 surrendered Texas to Spain, Benton could expound his dreams of national expansion. In the *Enquirer* he brilliantly attacked both policies, insisting that "American statesmen should have constantly before their eyes—(1) the acquisition of Cuba, (2) the independence of Mexico, (3) a trade to India by the Columbia and the Missouri Rivers."

America, wrote Benton, should have three new states on the Arkansas, Missouri, and St. Pierre rivers, each taking a river for its center. Then other states should be created to the rear of these, always with the river in the center. "Such a system would line the banks of the Missouri and other great rivers with a succession of great cities, capitals of States, rising above one another from the centre of the valley of the Mississippi to the foot of the Shining Mountains." The Florida treaty, he charged, would cut off Texas, dismember the Mississippi Valley, bring Spain to the neighborhood of New Orleans, and create a wilderness barrier between Missouri and New Mexico. A reasonable imperialist, Benton would keep Texas even at the cost of a war with Spain, but would surrender the Rio Grande Valley, not to please Spain, but "for the purpose of yielding an agreeable and permanent boundary to our future ally, the Republic of Mexico."

The Oregon question Benton saw in terms of a magnificent dream:

> The disposition which "the children of Adam" have always shown "to follow the sun" has never discovered itself more strongly than at present. Europe discharges her inhabitants upon America; America pours her population from east to west. . . . In a few years the Rocky Mountains will be passed, and "the children of Adam" will have completed the circumambulation of the globe, by marching to the west until they arrive at the Pacific Ocean, in sight of the eastern shore of that Asia in which their first parents were originally planted.

Trade with Asia and the Indies along a line from the Ohio to the Missouri to the Columbia rivers, he said, would shorten the voyage from America to the Indies by twenty-five thousand miles. The joint occupation of Oregon with the British, therefore, Benton denounced as a terrible and unnecessary mistake. The British had laid a "nest-egg" for a future pretension, and before the ten years should end, a "full-grown fighting chicken" would be hatched. The great competitors for the area were the fur traders, and the American traders, afflicted by a duty of fifty per cent on goods imported for the Indian trade, could not compete with the British traders who paid no duties. British traders, furthermore, were inciting the Indians, and America might well be "expelled by violence without waiting the slower, but equally certain process, of expulsion by underselling." [18]

The Chouteaus and their followers were probably unconcerned with the "circumambulations" of the "children of Adam," and apparently turned few handsprings of joy over the prospect of garbing East Indian peasants in American beaverskins. They could recognize a key to their own future, however, in the romantic imagination and Herculean energy of an aggressive giant like Thomas Hart Benton. When the booming cannon, ringing bells, and gleeful shouts announced the admission of Missouri to statehood in 1820, the fur traders had no difficulty in selecting their candidate for senator.

Though not a delegate, Benton, as editor, had considerable influence on the constitutional convention. He had been appalled by the bitter struggle in Congress over Missouri's admission, and in later years boasted that the constitutional provision against any future slave emancipation was his work. He had suggested it as a bar to any subsequent conflict on the issue.

The first General Assembly of the State of Missouri began its work in late September, 1820, in temporary quarters in the dining room of the Missouri Hotel in St. Louis. Among its first tasks was the election of senators. The first seat went unanimously to David Barton, generally regarded as the most popular man in the state, but there were several candidates for the second. Benton was opposed by Judge Lucas and three others, with Lucas the leading contender. After many ballots there was still no majority choice. The members finally asked Barton for his choice, and Barton, despite the friendship of his brother, Joshua, for Charles Lucas, chose Benton. Even with Barton's support, however, various plans, caucuses, and councils left Benton short one vote.

Thomas Hart Benton, however, had powerful friends. Legislator Marie Philip Leduc was a friend of Judge Lucas and had vowed that he would lose his right arm before voting for Benton, but he was also a wealthy Frenchman. On the Saturday evening before the election scheduled for Monday morning, Auguste and Pierre Chouteau, Sylvester Labadie, John P. Cabanné, General Bernard Pratte, and Gregoire Sarpy—all wealthy Frenchmen expecting the fur trade to make them wealthier—interviewed their friend Leduc. The meeting lasted all night, as Colonel Chouteau argued that Benton would work to have French and Spanish land titles confirmed by the Federal Government, while Lucas as a member of the board of commissioners had opposed such confirmation for nearly twenty years. Leduc was a stubborn man, but, perhaps from sheer exhaustion, finally surrendered and gave his word.

By election Monday, however, another problem had arisen. Benton had only a one-vote majority in sight, and member Daniel Ralls, pledged to Benton, had taken to his bed in a hotel room above the assembly and lay at the point of death. No time must be lost, because a replacement for Ralls might be less friendly, and the delay might enable Leduc and perhaps others to change their minds. When the legislature assembled in the dining room at nine A.M., four large, brawny Negroes were sent up to the room where Ralls lay dying. Each seized a corner post of the bed, and simply carried bed, man, and all downstairs into the assembly. Ralls could not lift his head, but when his name was called he could say "Benton" in an audible voice, and the victory was won. Ralls was carried back upstairs and died shortly afterward, thus ending his life on a note of excitement and in a burst of prestige. A county was later named for him.[19]

Nancy Ann Benton must have gazed upon her favorite son with much satisfaction as he departed to take his place among the councils of the mighty, but his mind was soon on matters unrelated to personal pride. Missouri had suffered far less from the panic of 1819 than most areas, but Senator Benton traveled to Washington in 1820 through regions filled with bankruptcy, debt foreclosures, despair, and anger. The Bank of the United States was everywhere assailed as the arch villain behind the collapse of the boom. Senator Benton agreed that the bank was a monster, and he recognized also the role played by the excessive use of unsound credit and wildcat paper money in the flamboyant era of land speculation which had ended in the debacle. The bank and soft money were already strong personal enemies long before he reached Washington.[20]

If the new Senator had expected to begin slaying dragons immediately, he was doomed to disappointment. The Missouri Compromise, admitting Missouri with slavery but barring the institution forever north of 36° 30′ in the Louisiana Purchase, had passed Congress in March, 1820, but certain members then objected to a clause requiring the Missouri legislature to pass laws barring free Negroes from the state. The debate raged again until February, 1821. The clause obviously violated the constitutional guarantee to all citizens of equal rights in all states, and Missouri was finally admitted only on condition that the clause should never authorize the passage of any law violating this guarantee. Not until August 10, 1821, did the Missouri legislature agree and Missouri become a state, and not until December 6, 1821, did the proud Senator Benton take the oath and assume his seat.

* * * * * * *

The months between September, 1820, and December, 1821, were not wasted. In his spare time the Senator learned the Spanish language and studied Spanish history, law, and literature—a necessary skill for the land title research planned for his constituents and a useful accomplishment in later years. More important, however, he renewed his assault upon the affections of Elizabeth McDowell and finally emerged victorious.

Despite her prolonged reluctance to exchange the comforts and grace of a beautiful Virginia plantation for the life of Thomas Hart Benton in Missouri, Elizabeth had been equally unwilling to accept any of her gentler suitors. Five years of French society may have added exterior polish and grace to the Benton personality, and Elizabeth was undoubtedly more impressed with the dignified and magnificently clad United States Senator than she had been with the fire-eating warrior of 1815. To suggest a relationship between his new success and her change of heart is not to question the genuine sincerity of her affection. That twenty-year-old Elizabeth McDowell could refuse Lieutenant Colonel Thomas Hart Benton of Tennessee on his way to Missouri because of his single great accomplishment, a pistol fight with hero Andrew Jackson, but could surrender to Senator Benton almost six years later, was a mark of intelligence rather than ambition. Marriage to a man like Thomas Hart Benton was not something for a thoughtful woman either to accept or reject lightly.

Thomas Benton was thirty-seven when he and Elizabeth became engaged, and had just passed his next birthday when they were married. She was twenty-five. His letters of the moment were the excited missives of any young man in love. Only to his mother did he confide the sedate information that Elizabeth "is a woman of sense, education, good breeding, accomplishments, and family equal to any in America, and of an age suited to my own, and presents the rare example of piety superadded." To a friend he apologized for not paying a visit—he had taken the "shortest route to visit 'One whom I find inexpressibly dear to me under every circumstance of my life.' " And to St. Louis friends he confided that "Time . . . has even put an end to my endless courtship." He hoped soon "for the happiness of imparting a part of my happiness to all my friends in St. Louis, both male and female, by presenting to them *one* who is *every thing* to me and I hope will be *something* to them."

After the wedding in March, 1821, Colonel and Mrs. Benton, with Elizabeth's cousin, Susan, made a long, overland honeymoon journey to St. Louis. From Wythe Court House, Benton wrote his new in-laws that Elizabeth was thriving on the journey. It was a pleasant summer in St. Louis, and Susan made many friends while providing much companionship for her cousin, "who would have been lonely without her."

The trip in the fall back through Kentucky and Virginia to Washington was less gay, because Elizabeth was expecting a child in February. The party left St. Louis on October 13 and had a pleasant trip through Kentucky, but were delayed in the Cumberland Mountains by Elizabeth's "alarming symptoms." Traveling slowly, they finally reached Abingdon, Virginia, where Benton was forced to leave the party and race on ahead to Washington in time for the opening of the Senate.[21]

Elizabeth Benton would later provide the Senator with a home life long remembered by their children for its quiet grace, simplicity, and charm, and a competent observer would describe her and Mrs. Washington as two women never affected by life at the seat of Government. Thomas Benton would earn a reputation even among his enemies as a tender and gallant husband and devoted father, "a house lamb and a street lion." But with all of his bridegroom's love for Elizabeth, December of 1821 found him hurrying alone to Washington. The eager new lawmaker had waited impatiently for a year, and did not propose that the ship of state should sail any further without his assistance.

CHAPTER V

———— ❦ ————

THE SENATOR

THE CHAMBER in which the Senate performed throughout the life and times of Thomas Hart Benton was relatively small and simple, but marked by great dignity. The room was seventy-five feet long, forty-five feet wide, and forty-five feet high, with the interior of a small dome for a ceiling and for light. At the rear was a wide arch upheld by a series of multi-colored marble columns with white marble capitals. On a dais in front of the marble columns stood the chair of the President of the Senate, and directly in front of the dais were the desks of Senate officials. The desks of the senators were arranged in concentric semicircles facing the President. A small gallery supported by iron columns encircled the room, and fine paintings overshadowed by a magnificently draped portrait of Washington decorated the walls. The chamber was also windowless and poorly ventilated. The fact that debates usually raged with greater heat and less reason during the longer summer sessions was probably no mere coincidence.

The members were rewarded financially with eight dollars per diem while in session plus forty cents a mile for travel. At twenty-five miles each day by stagecoach, the mileage allowance was no gratuity.

Thomas Hart Benton had been fortunate when Daniel Ralls lived long enough to cast a vote, and luck was still smiling.

74

Benton and David Barton, according to law, drew lots for the
six-year term ending in March, 1827. Barton lost, thereby facing another election in 1824, while Benton received an extra
three years in which to build a stronger base of political support
in Missouri.

The Senate before which Benton took the oath of office in
December, 1821, was outwardly a gathering marked by harmony of principle. The collapse of the Federalist Party through
its opposition to the War of 1812, the Jeffersonian party's adop-
tion of much of the old Federalist bank and tariff program, and
the almost unanimous election of Monroe in 1820 had led some
to consider American political parties a relic of the past and a
curse happily destroyed. But Thomas Jefferson, gazing upon
the scene from his Monticello mountaintop, knew better and
had a word of wisdom for his friend, Albert Gallatin: "You are
told, indeed, that there are no longer parties among us; that . . .
the lion and the lamb lie down together in peace. Do not believe a word of it." [1]

The Senate which received Thomas Hart Benton had come
to bury the era of good feeling, even if few of its members were
aware of it. A rapidly industrializing Northeast still Federalist
at heart, a Southeast plagued with depleted soils and competition from virgin western lands and already developing a persecution complex, and a West both north and south still angry
over the depression of 1819 and nursing a sense of destiny as
well as discrimination—these could not indefinitely flow har-
moniously along together in the same channel. And the absence of an opposition party could not fail to produce a furious
struggle within the ruling party for the mantle of Monroe. Already, the friends and followers of Lowndes, Crawford, Clay,
Calhoun, Jackson, and Adams were intriguing frantically for
their leader's success. And finally, new states with liberal voting
laws and a widespread movement toward universal male suf-
frage in the older states were creating a new kind of American
politics. America held in its arms a great mass of unprop-
ertied, often ignorant but never shy and always hopeful "expectant capitalists," who composed the so-called lower elements
in society from the factory work-benches of New England to the
tiny squatters' cabins firmly if illegally planted on unsurveyed

Indian lands in the frontier West. For better or worse the power of selecting national leadership was passing into their hands, and the ability to capture their hearts would soon be an indispensable asset for the aspiring politician.

To believe in the wisdom of the plain people was not easy in the America of 1822, but the political leader led by experience and philosophy to such a faith would possess a clear road to power. Thomas Hart Benton was such a man. The process of watching two frontiers evolve had left him with a devotion to equality of opportunity and a boundless optimism about the future of an America where he believed all white men, at least, would have such equality. Equality of opportunity to excel and become unequal was the practical meaning of democracy for most Americans in their young nation's great age of growing pains, and Benton saw a constantly expanding and ever-more democratic America as the answer to this dream. He had also gazed intently at the history of other nations and had developed an almost mystical faith in America and its democracy as a world force destined to elevate humanity.

First, however, there was the job of being a senator. Part of being a senator was looking like a senator, and Benton, the devoted student of the Roman Senate, knew that he had this attribute. Tall, broad, thick, and heavily muscled, his great physique was topped off by a large, majestic head, strong but even features, piercing gray eyes, and a large but not unhandsome nose which probably added to his feelings of identification with the ancient Romans. Occasionally a Senate visitor considered his demeanor excessively pompous, but most contemporary writers, both friend and foe, agreed as to the magnificence of his appearance. One observer described him as born with the traits of the bear, the bull, and the eagle—in physique, temper, and ferocity a Roman gladiator somehow imbedded in the nineteenth century. Another found him the "perfect embodiment of a great, inflexible, untiring will." [2]

Benton's three idols among his early colleagues were the three elderly senators, Nathaniel Macon of North Carolina, John Taylor of Caroline County, Virginia, and Rufus King of New York. King had been a major opponent of Missouri's statehood, but this did not decrease Benton's respect. Macon, who had been a friend of Samuel Benton in colonial days, always wore the finest linen and a fine cambric stock. To Benton, John Taylor's "whole character was announced in his uniform (senatorial) dress—the coat, waistcoat, and pantaloons of the same 'London brown,' and in the cut of a former fashion." Thomas Hart Benton himself appeared in the Senate splendidly clad in immaculate linen, the high, black silk neck-stock, and the double-breasted frock coat which were the fashion of 1821, and this uniform never changed. The materials varied with the seasons, but the style, which added distinction to his great size and dignity, remained the same throughout his life.[3]

The ancient Roman senators as well as Benton's contemporary models were men of great learning, and the new Senator from the beginning accepted eagerly the task of studying every possible detail related to any issue at hand. He made extensive use of the Library of Congress and finally came to be regarded by colleagues as something of a walking encyclopedia. Fluent in Spanish and French, he had a vast knowledge of history and geography ready for use at a moment's notice and could cite with equal facility from the classics, the Bible, the histories of Britain, Europe, and the Orient, and the documents and writings of the Founding Fathers.

As an orator his popularity actually suffered from the extent of his knowledge. Like the historian whose most difficult task is frequently the rejection of irrelevant material painfully gathered, Benton all too often literally smothered listeners with the volume of his research and erudition. Enemies described his voice as harsh and untuned; others found it agreeable or stentorian; none found it weak or had any difficulty understanding either his words or his meaning. Close friends on occasion felt that his speeches were more effective when read than when heard, and his orations on major issues after 1824 were often printed and distributed by the thousands as campaign documents for his party. Another who heard him debate in the heat of passion, however, found it "surprising how mildly the speeches of Mr. Benton read, compared to their spoken effect." When deeply involved emotionally in an issue, Benton was a debater second to none in effective presentation as well as preparation. When angry, he was fearful, raking opponents with icy contempt and biting sarcasm in a voice "cold enough to chill one's blood." Usually, however, he had the self-control necessary to disagree without being disagreeable, and constantly worked at curbing his fierce temper.

In this temper-curbing effort Benton at least tried to imitate Macon, Taylor, and King, being particularly impressed by the courteous treatment and deference which these gentlemen accorded each other. On one occasion after Benton had lashed the Senate with a particularly violent speech, King took him by the hand and offered friendly and wise advice. The old patriarch expressed personal affection for his young colleague and pleasure over his obvious abilities, but warned that his overbearing and authoritative manner when "heated by opposition" sat ill upon the older members, and advised him to show more restraint. As an expression of gratitude and respect toward King, Benton suppressed all publication of the speech and vowed to study moderation and forebearance in the future.[4] With great effort he managed to keep his manner mild and his oratorical delivery dull for a good many years. Only when the fierce struggles of his later career became no-quarter battles did he return to the biting sarcasm and blind fury of his younger days, and only then did his speeches fill the Congressional galleries.

But in December, 1822, such things lay in the future. The new Senator from Missouri had arrived in Washington to serve a western constituency seething with needs, both real and imaginary, complex enough to challenge the full abilities of a leader with energy and vision. The Senator had both and was ready for action.

CHAPTER VI

———————•◦⦚◦•———————

THE WESTERNER

THE SENATOR's first obligation was to the insecure Missouri landholders in need of American titles to their claims. He had already spent several months studying the French and Spanish land systems and law in the original languages, and on February 5, 1822, began to parade the results before the Senate.

Reviewing the Spanish colonial laws, Benton stressed the fact that the Louisiana land grants had been conveyed for services and for populating the region rather than for money. Pursuing this wise policy, argued Benton, the Spanish Government had given refugees of the French and Irish revolutions vast concessions, which, however, carried incomplete titles until confirmed by the Spanish Governor at New Orleans. Unfortunately for the grantees, the United States had confirmed only those grants surveyed before March 10, 1804, and most of the claims had not yet been surveyed. Such claims had been registered in 1805 and withheld from sale pending a decision by Congress. This, Benton insisted in great detail, was a violation of treaties and the laws of nations, and Congress must now make the decision. All holders of incomplete Spanish and French titles should be authorized to institute proceedings for validation in the United States Federal Court in Missouri.

The Senate was not prepared to act with haste. Reference of the claims to the judiciary was finally enacted in 1824, but un-

popular court decisions kept them a burning issue down till
1829. A law was finally passed which provided a new commission to make a final adjustment of the claims.[1] Benton had
worked for a quick victory, but the position of advocate in a
long-drawn-out struggle was in no way a political handicap.

The Senator's next assignment was perhaps closest to his
heart. He would convince the Senate that Oregon belonged to
the United States and must be retained at all costs. In further-
ing this aim he would promote the interests of his powerful
constituents in the ever-expanding fur trade.

This project had already begun. When Benton first arrived
in Washington in December, 1820, three fellow residents at
Brown's Hotel were Representative John Floyd of Virginia and
two heroes of the western fur trade, Ramsay Crooks and Russell
Farnham. Crooks and Farnham already knew Benton and
were not there by accident. Both had been among the founders
of Astoria on the northern Pacific coast, and had undergone
great danger, suffering, and hardship, as well as adventure.
Farnham was a "typical frontiersman of the better class," brave
and honest, but of ordinary imagination. Crooks, destined to
become general manager of the American Fur Company and
John Jacob Astor's right hand in the business, was brilliant,
imaginative, dynamic, and acquisitive. His driving force would
build the American Fur Company, although a careful historian
would later conclude that "in all his career, connected with a
business where the temptation to use lawless methods was so
great, there is no record of any attempt on his part to do anything that he had not a legal right to do." [2]

If Crooks was interested primarily in fur profits, he could
also understand the issue in larger terms, and he was a man
Thomas Hart Benton could appreciate. The four men had
many long discussions before Benton left for his wedding, and
Floyd henceforth served as Benton's *alter ego* in the House on
all questions related to Oregon.

Ramsay Crooks and the traders wanted Government protection in their competition with the British Hudson's Bay Company, but they had no enthusiasm for Government policies
designed to protect the Indians trapping the furs. To compete
with the British for the loyalty of the Northwest Indians, the

American Government had organized a trading system for the Indians' benefit. At various strategic points Government posts were established for trading goods to the Indians at fair prices, with the furs and hides received in exchange to be auctioned to the public in various American cities. Handicapped by the prohibition against use of liquor in the trade, which private traders could often violate, the Government in many areas had not been able to compete successfully with the private traders, and many abuses had developed. It was always possible, however, that reforms might enable the Government to trade more successfully and undercut the private traders in the fur market. Fearing this, those most responsible for failure of the system were loudest in their condemnation of its weaknesses.[3]

From his earliest days in St. Louis, Benton had been well instructed on the evils of the system. Charles Gratiot, his first host, had considered it a threat to the entire fur-trading business. The only effective defense of the system yet mustered has been the speculation that with needed reforms the Government could have served the Indians better than the greedy private traders, but to the Westerner of 1822 this was no argument at all. Perhaps most important, the system was stagnant, while the men like Crooks, Farnham, and the Chouteaus were dynamic adventurers in search of an empire. The Government traders hired to protect the Indians would never carry America to the Pacific, but Ramsay Crooks and Russell Farnham had already been there. If the empire they sought was financial, they were still the chief barrier to British domination of the Pacific Northwest. To Benton the Government factories were useless, expensive handicaps to those whom the nation should be protecting rather than hampering. His agreement with Crooks that the system was a "pious monster" to be overthrown was apparently born of sincere conviction.

On March 25, 1822, Benton delivered his onslaught with a careful summary of the institution's history, inefficiencies, and evils. Over the years, he said, six hundred thousand dollars had been spent, yet the system had not Christianized the Indians or kept them at peace, had not created respect for the Government among the Indians, had not prevented their going to the British for presents, and had not protected them from extortion.[4]

Various defenders answered Benton's charges of misconduct against the factories and pointed out the role of the private traders in weakening the system, but the Senate voted to abolish the factories. Crooks was duly appreciative. The result was "the best possible proof of the value of talents, intelligence, & perseverance . . . since to your unwearied exertions, and sound practical knowledge . . . the country is indebted for its delivery from so gross and holy an imposition." [5]

Later in the year a Federal agent in the Michigan area failed to close the factory rapidly enough to please Robert Stuart, another Pacific veteran, who wanted the factory to sell its stock to the American Fur Company. Stuart wrote Crooks that Benton should "give them another *rap*." Also during 1822 Benton served as attorney for the company in a succesful St. Louis lawsuit against Lieutenant Colonel Talbot Chambers. Chambers, in command at Prairie du Chien, had once stopped Russell Farnham and a partner en route to trade on the Des Moines River, refused to recognize their Mackinac licenses, and ordered them back to St. Louis for new authority. Attorney Benton won a five-thousand-dollar judgment for the company against Chambers for time and profits lost. And finally, Benton over a period of years worked to get tariffs levied on British furs. [6]

Modern critics of the American Fur Company have called Benton a lobbyist for the company, but a letter from Crooks to Benton concerning his fee in the Chambers case is the only evidence ever produced of a financial connection between Benton and the company. The letters from Crooks to Benton were those of an equal partner in a common cause based upon mutual conviction. Perhaps the best evidence that Benton's efforts to help the fur traders were based upon principle rather than mundane interest was the perpetually precarious state of his finances. Several of the Senator's closest friends in St. Louis became millionaires in the trade, and had he chosen to exchange his talents and influence for a share he could probably have done so, but such was not the case. Nancy Ann Benton must have remembered her long-dead husband in 1823 when she wrote son Samuel that his brother Thomas was "full of business and short of cash," and she was describing the Senator's most frequent condition. While he supported a large family in handsome style and the senatorial pay was low, Benton entered the Senate a large landowner, acquired other plantations through the family of Mrs. Benton, and continued his law practice. Over the years, piece by piece, the property, including the McDowell family homestead, was sold for maintenance of his family, while his income and debts ran a never-ending race. A debt of $878.43 incurred in 1822 was not finally repaid until 1844, accruing interest of more than a thousand dollars. In 1824 Benton lost his St. Louis home through foreclosure of a two-thousand-dollar mortgage, retaining possession, however, as a tenant. If Benton was a lobbyist in the modern sense, he was a grossly unrewarded one and there are no records to indicate that he was ever the American Fur Company's man except when its aims coincided with his own convictions.[7]

And the future of America on the Pacific was such a conviction. On April 25, 1822, he fought long and loudly for the western traders. The Rocky Mountain fur trade, he prophesied, would give America control of a vast and magnificent region full of rich products for the markets of China and Japan as well as Germany and Russia at three times their American price. Jefferson himself had suggested taking the furs *"direct to China, upon the line of the Columbia River and the Pacific Ocean."* Along the river routes from the Ohio to the Pacific and beyond, furs would bring in riches "such as were once carried some thousand miles upon camels, and constituted the wealth of merchants whose opulence is yet seen in the ruins of Alexandria and Palmyra." The American trader going to the Rocky Mountains to contend with the British and to the Columbia River to contend with the Russians deserved protection, said Benton. America should send a military expedition to the upper Missouri to overawe British traders and establish a fort as enlightened self-defense for the present as well as posterity.[8]

Soldiers and forts in the Rockies were strong doctrine for the Senate of 1822. The man from Missouri was obviously mad. His madness did not subside, however, and was matched only by his persistence. Two years later he offered a bill to exclude all foreigners from the Indian trade within American limits,

and demanded that four companies of soldiers be sent to protect the American fur traders.

Senator Dickerson of New Jersey protested the idea of troops
because "Thank heaven, that country does not admit of a white
population." Since Americans obviously would never leave the
Indians any cultivable soil, he had hoped that this region of
desert might become a haven for Indians where they might not
be disturbed. To Dickerson the rights of the Indians to their
buffalo, beaver, and game were as "sacred as our rights to our
property." This was sound legal and humanitarian doctrine,
but impressed only a minority. The Senate finally voted ten
thousand dollars which the President could use at his discre-
tion for soldiers to escort commissioners to treat with the Indians of the upper Missouri River area.[9]

The soldiers were not sent, and in 1825 Benton and Dickerson again collided on the issue.

America had sole right by law and by right of discovery to
Oregon south of 49°, Benton insisted, although for the only
time in his life he avowed the likelihood that the Pacific region
might become a separate American nation. As for Dickerson's
idea that the region was uninhabitable and so far distant that
any future representatives would spend each year just making
that trip to Washington, however,

> Within a century from this day, a population, greater than
> that of the present United States, will exist on the west side of
> the Rocky Mountains. . . . Within a century the population of
> the whole will be one hundred and sixty millions; of which a hun-
> dred millions will drink the waters which flow into the Missis-
> sippi, and sixty millions will be found upon the lateral streams
> which flow, east and west, toward the rising and the setting sun.

And, furthermore, this would have world-shaking significance:

> Upon the people of Eastern Asia, the establishment of a civi-
> lized power upon the opposite coast of America, could not fail to
> produce great and wonderful events. Science, liberal principles in
> government, and the true religion, might cast their lights across
> the intervening sea. The valley of the Columbia might become
> the granary of China and Japan, and an outlet to their im-
> prisoned and exuberant population. The inhabitants of the old-

est and the newest, the most despotic and the freest Governments, would become the neighbors, and, peradventure, the friends of each other. They have the same enemies, and by consequence, should stand together as friends. Russia and the legitimates menace Turkey, Persia, China, and Japan; they menace them for their riches and dominions; the same powers menace the two Americas for their popular forms of their governments. To my mind the proposition is clear, that Eastern Asia, and the two Americas, as they have become neighbors, should become friends; that they should stand together upon a sense of common danger. . . . [10]

The Senator's ideas were even bigger than himself, and a head-shaking Senate rejected the idea of a military base at the mouth of the Columbia.

The big Westerner was more successful in the cause of Missourians trading with Mexico. His long-standing sentimental interest in the Republic of Mexico had been supplemented by the fact that Missouri products could be exchanged for Mexican gold and silver. Past experiences and close association with Nathaniel Macon and John Randolph had also strengthened his conviction that true national prosperity must rest upon a non-inflatable hard currency, and this would require gold and silver. The trade between Missouri and Mexico needed a Government-protected road, even if the route did pass through hundreds of miles of Mexican territory.

Throughout the summer of 1824 in St. Louis the Senator carefully gathered evidence and returned to Washington armed with statistics, first-hand accounts of Indian depredations, and a petition from Missouri citizens. Then on Christmas Day, 1824, Thomas Hart Benton made his pilgrimage to Monticello for a visit with Thomas Jefferson. Presumably the younger dreamer and the aging patriarch discussed their mutual expectations for the future of America. More closely related to the matter at hand, Jefferson provided the Senator with the only existing precedent for building a road across foreign-owned territory. Jefferson reminded Benton that the United States had once built a road from Georgia to New Orleans across Spanish territory and told him where to find a map of the road in a volume in the Library of Congress. The young Senator apparently left the mountaintop with the great man's blessing.

Armed with this ammunition, Benton called for the road in a great speech on January 25, 1825. Painting a romantic picture of men and horses crossing the desert plains like the great caravans of Asia, he asked the Government to mark out a road and protect it from the Indian "Arabs of the desert." The trade, he argued, was already worth $190,000 annually and with protection would expand rapidly. Reciting various lurid accounts of Indian depredations, Benton insisted that the merchants' claims for protection were just as valid as the consuls, ambassadors, navies, and occasional wars demanded by seagoing commerce.

A second argument antedated the policy of hemispheric solidarity by more than a century. The United States and its republican neighbors, and particularly Mexico, said Benton, must stand together against the foes of their common systems:

> A speck of republicanism above the political horizon now throws all Europe into commotion. Telegraphs play, couriers fly, armies move, the Cossacks of the Don and of the Ukraine couch their lances, kings and emperors vault into their saddles; a million of bayonets turn their remorseless points against the portentous sign.

Building the road would

> bring together the two nations whose power and whose positions, make them responsible to the world for the preservation of the Republican system. And shall a measure of such moment be defeated by a parcel of miserable barbarians, Arabs of the desert, incapable of appreciating our policy, and placing a higher value upon the gun of a murdered hunter, than upon the preservation of all the republics in the world!

For the friends of the barbarous Arab, however, Benton the skilled advocate had another approach. Countless schools and missions to the Indians, he argued, had disappeared after great expense and effort. Only in areas dissected by the white man's roads had efforts to teach and Christianize the Indian really succeeded. The advanced condition of the Southern tribes was due entirely to roads, and the road to Santa Fe would thus eventually be a great blessing to the "preservation and improvement of their race."

And finally, there was the precedent and great example set by Jefferson in building the road to New Orleans. Several senators offered objections, but the bill passed both houses of Congress by wide margins and was promptly signed into law by President Monroe.[11]

The Senator had advocated the road to New Mexico as a national blessing rather than merely for the benefit of Missouri, and this principle was his fairly consistent lifelong approach to the question of internal improvements at Federal expense. He almost always supported appropriations of public land for roads, canals, schools, or any other worthy purpose, but when money was involved he could usually be found either supporting a project on national grounds or opposing it as purely local in character. This position was reached long before Andrew Jackson's famous Maysville veto.[12]

The Senator's efforts to get the Government out of the fur-trading business were related in philosophy and argument to his equally vigorous efforts to eliminate the Government from the lead-mining business. If there was inconsistency in denouncing the Government for protecting the mining lands while demanding Government protection for the fur traders and roads for the trade with Mexico, it was the inconsistency of which the American West has been guilty throughout its history. Thomas Hart Benton spoke his mind in a burst of true Western doctrine:

> I deny to the Federal Government the capacity to hold a body of tenantry within the limits of any State. The monarchies of Europe have their serfs and vassals, but the genius of the Republic . . . calls for freemen, owners of the soil, masters of their own castles, and free from the influence of a foreign sovereign. . . . God placed lead and salt in Missouri for the use of the people who go there to live; he gave them a surplus of both to sell to their neighbors; but by the intervention of a foreign Government, the people are denied the benefit of the use and the profits of supplying their neighbors.

The bill was tabled by an overwhelming vote, but Benton was not discouraged. After several more years of agitation, his plan was finally passed in 1829, only to be nullified by a later Court decision. Not until 1847 was the leasing system finally abandoned in favor of the policy advocated by Benton in 1823.[13] Meanwhile, however, the Senator's self-appointed position on the side of God's program for the free exploitation of lead and salt provided another downhill boulevard into the affections of his constituents in lead- and salt-rich Missouri.

The greatest bond of love between Thomas Hart Benton and his Missouri following, however, was forged on the anvil of the Westerner's hunger for cheap or free land. Benton not only sought to appease this hunger; he justified and glorified it as the natural and noble instinct of those engaged in carrying America and its democracy across the continent. On April 28, 1824, he launched the graduation plan to be synonymous with his name for the next thirty years. For two sessions the bill was held up in committee, but in 1826 the Senator took the floor for a full-dress speech on the subject. He would reduce the price of public lands annually by twenty-five cents an acre until the price reached twenty-five cents and would then give away the refuse. In a bid for Southern support, Benton insisted that the bill would increase greatly the sale of lands, thus bringing enough money into the national treasury to pay the national debt, which in turn would eliminate all necessity for a tariff. Above all, the sale of lands for the purpose of revenue and the resulting restriction of settlement were a subversion of democracy and a violation of natural law. The Senator spoke:

> The tenant has, in fact, no country, no hearth, no domestic altar, no household god. The freeholder, on the contrary, is the natural supporter of a free government, and it should be the policy of republics to multiply their freeholders, as it is the policy of monarchies to multiply tenants. . . . I say give, without price, to those who are not able to pay; and that which is so given, I consider as sold for the best of prices; for a price above gold and silver; a price which cannot be carried away by delinquent officers, nor lost in failing banks, nor stolen by thieves, nor squandered by an improvident and extravagant administration. It brings a price above rubies—a race of virtuous and independent farmers, the true supporters of their country. . . .
>
> I contend that the Earth is the gift of God to man. *I go for*

donations; and contend that no country under the sun was ever paid for in gold and silver before it could be settled and culti- vated.

God, announced Senator Benton, had given the Promised Land to the children of Israel free and not for a dollar and a quarter an acre. Indeed, the Senator would go further:

> We may open the page of ancient or of modern history—we may look to the example of Kingdoms or of Republics—we may go to Christians, Jews, or Mahometans—we may take in the extremes of Time, and embrace the entire circumference of the globe—we may traverse this continent, from Hudson's Bay to Tierra del Fuego—we may descend to the antipodes, to the Persians, whose feet stand opposed to our own—we may go to the thrones of Darius and Artaxerxes, to the successors of Tamas Kouli Khan— and every where (save in these United States) we shall find land, the gift of God to man, bestowed by the Governors of the earth, according to his bountiful intentions, upon those who will work it.

The Senator's constituents were impressed; his colleagues much less so. The bill was tabled and remained unpassed un- til 1854, but year after year the man from the West forced an unwilling Senate to deal with the question. Every leading statesman had to have a lands policy or follow one already sug- gested if he were to deal with the West. Benton's graduation speeches were printed and circulated by the thousands, and the time finally came when Senator Sevier of Arkansas could say that the graduation policy

> had endeared [Benton] to multitudes in the West. They called their counties after him; they called their towns after him; they gave his name to their children; and it had secured to him an influence which nothing else could have obtained for him. The Western people had gazed upon his proposition with admiration and delight. They had the terms of it by heart.[14]

And if the Government should not keep the Westerner from his God-given lands, neither should the Indian. As chairman of the Committee on Indian Affairs, Benton had clear-cut ideas with regard to the noble red man. He was to be protected and uplifted and dealt with justly, when possible without excessive inconvenience, but was in no way to be allowed to stand in the way of the white man's progress. Under the agreement of 1802 by which Georgia ceded its claims to Alabama and Mississippi, the Federal Government was pledged to liquidate all Indian claims within the state. There was the troublesome fact, however, that under solemn treaty pledges the Government was committed to protection of the Indians in their remaining lands. In January, 1825, William McIntosh, the half-breed cousin of the Governor of Georgia, and fifty other Creek chiefs signed a treaty ceding all Creek lands in Georgia and a vast tract in Alabama to the United States. By the time the Senate ratified the treaty, however, the ungratefully rebellious Creeks had charged their chiefs with treason, slain Chief McIntosh, and prepared to resist invasion. When Georgia began to mount an assault, President John Quincy Adams, a man of honor unmoved by Georgia complaints of discrimination and persecution, sent Federal troops southward to enforce the Government's treaty obligations to the Indians.

If Adams could see justice in the Indians' cause and was receptive to the pleas of missionaries trying to protect Indians, he was nonetheless a realist and had no taste for a minor civil war. In January, 1826, a new treaty was negotiated ceding most of the lands in Georgia, but nothing in Alabama. Benton and his committee promptly ruled this treaty distasteful because it seemed to justify the fate of McIntosh and his followers and did not cede enough land. With Georgia and the Federal Government facing each other with drawn weapons, Benton urged Secretary of War Barbour to negotiate a supplemental article which would make the treaty acceptable. All land in Georgia must be ceded and the Creeks must agree to move west.

This removal policy had already been advocated in the previous year by Senator Elliott of Georgia in a "bill for the preservation and civilization of the Indian tribes." Since the Indians always deteriorated when in contact with whites, they must be moved for their own welfare, and the Georgian thought Arkansas an ideal haven:

> Nature could hardly have formed a country more admirably fitted to such a purpose. . . . It is among the most beautiful and

fertile tracts of country I ever saw. .... There are delightful land-
scapes, over which Flora has scattered her beauties with a wanton
hand; and upon whose bosom innumerable wild animals display
their amazing numbers.

Flora's beauties did not at first make the desired impression
upon the chiefs, and Benton suggested a few judiciously distributed presents as "the only way of treating with barbarians."
Secretary of War Barbour, however, considered this bribery and
refused. Then Benton learned that the Indian diplomats in
Washington were already planning to divide $160,000 of the
$247,000 payment among themselves, leaving only $87,000 for
the remainder of a large tribe. Armed with this knowledge, the
Senator warned the chiefs that recalcitrance would mean no rewards for anyone. Under the spell of this argument the chiefs
signed the supplemental article agreeing to move westward.
Benton, however, was still not finished. With the documentary
evidence of the chiefs' intentions he persuaded the House of
Representatives to stipulate that the money be distributed
fairly among the Indians by American officials. Thus, the
march of progress continued in Georgia, and justice, such as it
was, was at least evenly divided among the Indians.[15]

As the election of 1826 drew near, Thomas Hart Benton no
longer needed influential patrons or dying voters. His base of
support in Missouri was broad and strong. He had enunciated
and served Western interests in the best Western spirit with a
clear-cut philosophy of nationalism in theory and states' rights
in application, and all with the accents of education and knowledge. His people understood this, and his position in their
hearts was secure.

He had also made or accepted another momentous decision.
He had rejoined the cult which surrounded another Western
hero. Andrew Jackson was preparing to bestow his character
and name upon an entire era of American history, and Thomas
Hart Benton stood ready again to march at his side.

CHAPTER VII

———————◦◦◦◦———————

DEMOCRATS AND
POLITICIANS

IN DECEMBER, 1823, Senator Benton struck a blow for democracy by proposing the direct election of the President and Vice President. His amendment would divide the states into districts equal in number to the senators and representatives, and the candidates winning the most districts by popular vote would be elected. To Benton the electoral system not only denied minority voters in each state a voice, but actually added their votes to the opposition. And as for the fear that direct elections would produce tumult, "Instead of violence, it is apathy which we have to dread in our Presidential elections." To the Missourian the American people were "the most enlightened upon earth." Indeed, he announced:

The whole course of an American's life . . . has become one continued scene of intellectual and of moral improvement. . . . Our juries, elections, courts of justice, the liberal professions, and the mechanic arts, have each become a school of political science and of mental improvement. The Federal Legislature . . . pours forth a flood of intelligence which carries its waves to the remotest confines. . . . The face of the country itself, its vast extent, its grand and varied features, contribute to expand the human intellect and to magnify its powers. . . . Under a free Government, the power of the intellect is the only power which rules the affairs of men; and virtue and intelligence the only durable passports to honor and preferment.[1]

The Senate did not question the "flood of intelligence" of which it had been accused, but tempers on the over-all subject ran hot for many weeks before the matter was postponed indefinitely.

If Benton was already establishing his place as a prophet of democracy for an approaching democratic age, its leader was to be another of perhaps lesser intellect, but equal determination and greater reputation. And a sensitive, delicate drama of reconciliation was necessary for the future harmonious combination of their highly complementary talents. In early December, 1823, tall, ramrod-straight, white-haired Andrew Jackson, a newly elected Senator from Tennessee, marched into the Senate chamber to take his seat. Only one desk was conspicuously vacant, and Old Hickory unhesitatingly took possession. Next to him sat Senator Thomas Hart Benton, if anything bigger and more irritatingly self-assured than ever. They had not met since 1814. Furthermore, Jesse Benton had written a pamphlet against Jackson for use in the coming 1824 campaign, and Old Hickory still considered Thomas an enemy. Other senators, perhaps fearing an explosion which might harm innocent bystanders, offered to exchange seats with first one and then the other. Both refused, all the while taking no notice of each other. Then both were assigned to the Committee on Military Affairs with Jackson as chairman.

The air about the two savage-tempered lawgivers remained charged with tension for several days, until Jackson finally broke the ice. Facing Benton squarely, he said calmly and politely, "Colonel, we are on the same committee; I will give you notice when it is necessary to attend."

The younger man was equal to the occasion: "General, make the time suit yourself." In committee they "did business together just as other persons," after which they exchanged inquiries as to the health of their respective wives. Mrs. Jackson had been "Aunt Rachel" to Benton in the old days, and Old Hickory may have been reminded of Benton's position of affection with the one whom Jackson adored above all things on earth. A few days later, Jackson called and left his card at the Benton lodgings: "Andrew Jackson for Colonel Benton and lady." Benton soon returned the courtesy: "Colonel Benton for General Jackson." Finally Colonel and Mrs. Benton found themselves with General Jackson at a White House dinner. Benton made the first bow, Jackson extended his hand which Benton took, Mrs. Benton was introduced, and the establishment of civil relations was complete.

Shortly afterward, Senator John Eaton wrote the always worried Rachel Jackson a reassuring letter: the General was now reconciled with his enemies, including "what you would never have expected Col. Benton." And Jackson added a benign postscript: "It is a pleasing subject to me that I am now at peace with all the world." [2]

Benton was impressed by Jackson's temporarily peaceful character, but not to the point of supporting him in the general Presidential election of 1824. Henry Clay was a cousin by marriage and quite popular in Missouri, and Benton was a willing if not particularly ardent supporter. But when Jackson won a popular and electoral plurality and received more Missouri votes than Adams, Benton switched to the banner of Jackson. Opponents suspected that various rumored political promises had influenced this decision, but in reality it was the only possible action consistent with the sentiments he had been shouting from the housetops throughout the preceding year. The people had spoken, and Benton would obey. Also, if he had not yet completely regained his old love for Jackson, the state of Missouri and the entire West had clearly chosen Jackson over Adams. Benton had already placed himself at the head of Western democracy, and Western democracy had spoken for Jackson. The Senator would not be run over by the very forces he had helped to generate.

Representative John Scott, who cast Missouri's vote when the House chose the President in 1824, had belonged with Benton to the Clark faction in early Missouri politics. David Barton, however, was wholeheartedly for Adams. Scott first wavered toward Jackson, but finally changed his mind and in honorable fashion informed Benton of his decision. Three times the Senator sought to dissuade him, and then wrote final words of warning and sorrow:

> The vote which you intend to give is not your own—it belongs to the people of . . . Missouri. They are against Mr. Adams. I, in their name, do solemnly protest against your intention, and deny your moral power thus to bestow your vote. . . .
> Tomorrow is the day for your self-immolation. If you have an enemy, he may go and feed his eyes upon the scene; your former friend will share the afflicting spectacle.[3]

Scott voted for the winner and paid for the privilege with his own defeat and permanent retirement from Missouri politics. Senator Benton's judgment on such matters was eminently sound.

* * * * * * * *

The administration of John Quincy Adams was one long procession of failures, as the Jackson supporters in Congress fought his every move. When Adams appointed Clay Secretary of State, the Jacksonians piously wailed that a corrupt bargain had been consummated—Clay's support for Adams in the House election in exchange for the Cabinet post. This charge was untrue, but Clay's reputation never quite recovered from it. The campaign for Jackson's election in 1828 began on inauguration day in 1824, and no opportunity was lost to gain the sympathies of the vast and ever-increasing new voting population.

On several issues designed to embarrass Adams, Benton was a leader. He did not support the story of the corrupt bargain, however, and on at least one occasion stated publicly if not too loudly that he had known of Clay's intention to support Adams as a second choice long before the election.[4] Also, Benton's opposition to the administration's Indian policy and criticisms of the Government's lead-mine and public-lands policies were genuine efforts to get his own programs enacted. His denunciations of the Government as a foreign landlord to Western citizens did not abate after the election of Jackson, and his position on internal improvements remained remarkably consistent. While voting with the Jacksonians against most of Adams' road and canal policies, he labored ardently if unsuccessfully for roads in the territories of Michigan and Arkansas.

In opposing the efforts of Adams to send ministers to the Panama Congress in 1826, however, Benton was inconsistent with his own convictions. Perhaps for his own conscience, the Senator developed an elaborate set of technical objections—several hours' worth on the Senate floor—but included his usual attachment to concepts of hemispheric and ideological solidarity. While American participation in this particular conference in the way proposed by Adams was inexpedient, if the Holy Alliance should reclaim the Latin American republics he "would go into the conflict not as ally, but as principal . . . with all our power by land and sea. . . . It would be the last struggle for human liberty, and should be worthy of the cause; great in the triumph, and greater still in the fall." [5]

When the bitter debates produced the celebrated duel between Clay and John Randolph, Benton attended as a mutual friend to both parties. The erratic Randolph assured Benton for several days that he did not really intend to shoot at Clay, and this resolve was strengthened by Benton's emphasis on the tragedy which Clay's death would be for his wife and children. At the last moment, however, Randolph, angry over a report that Clay had demanded a long count to have more time for a careful shot, took a quick though intentionally low shot at Clay. Furious with himself, Randolph on the second shot calmly allowed Clay to fire a bullet through his coattail and then discharged his own pistol in the air, thus vindicating himself for failure to perform quite so nobly on the first shot.

Randolph later went to Russia as minister and, not liking the atmosphere, left after a few days to spend a holiday of many months in London at Government expense. If the Virginian had no time for duties, he could still serve his friends, and, looking up a Benton coat of arms, had a medal struck for Benton, adding the motto: *Factis non Verbis*. He later decided the *non* should have been *et*. When Randolph finally died in 1833, he asked that no notice of his death be taken in Congress. A Virginia colleague rose in the House to begin an announcement of the sad event and fell dead on the spot. In the Senate the last wishes of the deceased were respected. Randolph's several conflicting wills included one which bequeathed a considerable estate to Benton, but Benton's own testimony with regard to his friend's struggles with insanity helped negate all wills except that which left the estate to the Virginian's relatives.[6]

In 1828 a tangled confusion of economic, political, and sectional interests enabled Congress to pass the so-called Tariff of Abominations, one of the worst tariffs in American history. Apparently the Jacksonians hoped that placing extremely high duties on raw materials used by New England might lead that section to oppose and defeat the bill—a result which would injure Adams in the tariff-hungry middle states. The profusion of amendments, however, added so many products that the representatives of every section except the Southeast felt compelled to vote for it. Opposing the principle, Benton voted for the final bill to get a high tariff on Missouri lead, and his part in the debate varied with the product. He supported duties on wool, but worked hard if unsuccessfully to eliminate all tariffs on woolen blankets used in the fur trade. He sought a heavy duty on molasses to help Western farmers making whiskey in competition with Eastern rum manufacturers. This, he said, was sound policy, because "whiskey was the healthiest . . . as men were known who had been drunk upon it for forty or fifty years, while rum finished its victims in eight or ten."

Perhaps Benton's most significant remarks in the tariff debate were aimed at the South in what may have been his only speech ever fully approved by the grim South Carolinian in the presiding officer's chair. If John C. Calhoun was already arranging the ideas which became nullification, he must have gained much comfort from Benton's plea for a tariff on indigo. The North, said Benton, should vote for it

> to show that the country south of the Potomac is included in the bill for some other purpose besides that of oppression. . . .
>
> Wealth has fled from the South, and settled in the regions north of the Potomac, and this in the midst of the fact that the South . . . had exported produce . . . to the value of eight hundred millions . . . and the North had exported comparatively nothing. . . . It is Federal legislation which has worked this ruin. . . . The twenty odd millions annually levied upon imported goods, are deducted out of the price of their cotton, rice, and tobacco, either in the diminished price . . . for these staples in foreign ports, or in the increased price which they pay . . . at home. Virginia, the

two Carolinas, and Georgia . . . defray three-fourths of the annual
expense of supporting the Federal Government; and . . . nothing
. . . is returned to them in the shape of Government expenditure.
That expenditure . . . flows northwardly, in one uniform, un-
interrupted stream.

Textile senators, led by Webster, screamed in anguish over a
high tariff on indigo, and amended it into oblivion. Senator
Benton later "concluded with a compliment to the vigilance,
sagacity, perseverance, and unity of action, which had enabled
the New England members . . . to appropriate . . . all the bene-
fits, and leave to others all the burdens of the different tariffs."
The Senator managed to support the tariff and still emerge as
a friend of the South.[7]

Another Benton contribution to the fight against Adams was
a widely heralded effort to reduce the executive patronage. As
chairman of a special committee, Benton reported a proposal to
forbid the appointment of any member of Congress to any Federal office until expiration of the Presidential term in which he
had served in Congress. Benton had not participated in the
corrupt bargain cry, but this proposition, obviously aimed at
Secretary of State Clay, was an effective if more subtle effort.
From another committee Senator Benton offered bills to regulate the publication of laws and public advertisements, secure
faithful collectors and disbursers in office and discharge de-
faulters, regulate the appointment of postmasters and military
cadets, and protect military and naval officers from arbitrary
discharge by the President. The bills were all tabled, but six
thousand copies were printed and distributed at Government
expense. Thus, even though the major weakness of the Adams
administration was its puritanical leader's refusal to fire his
enemies and hire his friends, the country was treated to the
spectacle of the Jacksonians saving the public morality from
the politicians. In old age Benton still defended the purpose
of these bills, but after 1828 he never proposed them again,
even though challenged to do so by opponents during Jackson's
administration.[8]

For the Jacksonians it was all a rather merry business, and
they did their work well, aided much by the stubbornness of
their prey. Adams fought hard, but his reliance upon morality,

ability, hard work, and good intentions to win through without attention to public relations with the new body politic was already outmoded. His desperate followers, however, made the election of 1828 even more disgraceful than it might have been otherwise. Jackson promptly suppressed all insinuations from his camp involving the moral character of Mrs. Adams, but Adams was apparently unable to perform the same service for Mrs. Jackson. The circumstances of her early divorce from a cruel husband before her marriage to Jackson were falsified, distorted, and echoed throughout the country, but the suffering inflicted was as useless as it was careless. The West and South swept Jackson to victory, and a new era began.

Old Hickory came to Washington alone, because the shock of the name-calling had taken the life of his beloved Rachel. In her place he brought a bitter, unquenchable hatred of Adams and Clay, and by association every principle or policy they had ever espoused. He needed friends to fill the aching void in a heart both fierce and tender, and those who fought by his side would be rewarded well. There were several waiting to serve his purposes, both from ambition and a genuine attachment to principle, and not the least of these was Thomas Hart Benton.

* * * * * * * *

Representative Scott's vote for Adams in 1824 marked an open break between Benton and David Barton, who found his burly colleague's increasing prominence almost intolerable. Slender, slight, and soft-spoken, Barton was nonetheless a fierce competitor who did not surrender his top position lightly. If Barton had helped elect Benton as a less formidable potential competitor than Judge John B. C. Lucas, the magnitude of the error must have broken his heart.

Anxious to remain Missouri's most popular and respected leader, Barton was apparently overwhelmed by the energy, imagination, and activity of Benton. On every question dear to the hearts of Missouri and the West, Benton had an immediately appealing if occasionally long-winded answer, and Barton was soon forced either to oppose his colleague or stand in his shadow. Barton was a proud man who accepted second position to none. By 1823 they were no longer speaking, and Barton's speeches were often deliberately insulting. Benton, on the other hand, had attained a new maturity and ignored Barton's attacks with the utmost dignity.

When Benton became a Jacksonian, Barton chose to remain a loyal Adams man and interpret his colleague's arguments for cheap lands and the sale of mines as political attacks upon the administration. Benton delivered his first great speech on graduation in 1826 just in time for its publication as a campaign document for his re-election, and Barton was stung to a savage answer. Government sale of lead mines, he charged, would help speculators rather than common citizens, and the public would be injured rather than served. Also, the mines were common property, and the people of all states were equally entitled to their use. And the graduation of land prices would only depress existing prices. The people of the West and of Missouri, he continued, did not consider the Government a monster crushing them with oppression by holding the lands, "and no one acquainted with my colleague will suppose I mean *him*, when I say, if we had among us a man endowed by nature with all the great qualities necessary to constitute a successful *TRAITOR*—even he could not disaffect the population of Missouri toward the Government of the United States." The graduation bill, he concluded, was a compound of "electioneering and speculation," and he would not follow the example set by Benton's "studied, popularity-hunting, Senate-distressing harangue."

The duel continued for session after session, and in 1828 Barton called for a decision. The graduation bill "has been for about five years . . . playing before the public imagination, in the Western States, without ever having been brought to a vote. . . . For five years it has hung like an impending guillotine over my neck, and I now call upon you to strike the blow, or take away your apparatus." The bill was defeated 25-21, and continued to hang.[9]

Barton's arguments that the Federal Government had rights as well as responsibilities in the Western states may have had logic and justice for the disinterested observer, but most Missourians were neither disinterested nor logical on such matters. Barton and his friends worked desperately to unseat Benton in 1826, charging him with subservience to Calhoun and Ran dolph and opposition to all anti-Virginian measures, including internal improvements and the tariff. All in vain. Benton had enemies in the assembly not yet ready to accept his leadership, but few dared risk a vote against him. Dr. William Carr Lane of St. Louis observed, "He will be elected— The voice of the people demands it, who dare disobey?" Benton received forty of the fifty-six votes cast.

By 1830 Barton had been on the wrong side too often. He had one last fling at Benton in the Senate, charging that his colleague had been elevated to the Senate by kinship with Clay's wife, aided by others who "thrust a finger under that collar and pulled, who have since had cause to regret it and have washed their hands of the whole affair." Later in the year Barton was defeated for the Senate. He failed also to win a seat in the House and sank into political oblivion, finally becoming a raving maniac before his merciful death.[10]

Missouri belonged to the Jacksonian Democrats after 1828, and Benton's personal popularity and his position of influence in the patronage-minded Jackson administration left him invincible in Missouri. Indeed, after 1826 the Senator did little personal campaigning again until 1844. And as his children grew older and travel interfered more and more with their education, there were occasional years when he did not return to Missouri at all. He made no effort to be a dictator in state politics, but few major decisions, nominations, or appointments were made by Missouri Democrats without prior consultation with the senior Senator. This was not true because of any affection in the minds of fellow politicians, but because his grip on the heart of the ordinary Missourian was unshakable. The Senator's own heart, mind, and rarely silent and always audible voice were in tune with his vigorous, ambitious, and noisy constituency, and his power would be unassailable as long as he remained on key.

CHAPTER VIII

──────•✦•──────

THE SECTIONALIST

THE AMERICA OF 1828 was a beehive of furious energy and creativity. The American genius for reproduction and sporadic European immigration were increasing the population by almost a third every ten years, and although the twelve-odd millions of 1828 were a tiny group in proportion to the vast continental empire already in use, there was little evidence that many of them considered it excessive. The conversion of Indian hunting grounds and howling wilderness into farms, towns, territories, cities, and states was roaring along at a merry pace.

Dynamic pioneers of the great southwestern cotton kingdom stretching from the western edges of the seaboard states to Texas were still riding the crest of an expanding world market for cotton, supported by fertile soils and a horde of expensive but temporarily profitable slaves clearing the forests and bringing the fields into cultivation.

The vast five-state area north of the Ohio River had already been settled heavily by upland Southerners unwilling or unable to compete with slavery or in many cases simply drawn by the greener grass in the distance and the urge to travel. And by the late 1820's, agricultural depression and a distaste for the seamier results of early industrialism were sending thousands of self-designated "God's children" from the holy commonwealths of

New England to the same region. People who surveyed their lands and used clotheslines were learning to live with those who set boundaries by guess and hung the clothes on bushes, and together they were rescuing the Northwest from the heathen darkness of Indian control and the sinful idleness of uncultivated lands. Irish, German, and Scandinavian refugees from hunger and political unrest would come later to assist in the process.

The great border states of Kentucky and Missouri were still a mixture of North and South. Both were growing wealthy on corn and livestock agriculture and small-scale manufacturing, with the mighty Mississippi serving as an outlet to world markets through New Orleans. Missouri was also busily mining its lead and iron and serving as the eastern terminus for an increasingly lucrative trade with Mexico.

Though agriculture was still of immense importance, the seaboard area from Maryland to Maine was humming with one form or another of industrial and commercial activity, as Americans continued to find new techniques for exploitation of their resources. And as might have been expected in New England and other areas where Calvinist traditions predominated, the grafting of urban industrialism on to a Puritan culture was stirring up an intense ferment of humanitarian reform movements projecting in every direction.

Only the older tobacco, rice, indigo, and cotton regions stretching down the Atlantic southward were not bubbling with one or another form of progress, and here worn-out and overexploited soils were bringing the section's former great wealth and power slowly to an end. Here too, however, men had not yet surrendered, and occasional sparks of imagination and ingenuity gave reason for hope that other avenues back to prosperity might be found to replace the declining gifts of nature upon which it had rested so long.

America was an overgrown child springing overnight into adolescence without the aid of an experienced parent. Long limbs and enormous muscles were seeking guidance and co-ordination from a brain eager and willing, but not yet adequately developed for the task of keeping all the parts working in harmony. Each geographic section needed or thought it needed national policies which usually conflicted with the equally firm desires of another region. And crossing sectional boundaries, the large and small among farmers, manufacturers, traders, bankers, settlers, speculators, creators, promoters, and mere adventurers, viewed each other with mixed feelings of dependency and mistrust. America was a land of competition, and its Government was a source of power which each section and group considered eminently respectable when in their own hands, but utterly dangerous when under the sway of others.

The horizontal competition among economic sections and groups was complicated further by the eternal struggle between the defenders of rule by the "rich, able, and well-born," and those welcoming the onslaught of democracy. To call this merely a conflict between rich and poor or even between vertical economic classes would be a gross oversimplification. The emerging Whig Party of Clay, Webster, and Adams, dedicated to the interests of commerce and industry, had its democrats and farmers, including Clay himself, while the roaring agrarian democracy of Jackson had its wealthy aristocrats and businessmen. The most vocal radicals of the period were often men of means and property. Simultaneously, the wealthy conservatives who looked with horror upon the coming of democracy may have been the most class-conscious group in America. As always, men forced to share or surrender long-unchallenged power felt deprived of liberty, and for many Adams followers the advent of the wealthy planter from Tennessee as President of the plain people appeared to be the end of property, stability, and civilization. The most vividly recorded accounts of Jackson's fateful inauguration day described in the words of terrified aristocrats the horde of hawk-faced, crude, hungry-looking barbarians from the hinterland who had swept over Washington to take charge of the event. The thoughts of the average barbarian were not noted, and it may be at least suspected that in his excitement over new scenes and events and his zeal to honor Jackson, he may not have recognized his defeated adversaries as class enemies at all. The man who had come many miles overland to attend the great affair was hardly a candidate for the poorhouse or the storming of barricades.

This is not to deny the existence of social evils in the America of President Jackson. Poverty, slums, crime, delinquency, unemployment, exploitation—all were present, and the great reformers of the period did sincere and valiant battle with them. True also, the social reformers were usually Jacksonians and their support for increased democracy rested upon concern for the underprivileged. Few of the Jackson leaders, however, were social reformers in any positive sense. Jackson and most of his lieutenants, including Thomas Hart Benton, showed little if any concern for slaves, Indians, or the inmates of poor-houses and sweatshops, although they were humane enough to their own slaves and were ready to use the welfare of labor as an argument against high public land prices and the use of paper money. "The People" in Jacksonian terms meant those like themselves, who with equal opportunity could develop the nation's wealth and perhaps rise to high station through the proper use of ability. To Thomas Hart Benton the people as a natural birthright deserved to have the nation's opportunities kept at least reasonably equal, and the Government was a citadel of privilege, not to be used positively to strengthen society's weaker elements, but to be defended to the death against those who would use it to gain unequal advantages in the race for inequality.[1]

A unified Government was not easy in the face of an array of increasingly complex problems which different sections and groups usually saw only in terms of their own interest. Statesmen willing to struggle honestly and tirelessly with involved political and economic questions were necessary if the democratic ideal of free debate as a means of public education were to be valid. And statesmen willing to subordinate their most painfully acquired and deeply cherished convictions to their basic respect for each other and faith in their system of government were required if the democratic methods of debate, compromise, and acceptance of compromise were to keep the nation's divergent groups together. The America of Jacksonian Democracy had a remarkable number of both. Some were motivated on occasion by mundane interest. Others saw nothing beyond the demands of their own section or group. Being human, none was entirely free from personal ambition, pride, or competitive spirit. A surprising portion, however, frequently veered away from expected sectional or class positions in their votes, and most of them probably thought they were doing what was best for all sections and all classes.

The observer of America's mid-twentieth century lawmakers, without denying the necessity for their well-paid research, administrative, and legislative assistants, cannot avoid feelings deeper than mere respect for those of the nineteenth century who did all their own work. Spending long hours over histories, documents, and statistics, seeking genuine policy guidance as well as support for predetermined prejudices, and scratching out in longhand an incredible volume of speeches on the great issues of their day, these titans earned their meager salaries as few public servants ever have.

*   *   *   *   *   *   *

Industry and commerce, dominant in New England and certain other parts of the Northeast and older West, found their great spokesmen in Henry Clay and Daniel Webster. The motives of Webster, the "God-like Daniel" and magnificent orator from Massachusetts, rested upon personal interest as well as principle. He was for a period in the direct employ of the Bank of the United States and invested heavily in certain industries he was most anxious to protect with tariffs. Clay, on the other hand, was a Kentucky farmer who defended the bank and favored the tariff because a flexible currency and strong home industries were integral parts of his dream of a rich and self-sufficient America. He saw commerce and industry not as rivals to agriculture, but as sources of wealth in which all might share. Others, including ex-President John Quincy Adams in the House of Representatives, followed the star of Clay's American system from a variety of motives, but the Kentuckian was the undisputed commander until the mid-1840's. Brilliant, witty, popular, persuasive, and tenacious, Clay believed sincerely that he had the key to America's future greatness in his program for high tariffs, subsidized banking, and Government-financed roads, canals, and river improvements for tying the nation together.

Andrew Jackson's hatred of anything related to Clay or Adams probably conditioned his opposition to their policies, but Thomas Hart Benton fought them entirely on principle. Benton and Clay were friends for many years until the fierceness of their opposing convictions drove them apart. To Benton Clay's American system was nothing but a scheme to strip the South and West for the benefit of the Northeast, and the advent of Jackson to power was to be his own opportunity to destroy Clay's plans and restore the nation to its Jeffersonian heritage.

Missouri was a state southern as well as western, and Benton had powerful emotional as well as economic ties with the older South. His respect for Nathaniel Macon and John Taylor had been genuine, and when he and Elizabeth in 1830 named their first son John Randolph, it was more than a mere effort to compensate the impotent Virginian for inability to produce one of his own. Aware of Randolph's constant struggle for sanity, Benton nonetheless loved him deeply and was clearly influenced by many of his attitudes. Also, Benton's personal and financial relations with the Virginia McDowells meant a powerful vested interest in the welfare of the older South. Standing with a foot in each section, Benton saw Virginia and Missouri as natural allies against the twin evils of high tariff and the National Bank, both of which were indirect barriers against his program for cheap public lands.

The oceans of Southern argument against the tariff boiled down to two major objections. It raised the prices they must pay for necessary Northern manufacturers to an unfair and artificial level, while their own productions were subject to an increasingly competitive world market. Equally important, the ability of foreign nations to pay high prices for a great volume of Southern and Western exports depended in the long run upon their own exports to America. Thus, by reducing American imports, the tariff was reducing Southern and Western prices and trade abroad.

No Southerner mustered more facts and figures to prove these contentions than did Thomas Hart Benton. In the sessions of 1828 and 1829 he tied the bank, the tariff, and his land policy into a single package. In heavily documented speeches he urged the application of the Government surplus in the bank to the national debt and demanded that the bank com-

pensate the Government for use of its funds. By paying interest
on its public debt while receiving none from the bank, charged
Benton, the American people had lost six per cent of three and
one-half millions of dollars annually for twelve years. A combination of this program and the increased revenues which his
land policies would bring, he insisted, would eliminate the
public debt in four years and make possible the abolition of
ten million dollars' worth of tariff duties.[2]

These efforts failed, but the Clay men recognized the dangers
to the tariff in Benton's land program and the fast-disappearing
national debt, and in 1829 found an answer. They would distribute the revenue from the public lands among all the states
for internal improvements. Benton violently opposed it as an
effort to avoid paying the national debt and keep the country
saddled with a heavy burden of unnecessary taxes.

These questions were still deadlocked when Congress convened in December, 1829, and at this point Senator Foot of
Connecticut led off with a different attack. He offered a resolution to have the Committee on Public Lands consider the
expediency of limiting the sales of public lands to those already
on the market and abolishing the office of surveyor general.
According to Foot, at the present selling rate of one million
acres annually, the seventy-two million acres of surveyed land
yet unsold should last for seventy-two years.

An angry Benton immediately demanded a full debate on the
subject before permitting even a resolution of inquiry. He
would "stand upon a great moral principle; that it is never
right to inquire into the expediency of doing wrong." This
touched off a sectional debate lasting from December 30 to May
21. Long after the resolution was dead, the speeches marched
on until virtually every subject of difference, past, present, and
future, among the sections had been covered. Arguments over
who had fought hardest against Britain joined constitutional
and philosophical debates over tariff, slavery, states' rights, nullification, and nationalism.

Benton defeated the resolution and almost won a triumph
for the low tariff. The Foot resolution, he proclaimed in a fiery
speech, was a black conspiracy against the West and South.
Only first choice lands would draw immigrants, and most of

the lands already surveyed had been picked over, leaving only the refuse. Thus, Western growth would stop, and great tracts of the newer states, including two-thirds of Missouri, would be taken off the market. Such lands, already cleared of Indians and now to be forbidden to white settlement, though meant by God for the use of men, would now revert to the wild beasts. This policy, he charged, came from obvious fears:

> The manufacturers want poor people to do the work for smaller wages; these poor people wish to go to the West and get land; to have their own fields, orchards, gardens, and meadows—their own cribs, barns, and dairies; and to start their children on a theatre where they can contend with equal chances with other people's children for the honors and dignities of the country.

The plan was to keep Northern labor from straying westward and to restrict the land revenues to make the high tariff necessary, "a most complex scheme of injustice, which taxes the South to injure the West, to pauperize the poor of the North!" The South, he insisted, was the only real friend of the West.[3]

This denunciation of the Foot resolution as a blow aimed at West and South alike found a willing listener in Senator Robert Y. Hayne of South Carolina, who enlarged upon the theme. Together West and South would extend the frontier and lower the tariff.

The high tariff senators were panic-stricken. Foot answered with an addition to his resolution: "or whether it be expedient to adopt measures to hasten the sales, and extend more rapidly the surveys of the public lands." This overture was followed by the massive Webster, who rose to spend hours seeking to prove that the Northeast and not the South had aided the West most. Among the blessings conferred upon the Northwest, Webster listed the Northwest Ordinance, claiming that this Northern production had saved the Northwest from the curse of slavery.

Benton answered with a long and sarcastic historical review to show that Thomas Jefferson was the real author of the anti-slave provision.

On this Benton had the last word, but Webster was playing for higher stakes than a historical argument. Both Benton and Hayne reacted hotly to the insult implied in the discussion of slavery and attacked the Northeast for its role in the Missouri Compromise struggle. And when Hayne cited the disunion sentiments of New England in the Hartford Convention of 1815, Webster found his chance. A rash of local meetings in South Carolina had recently avowed publicly the right of any state to pass upon the constitutionality of Federal legislation and their own subsequent right to resist the tariff. Webster challenged Hayne to oppose or defend these sentiments, and the Carolinian had no alternative but a qualified defense.

With this turn, Webster came forth with the great oration on American nationalism which remains the masterpiece of its type. As the packed galleries hung on every word, the majestic Webster's deep, organ-toned voice soared on and on in magnificent phrases which smothered Hayne's arguments with their eloquence and emotional power. His final words struck a chord of response in the hearts of the ultra-nationalistic West and drove a wedge into the developing Southern-Western alliance against the tariff:

> When my eyes shall be turned to behold, for the last time, the sun in heaven, may I not see him shining . . . on States dissevered, discordant, belligerent; on a land rent with civil feuds, or drenched . . . in fraternal blood! Let their last . . . glance, rather, behold the gorgeous ensign of the republic . . . not a stripe erased or polluted, nor a single star obscured, bearing for its motto. . . . Liberty *and* Union, now and for ever, one and inseparable.

To the sharp-eyed Benton it was a beautiful speech, but "too elaborately and too artistically composed for real grief in presence of a great calamity." Webster's "part was that of a prudent commander—to extricate his friends from a perilous position" by "starting a new subject and moving the indefinite postponement of the impending one." Why the "sudden proclamation for an earthquake, when the sun, the earth, the air, announced no such prodigy?" The speech would have been more proper at Hartford in 1815 than "here in this loyal and quiet assemblage, in this season of general tranquillity and universal allegiance. . . ." The Senator from Missouri strove mightily to deflate the spirit of crisis, but Webster had won, and the tariff was safe for three more years.[4]

Significantly, the subject of slavery played a minor role in 1830, with virtually no attacks from the humanitarian view-point. On this matter Senator Benton made himself clear. Slavery in the abstract, he said, had few advocates in the South and would have fewer if people unafflicted with it would leave it alone. Slavery had disappeared from Europe and from half the American states for economic reasons, the "calculation which, in a certain density of population and difficulty of sub-sistence, makes it cheaper to hire a man than to own him; cheaper to pay for the work he does, and hear no more of him, than to be burthened with his support from the cradle to the grave." On this principle slavery would ultimately end in sev-eral of the present slave states, and in some areas was already sustained only by habit and affection. In most ways, he con-tinued, slaves fared as the rest of the laboring community. True, there were cruel masters, but they were restricted by law and public opinion, and cruelty also extended to white ap-prentices, bound orphans, and children of the poor hired to the rich. These were all matters requiring time, and intrusive meddling with slavery could only prevent kind laws, cause severe ones, check emancipation, and deprive slaves of instruc-tion because of fears that they might read incendiary publica-tions. And finally, Benton the realist and working politician grappled with the possibility of slavery becoming a moral wedge between people of otherwise common political affiliation and economic interest:

The prevention of a world of woe may depend upon the democ-racy of the non-slaveholding States. . . . I beseech and implore them to suffer their feelings against slavery to have no effect upon their political conduct; to join in no combinations against the South for that cause; to leave this whole business to ourselves. I think they can well let it alone, upon every principle of morals or policy. Are they Christians? Then they can tolerate what Christ and his apostles could bear. Are they patriots? Then they can endure what the constitution permits. Are they philosophers? Then they can bear the abstract contemplations of the ills which afflict others, not them. Are they friends and sympathizers? Then they must know that the wearer of the shoe knows best where it pinches, and is most concerned to get it off. Are they republicans?

Then they must see the downfall of themselves, and the elevation of their adversaries, in the success of a crusade, under federal banners, against their natural allies, in the South and West.

As a partisan, and advocate of policies dependent upon party unity, Benton feared that slavery might finally split the Democrats of the North and the Old Northwest away from their Southern fellows, and his warning that agrarian power rode in the balance was prophetic.

Benton's attitude toward slavery never changed. He owned slaves until his death and was a kind master, but always considered the institution a temporary blight which would ultimately have no place in the modern world which he expected America to become. Never did he defend slavery, but he understood fully the magnitude of the human problems and the explosive possibilities involved in its demise. He saw slaves and masters alike caught in a web which zealots could only make worse—an hereditary misfortune for which almost any suggested direct cure might be worse than the disease itself. Slavery was perhaps the only problem of his day that Thomas Hart Benton faced with humility, and, like his friend John Randolph, he saw it as too complex and powerful an institution for direct human conquest. That time and changing technological, economic, and social circumstances might ultimately solve the problem as an indirect result of efforts aimed in other directions was his best hope. All that Benton ever asked of the North was tolerance for Southern slavery until the day when such processes might develop. And unless actual deeds proved otherwise, Thomas Hart Benton was prepared to assume that such tolerance marked the prevailing state of mind among most Northern people. On the subjects of human nature and the American future he was an optimist, and if he saw no answer to slavery on the horizon, he was equally unwilling to accept the inevitability of catastrophe. No slaveholder ever adopted a saner attitude.[5]

*   *   *   *   *   *   *   *

If the intellectual arrogance of the Senator from Missouri removed its hat only in the presence of slavery, the moral as well as intellectual self-confidence of the Vice President from

South Carolina bowed to nothing. The debates of 1830 might have been even more spectacular, but John C. Calhoun as presiding officer could not participate. Intense, humorless, self-exacting, and noted for a spectacularly pure life even in a relatively moral era, Calhoun moved in an aura of self-righteousness which left him impervious to ideas and facts alike when they collided with his own reasoning. Biographers have searched in vain for youthful escapades, adult sinfulness, or a trace of self-doubt or intellectual humility. Gifted with an extraordinarily able mind, Calhoun's experiences had somehow limited its growth to the single vertical dimension of depth or height. His best-known speeches and writings were towering skyscrapers of brilliance which all too often obscured the narrow, incomplete, and often flimsy foundations which made them dangerous when put to actual use. Observers marveled at his ability to examine the most complex question and with a few well-chosen words go right to its heart, but this attainment often meant the oversimplification of issues far less subject to logical analysis than Calhoun made them. If Calhoun's conclusions and prophecies were often harsh and difficult to face, they were usually easy to understand, and most Southerners seeking explanations for their declining wealth and power found them logical and emotionally satisfying. This was no guarantee of their validity. Pessimism and realism are not always synonymous.

Throughout his earlier career, Calhoun had been a strong nationalist, advocating the tariff and serving as an architect of the National Bank. By 1828, however, South Carolina was in economic distress, and by 1830 Calhoun was himself slipping from the pinnacle of national power. The supposed invalid in the White House was becoming stronger instead of weaker, and Martin Van Buren was rapidly winning the race for the succession. Jackson had learned that Calhoun as Secretary of War had recommended severe censure for the General's unauthorized seizure of Florida in 1819, and other misfortunes, including Mrs. Calhoun's unwillingness to associate with the ill-reputed wife of Secretary of War John Eaton, were contributing to a complete break between Calhoun and Jackson. In the detractors of Peggy O'Neill Eaton, Jackson found substitutes for those whose vicious gossip had destroyed his innocent and beloved Rachel, but the logic of this was small consolation for Calhoun. He and South Carolina would stand together against an evil world of unjust tariffs, excessive Federal power, Jacksonian tyranny, and Northern enemies of slavery. If these were not the South's real dangers, they were at least recognizable and could be opposed with direct action.

In 1830 Calhoun was "not a favorite statesman" with Benton, but the Missourian still "felt admiration for his high intellectual endowments, and respect for the integrity and purity of his private life." [6] Their opposite approaches to emotion-packed problems would lead ultimately, however, to a hatred which neither ever felt for Northerners. Benton finally came to regard Calhoun as a traitor to the Union, and to Calhoun Benton became an unprincipled deserter of the true Southern faith.

* * * * * * *

The great sectional debate occupied most of the 1830 session, but Barton and Benton, on the same side for once, did manage to win one triumph for the West. Congress passed the first of a series of temporary pre-emption laws which kept extending the principle in two-year periods throughout the 1830's. Thousands of optimistic and law-ignoring settlers throughout the West were happily working Government lands not yet on the market. Now they would have first chance to buy their lands at the minimum price when placed on sale. Congress, however, was not yet prepared to grant moral approval by promising such concessions in the future, and the bill was strictly retroactive. Settlers already on unsold lands would have two years in which to buy.[7]

Also in 1830, Benton offered an imaginative tariff program, anticipating the reciprocal trade system by a century. He would reduce duties on an enormous detailed list of products for all nations willing to "grant equivocal advantages" to American agriculture, manufacturers, commerce, and navigation. This program, he maintained in a long, long speech, would abolish twelve million dollars in duties at home and the same amount of duties on exports abroad, would discriminate be-

tween essential and non-essential imports to protect strategic
American industries, would increase international good-will,
and would greatly increase the gold and silver being traded into
the country from Mexico.[8] His arguments were intelligent, but
too novel for the Senate of 1830.

One section of this ill-fated tariff bill called for the elimination of the tariff on alum salt, and with it he launched a lifetime effort to provide the West and South with untaxed salt.
Benton had already added man's inherent right to free land as
a corollary to the natural rights of philosophy of the Declaration of Independence, and the effort to tack on free salt also
became an obsession. He attributed this almost mystical attitude to Nathaniel Macon, and though Congress could never
generate much heat either for or against his effort, for him it
was a deadly serious matter. He considered free salt "next to
the reduction of the price of public lands, and the free use of
the earth . . . as the greatest blessing which the federal government could bestow upon the people of the West." [9]

All in all Jackson's first two years kept the Missouri Senator
very busy. In the fall of 1829, he wrote a series of Missouri
newspaper articles demanding efforts to recover Texas peace-
fully from Mexico. The articles created quite a stir in Missouri, and in 1830 the Senator moved again to strengthen trade
between Missouri and New Mexico. Arguing that the expense
would be like a grain of sand compared to the amounts spent
for navy yards, lighthouses, and ships of war, he persuaded the
Senate to mount and equip ten companies of soldiers to guard
the caravans of the plains and protect the frontier.[10]

While an established friend of the administration and one
of Jackson's so-called "Kitchen Cabinet" of unofficial advisers,
Benton had surrendered no independence of judgment. Henry
Clay in 1830 pushed through Congress a bill to subsidize a
road from Maysville to Lexington, Kentucky, and Jackson,
who would have opposed a free highway to paradise if suggested
by Clay, vetoed it in a stirring message. His argument that it
was a local project of insufficient national importance for Federal expenditure was similar to Benton's usual position, but
Benton was on the other side. And when Jackson also vetoed
a subsidy to the same turnpike company to build a road from

Washington to Frederickstown, Benton voted to override the veto.[11]

The Senator was defending West and South with zest and ability, but the greatest enemy was yet to be faced. The power center of the industrial and commercial forces threatening his agrarian and Western policies was the Bank of the United States, and the bank's national power came from the privileges conferred upon it by the United States Government. To many the bank was an efficient public instrument and a source of financial stability, but to Benton it was a monster capable of destroying the people's welfare at the whim of its masters. Dragons were meant to be slain, and as 1831 dawned, the Senator from Missouri was polishing a shield and sharpening his big sword.

CHAPTER IX

———··⟨∞⟩··———

THE DRAGON SLAYER

THE SECOND BANK of the United States was America's answer to the problem of a stable and flexible paper currency in the days when Government-printed paper money and an actual Government repository for public funds were still dangerous ideas. It had risen out of the financial chaos of the War of 1812 to be chartered by Congress in 1816. The Government subscribed one-fifth of its thirty-five-million-dollar capital and the President could appoint five of the twenty-five directors. For the privilege of serving as sole repository for all Federal funds without paying interest for their use the bank paid a single flat bonus of one and a half million dollars. And its notes were in effect legal tender because they were receivable for all public dues.

The bank began by inefficiently and unwisely promoting the speculative boom of 1817-1818, and emerged from the crash of 1819 in possession of vast western properties. Other factors helped make the depression, but for Westerners the bank was the villain. In 1823, however, the suave, able and self-confident Nicholas Biddle became the bank's president, and for five years followed conservative, sound policies. He drove great amounts of state bank notes from circulation and kept his major loans in the Northeast where security was sound.

After 1828, however, Biddle suddenly became more reckless.

Between 1828 and 1832 Western loans increased to over one-half of the bank's total, and immediate demand liabilities increased by $12,340,000 while specie resources for meeting them rose by only $1,572,000. Biddle aimed at complete control of the nation's business in inland exchange, and bills of domestic exchange, which were usually loans on expected crops, were issued recklessly by the western branches of the bank until the total loans in 1832 doubled those of 1828. Bad weather and lowered crop yields in 1831-1832 ran the bank into serious trouble. Despite the appearances of prosperity and the popular confidence in the bank's notes, specie was running out of the country, and the bank was so hard-pressed for funds that Biddle had to beg help from the English banking house of Baring Brothers. Every western branch was bogged down with permanent debts, and in 1831 the bank began contracting Western loans, but this only increased the flood of angry complaints. Vigorous and imaginative Westerners, clamoring for the means of converting western resources into farms, plantations, mines, mills, industries, stores, towns, and cities, demanded credit and liquid capital, whether paper, specie, cheap, or expensive. The situation was in appearance enough like the condition of 1818 to give the critic, already anti-bank in principle, every cause for legitimate alarm.[1]

And the bank's capacity for harm if mismanaged was just as enormous as its ability to meet the nation's expanding credit demands was inadequate. It controlled the currency and credit of the United States, yet Biddle suppressed all dissent from fellow directors and insisted that the bank was responsible to neither the Government nor the people. The bank held powers of life or death over subordinate state banks and found the buying of influence from the average politician a very simple matter indeed. It could determine prosperity or depression for the country, and easily strengthen the economic power of any group or section at the expense of others. Such an institution was obviously inconsistent with the Jacksonian trademark of equal economic opportunity. That its power had not been recently abused and its performance had provided the nation for several years with a stable currency was less important than the democratic belief that its privileges were unfair and its power too great.

Studying his Western mail and plowing through all available statistics, the Senator from Missouri had grasped some of these facts, and his imagination and suspicions were prepared to generate still more. The mere fact that bank paper was replacing the gold and silver "currency of the constitution" was enough sin to damn the bank to perdition. If there was inconsistency between the Senator's vision of a future America of one hundred and sixty million people and his conviction that such a nation could develop on a currency limited to gold and silver, he had seen much to justify the vision and nothing to shake the conviction. The incredible American productivity which would one day replace gold and silver as the sole support for the soundest paper currency in the world was not yet visible in 1830, and the abuse and misuse of private bank-note currency had caused both America and Britain a world of trouble. His addiction to gold and silver may have lacked vision, but his opposition to private control of a national paper currency did not lack intelligence.

If Benton's philosophy was Western, his economic principles were Southern. The Western people condemned the bank for restricting their supply of cheap money, but to him it was an inflationary agent debasing the national currency. Perhaps more than anyone else, Benton fused the Western ideals of equality of opportunity and hatred of privilege with the agrarian economics of John Taylor, Nathaniel Macon, and John Randolph. His ideal was a simple, frugal government which spent money only for defense and western expansion, kept tariffs and taxes at a minimum, released the national domain to private enterprise as quickly, cheaply, and fairly as possible, and granted no artificial privileges to anyone. The bank was the agent of those promoting a national debt, high tariffs, high land prices, and the supremacy of the Northeast, and was therefore the mortal enemy of Benton's America.

The universal tendency to equate wealth with conservatism has left a distorted historical picture of Benton, the wild-eyed Western radical, making war upon the forces of order and stability in his attack on the bank. To Benton, however, the bank was leading the country away from the principles of the founders into new and dangerous paths and he, as the defender of the original faith, was the true conservative. He was no equalitarian leveler, and no more than his grandfather in long-past Carolina days did he question the rightness of a competitive order in which there would be winners, losers, and also-rans. The Benton economic creed was democratic, but not radical: the race should have a reasonably equal starting point, the road should be equally open to all (except slaves and Indians), no one should receive unfair assistance, and no one should use the rewards from one or more victories to monopolize all of the remaining races. The bank's Government privileges were obviously in violation of these rules and should be removed. The Government should protect all citizens equally and not confer monopoly privileges upon some at the expense of others. Temperamentally, Thomas Hart Benton was an imaginative, realistic pragmatist, and never a radical. He had once damned the "Atheist Tom Paine" and the "Sans Culotte Bloodhounds" of the French Revolution in no uncertain terms, and had not changed his mind in 1832. He was also a careful student and obvious admirer of Edmund Burke, the great British spokesman for enlightened conservatism, and loved to quote long passages from Burke in his own speeches. To Nicholas Biddle, Benton was undoubtedly a radical, but posterity should not make the same mistake.

While the bank's opponents had support from the new West, rival state banks and New York City banks, and workingmen's groups and intellectual reformers in the Northeast, the great majority of Americans in 1831 still favored the bank. America in general was prosperous in 1831, and the notes and credit facilities of the United States Bank appeared to be the soundest in the young nation's history. Two-thirds of the press supported it, and many nominal Jackson men were among its chief adherents. The Democratic Party of 1831 was already a loose coalition tending to treat party heresy and non-conformity with tolerance, and several lawmakers of the 1830's held power as Jackson men while opposing his policies more often than not.

The bank charter did not expire until 1836, but petitions and memorials for renewal were already bombarding Congress,

By 1831 Biddle was negotiating quietly with Secretary of the Treasury McLane for a recharter. Major William B. Lewis, now Jackson's private secretary and as vacillating as in the days when he had had no time for a duel with Colonel Benton, even assured Biddle that Jackson would not oppose it. Like a great steamroller the bank was sweeping toward an uncontested victory. Thomas Hart Benton, however, had not yet gone into action.

On February 2, 1831, Benton asked leave to introduce a resolution against recharter of the bank and delivered a fierce and powerful speech which soon filled a large pamphlet for nationwide distribution. His favorite British statesmen had succeeded after a long fight in reducing the power of the Bank of England, and, quoting their philosophy, the Senator drew a clear parallel. His language was grandiose; his message simple. The Bank of the United States was too powerful to be tolerated in a nation of free and equal laws.

Vice President Calhoun attempted to call him to order for discussing the bank before leave to introduce the motion had been granted, but might as well have faced a runaway locomotive. The Senator insisted that he must justify the motion and would invite a debate. Calhoun grimly nodded, and the hammer-blows continued to rain. The speech won few if any Senate converts, but the Senator was broadcasting to an unseen audience in the hinterland who would understand his words and their meaning:

> To whom is all this power granted? To a company of private individuals, many of them foreigners, and the mass of them residing in a remote and narrow corner of the Union, unconnected by any sympathy with the fertile regions of the Great Valley, in which the natural power of this Union—the power of numbers—will be found to reside long before the renewed term of a second charter would expire. By whom is all this power to be exercised? By a directory of seven, (it may be,) governed by a majority of four, (it may be;) and none of these elected by the people, or responsible to them. Where is it to be exercised? At a single city, distant a thousand miles from some of the States, receiving the produce of none of them, (except one;) no interest in the welfare of any of them (except one;) no commerce

with the people; with branches in every State; and every branch
subject to the secret and absolute orders of the supreme central
head; thus constituting a system of centralism, hostile to the feder-
ative principle of our Union, encroaching upon the wealth and
power of the States, and organized . . . to give the greatest effect
to the greatest power. This mass of power . . . must necessarily
become . . . the sole authority . . . to which the Federal Government, the State Governments, the great cities, corporate bodies,
merchants, traders, and every private citizen, must, of necessity,
apply, for every loan which their exigencies may demand. . . .

It tends to aggravate the inequality of fortunes; to make the
rich richer, and the poor poorer; to multiply nabobs and paupers;
and to deepen and widen the gulf which separates Dives from
Lazarus.[2]

The well-illustrated indictment roared on for several hours,
after which permission to introduce the resolution was denied
by a vote of 23-20, but the object had been gained. The administration press of Francis Preston Blair was soon at work, broadcasting the speech to citizens of every vale and hamlet from
Maine to Florida. And from North Carolina came encouragement from a venerated friend. "You deserve the thanks of
every man, who lives by the sweat of his face," wrote Nathaniel
Macon, adding in the gentle tones of master to pupil, "I observe some bad grammar,—you must pardon my freedom." [3]

Francis Preston Blair, a tiny, frail, hatchet-faced little man,
had come from Kentucky to edit the administration newspaper,
the *Globe*. Nine years Benton's junior, Blair had been such a
sickly youth that his prospective father-in-law had warned his
daughter that she would be a widow in six months. Her answer
that she "would rather be Frank's widow than any other man's
wife" was never put to the test, although Blair looked no
stronger throughout most of his eighty-five years of vigorous
and contentious life. Opposition to the bank united Blair and
Benton in the kind of friendship known only to strong men
sharing a common cause, and the little editor ultimately came
to consider the giant Missourian the greatest living American.
To the Benton children, "Father Blair" was another parent,
and in early manhood Blair's two sons moved to St. Louis to
practice law as Benton protégés. The Blairs did not bestow af-

fection lightly, and their lifelong devotion to Benton was a tribute to the gentler side of the Senator's complex personality.

In the fall of 1831 Benton girded for battle in Missouri as well as Washington, and warned his supporters that Jackson's personal popularity and the success of candidates running as Jacksonians would not necessarily defeat the bank. The bank party would run Jackson men against Jackson measures, he wrote Finis Ewing of St. Louis, and devotion to Jackson's principles rather than Jackson himself must be the true test of party loyalty. Two-thirds of Jackson's new appointments would "act under the banners of his bitterest enemies against his supporters at the next election," and the new party to be built upon support for the bank would be a "deep and permanent thing."

As for himself, the Senator was tempted by thoughts of retirement:

> My interest and the growing state of my family requires me to do so; & if I can get enough of the graduation bill passed this winter as will accomplish my great object, I shall then be for claiming my discharge. I wish to see every man have *land* & salt who *uses* these two articles. . . .
>
> As to voting *for* the Bk of the U.S. I presume I shall never do it. I consider it as Jefferson did, as an institution of the most *deadly hostility to liberty,* and *cannot* support it; but if my state is for it, I shall not *frustrate* her will.[4]

Talk of retirement continued for months and may well have been sincere. There were four little Bentons and another en route by 1831, and the financial rewards of statesmanship fell far short of the cost of his two households and the family's annual transportation to either Virginia or Missouri. Blair, who was forty thousand dollars in debt when selected for the *Globe,* lived to own most of what is now Silver Spring, Maryland, but for Benton the process ran in reverse. Thomas Hart Benton could never abandon a fight, however, and his America would enjoy tranquillity no more during his lifetime.

The Senator had every reason to look homeward with concern, and if opposition to the bank had been his only stock in trade, his senatorial future might have been highly insecure.

Missouri's lone representative, Spencer Pettis, and Major
Thomas Biddle, brother of Nicholas, had killed each other in
a duel which moved to its inexorable climax like a Greek
tragedy: opposition of Pettis to the bank; press attacks on Pettis
by Biddle; a public answer by Pettis; a cowhiding by Biddle; a
challenge by Pettis; an insane distance of five feet set by Biddle
to compensate for nearsightedness; and inability of either to
escape the web of pride and honor dragging them to certain
doom on Bloody Island. In the election of a successor to Pettis, Benton campaigned vigorously for Robert Wells against
pro-bank William Ashley, and called for Missourians to make
the vote a referendum against the bank. Senator Alexander
Buckner, who had replaced Barton, supported Ashley and the
bank, and Ashley won by a small margin.

An ordinary politician facing re-election within a few months
might have shifted ground or at least slacked the virulence of
his attacks upon an institution apparently favored by his constituents, but Benton's philosophy forbade such a course. He
would serve his constituents according to their best interests as
he saw it and not merely reflect their wishes. He would devote
uncommon energy to the task of understanding their welfare,
but the decision must be his. No legislative instructions or
fear of defeat would ever influence his conduct, and he would
hold power only so long as he could drive Missourians to accept his judgments or keep their faith in him despite his policies. Senator Benton returned to Washington in December,
1831, more determined than ever to slay the bank.

The dragon chose to attack its enemies at their greatest point
of strength. The emerging Whig Party nominated Clay for
President in 1832, and Clay and Webster persuaded Biddle to
make recharter of the bank the great campaign issue. Their
clear-cut majority in Congress and the hope that a veto of what
appeared to be a bulwark of prosperity would destroy Jackson
in the public mind were strong arguments, but they failed to
reckon with the significance of personality in American politics. Old Hickory's hold on the popular imagination transcended most issues anyhow. With enough arguments to make
the bank's virtue even doubtful, Jackson would be re-elected in
1832, and anyone risking his future on a different outcome

would be hurt. Indeed, the bank fight may have even strengthened the thread by which the frail old warrior clung to life. In constant torment from bleeding lungs and incessant headaches, carrying a varied assortment of lead in a body badly wounded in earlier duels and brawls, and defying medical science by the vigor of his personality, Andrew Jackson might have succumbed to even a brief period of genuine peace. In the midst of battle, however, Old Hickory had no time for consultations with the Grim Reaper. Perhaps the most sensible speech made for the bank was the presentation of its request for renewal by George Dallas of Pennsylvania. Dallas said that he had discouraged the application at that time, fearing that "it might be drawn into real or imagined conflict with some higher, some more favorite, some more immediate wish or purpose of the American people."

Knowing that the bank could pass the recharter, Benton's master plan was to fight a public battle fierce and colorful enough to rouse the people to support a veto. This would prevent a passage over the veto and bring Jackson's re-election despite the bank's opposition. Almost singlehandedly, he delayed the bill's passage for six months and kept the presses supplied with an almost inexhaustible stream of anti-bank arguments.

In the House, A. S. Clayton of Georgia secured the appointment of an investigating committee with a speech from notes twisted around his finger to conceal Benton's handwriting. After six weeks of examining records and witnesses, the committee issued a majority report against the bank and two minority reports in its favor. All three reports could probably have been written without the investigation, but each side now had its own organized and documented version of the facts.

In the Senate, meanwhile, Benton personally took charge with an arsenal of resolutions and amendments, each of which required a debate and each of which he was prepared to expound at interminable length. Some of his arguments, such as the insistence that the bank's foreign stockholders constituted a danger to America, were shaky, but many of them were unanswerable. In denouncing the bank's direct influence among politicians and the press the Senator spoke more truly than he realized. The bank had long given drafts for salaries of Congressmen payable at distant points without charging the usual exchange, often paid Congressmen before their salaries were due, and had made many large loans to lawmakers. John Watmough in the House and Webster in the Senate were in the bank's employ, and loan recipients included George McDuffie, Samuel Smith, Richard M. Johnson, and the redoubtable Davy Crockett, who came off the frontier to become a bank and tariff Whig. Biddle had also made huge loans to many prominent editors, including Blair himself at an earlier date. Significantly, Adams and Clay had no financial interest in the issue, and it was perhaps only poetic justice that Webster always pursued his great career just in the shadow of Henry Clay.

One of Benton's mightiest efforts was an attack upon the branch bank drafts circulating as currency. This illegal imposition of paper money, said Benton, proved that nothing was safe from the monster:

> It claps a foot upon a word here, and a phrase there—rears her gigantic form above all law, and boldly places an empire at defiance. . . . We are engaged with the real presence of that fabled monster—once believed to be the fabulous creation of frenzied poets—that monster which no art nor power could ever bind! which changed his form, at will, from man to beast—from lion to serpent—from serpent to water—from a river of flowing water to a column of blazing fire; and thus eluded, in the act of receiving them, the grasp and catch of every chain that was thrown upon him.[5]

Unlike many friends, Benton did not assault the bank without careful thought of an adequate replacement, and his mind ranged far beyond the plans of those eager to give the national finances to state banks. In Scotland three competing national banks of moderate capital had been models of efficiency and prudence, and here Benton found the blueprint for his own proposal. In America he would establish three banks, one north of the Potomac, one south of the Potomac, and one at New Orleans, all to establish taxable branches with the consent of the resident states. The capital of each should not exceed six million dollars and each stockholder would be liable if the bank failed to redeem its notes in specie. Neither the Government nor foreigners should own any stock, each bank should make adequate compensation to the Government for use of the Federal deposits, and the interest rate on all loans should be reduced to five per cent. The banks should own no real estate except for their own accommodation, no member of Congress or Federal officeholder should be a stockholder, and no person should be a stockholder or director of any two of the banks at once. No notes of less than twenty dollars would be issued, no state bank note of lesser amount should be paid, and all three banks would be equal in their relations to the Government.[6] This was a splendid program for a static agrarian democracy. America would have outgrown it, but in 1832 it was a sounder proposal than either the Bank of the United States or Jackson's pet state bank program. The Senate ignored it—probably for the wrong reasons.

The heaviest economic charge fired by the Missourian's task force was the indisputable fact that specie was constantly flowing from West to East and out of the country. To the degree that this was the bank's fault it was due to inadequacy rather than planned wrongdoing, but Benton drew no distinctions:

> All the flourishing cities of the West are mortgaged to the moneyed power. They may be devoured by it at any moment. They are in the jaws of the monster! A lump of butter in the mouth of a dog! one gulp, one swallow, and all is gone! [7]

The bank supporters fought with ability and confidence, defending its soundness as a fiscal agent, its creation of liquid capital for the West, and the dependency of the national economy upon its renewal. One at a time the amendments of Benton and his followers were debated furiously and voted down. On June 11 the Senate passed the bill by 28-20, and on July 3 a smiling Nicholas Biddle appeared on the floor for congratulations as the House followed suit by 107-86. Both votes indicated a wide divergence of sectional opinion. In the Senate, six states, New Hampshire, New Jersey, Kentucky, Mississippi, Illinois, and Missouri, had a senator on each side. The remainder of New England, plus Maryland, Delaware, Ohio, Louisiana, and Indiana, were for the bank, with New York and the six remaining Southern states in the opposition. In the House also, several states were closely divided. Missouri's William Ashley voted for the bank.[8]

The bill was a shot of adrenalin for the ailing President. Propped up on his bed of pain, the old soldier announced with grim determination and perhaps satisfaction that he was ready for battle. Attorney General Roger B. Taney apparently wrote the final draft of the veto, but every point had already been broadcast through the *Globe* by Benton. The veto charged monopoly, foreign influence, and the conferring of unequal privilege and artificial inequalities upon those already enjoying great advantages. It also stressed Jackson's conviction that each branch of the Government had equal power to decide questions of constitutionality. The veto was a powerful assertion of doubtful executive power and a ringing denunciation of unfair privilege, but it was no manifesto of economic radicalism. The insistence that the bank charter was a bad bargain for the people's Government and conferred unearned wealth and privilege upon a small group of favored stockholders was an argument which a nation of capitalists, large and small, could understand.

Clay and Webster had saved their big guns for the veto. Congress could not be persuaded to override it, but it could serve as a launching ramp for the 1832 election campaign. Webster warned direfully that only the defeat of Jackson could prevent economic and political catastrophe. He hoped Americans had not become "mere man-worshippers," but if the veto should receive general approval, the Constitution would perish. Clay's arguments that foreign investment was a boon rather than a threat and that the bank had provided capital for the West rather than withdrawn it were brilliantly presented, and he too closed on a note of impending doom.

Webster and Clay had no monopoly on the accents of calamity. The bank, roared Benton in answer, was

> a battering ram—the *catapulta*, not of the Romans, but of the National Republicans; not to beat down the walls of hostile cities, but to beat down the citadel of American liberty; to batter down the rights of the people. . . .
>
> If she succeeds, there is . . . an end of the republic. . . . The President of the bank, and the President of the United States will

be cousins. . . . They will elect each other. They will elect their successors; they will transfer their thrones to their descendants. . . .

The antagonists were well matched. When Benton charged the bank with packing the galleries to influence the lawmakers, Clay had another explanation: If, "impelled by curiosity, the galleries are occasionally filled, when it is understood some Senators are to speak, no member knows better than the honorable gentleman that, when others rise, the galleries are quickly emptied, with whatever else the Senate chamber may then be filled." Benton denounced the Kentuckian for disrespect to the Chief Magistrate, and Clay answered this also. At this period of his life he could not go to Benton for instruction on politeness to Andrew Jackson. Unlike the honorable Senator, he had never fought with the President, had "never complained of the President beating a brother . . . after he was prostrated and apparently lifeless," and had never predicted in the press that Jackson's elevation to the Presidency would require Congressmen to legislate with pistols and dirks at their sides. Benton hotly answered that while he and Jackson had fought like men, they had long since settled their differences, and the press statements had been lies. Three times Henry Clay pointed a long, bony finger at Benton and demanded, "Can the Senator . . . look in my face and assert that he never used language similar to that imputed to him?"

And like a battleship answering salvo for salvo, the angry Benton pointed an equally menacing finger and three times bellowed back an affirmative. It was a falsehood and "atrocious calumny," he roared, and Clay promptly returned the compliment. Amid the uproar the Chair called both to order. They were induced to apologize to the Senate, but made clear there would be no apologies to each other. On this note began the election campaign of 1832.[9]

*   *   *   *   *   *   *

The politicians made the bank the burning issue, but for some voters the tariff and land questions were equally important, and the Jacksonians were uncommonly lucky on both issues in the session of 1832. A fairly moderate tariff passed which neither fully pleased nor completely alienated any state except South Carolina.

Although he voted for the final tariff bill as an improvement over the one already existing, Benton's disgust almost equaled that of his friend Hayne. When the bill came from committee, the Senator pronounced his verdict:

> everybody had read of the mountain that was delivered of a mouse; but here was a great committee which was delivered of a bill which was not even a grown mouse; which is nothing, in fact, but a litter of young mice. . . . What would be thought of a man, who, being directed to fetch you a horse, should go and pull one hair out of his tail, and come and lay it down before you, and say, there is your horse, sir.

In good Western language, the proposed tariff was "the little end of nothing sharpened." [10]

Clay answered that the bill was similar to Benton's proposition of two years earlier for repealing tariffs on certain items, including essence and perfumery. His bill did not touch those items and therefore "was not so odoriferous as that of the gentleman just referred to."

Benton replied to humor with facts and imagery. Presenting a long list of articles which Clay claimed must have protection, Benton showed that they were being sold abroad in competition with foreign products at prices lower than those in America. The tariff, he said, was an unnecessary and iniquitous burden to South and West alike. Despite its natural wealth the West had

> none of the splendid works which imply the presence of the moneyed power. No Appian or Flaminian ways; no roads paved . . . no canals, except what are made upon borrowed means; no aqueducts; no bridges of stone across our innumerable streams; no edifices dedicated to eternity; no schools for the fine arts; not a public building [for] which an ordinary scholar would not apologize.

And for this there was no excuse:

> Behold the marching myriads of living animals annually taking their departure from the heart of the West, defiling through the gorges of the Cumberland, the Allegheny, and the Appalachian

Mountains, or traversing the plains of the South, diverging as they march, and spreading themselves all over that vast segment of our territorial circle which lies between the *debouches* of the Mississippi and the estuary of the Potomac! Behold on the other hand, the flying steamboats, and the fleets of floating arks, loaded with the products of the forest, the farm, and the pasture, following the course of our noble rivers, and bearing their freights to that great city which revives, upon the banks of the Mississippi, the name of the greatest of the emperors that ever reigned upon the banks of the Tiber.

The West obviously received enough gold and silver to "cover the face of the earth with magnificent improvements, and to cram every industrious pocket with gold and silver. But where is this money? . . . Sir, it goes to the Northeast!"

Two principles, said the Senator, would correct this discrimination: sell the public lands without regard for revenue and adopt his system of reciprocal duties to increase Western exports. New England, that "microscopic speck in the Northeastern corner of our America," would never furnish the "myriads of people who can consume the products of the West." [11]

When the bill passed, Robert Y. Hayne had the final word: "the hopes of the South are at an end; and, as far as their prosperity is dependent on federal legislation, their ruin sealed." South Carolina would be heard from again.

After much parliamentary maneuvering, the lands debate became a contest between the programs of Clay and Benton. Clay denounced the "restless men" who had "thrown before the public their visionary plans for squandering the public domain." Governor Edwards of Illinois had recently suggested that Illinois owned all its Federal lands, and the origins of this heresy, said Clay, were obvious:

> The Senator from Missouri was chanting, most sweetly, to the tune "refuse lands," "refuse lands" . . . on the Missouri side of the Mississippi; and the soft strains of his music having caught the ear of his excellency on the Illinois side, he joined in chorus, and struck an octave higher. . . . The Senator modestly claimed only an old smoked, rejected joint; but the stomach of his Excellency yearned after the whole hog! The Governor peeped over the Mississippi into Missouri, and saw the Senator leisurely roaming

in some rich pastures, on bits of refuse land. He returned to
Illinois, and springing into the grand prairie, determined to
claim and occupy it in all of its boundless extent.

Land remained unsold, said Clay, only from a shortage of
buyers. A landbuyer could "with no more propriety be said to
have 'refused' . . . all the other sections, than a man who, attracted by the beauty, charms, and accomplishments of a particular lady, marries her, can be said to have rejected or refused
all the rest of the sex."

The Senator from Missouri answered. His Kentucky colleague had resorted to

> song, anecdote, metaphor; many exhibitions and flourishes to
> entertain the ladies and bystanders; but very few arguments to
> enlighten the Senate. . . . He gave us the metaphor of the whole
> hog and the bacon ham; rather a swinish figure . . . and smelling
> strongly of the barbecue school. He gave us also the figure of the
> blanket pulled off of the old States by the young States. This was
> certainly a woolly metaphor and possibly owed its conception to
> the crowd of sheep memorials which were pressed upon the Sen-
> ate in the progress of the tariff debate. The metaphor of the ref-
> use lands and refuse maidens was doubtless a compliment to the
> ladies present . . . though it is difficult to perceive the congruity
> of the figure, or to comprehend how unmarried ladies could
> be complimented in a comparison with unsold lands which had
> been auctioneered without finding a bidder.

Distribution, he charged, was an "ultra-tariff" measure to
benefit the favored few.[12]

When the ammunition had been expended and each side had
a record for the election campaign, the Senate voted for Clay's
distribution, but the House promptly postponed the entire business. Clay was exultant, but no more so than Francis Preston
Blair and Amos Kendall at the *Globe*, happily running their
presses at top speed carrying the issue westward. Benton's program was firmly intrenched in the imaginations of Western
voters, and its defeat only added to the appeal of his party.

*   *   *   *   *   *   *

For distortion and exaggeration the election of 1832 was
quite the equal of 1828, with each party thoroughly dedicated

to the proposition that the nation could not possibly survive the election of the other. The Clay press outnumbered the Jacksonian papers by two to one, and vastly superior financial resources made its blanket of propaganda much thicker if no stronger in texture than that of the Democrats. To those who heeded both sides the country was doomed to perdition regardless of the result. There was no overwhelming mandate against the bank, but the people trusted Andrew Jackson. Clay carried only Massachusetts, Rhode Island, Connecticut, Delaware, and Kentucky.

To Benton the campaign was a "question of systems and measures," and provided a clear-cut popular mandate for his and Jackson's version of what was best for America. Clay's overwhelming defeat left his supporters and several future generations of historians with the same impression, but the Congressional elections did not support such a conclusion. Jackson swept the country, but his party gained only six seats in the House and lost five in the Senate.[13] The rebellion of anti-tariff Southerners was partially responsible, but the bank could probably have passed a recharter with equal ease in the new Congress. Benton returned to Missouri to campaign again for Wells against Ashley, but Missourians rejected his plea that they choose between Benton and the bank. Missouri supported Jackson by almost two to one, and the legislature re-elected Benton by an overwhelming majority, but the same voters re-elected pro-bank William Ashley and chose pro-bank John Bull to fill the new seat authorized by the increase in population.

For Thomas Hart Benton the fight to build an America in his own image had only begun.

CHAPTER X

HOUSE LAMB—STREET LION

For Elizabeth McDowell Benton, marriage to the Senator was all she had ever bargained for—much that she had wanted, and at least some of what she had feared. By all accounts he was a kind and adoring husband, proud of her beauty and accomplishments, attentive to her wishes, and demonstrative in his affections. He apparently submitted with eagerness to the regime of domestic harmony and order which she imposed, among other things joining the Presbyterian Church and escorting her proudly down the aisle each Sunday. And as the six children (in addition to one still-born) appeared with the usual regularity, he was a model father, giving them time and personal attention far above and beyond the usual call of parental duty.

Bitter opponents were often disarmed by his obvious love for the children, as he walked hand in hand to the Capitol with little Jessie Ann, pasturing her at the Library of Congress while he went on to work, or on occasion sat in the Senate chamber with baby Susan on his lap. As young John Randolph grew older, observers took admiring note of father and son out riding on sunny days, with Benton exhibiting his skilled horsemanship on a magnificent black charger and the little boy trotting happily and dutifully behind on a handsome pony. If suddenly given an inner view of the household, curious eyes on at least one occasion would have found the fierce and imperious

Senator delicately tuning a guitar for the younger children and reminiscing sadly of the distant past when he had performed the same service for his own long-dead sisters.[1]

And remembering the fate of his father and sisters, Benton waged a preventive war for the health of his children with a strict regime often considered Spartan by relatives and friends. Study room and nursery windows were kept open winter and summer, and long walks, daily breathing exercises, and exposure to sunshine were as much a part of their daily routine as morning calisthenics and a fierce cold-water scrubbing with a harsh brush were part of his. The children were allowed meat only twice a week, but received an abundance of milk, fruit, and vegetables. Five of the six grew to adulthood. In 1835, four-year-old James McDowell Benton died after a long period of illness. In days when the state of medical science often made treatment by the average physician even more dangerous than the usual diseases, the loss of only one child was an accomplishment, even for people as well-off as the Bentons.

Thomas Hart Benton had waited a long time for wedded bliss and had no intention of sacrificing any of it. Where many colleagues who lived any distance from the capital accepted, some with reluctance, others perhaps with enthusiasm, the advisability of separation from families and a jovial bachelor existence during Congressional sessions, Benton would live apart from his family only when absolutely necessary. Where Benton went the family went, except during the alternate summers when the long session did not leave enough time for a family expedition to St. Louis. In those years, the family would be left at the beautiful McDowell family plantation, Cherry Grove, near Lexington, Virginia, while the Senator would hurry to St. Louis and back again as soon as possible. When the session ended in March, however, the growing family year after year made the long pilgrimage together to St. Louis and back, often touching base at Cherry Grove en route. There were also trips to White Sulphur Springs and river expeditions to New Orleans, and always the entire family went along.[2]

This was glorious adventure for the children, but not always easy for their mother. On her first return from Missouri in 1821, Elizabeth almost suffered a miscarriage. The following

year, returning with baby Eliza in arms, the coach overturned
down a steep embankment; mother and child were miracu-
lously unhurt, while the Senator suffered severe head lacera-
tions. On the same route, a few years later, three-year-old
Jessie almost strangled from croup. The family quickly turned
off the road to the nearest house, where boiling water and the
usual poultices revived the little patient and presumably saved
her life. Their impromptu hostess, a Mrs. Crugar, made the
Benton home in Washington a regular stopping place for years
on the strength of this service. On other occasions when returning to Washington by boat, the family was forced by early
ice in the Ohio River to seek emergency overland transportation under difficult circumstances.[3]

Of all the children, brown-haired Jessie was most like her
father. Inheriting his drive, imagination, intellectual curiosity,
and ambition, Jessie if a man would have had a career comparable to that of the Senator. As it was, she later almost attained the pinnacle by supplying much of the ability behind
the rise of her courageous and honorable, but often maladroit
husband, John C. Frémont.

Jessie long remembered the excitement of preparations for
the long trek westward. The main baggage would be packed
and sent on in advance. Then one fine spring day a huge chartered coach drawn by four horses would wheel up to the front
door to be loaded with family supplies for the two-week journey
and packed with little Bentons. Overland they would go from
Washington to Wheeling, West Virginia, traveling from early
morning until late afternoon, stopping every ten miles to
change horses, and spending the nights in great roadside tav-
erns. The children were often rewarded for good behavior with
the privilege of riding outside, where they could enjoy the
scenery and sit fascinated by the adventure stories of the open
road exchanged by their father and the driver. Benton himself
loved to drive, and would often take the reins for the entire
day. Arriving at Wheeling, the family would go aboard a river
steamer and float the remainder of the journey, usually stopping at Louisville for rest and a visit with relatives.

The day would finally come when the still-small, but growing and lively city of St. Louis would come into view, and soon

Thomas Hart Benton, home at last, would bend down to kiss his aged mother, shedding tears of thanksgiving at finding her alive and well. Grandmother Benton was still a rugged personality whose advice and opinions commanded the respect of her children and neighbors. Unlike Grandmother McDowell, who specialized in the household arts, Ann Benton considered sewing bad for the girls' chests and admonished them to "never waste time doing what an uneducated person can do better for you."

St. Louis was still an exciting city, with its river front jammed with boats and people, its residential streets lined with beautiful locust trees, and its convivial French atmosphere. During his stay Benton would hold daily court for a stream of politicians, army officers, picturesque trappers, traders, and scouts, priests, constituents seeking favors, and old friends, who had come to see their Senator. Whether agreeing with all his policies or not, they were proud of him and had faith in his ability to speak for their interests. He had come for consultation and could expound and listen in terms they could understand. In later years he would on occasion tour the state, stopping everywhere on the way to visit informally with the people. Each town would proffer a public dinner and an opportunity for a formal address, but the Senator invariably declined in a long public letter which was in itself a blazing political speech. In this way he talked informally with more people, including many not yet Democrats, covered more ground in less time, conserved his strength and preserved his stomach, set a popular example of democratic principle, and still left behind a ringing declaration of his views for them to read.

At Cherry Grove, on the other hand, the family could enjoy the beautiful trees and flowers and the pleasant, relaxed atmosphere of gracious Southern living. There were weddings and parties and a continuous stream of house guests, as relatives came to compare their children and exchange the latest family gossip. Cherry Grove was often a welcome relief for Benton as well as the family from the excitement and tensions of Washington.

To the family, however, Washington was home. There Elizabeth was undisputed mistress in her own household, and there the Senator could return from a day of bitter anger and conflict at the Capitol to a household filled with love, tenderness, and pleasant responsibilities capable of absorbing his interest. Although tutors and private schools bore the brunt of the children's education, he gave the process much attention also. For several years he rose early to hear lessons before going to the Senate and returned in the evening prepared to hear more lessons after dinner. Father and children studied languages together, and foreign diplomats soon learned that when guests in the Benton home they could converse with the young ladies in their own languages and enjoy excellent music as well as gay talk. Susan would one day marry a French nobleman and play Chopin for Rossini in Paris.

At family meals quarrelsome conversation was forbidden, and anyone violating the rule usually dined alone on the following evening. After dinner Elizabeth would sit with her needlework and books, while Benton would work at a larger table using his own invention, four candles fastened in front of a large sheet of white blotting paper, for light. The children would find their work-bench at the great square dining table. The older girls attended a near-by private school for young ladies, and Sally McDowell, the lively daughter of Elizabeth's brother, James, joined the Benton household to be educated with them. Sally's letters home always pictured a gracious, happy atmosphere in which "Uncle Benton" was always respected, usually obeyed, and never feared. At least once the Senator penned his concern for the intellectual habits of the budding scholars, and their gay, young hearts must have been touched as well as amused by his grave admonitions:

My dear Sally,

I write to you as the eldest of the *three*, and impress upon you, and through you upon Eliza & Jessie Ann, the necessity of doing three things in carrying on your studies, *to wit: First*, to look for every word in the dictionary, the *exact* meaning of which is not known to you; *secondly*, to search for every place on the maps which is mentioned in your studies; *third*, to observe the chronology of all events.

Your affectionate uncle. [4]

Elizabeth's life with the Senator and her large brood was clearly an interesting and exciting affair and probably gave her many moments of supreme happiness. It must have been also an exhausting life, however, filled with enormous physical and emotional demands as she learned to share the atmosphere of constant activity and perpetual controversy in which the Senator moved. Small wonder, perhaps, that in 1842, the same year in which she watched twelve-year-old Randolph depart on a westward expedition with Frémont, Elizabeth suffered the first of a series of attacks which ultimately left her in a twilight of both mind and body. And consistent to the end, the grief-stricken Benton gave her twelve years of the most tender and loving care imaginable.

*   *   *   *   *   *   *

Like Jackson, Thomas Hart Benton knew a joy and contentment surpassed by few men in marriage and the companionship of little children. Yet there was little external evidence that the experience softened his conduct in dealing with men and affairs. His capacity for love and tenderness within the family circle and among friends never appeared to diminish his proclivity for implacable hatred and violence among enemies. Jessie, who knew his "Big Bully Bottom" reputation, would look at her great bear of a father at his work-table and see only a dignified, benign, gentle, kind, and loving parent. How could anyone think him otherwise? Yet the reputation began when he was sixteen, grew at the expense of Jackson, probably shook the aim of Charles Lucas, and was never weakened by his political habits. When Benton in 1850 informed the Senate in a chilling voice, "Mr. President, sir . . . I never quarrel, sir. But sometimes I fight, sir; and whenever I fight, sir, a funeral follows, sir," he was only stating what colleagues had believed for years. To opponents it was the reputation of a brutally overbearing and dangerous man, and he had earned every bit of it. This should not have been surprising. His formative years had been spent as lawyer, soldier, editor, and politician in areas where the moral code defined enemies as objects fit only for intense hatred and destruction. Elizabeth and the children rescued and developed his better nature, but the earlier emotional habits never fully disappeared.

Perhaps the Senator also found a vested interest in maintaining his earlier reputation. The story of his Chapel Hill disgrace was well known to opponents, yet only twice during his thirty years in the Senate was the charge hurled at him on the floor, and each time by imputation rather than direct charge. A sense of fair play undoubtedly influenced many, but others were probably deterred only by fear. A lesser man might have been driven from the Senate. That the story was never whispered loudly enough even to attract the serious attention of Benton's first three biographers is a remarkable fact testifying eloquently to the occasional value of a dangerous reputation.

And as time passed, the Senator's colossal egotism became as legendary as his towering rage, and served his purposes equally well. His bold conceit was well grounded, and matched well the temperament of the nation he served. At nineteen he had led his mother and brothers and sisters into a rugged, unsettled wilderness, where they had carved out a comfortable living. By hard work, study, and courage he had overcome a shattering disgrace and become a successful lawyer, soldier, and politician, rising to high position and power. Even the threat of tuberculosis had yielded to his fierce determination. Self-doubt was a habit he had had no opportunity to acquire. He informed America that he could and would conquer any situation, and a brash young nation feeling the exhilaration of manifest destiny took affectionate pleasure in his example and came to regard his self-pride as a national institution. It was a satisfying role, well-tailored for effective use by a skilled political leader, and Benton obviously cultivated and nurtured it. Expected to provide a performance, the great man rarely disappointed his audience.

The Senator's egotism was not the painful effort to bolster self-esteem so often practiced by those suffering feelings of inadequacy. His keen and robust sense of humor, utter aversion to fanaticism and firm grip on reality, readiness to forgive enemies, ability to separate policy decisions from personal animosities (although they often went together), and capacity for giving and inspiring deep and abiding love among family and friends were not the marks of a man driven by emotional insecurities.

Chapel Hill, however, was a long root. Friends were exasperated in 1840, 1848, and 1852 by his refusal to seek a Presidential or Vice Presidential nomination, and his early disgrace may well have been one of the explanations. Whispered or even written about a senator, the story remained a rumor considered ridiculous by friends and supporters. The records existed, however, and a Presidential campaign would probably have produced them. Every election from 1828 on illustrated the viciousness which the struggle for national power could generate in otherwise reasonable people. The Senator was vulnerable and knew it. The Senate was to be his one avenue to greatness, and he apparently never considered anything higher. There was a compensation. His independence of party discipline and disdain for easy avenues to popularity would have been impossible in a serious Presidential aspirant, and upon these characteristics rested the final claim to greatness of Thomas Hart Benton.

CHAPTER XI

———————·◦◦◦··——————

OLD BULLION

MOST OF ANDREW JACKSON's first message to Congress after the election of 1832 was a proclamation after Benton's own heart. The old General proudly announced the imminent extinction of the national debt, a magnificent achievement expected to produce a multitude of blessings. With the resulting decrease of the Government's financial needs, new tariff legislation could limit protection to those articles necessary for national defense, and the public lands could be sold to settlers in limited parcels at a price barely sufficient to pay for the system. There were, however, a few pending problems. The ungrateful Cherokees were still refusing to sell their remaining lands in Georgia; Congress should investigate the Bank of the United States to determine if it was still a safe repository for public funds; and people in a certain area were threatening to defy the laws and "endanger the integrity of the Union." The President hoped that prudence and patriotism would prevail in South Carolina, but if he should need help from Congress to enforce the laws he would ask for it.

Thus the inwardly boiling Jackson announced the emergence of John C. Calhoun as the politician of crisis. Sentiment against the tariff had smoldered in South Carolina since 1828, and the disappointment of 1832 only added fuel and a blast of air to the banked fires. The situation needed only a leader to become dangerous, and Calhoun was available.

Convinced by his own fall from national power that Jackson was a dangerous tyrant, Calhoun prepared to resist. He had already written a brilliant treatise defining the Federal Government as a creation of the states and proclaiming the right of any state to defy or "nullify" Federal legislation it might consider unconstitutional. His Washington paper, the *United States Telegraph*, had warned throughout the election campaign that if Jackson was re-elected, "those daring and corrupt politicians" using the General's popularity would "subvert the very foundations of liberty, and convert this government into the corrupt engine of the most odious and profligate despotism." Jackson and his "daring and corrupt politicians" were South Carolina's best hope for a low tariff, and the Democratic Party remained the bastion of Southern values until 1860, but Calhoun resolved the dilemma quickly. He and the South were inseparable. He had been wounded, and South Carolina must be defended. The brilliant Joel Poinsett led a powerful Union movement and kept the fuming Jackson informed as the crisis developed, but Calhoun's nullification treatise and personal influence were decisive. The Nullifiers won South Carolina, declared the tariff unconstitutional, and announced they would resist its collection, by force if necessary.

The crisis was peculiarly ill-timed. The tariff of 1832 was considerably lower than that of 1828, and there was every reason to believe that normal constitutional processes would relieve the situation still further in 1833. The debt was paid, the treasury was full, the administration was openly anti-tariff, and the elections of 1832 indicated that the Congress scheduled for December, 1833, would on this matter follow Jackson's recommendations. Clay, Webster, Adams, and others glumly feared that the protective principle was in danger, and Thomas Hart Benton was exultant for the same reason. Calhoun, however, could not wait. A principle was at stake. South Carolina was a minority interest, and the tariff issue must determine whether it was safe from Federal and executive tyranny.

Jackson, whose long, bony fingers itched for Calhoun's throat anyhow, did not intend to wait either. Five days before he announced the crisis to Congress in early December, 1832, additional troops and a fleet of warships were en route to South

Carolina. His reasoned yet stirring proclamation condemning South Carolina's unjustified threat to "the rich inheritance bequeathed by our fathers" followed. In response Congress began work on a bill authorizing the use of force if necessary to collect the revenues, and the overwhelming majority of both parties rallied to the President's support.

This single issue of Jackson's reign which commanded almost universal support found Thomas Hart Benton out of step with his leader. Benton considered nullification "madness" personified, but was fearful of the possible results if blood should be spilled. Apparently not yet sharing Jackson's personal hatred of Calhoun, the Missourian considered the President's spectacular approach much too strong. James McDowell assured him that a fiery nullification speech by John Tyler was highly regarded in Virginia, and Benton thought the issue might well lead to a Southern convention. "To carry off the storm quietly" was his aim, and for this purpose he wanted a special session of Congress called for April or May to bring in the newly elected Congress which he confidently expected to reduce the tariff. On December 16 he urged Van Buren to support this idea, warning that a continuing tariff would give Clay a huge surplus for bribing voters with his distribution plan. Jackson held firm, however, and two months later Benton was still calling for Van Buren to come to Washington and use his well-known talents for peacemaking on Jackson. Thus, Jackson's leading Senate spokesman sat silently while Daniel Webster, who had prophesied national catastrophe if the President should be re-elected, took the lead in answering Calhoun's arguments and getting Jackson's force bill through the Senate. The final vote was an overwhelming victory for Jackson and nationalism, but the roll call met only silence when it reached the Senator from Missouri.[1]

Benton was noisy enough, however, when Clay at the peak of the crisis suddenly presented a compromise tariff already agreed to by Calhoun and his followers. The somewhat relieved administration supported the measure behind the scenes, but Thomas Hart Benton was unimpressed.

In form a face-saving compromise for South Carolina, the bill was deceptive in its practical results. Duties were to be gradually reduced to a flat twenty per cent over a ten-year period, with the major reductions to come during the last two years. Clay, who had consulted his manufacturing friends fully, while saying nothing to Webster, did not disguise his purpose. The tariff was in danger and "must fall at the next session." To prevent this he wished "to place it on a bed of security and repose for nine years, where it may grow and strengthen, and become acceptable to the whole people."

To the realistic and angry Benton, the bill tied the hands of Congress for ten years, during which time many events might create new revenue needs and enable tariff supporters to regain the upper hand. Even Andrew Jackson, after all, could not live forever. The bill also restored to fifty per cent a duty eliminated in 1832 on cheap woolens used extensively by the South, and Clay surprised Calhoun with an amendment providing for evaluations at the American port of entry. This would add transportation and handling costs to all dutiable values. Calhoun complained bitterly, but was forced to swallow the amendment to save the bill.

The woolens tariff roused Benton's particular ire. Senator Smith of Maryland moved to strike out the provision, but Foot of Connecticut insisted that the Southerners had agreed to it and that "they were competent to guard their own interest." Clay added that without it the bill would fail. Benton was furious. This was an unfair tax, he said, entirely on the South and the laboring community of the North, and all for the sake of "two or three little factories in Connecticut." Obviously the South's so-called ability to guard its own interest "was a species of ability not confined to the South."

The bill passed, with Calhoun and the Nullifiers standing beside Clay and the Jacksonians, and Benton voting with Webster and certain disappointed high-tariff senators against it, but for opposite reasons. The tariff was thus nominally removed from politics for ten years, but neither Benton nor Clay expected the arrangement to last, and both knew that tariff considerations would remain part of all future arguments related to lands and the treasury.

Benton and Clay rarely agreed, but both remained convinced that Clay had used Calhoun's crisis to save the tariff from a real attack in the following session. The ratio of duties to imports did not decline appreciably, tending to fluctuate with the general economic situation, and the enormous amounts collected soon gave America its first and only treasury surplus problem. Calhoun's ill-timed application of brilliant theory to a practical situation had resulted in his defeat by Jackson on the states' rights principle and a virtual defeat by Clay on the tariff, when both might have been avoided. The lesson was not lost on Thomas Hart Benton.[2]

* * * * * * * *

In the spring of 1833 the Benton family caravan arrived in St. Louis to find a region filled with terror. Cholera was sweeping the area, and hundreds of people, including some of their closest friends, were stricken. Benton felt his family should stay and set an example of courage, and by organizing the household into a state of boiled sterility resembling a hospital they remained safe until time for their departure back to Virginia.

Others were less fortunate. Alexander Buckner, Benton's senatorial colleague and frequent opponent, was one of the victims. Governor Dunklin appointed in his place Dr. Lewis F. Linn, a practicing physician and a Democrat of the Benton school.

For Benton, Linn quickly became the ideal partner. Believing that Benton's "splendid talents, unwavering purpose of Soul, and expanded views entitled him to the Character of a great Man," Linn had a deep affection for his imperious colleague, and had no compulsion to compete for first place. Gifted with a keen intelligence and extensive knowledge, he was content to serve as an unusually talented lieutenant. The two men worked together in close harmony, and as the issues became more numerous and complex there was an efficient division of labor as each sponsored programs for which the other had less time. Thus Linn finally took up Benton's long-postponed program for the settlement of Oregon and ultimately sponsored the successful bill for its consummation. Like Van Buren, Linn was a peacemaker by temperament, and, understanding Benton's faults as well as his strong points, handled him skillfully, and occasionally served as a buffer in his relations with other politicians.[3]

In electing representatives, however, the Missouri Democrats were less fortunate. Democrats George Shannon and George Strother both insisted upon running despite Benton's advice to the contrary,[4] and this resulted in another Whig victory. The angry Benton would discuss matters with Mr. Strother later.

*   *   *   *   *   *   *

As the Bentons traveled back to Virginia in the fall of 1834, Andrew Jackson was already brewing another storm. He had returned from a triumphant tour of the Northeast in a state of dangerous physical collapse, despite the stimuli of adulatory crowds and an honorary doctorate from Harvard. As old Hickory rested on a Virginia beach, plans were laid for another attack on the bank. The bank had been guilty of a mild deception in delaying a required payment on the national debt, but a House committee, with James K. Polk dissenting, had whitewashed the incident and ruled the Government's money perfectly safe. Jackson and Blair did not think so, and they knew their big friend from Missouri would share their feeling. The bank would probably make another effort at recharter before 1836; so, why allow Government funds to be used for bank propaganda? To take the funds might violate a charter which still had three years to run, but Old Hickory would enforce the laws and defend the people as he saw fit.

Many close advisers and a majority of the Cabinet believed the step illegal and desperately dangerous politically, but on September 18, 1834, the President read his message to the nation. Because of its misconduct and misuse of funds for propaganda, no more Government money would be deposited in the bank after October 1. Routine Government expenses would soon strip the bank of the deposits.

Reading the announcement in the *Globe* while still resting at Cherry Grove, Benton "felt an emotion of the moral sublime at beholding such an instance of civic heroism." It was a call to battle, and the Missouri war horse galloped to Washington breathing fire and brimstone.

Nicholas Biddle's reaction was somewhat different, although

he was equally satisfied. At last Jackson had gone too far. The bank's power could now be used to cause economic hardship, and the illegal removal of the deposits could be blamed. If, as he wrote, "nothing but the evidence of suffering abroad" would "produce any effect in Congress," then suffering there would have to be. Thus, in fighting back, the bank justified almost every argument by Benton against its recharter in the first place. By suddenly curtailing loans, notes, and credit, the bank produced overnight a serious panic in all mercantile centers where business could not operate without credit. The collapse of stock values, numerous business failures, and growing unemployment were accompanied by countless well-organized mass meetings which flooded Congress with memorials and petitions demanding restoration of the deposits to save the country.

With the bulk of the press behind them and dozens of delegations pouring into Washington to lobby personally as well as present their memorials, Clay and Calhoun began a seven months' battle to force Jackson to restore the deposits. Clay opened with a set of resolutions condemning the removal and denouncing Jackson for dangerous, lawless, and unconstitutional action. The theme of the Kentuckian's three-day speech was summarized in his opening and closing paragraphs:

> We are . . . in the midst of a revolution, hitherto bloodless, but rapidly tending toward a total change of the pure republican character of the Government, and to the concentration of all power in the hands of one man. . . . If Congress do not apply an instantaneous . . . remedy . . . we shall die—ignobly die—base, mean, and abject slaves; the scorn and contempt of mankind; unpitied, unwept, unmourned!

This dire prophecy drew such long and loud cheering that the Vice President ordered the galleries cleared.[5]

Benton answered with a roaring four-day rebuttal which included his old charges against the bank plus a full documentation of Jackson's reasons for removing the deposits. The bank had "unnecessarily curtailed its debts, and oppressed the community, and used its immense power over the money market to promote its own objects." Instead of passing Clay's resolutions, the Senate should summon Nicholas Biddle to appear before the bar of the Senate for examination on the causes of the economic distress.[6]

Calhoun followed on a note of grim satisfaction. He and his followers had saved the country from the tariff during the preceding session, and would now help save the country from Jackson. If successful in this noble object, boasted the Carolinian, it would be owing to the success of the Nullifiers in maintaining states' rights the year before. From this doubtful point Calhoun proceeded to correct Clay's charge that Jackson was a Caesar. Caesar was a bold warrior, but the actors in this case were "of a different character—artful, cunning, and corrupt politicians, and not fearless warriors." Jackson, he said, had wounded the nation, which now stood "at a fearful crisis," over which "all who love their country, who have affection for their offspring, or who have any stake in our institutions," should pause and reflect.[7]

The constitutional arguments were a stalemate, but the practical issue was the panic, and here the bank had overplayed its hand. Biddle's mistake was in assuming that his opponents really were unprincipled, popularity-seeking politicians, dedicated only to pleasing the public and staying in power. Some of them, like Van Buren, were somewhat dismayed, but in Benton, Jackson, Blair, Kendall, Taney, and James K. Polk, Biddle was dealing with men of steel who would have fought the bank in the face of certain political disaster. The galleries jammed with supporters come to cheer the bank's advocates and jeer its opponents and the more than one hundred thousand signatures on memorials and petitions might have shaken lesser men, but Benton, speaking some thirty times himself, held his forces in line. Even Van Buren regained his confidence. Before a spellbound Senate and gallery Clay with tears in his eyes pleaded with Van Buren to inform Jackson of the tortured widows, orphans, and laboring people suffering from his policies. The little Vice President calmly stepped from the dais over to Clay's desk, asked for a pinch of snuff, bowed his thanks, and returned to his seat, thereby reducing a dramatic situation to a humorous incident and draining off the impact of Clay's histrionics.[8]

After a sensible and unrancorous compromise effort by Webster was tabled by the demands of Clay and Calhoun, the Senate on March 28, 1834, rejected Taney's reasons for removing the deposits and passed Clay's resolutions condemning Jackson. In the House, however, James K. Polk engineered a counter-report rejecting Clay's resolutions and approving Jackson's conduct. Thus, Old Hickory stood by his guns.

On April 17 Jackson submitted a long and dignified protest against the resolutions of censure, and again Thomas Hart Benton went on the warpath. Eulogizing Jackson in a long speech, he announced that he would never rest until the Senate by its own action had "expunged" the censure from the official record.[9] This was perhaps inadvertently a stroke of political genius. By attacking Jackson personally Clay had given Benton a political issue which transcended policy and struck where Jackson was strongest—in the hearts of countless Americans from Maine to Florida. Colleagues who dismissed the Senator's vow with ridicule were due a rude awakening. Several state legislatures in the business of electing senators came to find it very interesting indeed. The expunging resolution soon became an issue in state politics which ultimately drove a number of senators from their seats.

And Clay promptly followed with another error. As senator after senator continued to present desperate memorials from areas always described as "God's own country," where only the sins of man could prevent prosperity, Clay pushed through a resolution demanding an administration report on the national finances. Taney promptly complied and found that statistically the general situation of trade and income was excellent. Gleefully he and Benton laid their plans. When the report was presented, Webster listened briefly and promptly moved its reference to a committee. Benton, however, demanded a full reading and followed with a triumphant oration which rang throughout the country. It was "a report to make the patriot's heart rejoice! full of high and gratifying facts; replete with rich information; and pregnant with evidences of national prosperity." Yet those who had called for it sat with "downcast looks, and wordless tongues!" The panic, like the shade of the "noble Dane," had been exposed to light and must now quit the stage, and woe to him who would "grieve over the prosperity of his country." [10]

As the people read the report and Benton's speech, no statesman ever enjoyed greater success as a prophet. Eastern businessmen finally took Jackson's advice and began imploring Biddle to end the panic, and to his credit Biddle could recognize defeat, even if his political friends could not. Perhaps wearily, he ended the panic as quickly as it had begun. Credit was suddenly restored, and the nation shifted overnight from distress to a period of boom and inflationary expansion.

The Senator had not only beaten the bank. His program for raising gold to a sixteen-to-one ration with silver also passed, and gold circulation did begin to increase. As always, his plea for hard money rested upon the damage done by fluctuating paper to the laboring man and the small farmer. Back through history he ranged, contrasting the stability of the great empires from Rome down to modern France which had prospered on hard money with the problems of Britain and the United States stemming from the abuse of paper. His economic theories were out of step with the future, but they made perfect sense in the light of the past. Armed with history and the facts of 1834, the Senator was groping for answers to his nation's financial inadequacies, and it was hardly his fault that America faced a future too incredible for even his imagination. Hard money was one of the least successful of Benton's dreams, but it gave him a proud nickname among friends which made his financial theories unforgettable. "Old Bullion" was a sobriquet which implied a character as incorruptible as the precious metals, but when spoken aloud stimulated also the vision of a certain barnyard animal noted for power, energy, toughness, stubbornness, and temper. Both were appropriate.

There was no time for a trip to Missouri in 1834, but the Senator could bask in his new glory as the dragon slayer. On July 4 he helped Philadelphia celebrate the holiday by delivering the principal address at a great party rally, and a few weeks later served as toastmaster for a large Baltimore dinner honoring Taney. Fifteen tables seating a hundred people each, arranged beneath a huge canopy, and overlooked by giant portraits of Jackson, Washington, and Lafayette, provided the setting. As Old Bullion launched into a stirring account of the great triumph over the bank, a storm came up, and the Senator's choice metaphors and dramatic gestures were punctuated by great flashes of lightning and peals of thunder. The Senator was holding his own with both until a strong wind suddenly tore down the canopy and sent the guests fleeing for cover and further toasts in the adjoining tavern, where the inspiration already received mingled with further refreshment to send everyone home in an exalted frame of mind.[11]

It was a gala victory season for Benton, and still higher possibilities were dangled before him. A Mississippi convention unanimously nominated Van Buren for President and Benton for Vice President in 1836, and the Senator might well have had the national nomination. The office had often been a stepping-stone to the White House, but Benton, either remembering Chapel Hill or genuinely reluctant to surrender his Senate seat, declined in a long letter which as usual included a stirring declaration of principles.[12]

* * * * * * *

In the short but savage session of 1835, Benton renewed his demand for expunging the censure of Jackson in a mighty speech which added the bank's provable sins of the "panic" session to his usual indictment. The Senate was unimpressed, but Benton was speaking primarily to the general public in preparation for the coming election. State legislatures were beginning to bombard their senators on the expunging issue, and the Whigs were in a raw mood. Their counter-attacks against Jackson were so violent that when a slightly deranged young man tried to assassinate the President, the *Globe* charged them with the basic responsibility for inspiring the foul deed.

Amid the general vituperation, Calhoun proposed an inquiry into the Federal patronage, and the Senate selected a committee of six, including both Calhoun and Benton, to investigate. Calhoun's majority report charged that the public payroll and Federal expenses had been doubled by Jackson and that the enormous surplus rapidly accumulating in the treasury was a potential source of tyranny which must be removed from the President's hands. The Constitution, recommended Calhoun, should be amended to permit a distribution of the Federal surplus among the states. Apparently Calhoun saw no inconsistency between his position of extreme states' rights and a policy of Federal gifts to the states. Once again his hatred of Jackson and theories against executive tyranny had betrayed Calhoun into a position opposed to the practical interests of his section, since stripping the treasury could only generate a need for more revenue and higher tariffs. Again Calhoun was serving Clay in opposition to a President who had been friendly toward every Southern interest.

The angry Benton answered. Indian removals, Indian wars, and the pension act which the Democrats had opposed, were responsible for the increase in expenses. Ordinary expenses had increased but little, and the Senator from South Carolina had falsified the facts! Cries for order rang through the chamber, but Van Buren, obviously enjoying the scene, directed his friend to proceed. The Senate overruled the Chair, but the delay was only temporary. What an incredible scene, Benton gloated. Recently they had sat day after day listening to cries that the republic was sinking never to rise again, yet were now debating a proposition to distribute twenty-seven millions in surplus revenue. "Last year it was a bankrupt treasury, and a beggared government; now it is a treasury gorged to bursting with surplus millions, and a government trampling down liberty, contaminating morals, bribing and wielding vast masses of people, from the unemployable funds of countless treasures." This "dazzling, seductive, and fascinating scheme" was even worse than Clay's land bill. If there was money in the Treasury, why not lower the tariff, lower the price of public lands, and strengthen the nation's deplorable military defenses? Reading an eloquent plea for national defense written in 1822 by the then Secretary of War, John C. Calhoun, Benton called it "an elevated and patriotic conception, and worthy of the genius which then presided over the War Department." Little had he dreamed that he would ever defend those noble sentiments against their author, who now wished to give away the money sacred to national defense just to defeat all candidates in the next election who would oppose the "wretched and deceptive scheme."

Calhoun also had a memory, and replied with long quotations from Benton's long-dead patronage report prepared in 1826 for the benefit of President Adams. Benton, said Calhoun, had once agreed that too much executive power was dangerous, but had since gone over to the spoilsmen. It was a savage attack, quite equal to that of Benton, and senators bred on the tradition of Benton's violence sat transfixed waiting for the explosion. A duel was rumored, perhaps hopefully by enemies of both, but nothing happened. Neither forgot it. Hearing that Calhoun had been insulted by the "fiercest tiger in the den," New York merchant Philip Hone was certain that Calhoun would not challenge. "I would as soon think of challenging one of the hyenas in the geological institution for snapping at me as I passed his den," wrote Hone in his diary.[13]

As the Whigs followed Calhoun's lead with heartrending wails over Democratic extravagance, Benton and his friends had an answer the people could understand. On the anniversary of Jackson's victory at New Orleans, the Democrats held a well-publicized celebration, and Thomas Hart Benton, serving as the proud toastmaster of a great banquet for the faithful, gave the nation the word:

> This month of February, 1835 . . . Andrew Jackson being President, the national debt is paid, and the apparition, so long unseen on earth—a great nation without a national debt—stands revealed to the astonished vision of a wondering world. . . . President Jackson: may the evening of his days be as tranquil and as happy for himself as their meridian has been resplendent, glorious, and beneficent for his country.[14]

*   *   *   *   *   *   *

With the session ended on this happy note, the Bentons floated down to New Orleans, with the Senator leaving his usual trail of blazing manifestoes in the form of declined invitations to public dinners. His national influence was at a peak. Roger Taney, for one, was delighted with his friend's performances, and Benton had equally warm feelings for Taney. Writing to Van Buren, the Senator roared with glee over the torment of enemies who were unhappily spreading the direful

rumor that Benton would become Chief Justice upon the death
of the aging John Marshall. Such people, he wrote, could no
more comprehend him than old hack lawyers were "able to
comprehend the policy of an empire, and that was no more
than a rabbit, which breeds twelve times a year, could comprehend the gestation of an elephant, which carries two years."
He would accept no such appointment and wanted Taney for
the post.[15]

Back in St. Louis for the first time in two years, Benton accepted a gala public dinner. After a toast to his glorious contributions to the democracy and the nation, punctuated by a
band's energetic rendition of the "Missouri March," he delivered a masterful address on the general subject of Jackson,
Benton, and the People against the financial power and monopoly seeking to use the People's Government for special interest.
Reducing the issues to "People vs Money" was an oversimplification in the best political tradition, but there were germs of
truth in most of the speech. The bank had abused its power,
the Jackson party had discharged its public obligations with
considerable integrity, and whether gold money was the answer
or not, there was a desperate need to check the growing inflation. The Senator bowed to a standing ovation, and as the
remaining seventy-five toasts were being drunk, his message was
already being prepared for distribution to the press throughout the country.[16]

The summer of 1835, however, was not entirely happy. The
House election of 1835 found George F. Strother again in the
race as a Democrat. One afternoon Benton was seated on his
porch when Strother and a friend walked up. It was a bad
moment for Benton to encounter an enemy. He and Elizabeth
had been watching four-year-old McDowell waste away for
several months, and the little boy lay on his deathbed. As the
two men approached, Benton bowed to the friend and invited
him in, but had a different message for Strother: "Don't bow
to me, sir; you damned traitor. . . . You damned traitor, go
home."

Strother sent a duel challenge, which Benton declined.
Strother then announced that he would shoot Benton on sight,

but perhaps wisely for him made no such attempt. On the day of the challenge, James McDowell Benton died.[17]

* * * * * * *

Perhaps fortunately, new concerns quickly crowded in upon Benton's grief. The long and exhausting session of 1836 served the Democrats well enough as a prelude to the election of Van Buren, but the debates had their frustrations for Thomas Hart Benton.

From the bitter struggle over Benton's resolution to expunge the censure of Jackson came one of the only two blows ever struck in the Senate against the Achilles' heel of Benton's boyhood past. Senator Benjamin Leigh, when instructed by the Virginia legislature to support the expunging or resign, refused to do either, but knew his defeat was imminent. He was a waspish little cripple, who when angry settled back on his cork-supported shorter leg and delivered verbal projectiles with devastating effect. Gazing intently at Benton, Leigh in a low voice which grew louder and louder announced that "in that catechism which I learned at my mother's knee, I was taught 'to keep—to keep—to keep' my hands from picking and stealing, and my tongue from evil speaking!" As the Senate sat in stunned silence, Benton swung back in his chair, looked up at the wall, and gently patted his foot. When Leigh finally shifted his glare, a sigh of relief swept the chamber, and the debate continued. To avoid any possible doubt as to his meaning Leigh a few weeks later published a denial that he had been referring to Benton.[18]

Old Bullion's real struggle in 1836, however, was against the runaway inflation and flood of wildcat currency sweeping the country since removal of the checks previously imposed by the Bank of the United States. The West was delighted with the downfall of the bank, but not for Benton's reasons. Public land sales jumped from 4,658,200 acres in 1834 to 20,074,900 acres in 1836, with the rampaging purchasers gaily flooding the national treasury with depreciated money in payment. The resultant boom had the country throbbing with prosperity, speculation, and optimism, but Benton saw only catastrophe in the making. The state banks in which Jackson had placed the

national treasury were heavily involved, and the highly popular Calhoun-Clay program for distributing the surplus might
well bring them crashing down. To Benton the approaching
storm could be avoided only by requiring gold and silver payments for public lands and protecting the treasury from the
onslaught of distribution. Few Democrats were ready to agree.
Why tamper with prosperity in an election year?

The states were panting for the surplus, but Old Bullion
would not surrender without a fight. Jackson was involved in
an acrimonious controversy with France, and Americans were
locked in a bitter Indian war in Florida. For weeks Benton as
chairman of the Committee on Military Affairs scathed the
Senate for leaving America undefended and demanded defense
instead of distribution. He offered long and detailed bills for
major defense projects and demanded help for Florida. Senators interested in surpluses, however, preferred to trust the
Atlantic, and happily accepted Clay's view that the Florida war
was "seven thousand men engaged in a contest with six or
seven hundred miserable Indians . . . neither conquered nor
found." [19]

Few measures ever passed Congress under such a glow of
conscious hypocrisy as did the distribution of the Federal surplus in 1836. Both parties stressed the fiction that the bill was
intended only to safeguard the funds by removing them from
unsafe state banks. The money was to be immediately return-
able upon demand by the Federal Government. In vain did
the realistic Benton point out the inevitable results and insist
that the Government's growing commitments made the very
idea of a surplus an illusion. Alone among the important measures of the Jackson period, it passed both houses with overwhelming approval. In the Senate only five colleagues dared
join Benton in opposition,[20] and Old Hickory for once was not
in a vetoing mood, or at least was unprepared to veto something so clearly certain to pass over his objections. Thus the
Democrats had insured the White House for Van Buren in
1836, but had helped dig a pit for his administration which
would take them all down in 1840.

The Senate had rejected Old Bullion's demand for hard
money land payments. He could, however, submit the program

to Jackson, and the President unhesitatingly issued the policy
as a Presidential proclamation. With this Specie Circular,
Benton and Jackson thus pierced the land speculation bubble
at the very moment the state banks were being required to produce the treasury surplus for delivery to the states. The boom
and the banks collapsed together. The Federal treasury surplus
of twenty million dollars in 1836 had changed to a deficit of
over twelve millions by the end of 1837, and the final installment to the states was never paid. The Federal Government
never saw its first three installments again, and still holds a
meaningless lien against the states which spent them.

* * * * * * *

The slowly growing conflict between Benton and Calhoun
as opposing diagnosticians of Southern ills took still further
shape in 1836. In his message to Congress Jackson threw in a
brief notice that incendiary publications aimed at stirring up
slave revolts were circulating by mail throughout the South.
A law suppressing them might be in order.

Calhoun was immediately off to the rescue, and he and a
special committee of Southerners soon presented a severely
worded bill to serve the purpose. Benton also condemned the
publications as open incitements to violence and bloodshed,
but almost alone among the Southerners he saw also the
broader issue involved. He was unwilling that "the United
States should be made a pack-horse for the abolitionists," but
warned that investing ten thousand postmasters with censorship
authority would "lead to things they might all regret." Despite
the evil to be suppressed he could not support the bill. It was
finally defeated.[21]

A still-sharper divergence came when Congress was bom-
barded with petitions calling for the abolition of slavery in the
District of Columbia. Benton called for efforts to find the
policy best calculated to put down such efforts, and invited
the North to speak first. The abolitionists, he said, "had done
more mischief than the joint remainder of all their lives spent
in prayers of attrition, and in works of retribution, could ever
atone for." They had set the emancipation question back fifty
years and opened a gulf of misery for the free colored popula-

tion. He was confident, however, that the North would
continue to reject the doctrines of "fanatical, visionary, or incendiary" people congregated "to aggravate the disease which
they pretended to cure."

Most senators condemned the petitions, but argued that the
agitation could best be quieted by acceptance and immediate
tabling or denial of their request. To Calhoun, however, this
would be an admission that Congress had the right to grant the
petitions. Opposing the acceptance Calhoun initiated a debate
which raged for weeks and identified the abolitionists with the
sacred right of petition. Several colleagues charged him with
deliberately fomenting, exaggerating, and prolonging the very
agitation he was condemning. Isaac Hill declared that Calhoun's *United States Telegraph* had created more excitement
than any twenty abolition publications. For five years, Hill declared, this paper had "been laboring to produce a Northern
and a Southern party, to fan the flame of sectional prejudice
. . . to drive harder the wedge, which shall divide the North
from the South." Deliberately magnifying the number and
efforts of the abolitionists, it was libeling the North "by repre-
senting the almost united people of that region to be insincere
in their efforts to prevent a mischief of a few fanatical and mis-
guided persons who are engaged in the abolition cause."
Whether Hill correctly understood Calhoun's motives or not,
his estimate of abolition weakness in 1836 was correct.

Benton entered this argument only when Calhoun read ex-
cerpts from a violent abolition paper to the Senate as evidence.
Benton acidly suggested that this reading would multiply the
paper's notoriety and circulation ten thousand times, and asked
the reporters to omit it from the official record. After two
months of debate over the right of petition, which strengthened
the abolitionists immeasurably, the Senate voted 36-10 to accept
the petitions. The prayer of the petitions was then rejected
by 34-6, with Calhoun refusing to vote. None of the six dissenters defended abolition as a principle, but Calhoun had
the last word, denouncing the vote as an avowal of Congressional power over slavery.[22]

Still another event brought Calhoun marching into the
Senate waving the banner of slavery despite Benton's efforts to

haul it down. In a rousing revolution led by Benton's one-time
subordinate, Sam Houston, Texas had recently won its independence, and the American Senate faced the question of recognition. Various abolitionist writers were already screaming that
the affair was a plot to extend slavery and increase Southern
power. This was not true, because the settlement and revolution of Texas had nothing to do with slavery, but the abolitionists again found an inadvertent ally in John C. Calhoun. The
Carolinian called for immediate annexation to extend slavery
and redress the balance of power, and denounced all those unwilling to support such a move.

Benton remained silent throughout most of the debate.
Texas had been a special interest of his since 1818, Sam
Houston remained an admired friend, and two of his brothers
were in Texas. He was also a long-standing friend of Mexico,
and considered its gold and silver America's best hope for a
viable hard currency. And there was the question of slavery.
Delivering the final speech before the Senate recognized Texas,
Thomas Hart Benton spoke with the voice of reason. Denouncing abolition propaganda, he also castigated Calhoun by implication. The Texas revolution, he said, had nothing to do
with slavery. Indeed, it might "as well be said that our own
Revolution was a war for the extension of slavery . . . no revolt,
not even our own, ever had a more just and a more sacred
origin." Although he called down the wrath of heaven upon
those responsible for the massacres at Goliad and the Alamo,
Benton asked understanding for the Mexican people and
pleaded for caution on the question of annexation. The Texas
boundaries were not yet adjusted, and any discussion of annexation at this point would cause premature conflict with
Mexico and fan the slave issue within the Union. An unnecessary collision with Mexico would ruin Westward trade, cripple
New Orleans, and dry up America's perennial supply of solid
money. The Senate took Old Bullion's advice, but Texas and
Calhoun would be heard from again.[23]

All in all, the Senate of 1836 offered little justification for
Calhoun's excitement, and did much to strengthen Benton's
faith in Northern tolerance for slavery. The Senate greatly
expanded the area of slavery by approving Jackson's treaty for

the final removal of the Southern Indians, yet Calhoun and six slave-state colleagues opposed it. A similar, yet even more important, addition was granted to Missouri, which received seven large new counties in direct contradiction of the Missouri Compromise. And finally, Benton, the slaveholder, sponsored the admission of Michigan, while Buchanan, a Northerner, served as midwife for the new slave state of Arkansas.

CHAPTER XII

———◆◇◆———

THE VINDICATOR

In December, 1836, Old Hickory Jackson was just another
lame duck, and Benton was soon fighting like a tiger to
save the Specie Circular from the onslaught of his own political friends. The present "bloat in the paper system," he
warned, could lead only to catastrophe like that of 1819, and
he would not contribute to it. "I . . . promised gold, not
paper," roared Old Bullion. "I did not join in putting down
the Bank of the United States, to put up a wilderness of local
banks. . . . I did not strike Caesar, to make Anthony master
of Rome."

Mississippi Democrat Robert J. Walker charged that Benton's "wild, visionary, ruinous, and impracticable" schemes for
a metallic currency would wreck the state banks and destroy
the country, and assured the raging Missourian that if he
wished "an angry controversy with him, in all its consequences
. . . he could be gratified." Benton wished no fight with fellow
Democrats. He charged repeatedly that recision of the Specie
Circular was a bank scheme to discredit Jackson, but a bill
nullifying the circular passed Congress by overwhelming majorities.[1] Andrew Jackson, however, was still President until
Van Buren's inauguration. Filing the bill among his other
pocket vetoes was one of Old Hickory's last Presidential acts.

On December 31 the states received their first nine-million-dollar installment of the surplus, and as Congress hungrily began considering new ways to create more surpluses, Benton began his usual fight to reduce them. Ironically, when Wright and Benton pushed through a bill reducing the tariff on various items, Calhoun was their major opponent. The Carolinian insisted that any tampering with the sacred compromise of 1833 would be dangerous. The bill included Benton's beloved salt and Indian blankets, as well as calomel, quinine, and salts, on the plea of Senator Sevier of frontier Arkansas that his constituents "took large quantities of them." The measure failed in the House.[2]

The reign of Andrew Jackson was almost over, but one final triumph remained. If the Democrats were divided on policies, they remained united in gratitude and homage to their patron saint, and Thomas Hart Benton kept them provided with an opportunity to prove their orthodoxy. State legislatures had instructed several anti-expungers out of their seats, and the nominal friends of Jackson had a clear-cut majority. On January 12, 1837, Benton delivered his final full-length review of the glories of Jackson and the wickedness of his enemies. The people had spoken for Jackson, and the time had come to vindicate the hero against the infamous Clay resolutions. Jackson's "military life, resplendent with dazzling events," would "demand the pen of a nervous writer; his civil administration" would "require the profound, luminous, and philosophical conceptions of a Livy, a Plutarch, or a Sallust." The Senate must now pass an eight-paragraph resolution amounting to a full confession of every sin against the bank ever charged by Benton and ordering the words condemning Jackson stricken from the official record.[3]

On Saturday, January 14, Old Bullion mustered his forces at a famous Washington restaurant for an evening of planning and conviviality which ran past midnight. For members requiring conciliation, Benton remained in the background and called on the talents of his friends, Linn, Wright, and "Foghorn" Allen. A plan of action for the following Monday was unanimously adopted. They would simply keep the Senate in session until their measure should pass.

Expecting the debates to run well into the night and aware

of the weakening effects of hunger on determined spirits, Benton ordered "an ample supply of cold hams, rounds of beef, pickles, wines and cups of hot coffee" ready in a committee room for the evening session. The opposition debated all day, hoping to delay matters until adjournment, but every effort to adjourn was defeated. The word soon spread, and by the time the great chandeliers were lighted the galleries and lobbies were overflowing. The expungers traveled back and forth to the banquet table in small groups, always leaving enough men on guard to protect the cause. Opponents were gaily invited to join, and a few hungry enemies accepted. The great leaders like Calhoun, Clay, and Webster, however, were in no mood for festivity. Jackson's victory over the bank and the election of Van Buren were humiliating defeats, and the expunging was the final rubbing of salt into raw, gaping wounds. To Calhoun it was a deed reminiscent of the "times of Caligula and Nero," while Clay in sepulchral tones proclaimed it "a foul deed which, like the blood-stained hands of the guilty Macbeth, all ocean's waters will never wash out." To Webster it was a "ruthless violation of a sacred instrument."

As anger and tension mounted, some senators, remembering the recent attack on Jackson, sent out for firearms for their protection, and several people, including Elizabeth Benton, joined their friends and loved ones on the floor. Long after midnight, amid wild excitement, the final vote was taken—twenty-four to twenty-one in favor of expunging. Most of the opposition filed out of the chamber rather than watch the action, with Benton taunting them as they went. As the clerk drew a square of broad, black lines around the sentence condemning Jackson, a storm of hisses and groans went up from the gallery. The presiding officer ordered the galleries cleared, but the angry Benton opposed the order, insisting instead that the specific "ruffians" involved be seized and brought before the bar of the Senate. The victory was complete. In the wee hours of the morning, Thomas Hart Benton and Henry Clay met in the street for a final exchange of vituperation, after which Benton escorted Clay home and saw him safely to bed.[4]

On the following morning little John Randolph Benton knocked at the door of the White House with a gift for the

President. It was just an ordinary pen, but it had been an instrument of vindication, and to the tired, ill old President it was a symbol of sweet victory over his most hated enemies. Later in the day he wrote a grateful answer. The pen would be preserved and in his last will and testament be bequeathed to Benton "as an evidence of my high regard, and exalted opinion of your talents, virtue, and Patriotism." A few weeks later the expungers were invited to a triumphant dinner at the White House, where Jackson rose wearily but happily from his sickbed only long enough to thank his guests and place the chief expunger at the head of the table.[5] The ancient enemies, Old Hickory and Old Bullion, stood reunited in love and mutual respect, as well as at a peak in the affections of their fellow Americans.

On a beautiful sunny March 3, 1837, Benton looked down from a side window of the Capitol as Martin Van Buren took the oath of office, and Andrew Jackson, amid an earthshaking ovation, walked down the Capitol steps for the last time. To the emotion-filled Benton it was the grandest scene of his life— "a man and the people—he, laying down power and withdrawing through the portals of ever-lasting fame;—they, sounding in his ears the everlasting plaudits of unborn generations." [6] To Benton this man whom he had once tried to kill would remain the greatest of Americans, and one of the three men receiving Jackson's dying blessing would be Thomas Hart Benton. This long and turbulent relationship was of immense importance to both men and to their America. Jackson's initial opportunity for greatness in 1812, opposed on every side by jealous rivals, had come because he had an army on hand recruited in large part by the efforts of Benton. Then the great brawl had sent Benton into opportunity-rich Missouri, where his talents faced less competition on the road to achievement. History would come to rank Jackson as a great President, but at least some of the political victories supporting Old Hickory's claim to gianthood rested squarely upon the fertile imagination, courage, and relentless energy of Thomas Hart Benton. Generous, aggressive, tender, harsh, kind, utterly vindictive, and forgiving by turns, Old Bullion and Old Hickory personified much of the best and perhaps some of the worst of their America, and never more so than in their relations with each other. Working together, they had done much to weave their brand of democracy permanently into the American political fabric, and the nation would never again be quite the same.

* * * * * * * *

For the moment, however, Benton faced a more important challenge than eulogies for the retired. Van Buren and the Democrats were facing trouble and must be saved in spite of themselves. The new President had begged Benton to take a Cabinet post, but as always the Senator preferred his accustomed station. Serving the master politician, Van Buren, would be more difficult and less rewarding than fighting beside the iron-willed Jackson, but Old Bullion was prepared to offer his usual blend of dedicated loyalty and independence of judgment.

CHAPTER XIII

———◦◦◦———

THE DEFENDER

A FEW WEEKS before the inauguration, Benton tried to warn Van Buren that the inflationary boom was bound to explode, only to receive a rebuff as insulting as it was gentle and friendly. "Your friends," answered the New Yorker, "think you a little exalted in the head on that subject." Old Bullion pursued the matter no further.

The Senator's judgment was trustworthy. The deposit banks began reaching into their vaults for the money allocated to the states by the distribution act, but the funds were not there, and a frantic reduction of loans and tightening of credit ensued. The Specie Circular, meanwhile, despite the good intentions of its author, had destroyed public faith in the paper in circulation, and overnight the banks began to fail. In May, 1837, the New York banks suspended payments, and hundreds of others followed suit. Soon the boom had turned to depression from Maine to Florida, and this time, despite Benton's suspicions, it was no mere conspiracy to vindicate the Bank of the United States. In the spring Congress was debating the distribution of further surpluses; by September Van Buren was compelled to call a special session to consider the bankrupt Government's inability to meet its financial obligations.

Between sessions the Bentons raced home to the bedside of his ailing mother, and the Senator returned to Washington in

September fearful lest she die in his absence. He had found Missouri far less affected than most by the panic—his hard money policies had kept the boom within manageable proportions, and the collapse was therefore much easier. He was more than ever convinced that his theories might have prevented the panic and might yet save the nation.[1]

Back in Washington Benton found an unexpected ally. The retirement of Andrew Jackson had wrought remarkable changes in the thinking of John C. Calhoun. With the slave-holding Jackson as President, even though the Tennesseean had personally supported every Southern interest, Calhoun had worked with Clay on the side of Northern commerce and industry. Now that the libertarian New Yorker, Van Buren, who had no attachment to Southern values at all, was in the White House, Calhoun was ready to leave Clay and stand again beside Thomas Hart Benton and the Democrats.

Benton and Calhoun together, however, were not enough to make a success of the administration of Martin Van Buren. Even when ruled by the dominating figure of Jackson, the Democratic Party had never been really united in its policies and purposes, and with Old Hickory gone, the land, tariff, and currency policies of Benton had even less chance for success than before. With the personality of Jackson as a nucleus, Van Buren, the skilled politician, and his aides had forged a great national party which cut across sectional and economic lines to draw loyalty from every divergent and conflicting segment of American life. It was a tremendous force for national unity, but it paid for this usefulness with its inability to mount and execute anything resembling an effective party program. Year after year Benton continued to prepare bills and preach what he considered the true faith of Jefferson and Jackson. A number of colleagues continued to share his dream, but they soon ceased to be a majority even of their own party. With all of his determination and strength, Andrew Jackson had been able to steer his party in Congress only part of the time. Martin Van Buren could not even hold on to the reins.

Senators summoned in 1837 to deal with bankruptcy were still anxious to distribute surpluses. When a move began to withhold the fourth installment from the states, senators ranted loudly about the sacred duty of the Government to give the states their promised money. This time, however, Calhoun, the originator of the distribution, joined with Benton and the majority to stop the payment.[2]

Benton and Calhoun also stood together against the Whigs for a startling new idea—an Independent Treasury, which would separate the Government from banking altogether. To Whigs and some Democrats this was "the most alarming proposition" ever presented to the American people. Back and forth like bullets flew the charges and counter-charges as to responsibility for the depression and the sins and blessings of banks. Both sides aimed sound arguments at the general populace and spoke in the accents of democracy. The Whigs insisted that banks, by lending to new enterprises and enabling them to compete with older and richer businesses, had made vast contributions to democracy and freedom. After a bitter fight the Independent Treasury passed the Senate, only to be tabled in the House.[3]

The administration's solution for bankruptcy was the issue of treasury notes, and this measure passed easily. Almost stunned by this sacrilege, Benton did not vote on the final passage.

It was not a happy session for Benton. He and several colleagues spent at least one dinner period at Blair's warming themselves at the fire of their reminiscences of Jackson and better days. Old Hickory had written a letter condemning the new system of treasury notes, and the scrawling handwriting seemed to emit a glow of spiritual comfort. "He does not himself know how right he is," pontificated Benton. "Like a man who is so brave, that it costs him nothing of an effort to undertake the boldest achievement, and therefore does not consider it bravery the General's mind reaches just conclusions so easily, that he scarcely knows the magnitude of the truth which it gives him no labor to arrive at." At this the group drank Jackson's health as the man of the century, whose principles would yet put down the tyranny of *"The Paper Dynasty."* [4]

When the special session ended with the Government at least able to pay its bills, Benton raced home by stage, traveling night and day for ten days, to find his family well and his mother apparently no worse. In late November he and the family bade her farewell for the last time and returned to Washington. In January, 1838, Nancy Benton died after eighty years of vigorous, useful life, but her spirit lived on in the resolute stubbornness and unquenchable pride of her eldest son. Mother and son had shared equally and intimately a long, long road of hardship, anxiety, danger, sorrow, disgrace, achievement, and triumph, stretching back to the North Carolina grave of Jesse Benton. The final separation was a crushing blow.

Again, however, sorrow had come when the Senator had little time for personal grief. New attempts to pass the Independent Treasury and his old land policy, a successful extension of pre-emption for two more years, efforts to restrict the District of Columbia banks to hard money, a constant battle to prevent further treasury payments to the states, objections to his own party's financial policies, and a never-ending defense of Jackson against charges of responsibility for the depression—these and other issues kept the Senator going at his usual blazing pace.

Most of the debates were stalemated, but Benton sat with gleeful satisfaction as the former allies, Clay and Calhoun, took turns denouncing and insulting each other. He was less happy, however, when the Senate finally destroyed his cherished Specie Circular, and this time there was no Jackson to hurl a veto. To the end Old Bullion defied colleagues and popular pressures alike. "The whole current is for the recision," he warned, "but I never swim with the current when I see it flowing upon rocks and plunging into a gulf." [5]

The session of 1838 was also marked by another Calhoun effort to convince his colleagues that they were "reposing on a volcano" on the slavery question. The Carolinian presented a long set of resolutions on the inviolability of Southern institutions, but could stir up little controversy. Most of the resolutions were passed by overwhelming majorities, indicating clearly that the Senate felt no significant enmity toward the "peculiar institution." [6]

Adjournment finally came with Benton complaining to the end about the lack of achievement and protesting that "we are sent here . . . to work, and not to sit here for a given number of days."

The Senator then faced his fourth election. He did not go home until the people had chosen the legislature, although his lieutenants, led by Montgomery Blair, did yeoman service in reminding Missourians again of the mighty services of their Senator. Returning to Missouri to be on hand at his formal election by the assembly, Benton promptly squelched all talk of a Presidential nomination. Van Buren must be the candidate, and Benton wished nothing more than his own usual place in the Senate. His wish was gratified, as the legislature registered the overwhelming vote of a state grateful for his services and proud of his achievements.

*   *   *   *   *   *   *

The following session of 1838-1839 began on a note of humor. Senator James Buchanan presented a petition from a celebrated rain maker, who proposed to induce precipitation at his own expense under a Government contract guaranteeing a sliding scale of financial rewards dependent upon whether he made rain in a ten-mile square, a thousand-mile square, a five-thousand-mile tract, or kept the Ohio River navigable all summer from Pittsburgh to the Mississippi. Senator Crittenden of Kentucky objected on the grounds that such power even if it existed should not be encouraged without guarantees that sunshine might be produced with equal promptness. To start something which could not be stopped might be fatal. On Benton's motion the resolution was tabled.

Agreement on other issues, however, was not so easy. To Benton everything aimed at the approaching end of the compromise tariff, and Clay's policies for distributing funds and increasing pensions were aimed at an empty treasury and a high tariff for 1842. Though a former soldier, Benton could not justify the ever-expanding pension lists. Someone, he said, had once proposed a toast: "Soldiers of the Revolution, may you live forever! On that occasion, some gentleman proposed as a compromise, that they should live for nine hundred and ninety-nine years. Now it seemed this compromise had been carried into effect. . . ." The new pension bill passed.[7]

On two issues, however, the Senator refused to be niggardly. The war in Florida was still raging, but certain senators defended the Indians and opposed aid to a region which would become a slave state anyhow. According to reports, the Missouri volunteers had not lived up to their advance promise, and their commander, Colonel Gentry, had been killed. Senator Benton hotly defended his volunteer friends and demanded a Florida program which would roll back the Indians. He would grant three hundred and twenty acres each and a year's supply of grain and ammunition to a maximum of ten thousand men willing to settle and defend Florida. The war had already cost twenty million dollars without success. Why not give away four million dollars' worth of presently useless land to get the area settled. Also, he said, expelling the Indian by advancing population rather than by war and bloodshed would be far more humane. The Indians would "retire beyond the Mississippi when they hear, from the Okenfinokie swamp to Cape Sable, the sound of the ax, the crack of the rifle, and the fierce barking of the house-dog." The Senate passed the bill, but the House refused to agree.[8]

Benton was equally realistic toward the quarrel with Britain over the Maine boundary. The Senate debated seriously a resolution that Maine should go unsupported if it got into war while acting contrary to Federal advice. To Benton this was a dangerous absurdity. An attack upon Maine would be a blow against every state in the Union, and for Britain to think it could deal with Maine alone would be fatal to peace. Despite the opposition of Clay and Calhoun, Benton and Webster pushed through a bill to organize fifty thousand volunteers. The controversy was finally settled after several years of quarreling, and the realistic approach of both nations, which kept either from excessive temptation, made war unlikely throughout.[9]

When the session ended, Benton still had no time for rest. His own position was secure, but the Senator was concerned for his party and its principles in the coming election of 1840. Still a physical giant at fifty-seven, Old Bullion spent the hot summer of 1839 on an eleven-hundred-mile horseback ride back and forth along the dusty roads and trails connecting the farms and towns of the Missouri hinterland. Citizens of all degree turned out in droves to see the great man, and all along the way he stopped to meet and talk with his people. Everywhere his message was the same. He and Jackson had slain the bank, given them hard money and prosperity, eliminated the Indians, and given America distinction in its foreign relations, but much remained to be done. Graduation of land prices, permanent pre-emption, full protection for gold and silver money, repeal of the salt tax, and the Independent Treasury could be effected only if the people supported the Democratic Party.[10] Few political leaders ever gave more time and effort to his party and demanded less personal reward from it than did Thomas Hart Benton.

*   *   *   *   *   *   *

In 1840 Benton again happily observed his erstwhile enemies, Clay and Calhoun, denouncing each other and arguing furiously over who had been victorious in the crisis of 1833. To Clay's pointed inquiry about Calhoun's new personal relations with Van Buren, Calhoun hurled back the charge of Clay's personal collusion with Adams in the election of 1824. Clay's feelings were clear: "The Senator from South Carolina has been pleased to say that he has no confidence in me. Sir, I reciprocate it with all my heart, and go a step further, and say I have no confidence in the Senator, whether in the past, present, or future." [11]

With Calhoun again pulling with Benton, the Independent Treasury finally passed both houses, despite the wail that it would "reduce the value of property, the products of the farmer, and the wages of the laborer . . . destroy the indebted portion of the community, and . . . place the Treasury . . . in the hands of the President." The bill declared that after 1843 public revenues would be receivable only in hard money, and was thus a new Benton triumph, although it did not last until 1843.

Calhoun had traveled a long road. He and Benton had once fought like wildcats over the question of Jacksonian extravagance, but in May, 1840, Calhoun supported a successful move to print thirty thousand copies of Benton's report designed to show that Federal expenses except for Indian and military affairs had risen but little since 1828.[12]

Perhaps Benton's most vexing legislative problem in 1840 remained the Seminole War. His program for providing homesteader-soldiers was sound, but again the House rejected it after the Senate had approved. Defending the Florida effort against both the Indians and his colleagues was not an easy task. A wail had risen in some quarters because the army had imported some Cuban bloodhounds, and Benton was compelled to answer. The Federal Government, he said, had not imported the dogs and had given orders that they should not be permitted to attack the Indians. General Taylor had written a reassuring letter: "my object in employing dogs, is only to ascertain where the Indians can be found, not to worry them." [13] On the subject of Indians the Senator was more humane than many, but remained a child of his times—a Western frontiersman chiefly concerned with advancement of a nation in which the Indian could never play any significant role.

*   *   *   *   *   *   *   *

By seeking the Vice-Presidential nomination in 1840 Benton would have greatly strengthened his party's ticket, but again he refused, and the Democratic convention simply left the spot open for later selection by the electors. He had done his homework in Missouri well, however, and continued it with public letters, pamphlets, and speeches. Thanks to Old Bullion, Missouri held firm for Van Buren.

Nationally, however, the Whigs had finally learned some political lessons from their opponents. Choosing the ancient hero, General William Henry Harrison, forbidding him to speak on any matter of principle whatever, and adopting no platform beyond their candidate's alleged taste for a log cabin and plenty of hard cider, the Whigs campaigned for their "rough and ready" frontiersman against the "effete, effeminate, cologne-scented, Eastern aristocrat," Van Buren. The New Yorker stood squarely for Western policies and Harrison was clearly the instrument of a party tied to the industrial interests of the Northeast, but the issues were submerged in a gay, rollicking popularity contest of slogans and name-calling. Most of the

West voted for one of their own against "Little Van, the used-up man." To court the South the Whigs gave the Vice Presidency to John Tyler, a Virginia Nullifier who had resigned from the Senate rather than support Benton's expunging resolution. Tyler, they would soon learn, had left the Democrats from enmity toward Jackson and not for any Whig principles.

With no Jackson or any other magic name available, the Democrats campaigned industriously on Benton's favorite issues and suffered an overwhelming defeat. The people had spoken for "Tippecanoe and Tyler too," as well as for a Whig majority in both houses of Congress.

To Benton the Whig campaign tactics were a crime against popular government, and the people had been misled and defrauded. To admit that the people could be deceived was in itself a painful blow to his faith in democracy, and the vindication of the popular intelligence by a Van Buren victory in 1844 became for him almost a holy mission. The people must have another chance to demonstrate their capacity for wise voting on the basis of measures rather than men. The election had proven clearly that Van Buren was personally a weak candidate in the South and West, and various small fires for Benton himself had begun to flicker, but Old Bullion would have none of it. Comparing Van Buren to the defeated Jefferson in 1796 and Jackson in 1824, Benton announced that he was for Van Buren against the world,[14] and he never wavered until the Democratic convention of 1844 ended the fight. Meanwhile, the administration of Harrison and Tyler offered four years in which to teach Americans the magnitude of their mistake, and Senator Benton was prepared to assume this responsibility.

CHAPTER XIV

————◦∞◦————

THE DEMOCRAT

W HEN CONGRESS CONVENED in December, 1840, Senator Benton's program for "uncabining" the Whigs was ready. He immediately offered a bill for permanent prospective preemption for any family head, widow, or single man over eighteen to one hundred and sixty acres of public land if he would inhabit, improve, and "raise a log cabin thereon." If passed, any frontiersman for all time to come might settle on unsold or even unsurveyed land with the exclusive future right to buy it at one dollar and twenty-five cents an acre. It was a true "cabineer's" dream, designed to separate the true Westerners from the "inhabitants of the city 'log cabins'—the silk stocking and kid glove gentlemen." Every land program of the past ten years was promptly resurrected, and the usual stalemate began.[1]

In February, 1841, as the Whigs prepared to inaugurate their aged hero, President Van Buren graciously presented his victorious rival with a White House dinner. The old General, Harrison, half jokingly and half pleadingly asked his long-time friend, Benton, to keep his harpoon pointed at Clay and Webster rather than himself, and Benton, personally fond of Harrison, pleasantly agreed. Indeed, the old hero of Tippecanoe may have wondered if he had perhaps wandered into the wrong political party, because some of his own subordinates were much less courteous. The lordly Webster handed the new

President-elect an inaugural address all ready for delivery, but for once the godlike Daniel was a century ahead of his time. Harrison preferred to write his own—a flowery oration which Webster was still able to tone down considerably, boasting later that he had killed seventeen Roman proconsuls "as dead as smelts" in the process.

A month later the old President was dead, and the ordeal of the Whigs under John Tyler had begun. Seldom has a political party been so speedily and thoroughly punished for resorting to expediency in the selection of a candidate, although its adopted heir began well enough. Tyler promptly called a special summer session to consider means for the bankrupt Government to raise funds, and the two parties, with a Whig majority in both houses for the first time, faced each other in Congress for a blistering showdown on the great issues Clay had been nursing for more than a decade.

The President called for "discriminating" duties to meet the financial crisis and a fiscal agent to be neither a United States Bank, a state bank system, nor the Independent Treasury. His party responded by repealing Van Buren's one accomplishment, the Independent Treasury. Benton and Calhoun fought valiantly, but the institution was dismantled amid furious quarrels over just where the money would now be kept. Benton made the final speech, compelling his exhausted and overheated opponents to listen well into the night. The Whigs, he said, had misled the people. The repeal was demanded only by "politicians who want a National Bank, to rule the country, and millionary speculators who want a Bank to plunder it." And what would replace the Independent Treasury? "A nondescript, hermaphrodite, janus-faced fiscality, yclept, the fiscal agent? Or a third edition of General Hamilton's Bank? or a bastard compound, the obscene progeny of both?"

Throughout the summer, Old Bullion's vocabulary expanded with the heat, as he and Calhoun continued their war against "the great red harlot of Babylon, *THE NATIONAL BANK*," sitting "for Milton's picture of Sin, in the Paradise Lost—a monster, vast, foul, and hideous to behold—the mother of monsters, hell-hounds kennelling within her, creeping in and out, growling and howling for their putrid prey." [2]

The new bank passed both houses, but the celebrating Whigs had not reckoned with John Tyler, who promptly vetoed the favorite measure of his own adopted party. On August 16 the clerk read the veto message to a tense and excited Senate, and the gallery broke out in applause and hissing. Immediately Benton, whose external rage probably belied his inward delight, emitted an angry roar. These ruffians had "dared to insult the American President in the American Senate," and should be taken into custody. It was announced that an officer had arrested a man who had confessed and expressed proper penitence, and the Senator, perhaps with a twinkle in the back of his stormy eyes, withdrew his motion.[3]

The puzzled Clay introduced a new bill designed to answer Tyler's objections, this time for a "Fiscal Corporation of the United States of America." The jubilant Benton delighted his fellow Democrats with clever jibes at the new name. It reminded him of a Mississippi steamboat named after a beautiful Creole girl, *La Belle Creole*. The first name had been shortened to "Bell." Then, because Kentuckians pronounced Creole, "Cre-owl," it had been finally shortened further. The beautiful Creole had sailed up and down the Mississippi all its life under the "name, title, and description of, *The Owl!*" To get a proper name, continued the Senator amid roars of laughter, they should turn to the Aesop fable about the black cat which had fooled the mice by rolling herself in a meal-tub to become white. After a few massacres the mice had recognized their old enemy, and ever afterward called her the "meal-tub cat." Why not "call this corporosity the meal-tub Bank? A catish name would certainly suit it. . . . It has been killed several times, but here it is still, scratching, biting, and clawing." [4] Democratic laughter stopped temporarily as the bill again passed, but Benton's joy was quickly restored by another Presidential veto, this time with no explanation.

Meanwhile in a brilliant parliamentary effort Clay combined Benton's program for permanent prospective pre-emption with his own plan for distributing land proceeds to the states, even though the Senate had just authorized the bankrupt Government to borrow another twelve million dollars. Benton fought hard to amend the act to prevent any distributions while tariffs remained on the necessities of life. Such efforts failed, but ultimately an amendment was attached which negated all distributions if the tariff level should rise above twenty per cent. As part of this combination, permanent prospective pre-emption, perhaps the most important piece of frontier agrarian legislation in American history, passed the Senate with almost every frontier Senator, led by Benton, voting against it. A trademark of the Democratic Party for twenty years became part of the American scene during a Whig demonstration in a bill opposed by its advocates and supported by its bitterest enemies.[5]

Having disposed of its land revenue, the Senate promptly began a struggle to provide new tariffs to restore the national solvency. This debate continued into the next session, with Benton and Calhoun fighting to keep necessities off the list. Twice the Senate spent many weeks hammering out tariff bills ranging above twenty per cent, and twice President Tyler, who disliked tariffs on principle, vetoed them because they had retained the distribution of land revenues. On the third round, the distribution principle was abandoned forever, and a moderate if poorly planned tariff was signed into law.

Two days after Tyler's second bank veto, his Cabinet, except for Webster, resigned in disgust. Within a year after their great victory the Whigs had been demoralized by their own President.

The Democrats continued to enjoy themselves, stirred on by the modest oratory of Senator Benton:

> Sir, I have some . . . knowledge of history . . . and I can boldly say, that the annals of the human race present no example of a talent, of a patriotism, of a courage, of a devotedness, in any deliberative body of men that has ever existed, which is superior to that which we have seen in the twenty-one Democratic Senators who sustain the cause of their country at this most ominous and perilous extraordinary session. . . . The annals of intellectual warfare present no example of mental effort superior to their protracted, victorious, and magnificent debate.[6]

Jackson had been fined a thousand dollars during his 1815 occupation of New Orleans because of a technical illegality, and his friends now demanded full vindication and reimbursement. The first effort failed in 1841 only because the Jacksonians voted against their own bill because of an amendment denying that the act expressed Congressional opinion on the legality of Jackson's original action. The old General might have preferred less pride and more cash, but any disappointment was short-lived, because in the following year the fine was remanded. Old Hickory was vindicated.[7]

In 1842, also, Benton enjoyed a major triumph with the final passage of his Florida program despite a charge that it was a scheme to allow people to "turn sportsmen and range at pleasure over a vast domain in pursuit of game." The rapid growth of Florida alongside its finally docile but never-defeated Seminoles was a monument to the Senator's good judgment and perseverance.

All in all, until the middle of 1843 Benton and his party managed to be on the popular side of most issues while the Tyler administration drifted into semichaos. To Benton the administration was "an object of pity . . . no weight at all—no plans—no policy—no control or direction of any event . . . a drift in an eddy." On March 31, 1842, Henry Clay delivered a great dramatic effort and resigned from the Senate. Colleagues blew their noses and ladies in the gallery wept over his martyrdom. Even Calhoun shed tears and rushed to embrace his off-and-on friend and enemy, but Benton saw the performance as a histrionic effort to get completely free from Tyler in preparation for the Presidential election of 1844. While not entirely unsympathetic, Old Bullion sat with stern impassivity while the ancient foe recited his stirring lines and walked off the stage, and as he had predicted, Clay's retirement was of short duration. Even foreign diplomats echoed the obvious drift, going out of their way to court the good will of friends of Van Buren. The New Yorker, cruising leisurely along the Missouri and Mississippi rivers, contemplating the views so rapturously described by his friend, Colonel Benton, had every reason for satisfaction. His tour of the West was meeting wild enthusiasm everywhere, justifying Benton's faith in the people by showing "that it is not gunpowder popularity alone which can excite their enthusiasm." Benton was certain that the election of 1844 would vindicate democracy by restoring Van Buren to his rightful place in the White House. He had, however, failed to reckon properly with the versatility of John Caldwell Calhoun.[8]

*   *   *   *   *   *   *

The early 1840's were crucial years in the personal lives of Thomas and Elizabeth Benton. Their children were growing up, and at least one, the sprightly Jessie Ann, was maturing too fast for her father's comfort. Looking to the settlement of Oregon, Benton and Linn were promoting westward explorations, and the men involved often came to the Benton home. Among them was a dark, handsome, twenty-eight-year-old lieutenant, slender and slight of stature, but possessed of immense vitality, imagination, and ambition. To seventeen-year-old Jessie, John Charles Frémont was a romantic dream come true. Like her idolized father he was clearly marked for accomplishment, controversy, and potential greatness. Into the life of such a man she could pour the restless energy, steel-wire strength, and yearning for achievement which made her a true child of Samuel, Ann Gooch, and Thomas Hart Benton. Frémont was her first infatuation, and he remained the central project of her life for the next fifty years.

The usual manifestations of young love were apparent to Thomas and Elizabeth, and the Senator, while fond of Frémont, demanded a halt. Jessie was only a child, after all, and not yet qualified to make such major decisions. A promise to adjourn the romance for a year was painfully extracted, and Frémont departed westward on a tour of duty. Jessie, meanwhile, was taken off to Lexington, Virginia, where, despite the forewarnings and premonitions of Elizabeth Benton, Sally McDowell was married to forty-one-year-old Francis Thomas, soon to be Governor of Maryland. None of the assembled flower of Southern youth impressed Jessie in the least. She lived only for Frémont's return, and in October, 1841, after both were back in Washington, she defied her father and managed to overcome whatever resistance her lover may have offered. On October 19 the beautiful and imperious seventeen-year-old led her groom to a secret wedding ceremony, performed by a Catholic priest apparently because no Protestant minister dared brave the well-known wrath of her gentle father. The newlyweds then lived apart for several weeks until Benton returned from a western trip and the time came to beard the lion in his den. Family legend has it that when the young people made their announcement the raging titan they both loved ordered Frémont from the house. Jessie, however, had not been trained in her father's image for nothing. Quoting from Ruth, "Whither thou goest, I will go; and where thou lodgest, I will lodge," she watched Benton's anger melt in the face of his overpowering fatherly love. He had been beaten by the product of his own teaching and example and must have known it.[9] Frémont moved into the Benton home to become an elder son in every sense of the word.

Frémont's technical illegitimacy had apparently been a painful cross, but the young man found in Benton a father whose love and support could hardly have been surpassed by a natural parent. If Frémont was frequently short on wisdom and judgment, his daring, physical toughness, and skill in coping with the wilderness won the respect and affection of some of the most rugged human specimens ever produced on the American frontier, and these qualities quickly endeared him to Benton. As an organizer and promoter of Frémont's expeditions Benton probably relived some of his own quest for heroism and adventure on the Mississippi in 1813, and he clearly saw in the young Pathfinder the fulfillment of his own ancient dreams of a transcontinental America. In 1842 twelve-year-old Randolph Benton and his young cousin, Henry Brant, probably to the pride of their fathers and equal worry of their mothers, accompanied Frémont on part of an extended expedition to the South Pass of the Rocky Mountains. The exploit was a great success, and Frémont's report, embellished by Jessie's literary skill, soon made his name a household word.

Jessie was her husband's full and equal partner from the beginning. In 1843 Frémont prepared for a still-longer trek, this time with Kit Carson as guide and a small force armed with a small cannon secured at St. Louis. Frémont was not a West Point graduate, and both he and Jessie were prone to regard any impediments to his career as a form of discrimination. Thus, when orders came from the Secretary of War to the Frémont home in St. Louis commanding Frémont to return to

Washington and explain why he was taking the cannon, eighteen-year-old Jessie promptly destroyed the orders and sent an urgent message to her husband on the Missouri frontier. He must depart without delay. Having been married to Jessie for almost two years, the Pathfinder asked no questions and began what became his most successful expedition. Fortunately for himself, his powerful father-in-law, somewhat amazed at such audacity even in Jessie, approved her action and assumed full responsibility. This and the happy results of the trip kept Frémont out of trouble, but the regular army hierarchy probably did not forget the incident.

Meanwhile, the marriage launched with such public rejoicing at Lexington had gone a route which ultimately cost Benton many hours of worry, indignation, and valuable time when he could ill afford them. Young Sally McDowell found her much older husband, Governor Thomas, insanely jealous and ready to accuse her of infidelity at any sign of friendliness toward other males, including her favorite cousins. Unable to cope with such treatment, the distracted Sally returned to Virginia, from whence the remorseful husband's confessions of error, protestations of devotion, and pleas for forgiveness were unable to move her. The furious Thomas then launched public charges of adultery, accused the Bentons of trapping him into marriage with a previously seduced woman, and dared Benton and McDowell to challenge him to a duel. The dare was ignored, although the irate McDowell did strike his unloved son-in-law over the head with an umbrella. The alleged seducer named by Thomas was the recently deceased Senator Linn, who, old enough to be her father, had been friendly to the young Sally during her years in the Benton household. Mrs. Linn, neurotic and excessively jealous, had once written the young girl two angry letters, but had later retracted her statements and apologized. Seeking to discourage Thomas, Elizabeth Benton had showed him this correspondence, and though it had made no difference then, Thomas now threatened to call Mrs. Linn to Washington. With the honor of Sally and his dead friend at stake, Benton moved with customary energy. Thomas was sued for libel as well as divorce, and during the libel trial Thomas' own counsel declared themselves unable to proceed on the basis of their client's untenable statements. With Linn protected and Sally completely vindicated, Benton did not press for payment of damages. Thomas was later committed to an insane asylum for a time, but recovered to resume a successful political career. Sally in turn found a happy marriage with a famous Presbyterian clergyman, John Miller of the College of New Jersey (later Princeton University).[10]

Most serious, however, was Elizabeth's illness, which began with an attack in the fall of 1842 and continued for the rest of her life. She would undergo long periods of shattered nerves, poor sleep, slowness of speech and action, depressed spirits, and occasional wandering of mind, punctuated with occasional stretches of considerable improvement. No patient ever had a more faithful nurse. The big man rarely left her side except when absolutely necessary. Observers long remembered his gently carrying her into the parlor to greet visitors when she was unable to walk, and one incident moved even some of the most hardened anti-Benton hearts. Entertaining a handful of dignitaries one day, a startled Benton looked up to see Elizabeth wander into the room not fully dressed. With the utmost dignity he took his lady by the hand and presented her in the grand manner, passing off the affair without embarrassment for anyone.[11]

As always, the Senator faced the eternal problem of supporting an expensive brood in the style their position demanded. In the fall of 1841 Elizabeth's mother died, leaving the McDowell estate to be settled by her children. Elizabeth gave her husband full rein in settling such matters, and Benton's excellent relations with his in-laws made the task much less difficult than it might have been. Elizabeth was willing to draw lots or give the others first choice in most matters, but hoped they would remember that "mama" had promised young Sarah Benton a bed.[12]

Encouraged by their inheritance and the sale of a ten thousand-five-hundred-acre tract to a man named Youell, the Bentons purchased the house on C Street in Washington which the family had already been renting. The Senator bought his house on short term credit, expecting soon to receive four thousand dollars from Youell. Month after month he waited for the money. When his house payment came due, Benton could muster only a thousand dollars. A generous colleague, Representative John Miller, offered to lend him a thousand without interest, and he borrowed another thousand from the fur magnate and New York banker, Pierre Chouteau. The Chouteau loan was arranged with the utmost propriety, with James Mc-Dowell as co-signer. Chouteau owed much to Benton's earlier services, and probably would have been more lenient had Benton wished it. When the note had to be renewed Chouteau suggested that the interest rate be lowered to seven per cent.

Still waiting for Youell and struggling to keep his head above water, the Senator hit on a new idea. He would buy a newly invented, horse-propelled circular sawmill and cut the timber off his old Hart estate in Kentucky. Others thought the proposition risky, but Benton was like a child with a new toy. Investing almost a thousand dollars he sent it off to Kentucky and could hardly wait for spring to go see his dream in action. He found the plate too soft and the works too light and discovered further that a better mechanism was being produced in Kentucky at a price cheaper than he had paid in Baltimore.

Undaunted, he strengthened the machine, adapted several of the Kentucky principles, and ordered a tougher blade from St. Louis. Ultimately it was a success, although the property never produced the hundred thousand dollars' worth of lumber he had predicted. The Senator boasted of the exploit and relished the role of expert on the subject, but the exact amount of money yielded was never revealed. After several renewals he paid the debt to Chouteau by selling other property in St. Louis.[13]

The way of the full-time honest public servant was hard, and the Senator's atonement for Chapel Hill was a lifelong process. He probably would not have chosen otherwise. In opposing unsuccessfully a twenty-five-thousand-dollar appropriation for Mrs. Harrison in 1841, Benton took the occasion to expound his philosophy of the public life. Most outstanding public men, he argued, died poor, using up their patrimony while serving their nation. No one, he said, had recompensed Jefferson, Monroe, or Jackson for great losses suffered in the public service, and they would not have wished it.[14] The Senator clearly considered himself a member of the same company. He would never show concern for leaving a fortune to posterity, but would rely upon far more solid claims to fame. It was a *noblesse oblige* outlook in the classic aristocratic mold—an approach which has given American democracy some of its outstanding spokesmen and practitioners.

CHAPTER XV

THE PROPHET

THE YEAR 1843 marked a turning point in the lives of Thomas Hart Benton and his America. For twenty-three years he had fought for his ideas and principles as if the very fate of the nation were involved. He had often won, had as often been defeated, and had frequently compromised. He had occasionally succeeded when wrong and failed when right, but he and his colleagues in Government had enjoyed in common an immense underlying blessing. The issues they had fought with such magnificent energy and imagination involved basic conflicts of interest which could be compromised, and they had been dealing with a vigorous, freedom-loving people in a rich, vital, and expanding environment capable of progress despite almost any mistake they could have made. In truth, the ship of state had been sailing in an inland sea, relatively free from major storms, and with several safe channels to the same destination. Some routes were rougher than others, and some of the preferred itineraries might have been missed, but on the whole the pilots, while stirring up the passengers with their wrangling over which ones to take, had done well, and many of them had learned much. The experience and knowledge of these pilots were about to be tested in 1843, because the ship was nearing the end of the marked channel and was drifting into an open sea filled with rocks and shoals and beset with typhoons on a scale none of them had yet known.

A civilization which comprised a major part of the American Union was in trouble. Cursed with an institution out of step with the growing spirit of democracy in the other sections, the South was finding itself more and more on the defensive. Its relative political strength as opposed to non-slaveholding states was declining, although this minority status was in many ways more apparent than real. National political parties and mutual agrarian interests which crossed sectional lines enabled the South to have its own way on most vital economic issues until 1860. The section, however, was dedicated to slavery, an agrarian society, and a political philosophy of states' right in an America where all three were rapidly losing ground. To retain control of its own future the South would require leadership gifted with vision, wisdom, and patience, and, above all, willing to face complex facts and avoid oversimplification of the issues.

Thomas Hart Benton's attitudes toward slavery and abolition had changed but little since the Webster-Hayne debates. To him the peculiar institution remained an affliction which the South must and could settle for itself if given enough time, and abolitionists were still dangerous meddlers bound to worsen the ills they professed to cure. He believed that the overwhelming majority of the people in all sections wished no quarrel, and he was ready to grapple with politicians on either side anxious to foment one. The debates over the petitions and Texas recognition in 1836 had found him damning abolitionists and extreme Southerners alike.

From personal experience Benton knew that modern technology was shifting the center of wealth ever northward, but after the early tariff debates he no longer attributed this to Northern villainy. A realist, he never ceased to believe that the South must find its salvation within the Union, and he never doubted the possibility that this could be accomplished through democratic processes. Above all, he was a nationalist, with an almost mystical faith in the United States as a great experiment in human freedom which must not be allowed to fail.

He was convinced, moreover, that slavery had reached its natural and human boundaries and that any quarreling over its extension was mere shadowboxing for political advantage.

He was equally certain that Southern slavery was in no danger from the other sections if its practitioners would exercise moderation and reason in their demands. Unlike some other realists, however, he understood fully the explosive potentialities of the slave question, and never doubted for an instant that the South under the right conditions and leadership could be induced to break the Union and bring on a civil war. For this reason his personal hatred for John C. Calhoun was greatly enhanced by a healthy respect for the Carolinian's abilities and capacity for damage. For the next ten years Benton would consider Calhoun and his ideas the great threat to the Union, and act accordingly.

Benton's approach might have preserved the Southern civilization indefinitely and kept its necessary adaptations and changes under Southern control. That a civilization based upon slavery did not deserve salvation does not alter the basic fact that the South by avoidable actions brought on its own destruction.[1] In this story are universal lessons for those concerned with the problems of preserving a civilization under fire, and the contemporaries who truly understood the tragedy of their times deserve minute attention. Among these, Thomas Hart Benton stood in the forefront.

* * * * * * *

The year 1844 would be John C. Calhoun's final chance for the Presidency and vengeance for the betrayed hopes of 1832, and he had been building foundations since 1837. Defending slavery in the petition struggles had strengthened his already wide Southern following, and his return to Van Buren and the Democrats had restored much of his national standing. His liberal land position had been aimed straight at Western hearts, and overnight he had become a convert to internal improvements at Federal expense. In 1842 he even promised Eastern Whigs his approval for a moderate tariff in return for support against Clay's distribution schemes. Most astounding, he adopted a friendly attitude toward Jackson and even voted for refunding the General's ancient New Orleans fine. By the end of 1842 Benton was beginning to fret over rumors that Calhoun might reject the decision of a Democratic convention and run independently. Various leading Democrats were recommending conciliation, and Van Buren newspapers even suggested offering Calhoun the Vice Presidency, but to Benton this was heresy. He would eliminate Calhoun and purify the party once and for all.[2]

By the end of 1843 Van Buren was in firm control of the party machinery and on his way to an easy nomination, but Calhoun did not surrender easily. Desperately seeking an effective campaign issue and anxious to strike out at abolition anyhow, Calhoun and his supporters found a question laden with emotional dynamite. They would annex Texas to save and extend slavery.

President Sam Houston of the Republic of Texas, irritated by previous American rebuffs, was skillfully combining feigned indifference to the United States with well-publicized friendship for the British. Britain had arranged a truce in the stalemated but still-threatening conflict with Mexico, and the American chargé in Mexico soon feared that Texas would become a British satellite. As fate would have it, the British envoy to Mexico was Captain Elliott, an ambitious naval officer just recalled from Canton for losing a battle of wits to a Chinese viceroy. For standing by helplessly while the Chinese confiscated and destroyed some twenty-thousand chests of illegal British opium, Elliott had been judged by the London *Times* to be "notoriously unfit to manage a respectable apple stall." Anxious to retrieve his reputation the Captain lost no time in formulating a plan to bless Texas with free trade and the abolition of slavery. Slaveholders should be compensated by a profitable English loan and a free British market; the freedman should receive political equality. Thus the hearts of the Texas Negro citizens would be with England "beyond the third and fourth generation," and free trade might detach Texas completely from the United States.

These were stirring ideas, but they impressed Houston and his Texans not in the least. In England the suggestions brought wide publicity and much professional agitation. The English Government, however, was not so starry-eyed. Though admitting that abolition would be "desirable," Foreign Secretary Lord Aberdeen assured both the Texas envoy and the Ameri-

can Minister, Edward Everett, that Britain would never inter-
fere with Texas.[3]

These assurances were apparently sincere, but Calhoun's
confidant and former editor, Duff Green, reported from London that the definite promise of a loan in exchange for abolition had been made. Trusting Green provided Calhoun a
two-headed dragon ready for a knightly attack. The expanding
Northwest wanted all of Oregon up to the southern boundary
of Alaska at 54° 40′, and could now be united with the South
against the common enemy. The British must be driven from
Oregon; Texas must be annexed immediately to prevent British encroachments against slavery and the South. Green had
given the matter much thought, warning that only a prompt
and aggressive Texas policy could prevent Calhoun and their
friends from being "handed over to Van Buren as so much
political capital in the hands of Col. Benton." A union of
Texas and Oregon would "separate the non slaveholding N.
West states from the Northern States." Green was correct. A
handful of articles, editorials, and public letters set the snow-
ball in motion, and within a few weeks Texas and Oregon were
overshadowing all other issues.[4]

Simultaneously, the forsaken man in the White House also
came to life. John Tyler would annex Texas himself, and perhaps yet defeat his enemies. In 1842 Tyler had rejected two
annexation offers from Houston because of the well-known opposition of Congress and his Secretary of State. By 1844, however, Webster had resigned and been replaced by Calhoun's
friend Abel Upshur; and Thomas Gilmer, whose public letter
had launched the popular agitation for Texas, soon became Secretary of the Navy. Like Calhoun, Upshur conveniently accepted the word of Duff Green instead of the official words of
the British Government, and surprised Houston with a proffered treaty of annexation.

Thomas Hart Benton had been a Texas expert since opposing its abandonment in 1819, and had never doubted that it
must ultimately join the Union. He knew also that all talk of
Texas submitting to overnight abolition at the instigation of
Britain or anyone else was nonsense. Locked in a bitter political struggle to nominate Van Buren and sniffing the air and

scanning the horizon each morning for fresh signs of intrigue, Old Bullion saw the linking of slavery and annexation as a dangerous conspiracy, "on the part of some, an intrigue for the the presidency and a plot to dissolve the Union—on the part of others, a Texas scrip and land speculation."

His fears were not unsupported. The *Madisonian*, a Calhoun-Tyler paper, had already announced that the defense of slavery required either secession or the incorporation of Texas, and this theme expanded throughout the spring and summer of 1844 in a rash of Southern editorials, public letters, and public meetings. The private correspondence of Calhoun and his followers would have convinced Benton still further. Governor Hammond of South Carolina spoke for many: "If the Union is to break there could not be a better pretext. With Texas the slave states would form a territory large enough for a *first rate power* and one that under a free trade system would flourish beyond any on the Globe. . . ." Hammond believed that four-fifths of the South preferred Texas to the Union and would make the choice if necessary.[5]

Old Bullion understood also the magnetism of Texas as a get-rich-quick operation. Texas in 1841 had a debt of seven and a half million dollars in certificates, most of it in American hands, and had distributed enough land warrants to keep both farmers and speculators busy for years. Senator Robert J. Walker, Thomas Ritchie, and other high-ranking gentlemen were among those gambling for the rise and, in typical American fashion, doing everything possible to push their luck.[6]

Meanwhile, the patriarch of the Democracy, Andrew Jackson, still resisting both his infirmities and the cures of his physicians, had gone all the way for Texas in a letter carefully preserved for use in the coming convention. Robert J. Walker, head of the scrip and speculation forces, played upon the old man's inbred hatred of all things British as a skilled violinist draws his bow, and Jackson was soon commanding Houston to accept immediate annexation. Houston then added to the General's fears by answering that Texas, if rejected by the United States again, would seek friends elsewhere. Jackson confidently expected Blair, Benton, and Van Buren to follow his own lead.[7]

On February 28, 1844, fate took a hand. A happy gathering

of dignitaries and friends took a Sunday excursion down the Potomac aboard the U.S.S. *Princeton*. A new gun was much admired, and en route home in the afternoon someone suggested a final exhibition. This time the cannon exploded into its audience, leaving both Upshur and Gilmer among the dead. Benton himself suffered heavy shock and a burst eardrum and was saved from death only by a scientific curiosity to follow the ball's line of flight. Only a few seconds earlier, he had moved from the ranks of those hit by flying metal.

No prominent Whig or Democrat would have served Tyler as a replacement for Upshur, but Calhoun, by now aware that his final Presidential bid had failed, was soured on both parties and was immensely available. Tyler would have preferred someone less eminent, but the Carolinian was the only logical choice.

Accepting "reluctantly," Calhoun moved with speed and finesse. Military and naval protection departed for Texas, and on April 12 a treaty was signed, annexing Texas without mention of boundaries. Texas had defined its own boundaries to include a large area between the Nueces and Rio Grande rivers never included within the Mexican state of Texas and still occupied by Mexico. Unless accompanied by mollifying offers to Mexico the treaty meant either war or an abject surrender by Mexico, but Calhoun informed Mexico that the United States was ready "for all possible consequences."

Calhoun then played his top card. The British had written Upshur a strong official denial of any designs against slavery in Texas, adding, however, that "although we shall not desist from those open and honest efforts which we have constantly made for procuring the abolition of slavery throughout the world, we shall neither openly nor secretly resort to any measures which can tend to disturb their [the Southern states'] internal tranquillity. . . ." To this brief passage Calhoun dispatched an immediate answer addressed to Britain but written for Americans. He accused England of threatening slavery in Texas and the United States, delivered a sharp rebuke, announced his treaty of annexation, and concluded with a long and detailed eulogy of slavery as a wise and humane institution. Thus Calhoun asked the North to adopt a probable war with Mexico for the avowed sole purpose of extending slavery. If this defeated the treaty, Calhoun believed it could "only be explained on the assumption, that the spirit of faction and opposition to the South on the ground of slavery are stronger than the love of country." [8] An astute politician seeking votes for ratification of his treaty would have stressed commercial advantages, Texas resources, manifest destiny, or many other points aimed at Northern support, but Calhoun's purpose was far more complex. A showdown on slavery was his aim, and by making a vote for Texas a vote for the moral righteousness of slavery he had established the test. To Calhoun all men must be either builders or destroyers of slavery, and a Northern refusal to support slavery in Texas would be proof of mortal danger to the South. That people might oppose slavery on principle without wishing to risk anything against it Calhoun did not admit. The apathy, inertia, and self-interest which lead most humans to prefer goals far less exacting and more personally rewarding were factors rarely included in the dialectics producing the Calhoun version of Southern wrongs and dangers.

The treaty went to the Senate on April 22, and Clay and Van Buren, the expectant candidates of their parties, were flushed into the open. Wise politicians, they had already agreed to neutralize the issue, and on April 27 appeared their public letters opposing immediate annexation.

Two days later, Benton's manifesto appeared in the *Globe*. Old Bullion was ready to see "the old Texas" fulfill its inevitable destiny within the Union, but denounced the illegal boundaries being claimed. Arguing powerfully for delay until conclusion of peace between Mexico and Texas, he pled for avoidance of sectional views and partisan politics. The *Globe* pronounced him a wise and patriotic statesman, but Andrew Jackson shed bitter tears over both of his apostate protégés. Regarding Benton as the stronger, Old Hickory immediately concluded that he had probably misled Van Buren, and Francis Preston Blair, who loved both Benton and Jackson, assumed the task of preventing another break in their turbulent friendship.[9]

If Van Buren could have gained the nomination, his letter was politically sound, but Benton was courting political sui-

cide. He faced re-election in a state hot for Texas at a time
when he needed all possible strength. For many years his efforts to impose hard money and restricted banking on Missouri had been under heavy fire from powerful groups, and
numerous ambitious followers had begun to weary of his long
personal domination. Hard times had come to Missouri in
1842-1843, and the bitter truth was that people wanted and
needed liquid capital and credit which only banks and paper
money could provide. In deference to hard money supporters
in the central counties, Benton had also failed to support a constitutional convention effort designed to redistrict the state
along more democratic lines and abolish life tenure for judges.
Rumblings of discontent over this had begun to come from his
border county strongholds, allayed only in part by the appointment in 1843 of David Atchison of Platte County to replace
Linn in the Senate. Benton's opponents, shouting "dictator" in
the press, were just looking for sharp emotional projectiles to
fling at his broad back.[10]

This Benton knew, but again he would accept defeat before
compromising his view of the public interest. Bitter fury over
the impending threat to Van Buren, violent hatred of Calhoun,
the natural desire of a proud man to defeat his enemies and
have his own way, and resentment of blows to his own prestige
—all were whirling around in the complex boilerful of passions
that was Old Bullion Benton, but underneath were the basic
assumptions of a wise and farsighted man. He had earned his
self-appointed status of prophet by years of study and experience in the ways of men and nations. In Calhoun's treaty he
saw an unjust and unnecessary war with Mexico, loss of the
Mexican gold and silver trade supporting his dreams of a metallic currency, and a crippling blow to America's position as a
democratic example for Latin America and the world. And
above all, he knew that coupling the irresistible advance of the
American pioneer with the controversy over slavery could lead
only to secession and civil war.

Without hesitation Old Bullion opened fire on Calhoun's
treaty and exploded all chance for a clear-cut Senate division on
slavery. In the secret Senate sessions he roared for three days,
reviewing with full documentation the inconsistencies and ab-

surdities of the negotiations. The treaty clearly annexed Mexican territory, including the capital of New Mexico, and this outrageous misdeed was justified only by a non-existent British threat to slavery. Texas, he continued, should be annexed "for great national reasons, obvious as day, and permanent as nature" whenever possible "with peace and honor, or even at the price of just war against any intrusive foreign power," but not on "weak and groundless pretexts, discreditable to ourselves, offensive to others, too thin and shallow not to be seen through by every beholder, and merely invented to cover unworthy purposes." Reciting British denials, Benton met Calhoun's logic with the words of reality. Even if her denials were insincere, Britain's efforts to drive slavery from the "hearts, customs, and interests" of the people of Texas would take years, yet Calhoun had found no time to consult Mexico. The fear that Texas would jump "into the arms of Great Britain" was a "libel upon the people of Texas," whose "every feeling of their hearts, and every calculation of their interests, leads them as strongly to unite with the Americans as hold back from the British." For the foul purpose of nominating "a new Texas candidate, anointed with gunpowder," an unjustifiable sectional quarrel threatening the very life of the nation had been started.

Nearing the end of the attack, Benton offered fellow Southerners a personal testimony and sober advice:

> I am southern by birth—southern in my affections, interests, and connexions—and shall abide the fate of the South in every thing in which she has right upon her side. I am a slave-holder, and shall take the fate of other slave-holders in every aggression upon that species of property . . . but I must see a real case of danger before I take the alarm. I am against the cry of wolf, when there is no wolf. I will resist the intrusive efforts of those whom it does not concern, to abolish slavery among us; but I shall not engage in schemes for its extension into regions where it was never known. . . .

And for Missouri the Senator had a closing word:

> Twenty-four years I have sat in this chamber, and have had the gratification, all the time, and especially on many trying occasions, when I voted on my own convictions, to give satisfaction to my

constituents. If it should be otherwise now, it would be a source
of deep regret to me, but with my opinions of this treaty, it is
impossible for me to support it; and if the alternative should be
extinction of my political life, I should have to embrace it.[11]

In late May the debate shifted to the Democratic convention
at Baltimore. There Robert J. Walker and others engineered
a South-Northwest combination which torpedoed Van Buren
with a two-thirds rule and finally settled on James K. Polk and
a platform for immediate possession of Texas and all of Oregon. It was a bitter dose for Benton. Writing Jackson during
the deadlock, he compared it to 1824-1825, "when the will of
the people was put down in your presence by the intrigues of
members of congress. . . . Offices, 100 millions of Texas lands,
ten millions of Texas stock—are making fearful havoc among
our public men." The majority should "nominate Mr. V. B.
and go before the people with it." When Jackson's second
choice, Polk, was nominated, however, Benton informed the
public that Polk was innocent of "the intrigue which has nullified the choice of the people, and the rights of the people, and
the principles of our government, in the person of Mr. Van
Buren," and should not be "injured or prejudiced by it." With
his party's official platform, however, Benton would still move
only on his own terms.[12]

On June 8 the Calhoun treaty, weighted down by connection
with Calhoun and Tyler and staggering under Benton's attacks,
sagged to a 35-16 defeat, with only eleven of twenty voting
Southerners supporting it. Two days later Benton presented
the Senate his plan for annexing Texas: a carefully defined
boundary leaving the Rio Grande Valley to Mexico, admission
of a Texas state to be no larger than the largest existing state,
roughly equal division of the remaining area into slave and free
territories, and negotiation of Mexican consent by treaty unless
Congress rather than the President should declare such consent
unnecessary. Annexation of Texas without foreign war or sectional conflict was his aim, and the program offered sound
possibilities. Too many senators, however, were equally anxious to have their own way, and Benton's powerful arguments
struck well-barricaded minds. His bill was tabled by a vote of

25-20 along strict party lines, and much of the opposition came from those opposed to any annexation at all, thus paving the way for a future program far less in line with their own wishes.

Two days later, George McDuffie of South Carolina, tall, gaunt, ill-tempered, and eloquent, delivered a well-publicized reply to Benton before a packed Senate and gallery. McDuffie himself had opposed the annexation until January, 1844, but now appeared eager to atone for past heresy. Accusing Benton of seeking to prevent any future annexation without Mexican consent and dwelling mournfully on the Mexican atrocities of 1836 against Texas, McDuffie warned that Benton would have no place at a forthcoming Democratic gathering at Nashville. And comparing Calhoun's dead treaty to the ghost of Caesar who appeared to Brutus with the words, "Thou shalt see me at Philippi," McDuffie suggested that the ghost of the slain treaty might well haunt Benton before the election in Missouri. It was a long, able, and angry effort, and the tense galleries braced themselves for an explosive reply.

Rising as McDuffie concluded, Benton charged like a raging buffalo, hurling McDuffie's own former speeches like spears to show the inconsistency of the attack. To one observer "the way he thumped upon the desk, and gesticulated, and flourished in the face of Mr. McD., who sat immediately under and looking at him, would be, I would think, a caution to that gentleman ever after to express his sorrow and shed his tears at the proper moments and not let some seven or eight years intervene."

The Calhoun treaty, roared Benton, by dividing all Texas into slave states, was "an open preparation for a Missouri question, and a dissolution of the Union." And as for the Nashville convention, Burke had once described "a cluster of old political antagonists . . . all pigging together (that is, lying like pigs, heads and tails, and as many together) in the same truckle bed." Never was such a "medly of bedfellows" as would meet in Nashville, but they had better be careful around General Jackson, because "if he should happen to find old tariff disunion, disguised as Texas disunion, lying by his side . . . not only skin and fur, but blood and bowels, may fly."

As mention of Jackson and disunion electrified the gathering, Benton continued in a flood of angry eloquence, pausing finally to apologize for being arrogant, overbearing, or dictatorial, but justifying his conduct. He who hated intrigue and loved the Union could "only speak of intriguers and disunionists with warmth and indignation." The oldest Texas advocate, he must "speak in just terms of the criminal politicians who prostituted the question . . . to their own base purposes, and delayed its success by degrading and disgracing it." A Westerner, he "must be allowed to feel indignant at seeing Atlantic politicians seizing upon it, and making it a sectional question, for the purposes of ambition and disunion."

Here the conciliatory tone ended. Striking McDuffie's desk a resounding blow, Old Bullion trumpeted defiance in the most dramatic performance of his life:

> The senator . . . compares the rejected treaty to the slain Caesar, and gives it a ghost, which is to meet me . . . as the spectre met Brutus at Philippi. . . . I can promise the ghost and his backers that if the fight goes against me at this new Philippi . . . and the enemies of the American Union triumph over me . . . I shall not fall upon my sword, as Brutus did . . . but I shall save it, and save myself for another day, and for another use—for the day when the disunion of these States is to be fought—not with words, but with iron—and for the hearts of the traitors who appear in arms against their country.

Applause swept the galleries, and for once Benton did not demand silence. Moving to his seat, Benton looked into the eyes of an ancient and bitter enemy, but this time John Quincy Adams muttered a brief compliment and offered his hand. It was a remarkable concession, and Benton met it with equal grace. "Mr. Adams," listeners heard him say, "you are passing off the stage, and I am passing away also, but while we live, we will stand by *THE UNION*." For two veteran pilots the survival of the ship had become the overriding concern.[13]

Whether or not, as a reporter wrote, "McDuffie writhed in seeming agony of spirit and body," he submitted without serious protest—to the anger and sorrow of many Southern colleagues who never forgot Benton's alleged brutality on this occasion. Working for sectional peace, Benton had contributed much to the personal antagonisms which helped feed the strug-

gle and already found himself alienated from the section where
his influence was needed most. He had attacked neither slavery
nor the South, but his stirring defense of the Union against the
alleged treachery of certain Southerners made him something
of a Northern hero overnight and probably added much to a
rising distrust of Southern intentions.[14]

With Texas the stalemated heart of the election campaign,
Benton rushed home in late June to fight for re-election. The
Whigs were already distributing his Texas speeches as campaign documents for Clay against Polk, and waiting in Missouri
was a hornet's nest of opposition. "Texas or no Texas" was
such an easy oversimplification that his most loyal defenders
were sorely handicapped, and many of them did not even agree
with him. Closest friends considered his defense of Mexican
boundary claims a colossal political blunder. Jackson's Texas
letter was again dusted off, and Benton was roasted by Democrats on all sides for betraying the West, serving the British, and
going over to the Whigs. The *Missouri Register* set the tone
with a warning that Benton "must not be permitted to stand in
the way of the onward and upward march of our country to
those high and holy destinies to which God and nature seem
to have designed. May a dishonourable grave and a name forever infamous be the fate of him who will thus sacrifice the
highest hopes and the dearest interests of his native land." His
vote was challenged on the ground that he lived in Virginia and
Kentucky and used Missouri only for a political principality.
An opponent with a judgment against the old Bank of Missouri
had him arrested as a former director, and his necessary appeal
for Congressional immunity was widely publicized without benefit of explanation. The important question of why a successful politician would choose such an unpopular course as
opposition to the Texas treaty was dismissed with a reference
to Benedict Arnold, who, "in need of money, bargained for the
sale of West Point. . . . Mexico, France, and England are opposed to the annexation of Texas and they have the money and
to spare." And Secretary of State Calhoun apparently issued
secret orders to newspapers around the country blessed with
Government printing contracts to attack Benton as an enemy
seeking the defeat of Texas and Polk to secure the succession

for himself. A Cleveland editor later sold his copy of these instructions to Blair for fifty dollars, and Benton never doubted its authenticity.[15]

It was a bruising battle, but Old Bullion asked no quarter, proclaiming his position as more important than re-election. He continued to eulogize Van Buren and, expressing satisfaction that Polk wished only one term, even argued that the South had had too many Presidents. And citing recent South Carolina resolutions calling for "Texas without the Union rather than the Union without Texas," he pled everywhere for his own bill as the only safe solution. Honorable annexation without war or sectional conflict remained his theme, and everywhere he was well received. Missouri had come a long way with Old Bullion Benton, and not a few voters probably agreed with one citizen who, though "hot for Texas," was also "for Benton against the world." [16]

The issue remained in doubt until the legislature actually met, but party discipline and the Benton tradition held firm. This time, however, the margin was a slim seventeen votes, compared to a thirty-four-vote edge given the immediate annexationist, David Atchinson. Benton would have six more years in which to get back in line with Missouri, lead the state along his own path, or drive himself into political oblivion.

Meanwhile, the Senator's national party standing had also declined, as the older Jacksonians found themselves overshadowed by Polk and Texas. The ancient Sage of the Hermitage still wielded powerful influence, and his affections for the "great expunger" were undergoing a severe strain. Trying to serve both Jackson and Benton as well as help elect Polk, Francis Preston Blair maneuvered throughout 1844 with diplomatic skill worthy of the famed bigamist who lived together with two wives by convincing each the other was the housekeeper. An extra complication was the twenty-two-thousand-dollar wager Blair and his partner, John C. Rives, had made on the election of Polk, a situation causing sharp twinges of conscience when Blair sat down to pen editorials in the *Globe* against the profligate gambling of Clay. Convinced that enemies were trying to revive the ancient Benton-Jackson feud, Blair continued to print Benton's speeches, remind Jackson of the Senator's past services, and hope for the best. In long letters he explained to Jackson that Calhoun's treachery and disunion schemes had caused the trouble, but when Benton shook hands with Adams, Old Hickory needed "no better proof of his derangement." ". . . Do my dear Mr. Blair inform me if this can be true," he plaintively inquired, and sharply warned that allegiance to Benton would ruin the *Globe*. To Polk Jackson confided that Benton was demented by hatred of Calhoun, and suggested that the *Princeton* explosion might have injured his old comrade's brain. Benton sent regrets at inability to attend the Nashville convention, explaining that he was too busy saving the party in Missouri, but Jackson wrote that the "dilegation from . . . Ohio, Indiana, Illanoise, and Missouri" had convinced him that Benton had "lost the confidence of the democracy in those states." Francis Pickens reported to Calhoun that Jackson in discussing Benton's heresy had said, "Thank God! the party can do without him." [17]

On election day a bare majority of Americans spoke against immediate annexation, but fate again robbed Henry Clay. The Liberty Party, organized against slavery and Texas, took sixty-odd thousand votes for James G. Birney, and Polk won by only thirty-eight thousand votes. Less than half of Birney's New York vote would have elected Clay President by seven electoral votes.

For this vote-getting performance Clay owed much to his old enemy from Missouri. Jackson believed that Benton's speeches had hurt the Democrats "more than all the whiggs," but the old man's anger slowly changed to grief. He now resolved to save both Texas and Benton. In September, 1844, Jackson had begun working through Blair and Andrew Jackson Donelson (Jackson's nephew, soon to be chargé in Texas) to persuade Benton to re-establish himself with a Texas bill based on the Louisiana Purchase of 1803. Presumably the indefinite boundaries of the 1803 session would provide wide latitude for negotiations between the United States and Mexico, and the suggestion found Benton willing to listen. Jackson and Donelson were both very close to Polk, and Benton finally convinced himself that their assurances of an honorable treaty by Polk could be trusted. Writing from Texas, Donelson urged him to omit slavery and boundaries from the bill in order to get Texas back on the 1803 footing, and Benton answered that he would "expect from you all a treaty which I can candidly support." On December 22, 1844, Blair assured the relieved Jackson that Benton would support a Polk treaty, and Christmas Day found Senators Benton, Haywood, Allen, and others—probably Tappan, Bagby, and Dix, all of whom followed Benton on Texas matters—dining with Blair to discuss details.[18]

The Missouri General Assembly also passed a set of instructions for annexation, which Benton chose to interpret as backing for his own position. The instructions recommended that the Texas-Mexico boundary be left to future negotiations and declared acceptable any necessary and reasonable compromise. Benton praised them in the Senate, and his enemies criticized them sharply. Old Bullion's changing approach to Texas was clearly not dictated by the Missouri legislature.[19]

Through December and January the debate raged again between Benton's previous bill and efforts to restore the Calhoun treaty. Then, on February 5, Benton suddenly introduced a complete substitute omitting all mention of Mexico or slavery and calling only for admission of a proper-sized Texas state and cession of all remaining Texas territory to the United States. This new program, explained Benton, rested on faith in the incoming Polk's ability to handle the details wisely, and he would consider the importance of compromising the slave question and making peaceful adjustments with Mexico "as remaining just as fully in the mind of the President as if submitted to him in a bill."

Meanwhile the House had passed a joint resolution for annexation subject to boundary adjustments and permitting division of Texas into not more than four states. Those north of the Missouri Compromise line were to be free. This, of course, would make almost all of Texas slave, while Benton's new plan would leave the question unsettled. Both plans appeared doomed until the fertile brain of Robert J. Walker again bore fruit. This time he offered a compromise combining the two programs and adding a preamble giving the President free rein to choose between them. On this basis the United States Senate in a long, exhausting evening session before packed and excited galleries voted to annex Texas. The margin was 27-25, with Benton and four followers providing the deciding votes. At the last moment a colleague proposed Benton's former bill as an amendment. From his seat Benton avowed opposition. When asked if he would thus destroy his own child, Benton amid a roar of laughter and applause announced, "I'll kill it stone dead." For a brief moment Old Bullion had returned to orthodoxy.[20]

Benton's faith in Jackson, Donelson, and Polk was never put to the test. Tyler was still President, and the bill gave him a choice of programs. With only three days left in office, he and Calhoun ignored the Benton alternative and sent the original House resolution on its way to Texas. Polk took office to find this decision out of his hands. Benton later charged that he and his four friends had been cheated of their votes by assurances that Tyler would not dare take such action and that Polk would follow a Bentonian program. In a purely academic argument, Blair, Haywood, and Tappan always insisted that Polk had been so committed, although Polk himself denied this.[21] The conflicting statements probably resulted from the ambiguity of the final Benton program, statements of people professing to speak for Polk, and Polk's own ability to express himself in terms fully understood only by James K. Polk. Regardless, Benton for once had been influenced against his better judgment by the persuasions of others and had made possible a result which he had already opposed at the risk of political extinction. The way for his restoration to party ranks was now open, but the affair left him sore and frustrated. He would never be so amenable again.

The actual annexation was delayed several weeks because Houston disliked several parts of the resolution and preferred the Benton alternative. Several weeks of delicate handling by Donelson plus added appeals from the dying Jackson were necessary to bring The Raven into line. Texas and Benton were saved, and Andrew Jackson could now find the leisure time for a merciful and peaceful death. His final messages of affection and gratitude were to Francis Preston Blair, Sam Houston, and Thomas Hart Benton.

Thus ended the quarrel over the annexation of Texas. It

had divided the Democratic Party and overthrown its ruling dynasty, laid the groundwork for war and future expansion, and irrevocably linked the whole with slavery in a manner fraught with explosive possibilities for the future. Benton had foreseen these results from the beginning, but could claim small comfort from his vision. He had been the right arm and perhaps the heir of the dethroned Jacksonian dynasty and considered it America's only true democracy. His formerly invincible power in Missouri had declined sharply, and he was not in favor with the incoming administration, yet for once he had not even fought the good fight to the end. He had compromised in deference to faith in Jackson, Donelson, and Polk, and had led four trusting followers to the same fateful decision. It was an honest mistake—made after rather than before the Missouri election—but it was a decision obviously influenced by much wishful thinking. For better or worse it had made possible the timing and mode whereby the United States annexed the Republic of Texas.

Old Bullion, however, did not waste time brooding when work remained to be done. Convinced that America would "require all the prudence and firmness of temperate, considerate, and disinterested men to get along safely for some years," he was ready to continue his full-time service. He was sixty-three years old, somewhat advanced in years to begin learning the unfamiliar skills of peacemaking, but he would try. He was impatient, and opponents would remain objects for attack rather than candidates for conversion, but his vision was clear and remarkably unclouded by concern for his own welfare. James K. Polk would need help, and for many months would find Old Bullion a tower of strength.

CHAPTER XVI

THE STATESMAN

OPENING A LETTER from Senator Benton, Sarah Polk probably felt considerable curiosity. At the moment he and
her husband were not very friendly, and a letter to her from the
Senator at any time would be unusual. Its content, however,
could be appreciated by a lady of refinement and strong religious bent:

> The Rev. Mr. Sproule, the pastor of the Presbyterian church
> in which Gen'l Jackson had his last pew in this city, is desirous
> to know *before-hand* whether Mr. Polk & family will attend divine
> [services] in that church on Sunday, that a suitable pew &c may
> be in readiness. He spoke to Mrs. B. and myself about it last
> evening, and we will give him the answer. Mrs. B. and daughters
> sent their compliments to you this morning when I called on Mr.
> Polk, and we shall all do ourselves the pleasure to call on you
> tomorrow.[1]

The Bentons and Polks continued to meet in church for the
next four years.

As a party private in the ranks, James K. Polk had usually
obeyed orders. As President, this frail, grim, dutybound Scotch-
Irish Tennessee planter took instructions only from God, and
if the Sunday morning sermon disagreed with him he usually
concluded that the heavenly messenger in the pulpit had gar-
bled the transmission. Jackson urged him not to dismiss Blair

as party editor, but Polk did not forgive easily, and "Blaar" soon had his walking papers. Cabinet posts were offered to two Van Buren friends (it was known that one would decline), but when both refused, Polk promptly gave the War Department to Van Buren's New York enemy, William L. Marcy.

Still angry over Baltimore and the downfall of Blair, the Van Buren Democrats appeared to be Polk's worst potential foes, and Benton was thus expected to throw powerful influence against the administration. Old Bullion, however, had more important matters on his mind. The election was over, a new day had dawned, new battlefields lay ahead, and there was no time for sulking. Friendly social overtures were soon followed by restoration of an old political friendship. Benton in the Senate and Polk in the House had stood shoulder to shoulder in many a bitter fight during the days of Jackson, and both men, circling each other warily with cautious embarrassment at first, clearly needed allies in 1845.

The Calhoun forces were stunned with bitter disappointment. The Nashville convention had convinced them that theirs was the orthodox position of the party, and Calhoun apparently even hoped to remain in the Department of State. Instead, at Jackson's suggestion, the Carolinian was offered the mission to England, "there to combat with Lord Aberdeen the abolition question." The post was rejected, and by July, 1845, Calhoun's Washington editor was complaining that Polk's policy was "to forget his friends and buy up his enemies. Hence, Benton, Blair, and the New York regency can command anything." The Calhounites had thought the replacement of Blair by Thomas Ritchie a great event, but Duff Green was soon convinced that "Ritchie would sell the democratic party and Virginia too for the public printing and . . . is laboring to get up a coalition with Benton for that purpose." Benton, warned Green, was planning to "assume the control of the Government." [2]

Oregon was Benton's bridge into the new administration. Polk had appeared to acquiesce in the ardent Western conviction that "Oregon" extended all the way to Alaska, and many Americans had taken the party platform on Oregon as seriously as that for Texas. Polk, however, wanted California, and faced an angry and threatening Mexico. A face-saving compromise must be reached with Britain without ruining the Democratic Party's reputation in a large and growing Northwest determined to have "Fifty-four Forty or Fight!"

Announcing full legal rights up to 54° 40', Polk offered to follow the examples of his predecessors and compromise at 49°. The British as usual were prepared to bargain, and demanded the Columbia River Valley for themselves. His kindness rebuffed, the stern and righteous Polk ignored the war fears of timid Secretary of State Buchanan and answered sharply that he would settle only at 54° 40'. Polk understood his opponents. Looked squarely in the eye, John Bull retreated, and settlement at 49° appeared imminent. Shipping interests and the underlying prospects of British repeal of its grain duties and a reduction of American tariffs were also working for peace. Two-thirds of the American Senate, however, must be brought into line if a compromise were to be enacted and all risk of war removed, and the good faith of the Democratic Party must not be compromised.

Thomas Hart Benton had been urging the military occupation and settlement of Oregon since the days when colleagues thought the very idea madness, but he had never doubted that 49° was the legal boundary. He would go to war rather than sacrifice a foot south of this line, but the Frazer's River Valley north of this point he considered wholly English. The anxious Buchanan, fearful of his chief's belligerency, sent for Benton and with Presidential permission submitted the British correspondence and asked for advice. They had found their man. Over a period of several meetings the conscience-driven Polk presented every argument he knew in favor of 54° 40', and then listened attentively to Benton's opposing evidence.[3]

On December 2, 1845, Polk asked Congress to do what Benton had demanded twenty years earlier—abrogate the joint occupation and supply Oregon with American forts, soldiers, and legal jurisdiction. The message did not mention 54° 40', and received equally hearty approval from rabid Northwesterners and some Southerners who opposed any annexation at all. Benton, meanwhile, was conferring privately with the British Ambassador in efforts to reach an agreement.[4]

For weeks Polk kept the British, his Cabinet, his opposition, his followers, and perhaps on occasion even himself, in an uproar trying to fathom his intentions. His recommendations were bitterly debated, with few people entirely certain of the end being sought. The Whig position had already been suggested by Webster in a Boston speech. Oregon, he said, would never join either the United States or Britain, but would become "a great Pacific Republican nation . . . of English and American descent, whose power will be established over the country on the shores of the Pacific. . . ." If not all Whigs agreed, most favored any concessions necessary for peace, and the Calhoun Southerners were ready to surrender the Columbia Valley without protest. The Senate was sharply divided between those ready to concede everything and those determined to have war before surrendering anything. Benton, meanwhile, continued to counsel "calmness, firmness & moderation," while secretly writing Van Buren for a copy of the old New York military conscription bill of 1814 just in case war should come.[5]

As tension continued to mount, Benton on January 27, 1846, applied a cold compress to the war fever by sharply attacking as unnecessary a six-million-dollar appropriation for ten new warships. He would not "plunge into a war measure, when everything . . . indicated peace." Sighs of relief were noticeable on every hand, and the bill was defeated. Three weeks later, Senator Dix of New York, a Benton disciple, delivered an eloquent plea for settlement at 49°, and Benton followed with high praise for both Dix and Polk. With the issue moving to a head, Benton placed himself at Polk's call any hour of the day or night, and their personal relations attained a new warmth. Polk, meanwhile, would not be committed. He simply answered queries with brilliantly evasive replies accepting responsibility to God and country. The harassed President felt the party should support his efforts to solve the problem and blamed its divisions on Presidential ambitions for 1848.[6]

On April 1 Benton finally met the Northwesterners head-on. A recent book by Robert Greenhow had claimed the Treaty of Utrecht did not establish the boundary between the British and French in America at the forty-ninth parallel. The book was being cited everywhere as authoritative, but historian Benton delivered a long and well-documented refutation. Believing Polk to be serving "the great objects of the peace, the honor, and the rights of the country," Benton would "support him in what he may find it necessary to do." [7]

At this point Oregon was suddenly pushed aside by crisis from another direction. Texas had moved to its logical conclusion. With the annexation, Ambassador Almonte in Washington and the American Minister to Mexico had been recalled amid a wave of mutual denunciations, and aspiring Mexican politicians had so inflamed their populace that no Mexican officials dared risk the charge of collaboration with the United States. The ship carrying Almonte home also bore William Parrott, a secret emissary from Polk instructed to seek reconciliation and guarantees of safety for a new American envoy. Unfortunately, Parrott, with a much exaggerated financial claim against Mexico himself, was a foolish choice. As a diplomat he was inept, and his unpopularity provided endless fuel for Mexican newspapers attacking their Government. John Slidell then followed Parrott under circumstances making his reception impossible for any Mexican Government wishing to remain in power. Any knowledge or appreciation of the Spanish character or Mexican internal politics was conspicuously absent. Polk was willing to pay as much as forty million dollars for California, but the harassed Mexican Government could not receive Slidell, and his rejection was promptly taken by Polk to be ample justification for sending General Taylor's troops to the Rio Grande River.

Aware of Benton's tender feelings for Mexico and Latin America in general, Polk informed him of Slidell's rejection on April 9. Benton, who had hoped the United States Government as a basis for negotiations would pay the two million dollars owed American citizens by Mexico, remarked that "our ablest men should be Ministers to the South American States; that we should cultivate their friendship and stand with them as the crowned heads of Europe stood together." [8]

On April 28 Polk and his Cabinet agreed that action must be taken to avenge "the aggravated wrongs done to our citizens . . . by Mexico," but Benton remained unconvinced. On May 3 he repeated his opposition to war with Mexico if avoidable "consistently with the honour of the country." Presumably this objection was met when word came that Mexican soldiers had attacked General Taylor's army on the Rio Grande. Still Benton could not swallow the war message, and advised Polk that he was "willing to vote men and money for defence of our territory, but was not prepared to make aggressive war on Mexico." Again he stubbornly insisted that Taylor's army had been on Mexican soil.[9]

It was a painful situation for an ardent patriot convinced of the error of his beloved country. In the Senate, Benton prevented the debate on the war message from delaying the mobilization of men and supplies by moving a division of the message according to content between his own Committee on Military Affairs, which could proceed immediately to military preparations, and the Committee on Foreign Relations. But when the House of Representatives passed a war declaration after only two hours of debate, Benton was exasperated by such a lighthearted approach, and Polk feared he might muster enough Whig opposition to defeat the measure in the Senate. Such fears were groundless. Benton voted for the declaration, and a moment of rare unity found the Senate passing the declaration by forty to two (both Whigs), with Calhoun and two followers abstaining. Another Benton prophecy had come true.[10]

Having reluctantly and painfully proved his loyalty to Polk in the Mexican crisis, Benton now moved to liquidate the Oregon controversy in a three-day speech covering the entire history of Oregon. Again he proclaimed the inevitable destiny of the American people and American democracy in terms rarely equaled for sheer breadth of imagination. The Columbia River Valley, he prophesied, would be the North American road to the Orient. Through it the untold wealth of Asia would shower down upon America, and over it would go an advance guard of American democracy which through intermarriage and cultural exchange would raise the entire yellow race to a new level of human existence. He had said the same things twenty-five years earlier, but fewer heads were shaking now. At the end little doubt remained as to the legal boundary of Oregon. On June 6 the British offered to accept 49°, and on June 12 the Senate passed a resolution advising the President to accept, with a handful of angry Northwesterners, including Atchison of Missouri, in defiance to the bitter end. Polk had thus avoided primary responsibility throughout. Never once had he been personally committed to anything beyond the vague assertions of his inaugural. For this result he owed much to Senator Benton.

Benton did not hesitate to admit his starring role in the Oregon drama. He had "performed a painful duty . . . to set a nation right that had been led astray. . . ." The people loved "truth and justice," and if Frazer's River was British they did not want it. The people were "just, and ready to act on Jackson's great maxim: *ASK NOTHING BUT WHAT IS RIGHT —SUBMIT TO NOTHING THAT IS WRONG.*" He had saved the country "from the calamities of a war upon mistakes and blunders," and would "rely upon the equity and intelligence of the people, and give defiance to ignorance, malice, and misrepresentation." [11]

He had indeed served the nation well, but had broken another link with his former position as Western champion without regaining his lost standing in the South. Northwesterners, angry with the submissive approach of Calhoun and McDuffie, openly charged the South with bad faith in an election bargain calling for all Oregon as well as Texas, while Benton remained a villain for many of both sections. The *Missouri Reporter* in St. Louis piously commented: "We are sorry, it is true, that Col. Benton does not think our title good to the 54th; but that is a matter between him and his God."

Benton, however, had no time for either concern or gloating when his country was at war. He was a realist, and when the unwanted war became a fact, he promptly turned his authority as chairman of the Committee on Military Affairs to the task of organizing a rapid and profitable victory. He immediately took charge of a bill to organize volunteers and appoint generals and, despite Whig efforts to keep generals "away from the vortex of executive patronage," guided the bill to quick passage.[12] And with a superb command of geography, competent knowledge of the Spanish language and Mexican history, and numerous frontier contacts and friends, Benton was admirably equipped for the role of Presidential adviser. His brief opposition to Polk's war message was apparently forgiven, and soon few important decisions were being reached without his advice.

The relationship produced quick results. Polk and Benton immediately recognized the need to counteract Mexican fears that an American invasion would destroy the Catholic religion. Unfortunately, Mexican leaders had numerous instances of open anti-Catholicism in the United States to cite in their propaganda, but Polk now countered by sending Catholic priests as chaplains with the army. After Polk had discussed the matter first with Benton and then with the Bishop of New York, Benton brought the Bishop of Missouri to the White House and arranged with the Secretary of War for the Missouri Bishop to select the desired personnel.[13]

At the first approach of war Benton had already sent for Colonel James Magoffin, a twenty-year resident of Chihuahua, and on June 15 presented him at the White House. In Polk's words, Magoffin provided valuable information "in relation to the Northern provinces, the character of the country, and the means of conducting a campaign in them." This was an accurate but highly restrained description. Magoffin was one of the shrewdest, best-informed, and most strategically situated men in the West—rather typical of the circle of friends Benton had accumulated through the years. Largely through this wily trader's "fifth column" activities, namely bribing Mexican generals, General Kearney later took New Mexico without any fighting. Some confusion remains as to Magoffin's exact deeds, but a secret session of Congress eventually voted him thirty thousand dollars for services rendered. Also, in selecting commanders for the New Mexican and California expeditions Polk took Benton's advice, promoting Colonel Stephen Kearney of St. Louis to brigadier general and appointing Sterling Price, a later Confederate hero, as commander of the Missouri volunteers. Kearney proved an able commander, and Price rendered valuable service as Governor of New Mexico.[14]

Despite his sympathies for Mexico, Benton agreed fully with Polk that California should be purchased as soon as possible and should never be allowed to fall into other hands. California, with a rebellious minority of United States citizens, was poorly administered, could not be controlled or protected by Mexico in case of trouble, and was rumored to be menaced by the supposedly omnipresent British. In the summer of 1845, Benton and Secretary of the Navy George Bancroft had already sent Frémont on a long overland trek to California with a "scientific expedition" of sixty well-armed, straight-shooting adventurers. Frémont's exploits, achievements, and misadventures are still debated, but in spite of his foolishness before and after the event, the Pathfinder did help conquer California, and young Jessie was soon writing joyfully of her husband's promotion to lieutenant colonel. The initial seizure of California by Frémont and Commodore Stockton was followed by the major overland expedition of General Kearney—a venture which Benton helped plan also. From the map and book compiled by Frémont on earlier expeditions, Benton briefed Polk on the route and its difficulties, assured him that the soldiers would not be caught by winter in the mountains if they could leave Missouri by August 1, and provided a written outline for the expedition. And finally, a later regiment of volunteers sent from New York by sea went, on Benton's advice, under agreement to settle in California after being discharged from service —a modified version of Benton's old Florida program. Benton was clearly a major architect of Polk's highly successful and relatively bloodless military policies in both New Mexico and California.[15]

Near the end of June, 1846, the President asked for a written summary of Benton's views on conducting the war, and this document, after minor editing by Polk, was included in a set of instructions to General Taylor. The summary revealed a profound knowledge of Mexican political and social history and a keen understanding of psychological warfare. Taylor was to counteract by honorable behavior the Mexican charges that the war was for national survival against American plunder and rapine, and every opportunity should be taken to convince enemy soldiers as well as civilians that America wanted only an honorable negotiated peace. Mexico, explained the Senator, was sharply divided into races, classes, parties, and factions: "the Spaniards, who monopolize the wealth and power . . . and the mixed Indian race who bear its burthens . . . the lower and the higher clergy, the latter of whom have the dignities and the revenues, while the former have poverty and labour . . . the political parties . . . some more liberal, and more friendly to us than others . . . rival political chiefs, political and military." Among them existed much bitterness which might be skillfully exploited to win a just and speedy peace from the more liberal Mexican elements. And above all, concluded Benton in words of genuine statesmanship, the war should be conducted so as "to leave no lasting animosities behind, to prejudice the future friendship and commerce of the two countries; nor to permit injurious reports to go forth to excite the ill will of the other Republics of Spanish origin, against us." [16] It was a tall order, but an objective worth pursuing. Few enough leading Americans shared his concern for the nation's reputation among its neighbors.

Waiting impatiently for word from the family hero, Frémont, the Bentons found another special excitement. Secretary Buchanan could not read Spanish and often needed help with documents from secret agents in Mexico. Robert Greenhow was the official translator, but his wife, later a famous Confederate spy, was apparently in the pay of the British. Buchanan knew this, but, preferring to keep her unaware of exposure, dispensed with the services of her husband, and left the translations to the Benton household. Benton and Senator Dix would read the documents to the Secretary, after which the multi-lingual Benton daughters would write them out in English.[17]

If the war was a romantic affair for some, for many others the early excitement soon gave way to sullen anger. Though only some fifteen hundred men were killed in actual battle throughout the war, more than ten thousand fell by the sun-baked Texas and Mexican waysides from accident and disease. Among the bereaved parents were Henry Clay and Daniel Webster, both well-known opponents of the policies which had led to war. Clay's eldest son was killed, and General Taylor sent the grieving father a well-publicized letter of personal sorrow, shared by sympathetic readers throughout the country. The generals did their best to maintain discipline, but reports of American, and especially Texan, atrocities and plunder filtered back into the American press to disturb consciences already sore enough. General Taylor made no effort to conceal his own longing for the war to end and his open disagreement with the President's territorial aims. Exciting headlines became rare, and the Whigs incessantly hammered at the growing disillusionment by charging the administration with starting and prolonging an unjust, useless, and apparently endless war. In the fall elections of 1846 the Whigs won control of the House of Representatives.

And the administration had other peace-loving enemies. Unwilling to accept any personal responsibility for events he himself had set in motion, Calhoun denounced Polk for starting the war and, fearing future tariffs, devoted himself to limiting its cost. He and three friends supported a military policy of "masterly inactivity," or holding the existing line of advance until Mexico sued for peace. Voting with the Whigs, these senators were able to delay or block much of Polk's war legislation.

Benton, meanwhile, spoke twice and lined up his personal following solidly behind the administration's low-tariff bill, which passed the Senate by only one vote. And when Polk vetoed a bill for the American Government to pay certain American citizens for some ancient spoilation claims settled with France, Benton defended the veto successfully in a brilliant debate with Daniel Webster. It was a high point in the restored friendship of the imperious Senator and the stubborn President. Reminding Polk of his reconciliation with Jackson, Benton asked that all past differences be forgotten and offered to serve Polk as he had served Jackson. Polk was grateful and as a reward offered Benton the mission to France. He probably made the gesture knowing the honor would be refused.[18]

For Benton felt needed as never before. Personal feuds, sectional quarreling over Oregon, the new tariff, the war itself, and "masterly inactivity" in general were sucking away at Democratic harmony and strength. With dangerous cracks in the structure of national unity visible everywhere, Benton fretted and fumed with impatience. His bombastic energy and fertile imagination could not endure a policy lacking in force or direction. Down in Kentucky during the early fall of 1846, perhaps inspired by watching his favorite machine chew forests into lumber, he sprouted new ideas and returned to Polk urging the immediate seizure of Vera Cruz and the advance of a powerful force overland from Vera Cruz to Mexico City. This army should be accompanied by a peace commission of distinguished leaders from both parties, authorized to offer peace "before a battle, during the battle, & after it was over." Only immediate action could prevent the unhappy war from overthrowing the party, and the modest Senator would be happy to serve on the peace commission.

Polk was impressed, but had found new problems in a conviction that his leading generals, Scott and Taylor, were utterly incompetent and untrustworthy. Like Jackson, Polk considered any Whig slightly sub-human, and Scott and Taylor were both reportedly guilty of such tendencies. Neither respected Polk, both were often unco-operative and indiscreet in their public statements, and Polk was certain they were aiming for the Presidency in 1848. This unhappy situation created a form of Presidential paralysis, but Senator Benton had a further suggestion. Polk should ask Congress to create a new rank of lieutenant general and appoint a new supreme commander authorized to make policy and negotiate for peace at the proper moment. The post would require "a man of talents and resources as well as a military man," and "with a view to obtain peace more depended upon the talents & energy of the officer than mere bravery." Such a man was clearly available; Benton would accept the command himself.[19]

The President was apparently delighted with the prospect of a Democratic general and agreed that the Whigs must not be allowed to use the war as a successful political weapon. Other party leaders threw cold water on the idea immediately, but Polk persisted, and assured Benton that if Congress refused to create the new rank he could still be a major general. Benton politely declined the promise of any such junior position, but Polk repeated his earlier promise that Benton should head any mission for peace.

The Cabinet agreed that Benton's war strategy had merit, but concluded that General Taylor was unfit for command. "All were at a loss to designate who would be chief in command . . . against Vera Cruz." At Polk's request Benton presented a written version of his war plan. With this in hand, the Cabinet also agreed that Vera Cruz should be attacked, but would not commit themselves to the Mexico City venture. General Scott, meanwhile, presented a detailed analysis of the requirements for the move against Vera Cruz, and as senior officer was the only possible choice for command. The unhappy Polk, however, refused to make the choice until Benton insisted that Scott must be appointed.

By December, 1846, Benton was assuming the role of a one-man Kitchen Cabinet without portfolio, probably to the increasing irritation of the official Cabinet. As Congress prepared for the unruly session of 1846-1847, Benton reviewed the President's annual message and objected strenuously to certain passages. Polk was prepared to ask Congress for authority to establish permanent occupation governments in conquered territories, but Benton insisted that the President already had this power under international law. To wait for legislation would be just another form of masterly inactivity. Some Cabinet members disagreed, but all felt that the mere fact of Benton's objection was enough to make the request inexpedient. The Senator had his way.[20]

On December 3, however, the President and the Senator met head-on in disagreement. Polk decided to appoint the peace commission, and Benton suggested Silas Wright, John J. Crittenden, and himself. Polk agreed, but wished to add John Slidell. As prospective head of the mission, Benton objected violently to Slidell and refused to yield. The irresistible force thus met the immovable object, and Polk simply dropped the entire project. Benton's objection was sound—the former envoy would have been a burning irritant to Mexican sensibilities—but any mission might have been a step forward, and the inclusion of Whig Senator Crittenden was expected to carry some Whig support for the lieutenant-general bill. Mutual stubbornness had cost Benton and Polk an opportunity with considerable possibilities.[21]

Francis P. Blair thought Benton's war plan "perfectly Bonepartean in character," beneficial "to Mexico politically—To us territorially and commercially." Taylor was to advance with twenty-five thousand men along the tableland by San Luis Potosí and, leaving garrisons in conquered districts, arrive at Mexico City with ten thousand men. Scott would simultaneously occupy Vera Cruz and march from there up the excellent road to Mexico City, joining Taylor to render the Mexican capital at the mercy of the combined forces. With Scott's army would be the new commander-in-chief and his distinguished bipartisan council of leading statesmen, prepared to negotiate for peace on the spot. The commander could settle any dissensions between the generals without the interminable delay of communications with Washington, and the council could work for the political success of Mexico's more liberal elements and stop all bloodshed immediately at signs of surrender.[22] It was a sensible, comprehensive program, planned for one of the most drifting, directionless little wars ever fought.

Political distrust and poor communications had made Polk and his leading generals almost incomprehensible to each other and left his control over them practically negligible. Presence in the field of an eminent, highly respected and trusted, Democratic aide ready to accept full responsibility and credit for ending the war was an appealing prospect for the weary President, and he did his best to accomplish it.

But the new office never had a chance. The Whigs saw Benton's military ambitions as a last effort by the Jacksonian Democrats to regain their fading national power, and the Calhoun Democrats would have voted first for Santa Anna himself. The disgruntled Calhoun believed Benton's emergence as the "organ of the Administration in the Senate" to be part of a plan to rebuild the Van Buren faction, and was determined to block it at all costs.[23] Various other Democrats, agreeing with Calhoun on almost nothing else, had had enough of Van Buren, and Benton proudly remained a Van Buren man. Also, in the Cabinet, Secretary of State Buchanan naturally enough resented Benton's role of foreign-policy-maker, Secretary of War Marcy was Van Buren's most bitter New York enemy, and Robert J. Walker had once battled furiously with Benton for weeks over the legality of the Texas claim to the Rio Grande. Walker wished to annex all of Mexico, and could not support a plan giving Benton control of the final settlement.

Benton's suspicions of the Cabinet soon brought further mis-understanding with Polk. After Benton had been consulted by the Cabinet on the advisability of annexing California and New Mexico and extending the Missouri Compromise line to the Pacific, the House began debating a resolution to bar slavery in all conquered areas. Knowing that the lieutenant-general bill would need Democratic Party unity, Benton angrily concluded that the Cabinet had leaked its discussions to foment a slave argument which would defeat the propo-sition. He wrote Polk that "strange work had been going on. . . ." The sensitive President felt unjustly accused of per-sonal deceit, and the sting was not entirely removed by Ben-ton's explanation that he meant nothing of the sort.[24]

On January 9, 1847, the House rejected the lieutenant-general bill, and a week later the Senate followed suit by a six-vote margin. The Calhoun group voting with the Whigs provided the edge for defeat. The opposition charged Polk with trying to dictate his successor, and the arguments were political and factional throughout. On a measure of enormous national importance the competence or incompetence of the prospective commander was never an issue.

Two weeks later the frustrated would-be commander de-livered an angry vindication of the President and himself. Hotly denying that Polk was seeking to select the next Presi-dent, he reminded colleagues that he had been a lieutenant colonel before any of the present commanders had reached that rank, and described his war plan in detail. He had planned a combination of the sword and the olive branch—a sword for the war party and diplomatic negotiations for the peace party. He had hoped only for an honorable victory which would leave no lingering hatreds between the United States and its Latin American neighbors.[25] The Senator's objectives were worthy, but they did not move a Senate seething with political partisan-ship.

Throughout February Benton and his friends, Dix and Bagby, led the fight for ten additional regiments and a fund of three million dollars for general use in ending the war, while Calhoun spurred the opposition at every turn. In the House the Wilmot Proviso, a proposition to bar slavery from the new

territories, entered the struggle, and Calhoun countered in the
Senate with resolutions denouncing the Missouri Compromise
and guaranteeing slavery in the newly conquered areas. Few
men have been subjected to more epithets and accusations than
Polk during this session, but at its end both of his important
measures had passed, thanks in large part to the efforts of
Thomas Hart Benton.

These debates provided the arena for another round of bitter conflict between Benton and Calhoun. The Carolinian
eloquently defended "masterly inactivity," denounced the administration for starting an unnecessary war, and called for
support for his slave resolutions. The exasperated Benton,
struggling to get Congress to vote men and supplies for the
war, charged Calhoun with injecting abstract firebrands to
ignite the Union when he should be assisting in the practical
business of ending a war he himself had started. Calhoun answered that he had expected Benton as a slaveholder to support
his resolutions, to which Benton thundered back, "I shall be
found in the right place. I am on the side of my country and
the Union." And a few days later Benton answered Calhoun's
attacks on the administration with a barrage of his own. On
all Texas matters from beginning to end, said Benton, Calhoun
had been tragically wrong:

> wrong in 1819, in giving away Texas—wrong in 1836, in his sud-
> den and hot haste to get her back—wrong in all his machinations
> for bringing on the Texas question of 1844—wrong in breaking up
> the armistice and peace negotiations between Mexico and Texas—
> wrong in secretly sending the army and navy to fight Mexico
> while we were at peace with her . . . wrong in writing to Mexico
> that he took Texas in view of all possible consequences, meaning
> war—wrong in offering Mexico . . . ten millions of dollars to hush
> up the war which he had created—wrong now in refusing Mr.
> Polk three millions to aid in getting out of the war which he
> made—wrong in throwing the blame of this war of his own
> making upon the shoulders of Mr. Polk—wrong in his retreat and
> occupation line of policy . . . and more wrong now than ever, in
> that string of resolutions which he has laid on the table, and in
> which, as Sylla saw in the young Cicero many Mariuses, so do I
> see in them many nullifications.[26]

If the indictment was exaggerated in spots, its essentials were accurate and must have hit Calhoun hard despite his brilliant defense. Texas had boomeranged to make Calhoun again a party outcast, rejected by all sections except the deep South and stripped of every issue but slavery even in his own stronghold. National power gone forever, Calhoun would retreat ever further into the role of sectional agitator.

Meanwhile, the chain of command between President and generals was growing weaker. Scott's plan of campaign appeared in a New Orleans newspaper, and Polk immediately blamed the General himself. Then some New York papers carried a letter from Taylor to General Gaines criticizing the administration sharply and discussing various projected troop movements. Both incidents fed Polk's bitter distrust and anger over the refusal of Congress to provide a satisfactory commander.

Then, on February 26, the House passed a bill authorizing the President to select a commander-in-chief from among his major generals, and overwhelmingly defeated an amendment declaring members of Congress ineligible for the post. The Senate, however, promptly reversed this decision. On March 3, the final day of the session, the House re-inserted the amendment to elevate Benton, but administration friends, fearing the deadlock would kill the war appropriation bill, reluctantly shelved the proposition. Thus Polk and Benton were again thwarted by Southern opposition in the Senate.[27]

A few hours before the session ended, Benton was appointed and confirmed as a major general, but General Benton soon qualified his acceptance. He would serve only if given command of the army and sufficient diplomatic power to negotiate peace on terms to be specified by the President. He "had no desire to go to Mexico simply to have a plume and bunch of feathers in his hat."

The Cabinet advised Polk that Benton could not legally take command without the recall of the four major generals already in the field, and Buchanan and Walker objected strongly to the granting of diplomatic powers. Polk agreed with Benton's terms and was ready to recall Scott and Taylor without hesitation, but could think of no reason for recalling Butler and

Patterson. Two days later, however, Polk learned that General Patterson, from either wounds or illness, was in New Orleans. In the President's own words, "I did not still see my way entirely clear to remove three senior Major-Generals who had rank of Gen'l Butler, but thought it probable that I might do so in a short time." Off went the Presidential secretary to ask General Benton to postpone any final decision until further consultation, but the envoy reported an hour later that Benton had already addressed letters to the President and the Adjutant General declining the appointment. The rebuffed Polk received both copies an hour later and carefully noted the time in his diary, apparently suspecting that the refusal had been written after rather than before his own plea.

Polk immediately summoned his reluctant tiger to an evening conference and explained the new possibilities involved in Butler's absence from Mexico, but Benton's decision was final. He would be part of no such plan, and was blazing with anger over certain newspaper letters which he believed to have been written by members of the Cabinet. Polk answered sharply that all the Cabinet had favored the appointment, and was clearly displeased by Benton's refusal to obey his wishes.[28]

Benton's note of refusal emphasized that in a subordinate position his presence in Mexico would be "improper and mischievous," because his well-known attitudes would make him a "nucleus of discontent and insubordination." The reasoning was sound, but relations between the President and the Senator were never again quite the same. On March 12 they argued again over Benton's accusations against the Cabinet, and three days later Polk recorded a significant conversation with Brigadier General Franklin Pierce. Pierce "expressed deep regret that Gen'l Benton had declined to accept the office of Maj'r Gen'l, and said he had utterly ruined himself with the masses of the people of the country." And Polk added, "I think myself that Gen'l Benton will have reason to regret his course." On March 18 Polk attended the wedding of the eldest Benton daughter, Eliza, to attorney William Carey Jones of New Orleans and personally escorted the bride to the supper table. For many months he had found Benton pleasant and friendly, but on March 29 "Gen'l Benton called and read . . . a letter which he had addressed to the people of Oregon." Polk disapproved, "but knowing his domineering disposition and utter impatience of contradiction or difference of opinion," objected only briefly. Benton then asked about a diplomatic appointment for his new son-in-law, and Polk flatly refused. There was no spot open and there would be none in the future. And in the ever-present diary Polk predicted that failure to appoint Jones would cause "a violent outbreak of opposition . . . by Gen'l Benton." [29]

Thus Polk recorded his new feelings toward the Senator. True, William Carey Jones had been a Whig, but Benton had more than earned the right to make such a request, and Polk had been quite generous to Benton in patronage matters earlier. The frail Tennesseean, literally working himself to death, apparently considered Benton's refusal of anything but the top command and unwillingness to wait for the opportunity as selfish and unpatriotic. Polk desperately wanted a trustworthy general and after following Benton's wishes and advice for months felt entitled to the same consideration. The two men still needed each other, but Benton served no man except on his own terms, and Polk, equally unable to retreat from a conviction, had reached the point where disagreement and distrust were almost inseparable.

Benton's refusal, however, was a wise decision. Legally empowered to enforce co-operation between Scott and Taylor and work for a peace treaty, Benton might have served with distinction. As a field subordinate he could easily have become a focal point for jealousies, quarreling, and confusion in a war already amply distinguished for these commodities. Indeed, Old Bullion's rejection of a field command even with full Presidential backing was consistent with his proposals all along. Never had he expressed any wish to supplant either Scott or Taylor as director of field operations. The position he sought was similar to the later chief-of-staff function, supplemented by a diplomatic assignment requiring knowledge and imagination clearly lacking in Secretary of State Buchanan. And for this role Benton was well qualified. He had the prestige of a famous senator and a reputation for good-will toward Mexico, spoke Spanish fluently, understood the issues, knew the geography and history of Mexico, and was a keen student of military affairs and history in general. The confidence motivating Polk's efforts to make Benton the commander had been well earned and was justified. Their program was not a harebrained project, and was not so regarded by contemporaries. Indeed, the fear of opponents that Benton would emerge as a national hero was the chief obstacle blocking its enactment. Only when Polk began talking of replacing both Scott and Taylor did the plan become untenable, and at that point Benton himself withdrew.

In the late spring and summer of 1847, Benton swept through Missouri again, reminding voters of the past services of the Democratic Party and sounding a long and loud alarm against Calhoun and his slave-extension resolutions. The issue was dangerous in slaveholding Missouri, and a wise politician might have side-stepped it as long as possible. When Thomas Hart Benton saw national danger ahead, however, his concern for political expediency was roughly akin to that of an Old Testament prophet. These "firebrand resolutions" aimed at subversion of the Union and would destroy "all compromises, past and future, on the slavery question." They could only lead to the same practical consequences as the agitation of Northern abolitionists—"fanaticism, for or against any *dogma*, terminates at the same point of intolerance and defiance." There "was no Jackson now to save the Union by a voice, like the command of destiny," and all true friends of the Union must take up the challenge. Thus the Senator drew the battle line upon which he would stand for the rest of his life.[30]

Before returning to Washington in July, Benton addressed a wildly enthusiastic reception for Colonel Alexander Doniphan and the returning Missouri volunteers, who had marched brilliantly across northern Mexico despite incredible hardships. Doniphan answered the Senator's words of praise by assuring the huge crowd that if Benton's ideas had been followed "the war would have terminated long ago."

Benton thought so too, and returned to Washington still hoping to help shape events, but an event in faraway California would soon tear his relation with Polk past the healing point. Commodore Stockton, Lieutenant Colonel Frémont, and General Kearney had finally consolidated the conquest of California, only to continue with a private war among themselves. The erratic Frémont found himself receiving conflicting orders from Stockton and Kearney, and since Stockton had directed him to retain the post of Governor of California, Frémont chose to obey the navy. Orders from Washington finally vindicated Kearney, and the proud Frémont, demanding a public court-martial on all charges, was sent home under arrest.

Thomas Hart Benton had been defending his loved ones since his earliest days as eldest son in an orphaned family. Brother Jesse, Andrew Jackson, and Sally McDowell, among others, had found him a fierce and effective champion, and Frémont was to be no exception. To Benton in 1847 the Pathfinder was young Galahad with the pure heart being persecuted by jealous West Pointers resenting his achievements, and the old man sprang to the rescue with all the fury of a mother bear defending a cub. During late summer and early fall he pled Frémont's case to Polk without encouragement, making plain that his "deepest concern in this life was to see justice done to Col. Frémont in this matter."

The anxious Jessie and Frémont's stalwart friend, Kit Carson, also poured their versions of Frémont's troubles into the Presidential ear, and in October Randolph Benton, not yet eighteen, added a sour note which left the harassed President feeling surrounded by Bentons. Randolph burst into the White House, apparently intoxicated, and demanded an army commission, and when Polk refused the angry boy stormed out swearing that " 'By God' he would do something." Young Randolph apparently spent his short life in the shadow of his famous brother-in-law and brilliant sister, which was not easy for a boy anxious to impress an idolized and exacting father. Again Polk gloomily prophesied that the Senator would probably become an enemy "if all his wishes in reference to his family and their appointments" were not granted.

This was not entirely fair. The inquiry for Jones was no demand, and Benton had asked nothing for Randolph. Frémont, however, was another matter. In November Benton gave up his beloved post as chairman of the Committee on Military Affairs because of Marcy's alleged conduct toward

Frémont, and from November into January the trim Pathfinder and his ponderous father-in-law sat shoulder to shoulder in one of America's most famous military trials. Savagely the Old Buffalo cross-examined the young man's detractors, and at one point the very fierceness of his gaze led to an angry protest by General Kearney. In the end, however, Frémont was found guilty on all counts and sentenced to dismissal from the service, but with a recommendation for clemency.

The last hope then rested with Polk. Except for Marcy the Cabinet agreed that the sentence was entirely too harsh and unwarranted, and Buchanan defended Frémont in several sharp encounters with Marcy. As Secretary of War, Marcy felt the honor of the army to be at stake, and finally suggested that Polk approve the findings, but remand the sentence. Except for a complete reversal on the charge of mutiny this procedure was followed. Polk ruled Frémont guilty of insubordination, but ordered him back to duty with full rank. Polk considered this generous enough, but the proud Pathfinder and his angry champion felt differently. Frémont resigned, and except for a brief nod at a senatorial funeral, Benton never spoke to Polk again. The President dated their break with the Frémont affair, although there had been no real co-operation since Benton's refusal to go to Mexico.

The final chapter of the Frémont episode was played out in July, 1848, when Benton spoke for thirteen straight days against Kearney's promotion to major general, reviewing the Frémont case again from beginning to end. Frémont emerged with added publicity for his already heroic legend, and though the promotion was confirmed, Kearney's reputation never quite recovered from the old battler's sledge-hammer blows.[31]

Thus ended the usefulness of Thomas Hart Benton to James K. Polk and the vexatious war—perhaps a serious loss to the United States. A modified version of Benton's combination of sword and olive branch finally ended the Mexican War. Scott moved upon Mexico City, but the celebrated peace mission, as well as authority almost equal to that requested by Benton, was vested in Nicholas Trist, a chief clerk in the Department of State. General Scott could have deferred without loss of face to a legally superior officer or a council of distinguished senators, but could not abide the tactless orders of a mere clerk. Before Scott sent a jug of guava jelly to soothe the upset stomach of Trist and the two men were finally united against Polk by a sense of shared persecution, the war had been prolonged many weeks by their juvenile squabbling. Trist's incompetent bargaining and prematurely granted armistice enabled Santa Anna to recover from a total defeat and regroup his forces for the bloody battles of Molino del Rey and Chapultepec.[32] The amoral dictator, Santa Anna, represented a Mexican element Benton wished to see destroyed, and Benton would have been far less susceptible to the deceits practiced on Trist. With Scott, Taylor, and the other generals directing operational details, it is unlikely that any battle would have been fought any differently with Benton in command, but much costly delay and political bungling might have been avoided. In checking Benton, the partisan, sectional, and personal politics and jealousies in the Senate and Cabinet, and the headstrong misjudgment of young John Frémont probably cost America more in blood and treasure than has commonly been realized.

If Benton's attitude toward Polk became one of malevolent neutrality, it did not shape his senatorial conduct. He did not attack the administration and continued to support its war appropriations. When Trist, after being discharged by Polk, ignored the President and negotiated the treaty ending the war, Benton, along with Webster and two others on the Committee on Foreign Affairs, recommended rejection and the "appointment of an imposing commission to be composed of three or five persons belonging to both political parties, to proceed to Mexico to negotiate a treaty." They opposed the mode of negotiation, and Polk, who detested Trist, shared their distaste, but was willing to accept the treaty. Trist's conduct had been impudent and undignified, even if successful, and, despite the excellence of the treaty, the ratification of an international agreement negotiated by an unemployed civilian was a new departure. Polk thought Benton's opposition motivated by vindictiveness, overlooking a much simpler explanation. By sending a clerk instead of a prominent Democrat, Polk had thrown away the last hope to counterbalance for his party the fame already won by Taylor and Scott. With Mexico beaten, a new commission of prominent senators would be guaranteed success and might have still rectified this political error. Indeed, both Benton and Webster were probably hoping for the prestige of membership on a successful and well-publicized peace mission.

Both ultra-annexationists and "no territory" extremists attacked the treaty, and defeat was probable until the sudden death of John Quincy Adams in the House quieted the spirit of partisanship. Although Benton voted against the treaty, he voted for almost all the important amendments which made it acceptable, and in later years commended it. Thus ended the first calamity prophesied by Benton in 1843—the war had been fought, and the nation must now digest the spoils.

The war had been a painful experience for Benton, but, as he wrote Van Buren, he had "managed to discharge the first duty of a citizen toward his country without compromising . . . his actual political position." [33] Unlike his friends he had put aside personal feelings and given invaluable aid to the President when most needed. On the Oregon issue he had openly opposed Missouri even though aware of his ever-weakening hold on its voters. Although emphatically opposed to war with Mexico, he had calmly accepted an accomplished fact and worked diligently for Polk's objectives. He had made essential contributions to the conquest of New Mexico and California, the provision of soldiers and money, and much of the political and military strategy of the war. The temptation to go to Mexico as a powerful administration-backed major general must have been great, but with admirable restraint he had refused to risk a situation which might harm the nation's total military effort.

But for the Frémont affair he might have yet regained Polk's favor and continued to serve, but such action was too much to expect from a man so intensely human as Thomas Hart Benton. As always, his loves, hates, furious temper, and impatience with opponents were his major handicaps. His judgment would remain sound, and he would struggle incessantly and sacrifice every personal ambition to keep America united in peace and harmony, but he would always remain out of character in the role of peacemaker.

* * * * * * *

The angry years of the reign of Polk were not entirely unhappy for Thomas Hart Benton. The family continued to provide warmth, love, and satisfaction, and Jessie by now had produced little Elizabeth Benton Frémont for the proud grandfather to idolize. Eliza's happy marriage to William Carey Jones provided another son-in-law as steady and trustworthy as Frémont was romantic, and in the long run Jones would stand closest to the old man in his hours of trial. Sarah, meanwhile, had met young Richard Taylor Jacob, a Kentucky adventurer who had come to Washington for the Frémont trial after serving the Pathfinder in California. In January, 1847, they were married and moved to Missouri for a happy life on a prosperous farm.

Perhaps most important, Elizabeth's health, though precarious, settled down to a chronic condition diagnosed, probably inaccurately, as a form of epilepsy. Medical assurances that she was in no imminent danger eased her husband's gnawing fears, but her comfort remained his major domestic concern.

If Benton found joy in his sons-in-law, his chief disappointment within the family circle may have been his own son, John Randolph, whose brief life remains something of a mystery. From the sparse facts available, Randolph was intelligent and sensitive, adored his father, traveled west with Frémont at the age of twelve, and suffered from poor health which caused his mother much concern. He was also pronounced "worthless" by James K. Polk and "an utter ruin" by his father's close friend, Francis Preston Blair, and as a family problem attracted the attention, sympathy, and advice of the famous St. Louis Jesuit missionary, Father De Smet.[34] Such judgments might have been proven premature, but the young man was destined for a tragic death at the age of twenty-two.

Meanwhile, the process of surrendering the family patrimony to leave the Senator free for public service continued toward its inevitable end. In October, 1847, Benton sold three hundred acres next to his sawmill tract in Kentucky for $20,100.[35] It was a fair price, but payment would be slow and the money would not last long. Such matters, however, were only incidental to the Senator's major purposes. Oregon, New Mexico, and California would need government, the inevitable clashes over slavery were pending, and a new President must be elected. The ship of state needed steady guidance, and Senator Benton stood ready to help as long as the passengers would approve his course.

CHAPTER XVII

THE REALIST

ON MARCH 24, 1848, Thomas Hart Benton rose in the Senate to deliver a glowing eulogy of the dead John Quincy Adams. The resulting explosion in the Andrew Jackson sector of heaven or some less temperate habitat can only be imagined, although conceivably Old Hickory and Old Man Eloquent Adams shook hands and enjoyed it together. Benton's words were as sincere as they were eloquent. The ancient enmities had faded before the common cause of devotion to the Union, and here he and Adams had stood together. Other veteran senators added praise to the Adams epitaph, but John C. Calhoun remained silent.

* * * * * * *

Peace came to America in 1848, but two new events quickly snapped the tension back into the slackening lines of political excitement. Oregon was given a territorial government with an anti-slave restriction, and a Whig general was chosen to occupy the White House. Oregon fanned the question of territorial slavery to a white heat which did not cool until the Compromise of 1850. The election was a dull affair between two mediocre and uninspiring candidates, but it splintered the Democratic Party in New York and spawned the Free-Soil Party under the leadership of a former President. It thus became an important milestone on the road to civil war.

In January, 1847, the House had overwhelmingly approved an Oregon territorial government with an anti-slave provision, only to see the measure die in a Senate committee because of the slave issue. Considering slavery a ridiculous question in an area so far north, Benton angrily concluded that Calhoun was stirring another false issue to divide the Democratic Party along North-South lines. Despite the objections of President Polk, the Senator dispatched a sharply worded letter to the people of Oregon. They would not be abandoned, he wrote, for adhering to the Ordinance of 1787, "the work of the great men of the south, in the great days of the south, prohibiting slavery in a territory far less north than yours," because of a "home agitation for election and disunion purposes." He could promise "in the name of the south as well as of the north" that the Senate would "scourge it out!"

The grateful Oregonians replied with a letter of thanks and a petition for Congress. When Congress met in December, 1847, an elected Oregon representative was present to plead for a government, and a special envoy appeared shortly afterward to report an Indian war. The two were soon filling the air with pleas for military aid and the blessings of law and order.

After almost five months in committee, an Oregon bill finally reached the Senate floor on May 31, 1848. The Senate immediately approved Benton's amendment to send a regiment of mounted volunteers, but it was the last peaceful moment in the debate. The New Hampshire abolitionist, John Hale, moved an amendment prohibiting slavery, and the battle was on. To Calhoun this meant "the degradation of nearly one-half the States of this Union, who claim to be full equals here, and who intend never to yield that full equality."

The angry and realistic Benton saw the entire argument as a piece of monumental folly. Colonists in mortal danger from Indians were pleading for help, he said, yet Congress was paralyzed by a meaningless question. No laws could affect slavery in Oregon. Climate, latitude, nature, and the people themselves, largely from slaveholding states, forbade it. Here was

the real business of the country stopped, prostrated, defeated by thrusting this question upon us. We read in Holy Writ, that a certain people were cursed by the plague of frogs, and that the plague was everywhere. You could not look upon the table but there were frogs, you could not sit down at the banquet but there were frogs, you could not go to the bridal couch and lift the sheets but there were frogs! We can see nothing, touch nothing, have no measures proposed, without having this pestilence thrust before us. Here it is, this black question, forever on the table, on the nuptial couch, everywhere!

The anti-slave amendment, he insisted, should be voted down as impractical, and opinions for or against slavery should not prevent government and protection for Oregon.[1]

The Senator's practical good sense and grim humor were wasted, as the quarrel raged for many hot and dreary days. In Oregon the irate citizens were happily clubbing their Indian foes into submission, but Congress did not know this, and the question remained on an emergency basis. No one suggested that slavery might go to Oregon, but the right of Congress to forbid it was a burning issue. Ignoring the Ordinance of 1787 and the Missouri Compromise, both enacted primarily by Southerners and long accepted as part of the American tradition, the Calhoun men insisted that slave property was guaranteed in the Constitution and that neither Congress nor any territorial government could exclude it. Keeping them well supplied with arguments were those at the opposite pole insisting that slavery must be officially prohibited. Among those pleading for a common-sense, practical approach, the voice of Benton was loudest.

A select committee finally met on July 14 in an effort to break the angry deadlock, and five days later Chairman Clayton of Delaware announced its recommendations. Oregon should be organized with its existing anti-slave laws, California and New Mexico should be organized with their territorial legislatures forbidden to deal with the subject, and any actual case involving the legality of slavery should be settled by the courts. This plan would enlist the aid of nature. If, as many thought, slavery was barred by geography and climate, the issue would never be tested, but Southern pride would be saved. Meanwhile, Oregon would receive government and military aid, and if a case should arise in the other regions, the Supreme Court might presumably work under less tension than Congress in a heated debate.

Powerful opposition was immediate from both sides, neither of which trusted the Court. Calhoun, however, was willing to accept the compromise as "a permanent and not a temporary settlement of the whole question." Finally, on July 26, the Senate remained in session for twenty-one consecutive hours. Throughout the day and night the interminable speeches droned on, punctuated with occasional bursts of temper from the tired and irritable lawmakers. At two A.M., finding himself addressing one colleague, Senator Niles moved an adjournment, but bleary-eyed senators quickly appeared from all directions to vote for continuance, and Niles "very cooly" continued. At seven minutes before eight A.M., the Senate finally voted 33-22 for the bill, with overwhelming support coming from the slave-holding states.

It was an intelligent effort with long-range possibilities for peace, but the Senate had no time for rejoicing. The weary members were still recovering from loss of sleep when the House tabled the bill and the long grind had to be resumed.

The House returned another bill again including the anti-slave Ordinance of 1787, and late in the night of August 10 the Senate after a long, angry session passed it, amended this time to extend the Missouri Compromise line to the Pacific. Benton supported this plan, while Calhoun and Westcott, alone among the Southerners, voted with the Northern extremists against it. The House, however, remained in an uncompromising mood and threw out the amendment. Again the Senate received the bill with an anti-slave restriction.

Two days before the end of the session, Oregon appeared doomed again to be without government or protection. At this point Benton moved that the Senate recede from its amendment and accept the House bill. He had waited patiently, he said, for conciliation, voting for both compromise efforts, but the Senate had a solemn obligation to the people of Oregon, and, slavery or no slavery, it was time to act.

John C. Calhoun answered. Admission of Oregon without slavery would "convert all the southern population into slaves; and he would never consent to entail that disgrace on his pos-

terity. . . . The separation of the North and the South is completed. . . . This is not a question of territorial government,
but a question involving the continuance of the Union." [2]

Calhoun had reasoned the South into a preposterous position, but Benton found only one Southern ally. The picturesque new Senator from Texas, Sam Houston, stopped his usual
pastime of whittling on a block of wood, and rose "to make his
position known, not only on this continent, but that it should
be blazoned forth to the world." Slave restriction north of 42°
could never harm the South, and he would vote for Oregon
with or without slavery. The cry of disunion and nullification
in 1832 had once "reached him in the wilderness, an exile from
kindred and friends and sections; but it rung in his ears and
wounded his heart." Now in this crisis, he was ready to defend
the South, but "the Union was his guiding star. . . ." What
did the South wish anyhow? "Would it raise troops to cut off
emigrants to Oregon, because they were going there without
negroes?" [3]

After further arguments and a recess, the tired members
reconvened for an evening showdown before galleries overflowing with tense and excited onlookers. Shortly after midnight,
when fatigue was sapping any remaining reasonableness, Butler
of South Carolina tried a new move. Benton's remarks in secret
session against General Kearney had, of course, been repeated
in public attacks. Butler had prepared written charges against
Benton for betraying Senate secrecy, and now, with the furious
Oregon debate at a climax, suddenly moved that the galleries
be cleared and the Senate go into executive session to consider
his accusations. Benton's self-control had come a long way, but
the old temper was always near the surface, and fifteen hours of
listening to rancorous argument was not easy on patience. Out
of his seat he bounded with a roar. If Butler meant to impute
anything dishonorable to him, "he would cram the lie down
his throat!" This feat was prevented only by the rapid interfer-
ence of colleagues, and the scene, recorded as "more than
usually exciting at one time," subsided when the Chair ruled
Butler's motion out of order. [4]

Henry S. Foote, a waspish, aggressive little man from Mississippi, urged Benton to withdraw his motion to accept the

House bill, but Old Bullion "playfully observed that he always had an objection to retreating. One of his earliest recollections was the old Roman maxim, *non retrahit pedem;* and, if the object of the gentleman's speech was to induce him to draw back his foot, he might have saved himself the trouble." Men in deadly earnest do not like "playful" opponents. Henry S. Foote would hate Benton for the rest of his life. The little Mississippian declared himself ready to speak for two days and nights without inconvenience, but his lungs surrendered long before nine o'clock on Sunday morning. By a margin of 29-25 the Senate accepted the will of Oregon and provided a government without slavery.

As the only Southerners supporting the measure, Benton and Houston found themselves outside the pale of Southern respectability, and Benton as author of the final motion was now the heretic of heretics. Butler sent a note demanding an explanation of the words, "cram the lie down his throat." Benton ignored the inquiry, whereupon little Henry Foote knocked at the Benton home on Sunday afternoon to deliver Butler's formal challenge to a duel. The family was much disturbed, but Old Bullion felt no need to prove his courage. He kept the challenge, but declined to answer, assuring the worried Blair that "nothing would come of it." [5]

Thus Oregon received a government, and the South had not been injured in any practical sense, but the power of Congress over territorial slavery, as established by Southern votes in the Northwest Ordinance and the Missouri Compromise, had been reaffirmed. Perhaps most important was the bitterness of the struggle itself. Committed still further to the idea that failure to achieve abstract rights, however meaningless, in the territories meant danger to slavery at home, the defeated South must fight still harder for the remaining territories. Operating from an inaccurate premise which in turn was their chief weapon in debate and major political issue at home, Southern extremists were to become more and more the prisoners of their own self-generating blindness. Northern tolerance for slavery where it existed was to be had for the asking, but increased demands for concessions implying outright approval could lead only to disaster. Thomas Hart Benton saw this with crystal clarity, but his fellow slaveholders had an implacable distrust for one of their own unwilling to defend the system, and Benton was ill equipped to break down such feelings. He was equally ready to distrust opponents, and, once convinced that his beloved Union was threatened by either the ignorance or the wickedness of his enemies, did not know the meaning of conciliation or persuasion. There would henceforth be no place for him in high Southern councils, however badly his brand of reasoning might be needed.

*   *   *   *   *   *   *   *

Interlocked with the Oregon struggle in 1848 was the Presidential election. As usual, various newspapers tried to launch a Benton movement, and as always the Senator throttled it in the cradle. Again in speeches and public letters he called for the choice of a Northern candidate. The Nullifiers, he wrote, were trying to make the planting of slavery by law in areas unwilling to have it the test for Presidential candidates, and such a move would destroy the national party organizations. The Democrats must meet the challenge and serve the Union by electing a candidate from that section which had provided only one Democratic President in almost sixty years.

At first the Blair, Benton, Van Buren faction was united behind Silas Wright of New York, but in August, 1847, the able candidate died. New York Democrats were already badly split by enmity between Van Buren and William F. Marcy. The Van Buren group had absorbed the old Loco Focos and other radical reform organizations, and had almost smothered the Marcy faction by 1844. In the Polk Cabinet, however, Marcy had used the Federal patronage to rejuvenate his New York friends, and Wright's defeat for the governorship in 1846 was widely blamed on the administration. Blaming Wright's death on the disappointment of defeat was only a short step further, and any cause graced by martyrdom requires careful handling. When the Democratic President-makers gathered at Baltimore in May, 1848, they were confronted with two delegations from New York. In good political fashion, the convention voted to seat both factions with each delegate to have only half a vote, but this and a rule pledging all delegates to support any candidate chosen was more than the Van Buren "Barnburners" could take. They angrily withdrew and prepared to hold their own third party convention at Utica, New York.

The Democrats then proceeded to nominate the fat and colorless Lewis Cass of Michigan, a long-time political figure who had found a middle ground on the slave issue with a letter advocating that the settlers in any new territory have the right to settle the question of slavery for themselves.

Among the Barnburners were almost all of Benton's closest friends, including Van Buren, Dix, and Butler, and he had long disliked Cass. Followers of Cass had allegedly betrayed Van Buren in 1844, and Benton had fully shared his friends' anger. In 1848, however, he had nothing for his friends but practical advice: any third party move would be a mistake. To Benton a united Democratic Party was the nation's best hope for sectional peace, and Cass, however distasteful personally, was the best hope for unity in 1848.

The Whigs were delighted with the Democratic split. The Whig press reported that Benton, seeing the aged Thomas Ritchie, lantern in hand, ascending the Benton steps to ask support for Cass, had remarked, "There he is . . . like the Athenian, with a lantern in his hand, seeking for an honest man." [6]

In answer Benton took a course never before followed even for Jackson and Van Buren. Invited to accompany Cass and several other leaders, including Houston and Foote, on a campaign tour of Baltimore, Philadelphia, Trenton, and New York, he accepted and took the stump for his former enemy. It was a decision over and beyond the call of party orthodoxy or duty; otherwise, a public letter could have served the purpose. Mrs. Benton's illness, the discomfort of travel in hot weather, the pressure of his own business—any number of valid excuses were available had he not wished to make the tour. New York friends were soon dismayed to learn that their old champion was about to invade their stronghold in the army of the enemy. [7]

The tour was a Bentonian triumph. Old Bullion consistently overshadowed the candidate himself in the press reports, as editors worked overtime on the theme of Benton's allegiance to Cass. On the boat from Baltimore to Philadelphia, Benton delighted an impromptu audience by fighting over "in a most admirable vein of wit and humor, some of the trying battles in which he had participated in the Senate Chamber, and convulsed his hearers at times with laughter at the dry sallies which he made at the Whigs." Arriving at Philadelphia, each man "spoke in the happiest and most eloquent strains," and beautiful bouquets were presented to Cass and Benton. When the visiting statesmen reached their lodgings, Benton spoke again to a wildly cheering crowd, reviewing the "immutable principles" of the party. Next day Benton and Cass stood in Independence Square at the "foot of one of the most venerable-looking trees in the sacred grove in which was first heard the infant voice of liberty" and for two hours shook hands with all comers. "Senator Cass stood with his back against a tree, with the perspiration standing in large drops upon his face, which was red with exertion. By his side stood the venerable Senator Benton, smiling affably and benignantly upon every individual, and bowing to each person whose hand he shook."

Through New Jersey went the parade, finally arriving at New York, the focal point for Benton's influence, and here Old Bullion received the lion's share of the attention. Van Buren followers were angry that he had come, but most Democrats were prepared to do him honor. When the party arrived at the Battery, nine cheers for Cass were followed by nine more for Benton, and after Cass spoke briefly, the immense crowd demanded the same from Benton. Riding through flag-bedecked streets to the Astor House, Benton sat beside Cass in a barouche. At their quarters another crowd began calling for Cass, but the candidate was too overcome with fatigue to comply. Benton, however, emerged and was "received with the most deafening plaudits." Thanking his audience "in a brief but exceedingly happy manner," Benton announced "that the ardor of their enthusiasm had exerted such an electrifying influence, that it had revived Gen. Cass sufficiently to enable him to appear before them and respond for himself." This was only a slight exaggeration; the weary Cass could drag himself to the window for an ovation, but did not speak.

On the following evening the group addressed an immense crowd at Tammany Hall. Some four thousand vociferous Dem-

ocrats jammed into the building, while Houston was assigned
to enlighten the throng arriving too late to get inside. Received
"with the most deafening cheers, which lasted several minutes,"
Benton electrified his audience with an eloquent appeal for
party unity. For a quarter of a century, he said, he had worked
with New York senators, and "one who was worthy of Rome in
her best days" had been his friend—"the lamented Silas Wright.
(*Sensation*.)" He had long been convinced that "harmony, union, and concession among the democrats" were "the only sure
guaranty of success." Cass would be a President "honorable to
the country" and "satisfactory to the whole democratic party."

Cass shortly afterward departed for Michigan, but Benton
remained in New York for the ratification meeting on June 12,
where before several thousand outdoor listeners he again recommended "coolness" and "a sober second thought" to his
Democratic friends. The speeches were interrupted by the
collapse of the platform, but the affair was apparently a success.
One resolution read: "[Cass] is, in the language of the illustrious Benton, 'a distinguished, worthy, and elevated man; and
should he be elected, his administration will be such as will
prove honorable to our country, and satisfactory to the whole
democracy.' " [8]

It was all a valiant effort, but a failure. New York Demo-
crats might love Benton, but they would not take his candidate.
Van Buren shortly afterward accepted nomination by a new
Free-Soil Party on a platform of "Free Soil and Free Men," and
when the votes were counted in November, the Barnburners
still led the New York Democracy. Cass ran a poor third in the
state, more than six thousand votes behind Van Buren. The
Whigs, however, won the Presidency, as the calamity feared by
James K. Polk for three years came to pass. General Zachary
Taylor, slaveholder and Mexican War hero, took the victory by
virtue of his New York margin. The Democratic Party had
gone down before its own internal divisions and the issue of
keeping slavery out of the new territories. Thanks in large
part to the meaningless Southern agitation over Oregon, the
Free-Soilers moved far ahead of the Liberty Party's performance
in 1844. Van Buren ran ahead of Cass in Vermont and Mas-

sachusetts, and did well in Maine, Ohio, and Wisconsin. His total vote was 291,203, some ten per cent of all votes cast.

Missouri enemies denounced Benton for not making a special visit to Kinderhook to persuade Van Buren against bolting, but this was unjustified. He had carefully written his views to the New Yorker, and if this and his tour for Cass had made no impression, a visit could have only strained their friendship without practical result. Van Buren, after all, could be stubborn, as Benton well remembered from his own unheeded warnings of the coming depression in 1837. It was characteristic of Benton that in Missouri, where appearances for Cass would have strengthened his own position and were not really needed by the candidate, supporters waited in vain for a visit. He had given his all in the Northeast, the only place where it really mattered, and now spent the rest of the summer and fall taking Elizabeth to Virginia and Kentucky, stopping to sell land in each place. Not until after the election did Blair discover that "instead of being any longer a follower of the late standard bearer of Democracy, he was looked upon in the light of a rival, who had taken his throw & was not entitled to another." Still unable to believe the sincerity of their friend's persistent protests, Blair and Van Buren again began thinking in terms of a Benton ticket for 1852.[9]

In 1848 it was still possible to be a national leader without approving either the Wilmot Proviso or the doctrines of Calhoun. Whether Benton could remain neutral without losing the necessary support of slaveholding Missouri remained to be seen, and powerful enemies were now busily marshaling their forces to drive him from the Senate.

CHAPTER XVIII

PROPHET REJECTED

Among Missouri Democrats the anti-Benton revolt so well planted in 1844 needed only a ray of hope to burst forth again into full bloom. Jacksonian Democracy had taught the principle that public offices should be shared in rotation by the common herd, but Old Bullion's thirty-year domination had produced a political stratification which many ambitious politicians were anxious to break. Three of his bitterest enemies, William H. Napton, James H. Birch, and William C. Price, were judges hoping for advancement, and sixteen of the state's twenty judges were eventually against him.

Even with Texas Benton's enemies had failed to unseat him in 1844, and the Senator had redeemed himself finally on the annexation issue. His opposition to Fifty-four Forty for Oregon had been headlined, but this had been offset considerably by his well-publicized influence with Polk and continued control of the Federal patronage in Missouri. The state remained overwhelmingly Democratic, and Benton still controlled the party machinery and enjoyed much public affection, although the old Bentonian land policies had lost much of their meaning for new generations of voters. Barring another extraordinary issue, his opponents were doomed to continue gnashing their teeth in frustration.

The Senator's concern for the Union and impatience with

impractical and impossible Southern demands provided just such an issue. While many Missourians sincerely believed him an enemy to the South, his position was an excuse and a glorious opportunity as well as a reason for local political rivals. Emotional issues easily oversimplified are always dangerous to the politician bound by conscience to take a stand requiring complex explanations. Appealing to the people of a slaveholding state, Benton's enemies promptly began the process of reducing his practical and farsighted reasoning to a simple and easily attacked position of opposition to slavery.

In December, 1848, a coalition of anti-Bentonites and radical pro-slavery elements in the Missouri General Assembly passed a set of resolutions proposed by Claiborne F. Jackson, an aspiring anti-Benton politician. These placed Missouri on record in support of the extreme Southern position on territorial slavery and instructed the state's national senators and representatives to act accordingly. The action was aimed straight at Benton. He must enlist in Calhoun's army or openly defy the legislature of his own state.[1]

A qualified obedience or perhaps even silence would have kept his re-election safe, but neither obedience nor silence were among Benton's habits. By now sixty-seven years old, he had lost but little of the old fire and dynamite which had carried him through half a century of contentious life. Blair was saddened by the thinness and whiteness of his temples, but found him "strong and vigorous within with all the look of resolution in his face that ever characterized it." [2] A challenge had been issued, and the Old Buffalo would meet it in the only way he knew. The Jackson resolutions were aimed at the Union and himself, and he would do battle for both, usually unaware of just which he was defending at any given moment.

The course had already been set. In August, 1848, John C. Frémont was ready to search for a shorter route to California and this time remain there to seek his fortune. Before the expedition departed Benton offered the Pathfinder's services to Secretary of State Buchanan as an agent "to pacify the Californians and hold them on to the US despite the loss of all their bills." When this overture went unanswered, Benton as in the case of Oregon wrote his own letter of advice to the people of

California and New Mexico. Frémont left too late in the season and lost half his party to cold and starvation in the mountains, but finally arrived with the letter.

The Senator offered sound advice. Suggesting that the people meet in convention and form a simple government, he urged patience. When a state they could settle slavery for themselves, but for the present he "would recommend total abstinence from the agitation of the question." His promise to Oregon had been fulfilled, boasted Benton, and he could guarantee the same service for them, regardless of slave agitations.[3]

New Mexico soon responded, but disobeyed Benton's wishes on slavery. On December 13, 1848, Benton presented that region's petition for territorial government, including a request that Congress prevent the introduction of slavery. Calhoun attacked the petition immediately as a vile insult to the very people who had conquered the province. Benton answered that the signers had the right to have their petition printed regardless of opinions for or against it. An observer later remembered vividly that Old Bullion's "voice struck a higher key and rang out with increased power; his mighty arm swept through the air with majestic gesticulation, his eyes blazed, his massive form dilated and towered with indignation, and he looked as though he was ready to sink the Senator in the gladiator at the slightest physical provocation." The petition was printed, and opponents knew there would be no concessions from Thomas Hart Benton.[4]

When Calhoun led the Southern members of Congress into secret caucus in January, 1849, Benton and Houston were not invited. The Texan, however, attended without invitation and worked to keep the affair within moderate channels. Benton considered the movement sheer treason. His Missouri colleague, Atchison, however, played a leading role and signed the memorable Southern Address, a document bulging with exaggerated complaints of Northern aggressions and frightful predictions of eventual race war and Negro supremacy.

The next step was a foolish charge of treason cooked up by Henry S. Foote. The envoys carrying the peace treaty to Mexico had drawn up a protocol assuring the Mexicans that the Senate amendments to the original treaty made no significant changes. This protocol was never communicated to Congress until February, 1849, when Benton got a copy from the Mexican Minister and showed it to several colleagues. Whig leaders complained that it could have no legality without Senate ratification, but when Polk submitted copies, the matter was dropped. Foote, however, in a long, virulent diatribe, accused Benton of risking the loss of California and New Mexico by treacherously stirring up the matter. Benton maintained a dignified silence, although several senators of both parties came to his defense. The charge was too flimsy for use even by Benton's worst enemies, and was not heard from again until Foote wrote his memoirs twenty-five years later.[5]

Also in February, Benton found a sharp new arrow for his big bow. America was on the verge of a great railroad-building spree, and Old Bullion was never one to lag behind the times. On February 7 he introduced a bill for a national railroad from St. Louis to San Francisco. Opponents immediately complained that it was merely a scheme for re-election. Most people expected only one transcontinental road to be built, and Missouri voters naturally wanted St. Louis to be the eastern terminus. The project was well timed politically, but consistent with Benton's thinking and habits for a lifetime. The original father of the Santa Fe Trail was a natural advocate for linking the two great oceans with iron rails.

Unlike most would-be promoters working for Government land grants and subsidies to private interests, Benton wanted the Government to own the road as well as build it. He would finance it with seventy-five per cent of the California land sales and fifty per cent of the sales of all other public lands. The right of way should be a mile wide to accommodate additional tracks in the future—"a national, central road, a highway, not merely for ourselves, but for our posterity, for all time to come."

The Benton railroad plan was soon a national question. On April 23, 1849, the Senator addressed a Board of Trade meeting in Pittsburgh, met to discuss an extension of the Ohio and Pennsylvania Railroad. To a wildly cheering audience he declaimed that "one end of this road points to St. Louis; and St. Louis is on the high road in a direct line to the Pacific Ocean and to Canton." Children already born, he prophesied, would live to see a completely encircled world.[6] It was a splendid issue, with all the fresh appeal of his graduation program of twenty-five years earlier, and might have carried the Senator into a new cycle of invincible popularity had he been willing to act with benevolent neutrality toward Calhoun and pro-slave radicals in Missouri.

On May 9, 1849, Old Bullion roared his answer to the Jackson resolutions:

> The General Assembly . . . adopted certain resolutions . . . and gave me instructions to obey them. From this command I appeal to the people of Missouri . . . and if they confirm the instructions, I shall give them an opportunity to find a Senator to carry their will into effect, as I cannot do anything to dissolve this Union, or to array one-half of it against the other.
>
> I do not admit a dissolution of the Union to be a remedy, to be prescribed by statesmen, for the diseases of the body politic, any more than I admit death, or suicide, to be a remedy to be prescribed by physicians for the diseases of the natural body. Cure, and not kill, is the only remedy which my mind can contemplate in either case. . . . [7]

While echoes of this appeal were still reverberating, Benton at Jefferson City, Missouri, delivered a savage, biting address which answered all questions and split the Democratic Party of Missouri down the middle. Comparing the Jackson resolutions one by one with those of Calhoun, Benton charged a subversion which he could never cease opposing without dereliction of public duty. He repudiated the Free-Soilers, pointing to his eastern tour for Cass, but described the Wilmot Proviso as constitutional and, if enacted, binding upon all law-abiding citizens. The Proviso's real crime, he said, was inexpediency, since California and New Mexico were already free from slavery both by law and fact. The Proviso advocates had only strengthened Calhoun, and its defeat would remove his last card of disunion. Benton then thundered out a full review of Calhoun's enigmatic career, some of it exaggerated, but with the weight of the indictment resting soundly upon the practical meaninglessness and terrible danger of the issues being utilized by the great Nullifier to frighten the South and wreck the Union. Personally, said Benton, he was against slavery and its introduction where it did not exist, and he therefore could not vote for sending it to New Mexico or California, "a declaration which costs . . . but little, the whole dispute now being about the abstract right of carrying slaves there, without the exercise of the right. No one asks for a law for the exercise of the right and cannot ask it in the face of the *dogma* which denies the power to grant it. States do as they please." Thus the only practical difference between himself and Calhoun was "the difference between refusing and not asking. And for this the Union is to be subverted!"

The Senator left no question or challenge unanswered. His "profession and conduct—no unusual thing for frail humanity—" did not agree. He "was born to the inheritance of slaves" and had always had them. He had "bought some, but only on their own entreaty, and to save them from execution sales." He had "sold some but only for misconduct." He had lost two to abolitionists, "and never enquired after them and liberated a third who would not go with them." And he had slaves in Washington, and was "not the least afraid that Congress will pass any law to affect this property either here or there." Knowing slavery to be perfectly safe everywhere it existed, he would not alarm slaveholders with a non-existent threat. The American Union was too important to the world:

> We are a republic—the head of that form of government—and owe a great example to a struggling and agonized world. Liberty is now struggling in ancient empires, and her votaries are looking to us for the exemplification of the blessings of which she is in search, and for an argument in favor of her efforts; what do they see? wrangling and strife, and bitter denunciations, and threats of disunion. They see a quarrel about slavery! to them a strange and incomprehensible cause of quarrel. . . . They see us almost in a state of disorganization—legislation paralyzed—distant territories left without government—insult violence outrage on the floors of Congress. . . . Once called the model republic by our friends, we are now so called in derision by our foes; and the slavery . . . dissensions quoted as the proofs of the impracticable form of government which we have adopted. I cannot engage in such discussions, nor do anything to depress the cause of struggling freedom throughout Europe.—Nor can I disparage the work,

or abuse the gift of our ancestors. . . . They left us the admiration, and the envy of the friends of freedom throughout the world. And are we, their posterity, in the second generation, to spoil this rich inheritance—mar this noble work—discredit this great example—and throw the weight of the republic against the friends of freedom throughout the world? I cannot do it. Taught to admire the founders of our government in my early youth, I reverence them now; taught to value their work then, I worship it now. A Senator for thirty years, I cannot degrade the Senate by engaging in slavery and disunion discussions. Silence such debate is my prayer; and if that cannot be done, I silence myself.[8]

It was only natural that Benton should see the slavery and disunion quarrels as a threat to democracy everywhere. Abraham Lincoln would say the same thing in simpler language in a different context at Gettysburg fourteen years later.

This widely circulated speech brought national repercussions which in turn reacted upon the local scene. Extremists of both sides emphasized his constitutional defense of the Wilmot Proviso, although his Free-Soil friends felt harshly treated. The forces of Calhoun soon answered. In a bitter public letter Henry S. Foote charged Benton with betraying the South to further his unholy Presidential ambitions. Once expecting proslave elements to make him President, Benton, wrote Foote, was now looking toward the more populous North for the great honor. Foote missed no possibilities, ridiculing Benton's program for a mile-wide railroad to the Pacific and reminding all friends of Scott and Taylor that Benton had tried to supplant them in the late war.

The big gun, however, was fired by Calhoun himself in a ten-column public letter of defense and reaffirmation, denouncing Benton as an enemy to all Southern interests, involved "at every step in false statements, contradictions, inconsistency, and absurdities." What an insult and injustice, wrote Calhoun, that those who had spent their blood and treasure to conquer new territory should be excluded "while it is left open for the use and enjoyment of all that rabble of foreigners which he enumerates with such zest as the efficient means of our exclusion." Warning the South against its traitors, Calhoun listed the spots by which such leopards could be identified: "a strong profession of attachment to the Union, and condemnation of what is called the violence and ultraism of the South, accompanied by a volley of abuse of me, and the absence of all censure or condemnation of your assailants." After denying all disunion sentiment, Calhoun closed with a striking parallel: Washington had remained loyal to the British Union until the folly of Parliament had produced the necessity for revolution, and the South could but follow his example. Friends wrote Calhoun that the effect of this letter upon Southern public opinion was tremendous.[9]

In Missouri, meanwhile, Benton's Jefferson City keynote speech had launched one of the fiercest, rowdiest political battles ever seen in America. Throughout the summer and much of autumn Benton rode the length and breadth of Missouri, invading the domains of his most bitter enemies in the most radically pro-slave sections of the state. He had reportedly announced, "I shall crush my enemies as an elephant crushes piss-ants under his tread," and this was an accurate description of his intentions. His arrivals were heralded by political meetings and resolutions for weeks in advance, and speech days found the dusty trails teeming with wagonloads of citizens from a forty-mile radius. Many came armed, to attack or defend according to taste, and the Blairs constantly feared Benton would be assassinated. The artillery was apparently fairly evenly distributed, however, because violence never went beyond numerous awesome threats. The old warrior's utter fearlessness apparently caught the imagination of potential attackers as well as friends. His speeches followed the Jefferson City pattern, but shifted much emphasis to local enemies and were often filled with language somewhat less than polite, particularly when objects of his wrath were present.

Pro- and anti-Benton newspapers gave opposite versions of the campaign, while the Whig press, almost dizzy from the unfamiliar scent of possible victory for themselves, gleefully printed both versions to show what scoundrels all Democrats were in general. "The Whigs in all their opposition," chortled the *Missouri Republican,* ". . . never charged *half so much* against them as these two factions now charge and *prove* on each other." The paper closest to the actual thinking of Ben-

251251251251

ton was probably the *Jefferson Enquirer,* which from June, 1849, down into the Civil War, proudly carried at its masthead the words from Benton: "Taught to admire the founders of our government in my early youth, I reverence them now; taught to value their work then, I worship it now." Of sixteen Democratic newspapers, apparently ten were anti-Benton.[10]

Though Old Bullion was a one-man host, his adversaries had a decided edge in quantity, as Atchison, Claiborne Jackson, Birch, Green, Napton, Dr. John J. Lowrey, and others took turns on the stump or in the press against him. Once a close friend, Lowrey professed to "mourn over him as . . . a great mind in perfect error," and though it caused his "heart to bleed," the doctor became a bitter enemy. The *Palmyra Whig* observed with clear discernment:

> With these men Col. Benton can take no course to satisfy them. . . . No one of them possesses the ability and learning to meet him in debate; and not one will attempt it; and yet in their own way they will wage an exterminating war against him. His policy is to draw them out in debate. But he will fail that; and when he removes one objection, they will disseminate others, and thus effect their purpose.[11]

Senator Atchison warned his fellow citizens of Platte County that Benton would reduce them "to the social and political level of . . . slaves," and pledged himself to drive the base traitor from the Senate. Another star anti-Benton orator was Judge Birch, who blasted Benton for abolitionism, betrayal, Presidential intrigue, and colossal arrogance in disobeying the legislature. From the Birch-Benton exchanges grew a libel suit which was still in the courts when Benton died nine years later. Among other mild compliments, Benton, with apparent accuracy, remarked in a conversation that Birch was a wife-beater and implied that the Judge's relations with a certain mulatto girl were somewhat more than platonic. Birch sued against Benton's defense that he had spoken nothing but the well-known truth. Others revived the ancient charges against Benton of debt evasion and non-residence, and when Governor King supported Benton, the anti press charged that King feared exposure by Benton of some long-past scandal in Tennessee.

Omitting the obvious implication, a lady reported to a friend that shortly after Benton's speech at Alexandria, "thirty 2 of the coloured population . . . hitched their master's Horses to the waggons and set off for Canada, fortunately for the owners they were taken before they crossed over into Illinois." Even religion entered the picture, when enemies charged that all the Whigs, abolitionists, and Northern Methodists were for Benton.[12]

Thus the battle raged, with Benton, in Blair's words, "like a great Bear surrounded by a yelping pack of whelps. He slaps one down on this side—another on that—and grips a third with his teeth—then tosses him with his snout. . . ." At New Franklin Benton "laid the rod on the backs of the transgressors with an unsparing hand," and kept the crowd alternating between laughter and indignation for two hours. At the finish, Claiborne Jackson rose to defend himself, but "Col. Benton took his hat and marched off without deigning to cast a look even of scorn upon the pigmy defender of the disunion resolutions—so called by Col. Benton."

At Lexington Benton brought roars of laughter by describing the genealogy of the Jackson resolutions as "CALHOUN, *the father;* NAPTON, *the Granny;* CLAIB JACKSON, the nurse, and clout washer." On another occasion he effectively silenced Jackson and two front-row companions by pointing them out with the description, "as demure as three prostitutes at a christening."

Citizens of Atchison's home town of Platte City, however, apparently gave Old Bullion a rough afternoon. The opposition press announced that after speaking there he was heard to say, "*GOD DAMN* Platte City,—*GOD DAMN* it, I wouldn't make another speech there to save it from the fate of Sodom and Gomorrah. . . ." The reporter added: "Such were his denunciations of a whole community, whose only offense was that they did not agree with him in his opinions. We want no such tyranny as this. . . ."

Before arriving at Fayette, Benton received threats that he would answer questions or walk over dead bodies in leaving the building. Atchison, no stranger to colorful language himself, had preceded Benton there with a rousing plea for a reception of tar and feathers. At the appointed hour Old Bullion marched into the hall before an overflow crowd of some twelve hundred people. His opening words were greeted by a storm of groans and hisses, but the old dreadnaught continued to thunder away above the crowd and within fifteen minutes had the situation under control. In this speech, as in others, Benton tore into the notion that all Northerners were abolitionists, piling up both evidence and logic to show that most Northerners had no practical designs upon the South's peculiar institution at all. When he had finished, three-fourths of the audience enthusiastically followed him from the building, while the remainder sat in sullen silence.[13]

Near the end of Benton's march through Missouri, the railroad seed he had so carefully cultivated began to sprout. In the early summer a group of prominent St. Louis citizens had issued invitations for every state and territory to send delegates to a national railroad convention in St. Louis during October. Benton contributed only an address to the convention, but its invitation might have been copied from one of his "mad" speeches of a quarter century earlier. The road was to be a "Western route to Asia," which would have "the effect abroad, of carrying and diffusing the lights of American civilization to regions remote and hitherto involved in the darkness of pagan idolatry and imperial despotism; the effect at home, of producing a more perfect fusion of the different elements composing our own National Union." Down the railroad would come a trade

> embracing the furs of the north, the drugs and spices of the south, the teas, silks and crapes of China, the Cashmeres of Thibet, the diamonds of India and Borneo, the various products of the Japan Islands, Manchooria, Australasia, and Polynesia, the results of the whale fishery, the gold, silver, quicksilver, jewels, and precious stones of California, and the innumerable and unimaginable elements of commerce which could be brought into life from the depths of the sea, and from new and unexplored regions, by the enterprise and ingenuity of our countrymen. . . . Our surplus . . . products would find a new . . . market in return, while the Bible, the Printing Press, the Ballot Box, and the Steam Engine, would receive a welcome passage into vast and unregenerated fields, where their magic powers and blessed influences are greatly needed.[14]

It was a noble dream, this concept of a miraculous transcontinental railroad, but other cities were dreaming with equal energy of themselves being at the end of the rainbow of wealth to be gathered. Memphis promptly organized its own convention to follow that of St. Louis, and Chicago carefully selected a delegation for St. Louis dedicated to keeping any western railroad on a path north of St. Louis aimed at Chicago.

If all invited had come, the convention might have proved quite a forum. Declining were Calhoun, Foote, and Clay, as well as anti-slave radicals, Preston King, John A. Dix, and William H. Seward. Foote and Calhoun discussed making an attack on Benton, but abandoned the idea when assured by Atchison that Benton had "as good a chance to be made Pope, as to be elected Senator." [15]

Fearing a Benton success, anti-Benton Democrats welcomed the opposition to St. Louis offered by those favoring Memphis, New Orleans, and Chicago. Thus pulled in different directions, the Missouri delegation could agree upon no line of action at all, but the Chicago group suffered no such disability. Led by the Little Giant, Stephen A. Douglas, the Chicagoans invaded St. Louis already committed to a route from Chicago via Council Bluffs, Iowa. Except for Benton, the most consistent defenders of St. Louis were the Whigs. Colonel John Darby, a leading Whig, in tendering Benton a personal invitation to speak, warned that Douglas was trying to shift the road to Chicago and might succeed by becoming President of the United States. Benton accepted and reassured the Colonel that "Douglas never can be president, sir. His legs are too short, sir. His coat, like a cow's tail, hangs too near the ground, sir." [16]

The convention was a gala event. Fortunately the cholera epidemic which had shared news space with Benton by taking six thousand St. Louis lives during the summer had subsided by October, and over a thousand delegates from fourteen states could gather in relative safety. For days the press urged all good citizens to provide housing and entertainment, and the city throbbed with activity and excitement. The picturesque little village Benton had marched into so confidently thirty-four years earlier had exceeded even his great expectations, and was now a thriving metropolis of seventy-eight thousand people.

The broad, tree-lined streets were adorned with scores of large, handsome buildings, and new residents were pouring in and being born at a rate which would double the population again within ten years.

When proceedings finally began before a jam-packed hall, the great orator, Douglas, was temporarily sidetracked by the simple expedient of electing him to the chair, and Benton dominated the first day with perhaps the most famous speech of his life. It was a masterly blend of shrewd understanding, stirring nationalism, and magnificent dreams stretching back to the days when a rough, overgrown, ill-tempered, aggressive boy had sat enthralled by every book of history and geography he could find. Describing the ardor, love of enterprise, intelligence, and irrepressible activity of the American character, Benton said it must have employment; if no war or great object was available, it would take up speculation, "and the whole country go a planting bushes, and counting fortunes at the rate of thousands of dollars for each opening bud." That "restless spirit of enterprise" was "panting for employment." Build the railroad, and a hundred thousand men would finish it in seven years. Such a road would be "a band of iron, hooping and binding the States together, east and west" and "a cement of union north and south." People of North and South "would meet in the great line which would go east from the Mississippi, and feel again as their fathers did in the time of the revolution—feel that they were brothers, children of the same mother country, with a heart to love and a hand to support each other." The Senator's imagination began to soar:

> Three and a half centuries ago, the great Columbus . . . departed from Europe to arrive in the East by going to the West. It was a sublime conception. . . . A king and a queen started him on his great enterprise. It lies in the hands of a Republic to complete it. It is in our hands—We, the people of the United States, of this first half of the nineteenth century. . . .
>
> Let us rise to the grandeur of the occasion. Let us complete the grand design of Columbus by putting Europe and Asia into communication . . . through the heart of our country. Let us give to his ships, converted into cars, a continued course. . . . Let us now rise above everything sectional, local, personal. Let us beseech the

National Legislature to build the great road upon the great
national line which unites Europe and Asia—San Francisco at one
end, St. Louis in the middle, New York at the other; and which
shall be adorned with its crowning honor—the colossal statue of
the great Columbus—whose design it accomplishes, hewn from a
granite mass of a peak of the Rocky Mountains, overlooking the
road—the mountain itself a pedestal and the statue part of the
mountain—pointing with outstretched arm to the western horizon,
and saying to the flying passengers, "There is the East; there is
India."

If the mention of St. Louis following the exhortation to rise
above localism was inconsistent, Missourians did not mind.
Frequent cheers were long and loud throughout, and after
pointing the way to India Old Bullion took his seat amid a
storm of applause.[17]

The convention made few converts. After two more days of
bitter wrangling, the delegates finally compromised with a resolution declaring Congress dutybound to provide a Pacific railroad with branches to St. Louis, Memphis, and Chicago. The
eastern terminus was still a wide-open question and would
provide Benton and Douglas a fierce bone of contention for
several more years.

Thus ended Benton's effort to win re-election by again leading the people of Missouri along his own path. He returned to
Washington in November confident of victory, and perhaps at
this point could have been re-elected. For the next nine
months, however, his foes would have the Missouri field un-
hampered by the presence of the Great Bear himself, while
Benton would again take an unpopular road in the great debates of 1850. Whig support gained by his railroad efforts was
shattered by Benton's bitter debates with Clay in the late summer of 1850, as the Missouri Whig press consistently defended
their old champion and castigated Benton.

In the late winter of 1850 a group of anti-Benton Democrats
took a long second look at the prospects of a Whig victory and
offered peace. Old Bullion roared back that he "would sooner
sit in council with the six thousand dead . . . of cholera in St.
Louis, than go into convention with such a gang of scamps."
The disunionists were counting on Missouri, he wrote, and

must be kept segregated and defeated as a blow against disunion everywhere. Even a Whig victory would be a "victory in behalf of the Union," and this was "the over-ruling consideration." He could never be moved by "fear of seeing a Whig elected in my place." And to a prospective editor he wrote that the time was past for "holyday professions in favor of the Union." Action was required: repudiation of the General Assembly's "disunion resolutions"; repudiation of "secession, nullification and disunion, as remedies for political evils—submission to the laws of the land, until repealed by the people, or invalidated by the judiciary." He would associate with no one unable to serve these principles.[18]

The assembly elections in August, 1850, were a personal tragedy for Benton, but a triumph for his principles. Sixty-four Whigs, fifty-five Benton Democrats, and only thirty-seven antis were chosen. The thirty-year reign of Benton was coming to a close, but a cause had been won. The term "disunionist" was a universal term of approbrium, and Missouri had sent no delegation to the radical Southern convention at Nashville. If the cruel defeat of an old man who had served his people faithfully and well for thirty years was a heavy price, there is no evidence that he ever considered it excessive.

* * * * * * *

Benton's great march through Missouri in 1849 was a national event. For radical Southerners the honor of the South was involved, and Calhoun's reply was a sectional rallying point. To Southern editors Presidential ambition seemed the only possible explanation for a slaveholder gone so far astray, and an occasional note of sadness blended with the general indignation. The *Fredericksburg* (Virginia) *News* declared:

> The Platte, the Osage, the Jackson, and the St. Genevieve have all been trampoosed by the great champion of free soil, and the thunders of his declaration made to reverberate from the confluences of the Missouri and Mississippi to the base of the Rocky Mountains. There is a slight touch of the moral sublime in the majestic stride of the old Bison, as he wends his way over the stamping grounds it was his wont years since to claim as his own undisputed possessions. Like Selkirk, with equal truth he could

exclaim, "I am monarch of all I survey," until failing to achieve a nomination for the presidency by honest and honorable means, he threw away his birthright in the fruitless effort to attain the object of his unhallowed ambition. . . . Benton . . . will be consigned to that obscurity which is justly due to such moral degeneracy.[19]

Newspapers and citizens in Iowa, Illinois, Michigan, Massachusetts, and New York did begin booming Benton for the 1852 Presidency. Even Horace Greeley's New York *Tribune* remarked:

> Col. Benton has some faults besides his wrong politics, and conspicuous among them is his excellent opinion of his own opinions. But he is a laborious, pains-taking Senator, who seldom speaks without knowing whereof he is talking, and it would be rather hard to find another Loco-Foco in Missouri to fill his place, though there are many ready enough to *take* it. That you see is quite another thing.

Thus, despite all his efforts to assume a national position and remain a Southerner, Old Bullion returned to the Senate in December, 1849, again stamped with a Northern label.[20]

Americans had watched a local political struggle in which the issues were free soil versus slave extension, opposition versus obedience to the Constitution, centralization versus states' rights, freedom versus slavery, or Union versus disunion, depending upon the observer. These questions involved the fate of a nation, yet they were sharply conditioned in this instance by the anxiety of a small group of ambitious country judges to cast off the domination of a man whose long tenure violated the Western idea that offices should be shared. The separation of life and death issues from the vicissitudes of personality conflicts and partisan politics is not a new American problem.

The campaign destroyed Benton forever as a Southern statesman just when the section desperately needed his kind of realistic thinking. He must henceforth depend for national influence upon anti-slavery elements whom he could not follow and whose proffered honors he would steadfastly refuse. In Missouri, however, the great purpose had been served. Benton repeated his stump performances in 1852, 1854, and 1856, and though many Missourians finally joined the Confederacy, in 1860 the people as a whole had had no conditioning toward the ideas of secession. The statue of Union General Frank Blair stands beside that of Benton in the niche at Washington reserved for the two greatest men of each state.

Just as the Lincoln-Douglas debates would help promote the crisis of 1860, the Benton struggle contributed much to the great debates of 1850. His personal attacks upon Calhoun provided the Carolinian with an opportunity to propagandize the extreme Southern position in the form of a personal defense. And in the North Benton's eloquent phrases had probably added much to the growing idea of national destiny being thwarted by the "slave power." Trying to stand with a foot in each section, Benton had helped the radicals of both. He had attacked the Wilmot Proviso as inexpedient and dangerous, but had defended its constitutionality. He had insisted that slave property was in no danger, but had criticized the institution. He had pled for harmony and unity while carrying on a savage political campaign. And finally, he had helped open a railroad question, designed to unify, but destined to be a major source of the most bitter sectional issue of the 1850's.

Yet the loud voices of Southern emotionalism had to be outshouted and outfought by a voice of realism somewhere, if reason were to have any chance at all against the sensitivity, fear, pride, and frustration in the Southern mind and soul. Southern fearmongers, caught in the grip of their own arguments, were hammering away at minds frozen and paralyzed in the presence of any discussion involving slavery. To most Southerners, only twenty-five per cent of whom owned any slaves, the unpredictable possibilities which might follow the sudden release of several million exploited, ignorant, propertyless bondsmen were a nightmare in no way softened by inescapable pangs of conscience. The peculiar institution was more than an economic system. It was a loaded bomb which despite its deadening weight and corrosive psychological effects must be cherished and protected for fear of the fatal explosion which might result from any tampering with the mechanism. In its essence the Southern demand for impracticable and unusable rights in the territories was an effort to test the length of the fuse. Thomas Hart Benton did not fully grasp this, but he saw clearly the absence of any Northern fire hot enough to ignite the fuse unless the South should continue fanning the blaze and push the fuse within reach. The peace and perhaps the life of the Union would require keeping the fuse and the fire apart, and to this end the Senator was prepared to continue fighting regardless of personal catastrophe.

CHAPTER XIX

VALEDICTORY FOR GIANTS

> When an American citizen . . . contemplates the meeting of these distinguished men once more in the United States Senate, his mind is wrapt in admiration of the times when the esquires of that body were worthy the steel of a templar, and every [k]night was terrible "like an army with banners." There were giants in those days, and these were greatest where all were great. [1]

THUS A WASHINGTON EDITOR anticipated the return of Benton, Clay, and Webster in 1850, and his expectations would not be disappointed. Driven by a hurricane of oratorical wind the ship of state was drifting toward fatal shoals, and the most experienced seamen were needed at all key stations. Issues involving pride, fear, genuine humanitarian impulses, personal animosities, partisan politics, and competing interests lay ahead. Unless the statesmen could chart a safe course through them, the democratic process of settling quarrels with words instead of weapons would be destroyed.

The great portrait of Washington was truly gazing down upon the last gathering of the giants. The godlike Daniel, Presidential hopes gone, was ready for once to use his great talents in a cause inimical rather than favorable to his own personal interests. Emaciated and dying of tuberculosis, John C. Calhoun was prepared to pursue his path of God-given self-

righteousness and brilliantly spun logic to their bitter conclusion. Henry Clay, like Webster no longer dreaming of the
White House, was ready to add a final chapter to his well-
earned title of Great Pacificator. Some attributed his weakened
condition to the ravages of fast living, but Clay at seventy-three
had little reason to regret past habits. And as always, Thomas
Hart Benton was the tireless dynamo of the quartet, trained to
the vigor of an athlete by his tremendous exertions of the summer.

Each would remain in character and leave his particular
stamp on the proceedings, but others were also important.
The mighty little Giant from Illinois, Stephen A. Douglas,
almost as wide as high and every square inch a fighter, was
only thirty-six, but deferred neither to age nor to longer coat-
tails. At one point the rugged Texans, Houston and Thomas
Jefferson Rusk, may have held the balance between compromise and civil war. Much responsibility for the pattern followed by the debates rested upon the histrionic exertions of
Henry S. Foote.

Short, bald, and extremely homely, the forty-five-year-old
Foote combined a sharp mind and nervous temperament with
the bitter pugnacity so often found in able men of small physical size. His past included four duels, a tribute to courage
rather than marksmanship, since he had been shot down in
three of them. His flair for invective was unexcelled. In the
previous year he had promised Hale of New Hampshire the
honor of being hanged to the tallest tree should he visit Mississippi, and on the last evening of the session had lost a wrestling match in the Senate aisles to Cameron of Pennsylvania.
An 1850 observer, hearing of his duels, was mystified as to "how
he ever stood still long enough to be shot at" and "how any man
could look into such a funny face and fire." A daily ritual with
Foote was his motion to admit the ladies, and his frequently
inconsistent and pointless outbursts were clearly the performances of a frustrated showman anxious to steal every possible
scene. With all of this, however, Foote had a purpose and
pursued it effectively.

Foote came to Washington in December, 1849, prepared to
serve Calhoun. On the Cass tour in 1848 he had praised Ben-

ton as a *"statesman superior to Edmund Burke,"* but in the
Oregon debate had accepted Calhoun's judgment of Benton
as a Southern traitor. Carrying Butler's challenge to Benton,
he had perhaps also been impressed with Benton's refusal to
fight. At any rate, the little Mississippian henceforth rode the
Senate aisles as a self-appointed St. George, dedicated to the
extermination of the Missouri monster.[2]

The drama moved on schedule as Calhoun for the first time
in his life joined the Democratic caucus and with Foote and
Atchison succeeded by one vote in striking Benton's name off
all committees except that on Foreign Affairs. Atchison patron-
izingly interceded for Benton's inclusion on the latter committee, but Old Bullion resigned without comment and
prepared for the great clash with Calhoun. The pro-Calhoun
Richmond *Republican* expected a meeting comparable to "a
contest between the bright stars of an Italian sky, and the
yawning mouth of Vesuvius casting up its murky volumes of
flame and smoke as if it hoped to extinguish the immortal
lustre of the heavens."

Fate, however, intervened. Locked in a grim race with death,
Calhoun made only limited appearances, and Benton would
not attack a stricken enemy. Reportedly, he announced on one
occasion; "Benton will not speak today, for when God Al-
mighty lays hands on a man, Benton takes his off."

The issues were another matter. On January 3, Atchison
presented the Jackson resolutions, and Benton answered: The
people of Missouri would "abide the law . . . be it what it may,
subject to the decision of the ballot box and the judiciary."
The Founding Fathers had formed a sacred and perpetual
"Union—not a league—a Federal Legislature to act upon persons, not upon States, and they provided peaceful remedies for
all questions which could arise between the people and the
Government."[3]

Although anxious for national harmony, Benton had a strong
personal interest in two burning questions. He regarded both
New Mexico and California with paternal concern. Also, the
Frémonts had gone to California in 1848, and the Pathfinder
had now returned to Washington a millionaire gold-miner and
one of California's prospective senators. Benton had promised

California his support long before Frémont's election, however, and had numerous contacts with the sprawling, brawling new territory whose swarms of gold-crazed immigrants desperately needed law and order backed by state and Federal authority.

New Mexico had been a Benton-child since his bill for the Santa Fe Trail in 1824. Friends like Kit Carson and Magoffin had lived there, and his friend W. Z. Angney had come to St. Louis for advice before heading the constitutional convention in September, 1849. Texas in 1836 had claimed almost two-thirds of present-day New Mexico, but in 1846 General Kearney had promised New Mexico its original boundaries. Twice during the interval Texas had unsuccessfully invaded New Mexico. By the end of 1849 the Texas legislature had passed bills organizing New Mexico east of the Rio Grande into four Texas counties. The New Mexicans had responded by threatening any prospective Texas judges with robes of tar and feathers. Did the disputed area belong to slave-state Texas or the anti-slave territory of New Mexico? With a national slave quarrel on the issue in the making, New Mexico prepared to resist by force and appealed for Federal protection.[4]

With petitions and resolutions on slavery pouring in daily from both North and South and Congress deluged with a flood of bitter oratory rising daily, Congressional business reached a standstill. President Taylor, meanwhile, insisted upon immediate statehood for California. The President's attitude soon became known as the "do nothing" policy, and his close connection with the anti-slave New Yorker, William H. Seward, led to bitter Southern accusations. In Taylor the South had found another heretic.

Behind the scenes, meanwhile, Henry Clay and Stephen A. Douglas were seeking a practical adjustment. Clay made his famous stormy night visit to ask Webster's support on January 21, and eight days later introduced his program for compromise: admission of California without Congressional action on slavery; territorial government for New Mexico and Utah without mention of slavery; surrender by Texas of some of its claims in return for Federal assumption of the Texas debt; abolition of the slave trade in the District of Columbia but guarantees of the institution there as long as it existed in Mary-

land; a new and effective Federal fugitive slave law; and a resolution denying Congressional jurisdiction over the domestic
slave trade. With a magnificent plea for mutual tolerance, Clay
emphasized the superior power of the North and begged for
understanding of the problems of the South.

Thomas Hart Benton had been fighting Clay for twenty-five
years, but now rallied promptly to the Kentuckian's side. On
February 13 President Taylor transmitted the California constitution to the Senate with a request for immediate admission,
and Benton urged Clay to propose a select committee and serve
as its head. America looked to the Senator from Kentucky, said
Benton, and if Clay were unwilling to make the motion he
himself would do so.

Henry Foote immediately protested that he was planning for
a committee which would deal with all the questions together
and was anxious that they not be divided. Thus Foote announced the strategy of the realistic Southerners. By tying the
questions together in a single bill, the highest possible price
might be exacted for the admission of a free California. Favorable amendments might be passed during the debates, and if
these failed, the combination of radicals from both sections
could stall the program forever. In the words of Senator
Butler, ". . . there were three vessels at sea—one of them
[California] was strong enough to carry the other and weaker
vessels into port, if connected with her. California was a large
and safe ship, and the other smaller boats in danger were to be
attached to her, and she would carry them all safely into port." [5]

This plan would require the support of Clay, but Clay at
first agreed with Benton, Webster, and Douglas, that the compromise resolutions should be divided into separate bills. Foote,
however, had a trump card in the ancient rivalry between Clay
and Benton. On February 14 Douglas and Clay advocated
keeping California separate, and Foote answered with a savage
attack upon Clay. After posing as a friend of compromise,
snarled Foote, Clay had suddenly come under the influence of
Benton, who was betraying the South to help his son-in-law.
Clay answered sternly that he knew "no South, no North, no
East, no West." He owed allegiance only "to this Union and
to my State."

Others continued the assault. On February 20 Clemens of
Alabama taunted Clay unmercifully:

> I have read indeed that a time was coming when the lion and
> lamb should lie down together, but I did not expect to witness
> anything approaching that happy state in my day. All incre-
> dulity, however, is now at an end, and I am prepared to believe in
> any miracle, and treat with grave consideration any prophecy.
> When Thomas H. Benton and Henry Clay, "the great expunger"
> and "the great embodiment," are found holding sweet converse
> with each other, forgetting the animosities of thirty years, and
> lovingly pulling side by side in the same team, there can be noth-
> ing so wild and fanciful as to defy belief.

Foote and Clemens had found a soft spot. Clay hotly denied
that he was following Benton, but insisted that he would gladly
address his worst enemy as friend if it would conciliate the
Union. Again Clay called for admission of California.

Foote answered viciously. Benton, he said, was using Clay,
and Clay's speech had wounded the South even more than the
professed abolitionists, "not excepting . . . Garrison, and Phillips, and Douglass." [6]

Again the weary Clay defended himself, but his words lacked
defiance. Apparently convinced that co-operation with Benton
was destroying his influence with the South, Clay now joined
Foote as the best hope for success. Foote also carried the influence of the Democratic *Daily Union* and arranged an interview between Clay and Ritchie, the editor. When Clay agreed
to support a select committee to organize a single "omnibus"
bill covering all subjects, the *Union* changed overnight from
harsh criticism to lavish praise of Clay.

Benton, meanwhile, continued to receive pro-Union and
anti-Southern publicity. Representative Bissell of Illinois
apologized publicly. He had denounced Benton for the Missourian's charges of disunion against Calhoun and the South.
"May God forgive me for the wrong I did him. *I* was wrong—
he was right." And at a great mass meeting in New York, ten
thousand listeners heard a speaker urge expressions of "admiration and love for Lewis Cass, Samuel Houston, Henry Clay, and
Thomas Hart Benton, four congenial spirits who will live for

all future time in a glorious immortality for their achievements in defense of the Union." [7]

Events had eluded the control of John C. Calhoun, but the dying Carolinian played his role to the end. On March 4, before packed galleries, he tottered to his seat and in a hoarse voice announced that Senator Mason would read for him. The danger, Calhoun had written, lay in the fears of Southern people that they could no longer remain in the Union with honor and safety. The South had fallen behind in population and political power, because soon the Senate balance would be forty to twenty-four against the South. This, said Calhoun, was due entirely to Government legislation: to acts like the Northwest Ordinance, the Missouri Compromise, and the recent Oregon bill, which had excluded Southerners from the areas involved; to financial policies which had shifted wealth from South to North, thereby preventing immigration to the South; and to those acts which had changed the Government from a Federal republic to a consolidated democracy, in which the minority had no rights. With its protection gone, the South could only look forward to abolition, race war, and chaos from its connection with the Union. Clay's compromise was inadequate. The North, said Calhoun, could save the Union only by conceding equal rights in the territories, enforcing the fugitive slave laws, suppressing the abolitionists, and providing a constitutional amendment by which the South could protect itself. Otherwise, the South must follow the example of the immortal Washington when oppressed by the British—either depart in peace or defend itself against attack.[8]

Thus Calhoun reviewed the beliefs and philosophy against which Benton had staked his political life. If fear dominated the South, Calhoun was to a large degree responsible, and here lay the tragedy. The threats and injustices described by Calhoun did not exist in fact. Party lines had always crossed those of section, and the South in combination with the West had had its way on most issues, including the recent acquisition of Texas. Common agrarian interests, it was reasonable to believe, would always provide a basis for affinity between Northwest and South unless they should be split by other factors. Calhoun assumed also that all Southerners were slaveholders and that except for anti-slave restrictions enough slaveholders would have emigrated to the old Northwest, Iowa, and Oregon to shape the political complexion of those regions. Three-fourths of the Southern population had no connection with slavery, a vast number of Southerners had gone to the areas cited, and slavery could have survived in none of them. Both prospective senators, the Governor, and the Secretary of State of California were from slaveholding states, and Senator Gwin was a long-time Calhoun follower, but California had rejected slavery. As for financial policies, tariffs except for a brief time had been relatively low and in 1857 would be virtually eliminated. Slavery and not Northern economic policies had deterred foreign and Northern emigration to the South. The center of wealth had shifted northward, but this had resulted from science, invention, and the coming of industry, rather than Government discrimination. Calhoun's complaint that America had become a consolidated democracy in which the minority had no protection if overruled by a majority was a penetrating analysis, but his corollary assumpton that Northern strength would compel the South to choose between secession and abolition had no historical basis. As Benton had pointed out, Congress had a long and consistent record of non-interference with Southern slavery. A constitutional abolition would have required an amendment which a century later the former slaveholding states would still have the power to block. And the representatives of a nation dedicated to the sanctity of private property were hardly likely to enact an unconstitutional law destroying Southern property and then organize a military crusade for its execution. Abolition sentiment became dangerous to the South only after 1860, when it became united with Northern determination to save the Union. Benton's judgment of Calhoun's motives may have been excessively harsh, but his rejection of such unreal basic assumptions and his understanding of the disaster which must inevitably follow action based upon such reasoning were eminently sound. Calhoun had been captured by the "Devil" theory of history, which decreed that Southern misfortunes must be explained in terms of Northern enemies, and in spinning his web of sinister explanations had strayed off into the realm of fantasy. With his own personal ambitions reasonably satisfied and with no emotional attachment to the cause of slavery, Benton was remarkably free of such illusions.

Calhoun found himself rejected, as Foote and other Southerners opposed his opinions, and none supported his demand for an amendment. Asked why he did not reply, Benton answered that as a lawyer he "never interrupted the adversary counsel while he was proving up my case for me." A few weeks later Calhoun was dead, leaving on a few scraps of paper his last effort—a projected amendment whereby North and South would each elect a President, and no law would be valid without approval of both. Dying in loneliness, Calhoun received the most magnificent funeral Washington could provide. Clay, Webster, and the other veterans rose to pronounce brilliant eulogies, but Benton was as silent as Calhoun had been at the death of Adams. When Webster urged him to show magnanimity to the dead and speak, Benton reportedly answered, "He is not dead, sir—he is not dead. There may be no vitality in his body, but there is in his doctrines. . . . My people cannot distinguish between a man and his principles—between a traitor and treason. They cannot eulogize the one and denounce the other." [9]

Webster's great speech for compromise on March 7 ruined his popularity in Massachusetts, but the nation sighed with relief. Men wanted the peace, but the process of creating the compromise lay ahead. Clay had supplied the spirit of tolerance and understanding, Calhoun had remained the prophet of self-induced doom, and Webster had again evoked the spirit of nationalism. Benton, equally in character, was still the practical man of action, throwing himself headlong into the business of getting satisfactory measures passed and continuing to speak words of wisdom in the tones of impatience and controversy.

On April 8 Benton attacked the omnibus committee proposal and indirectly answered Calhoun. The slave states, he said, were agitated without cause. The refusal of Congress to touch slavery for sixty years should satisfy the slaveholder, but if not, "let him go to the market—that quick and truthful reporter of all danger to property; and he will quickly find, from the price that is offered him, that nobody is afraid of abolition but himself." Congress had followed the Constitution faithfully, and there was no reason to expect a change. "We should no more look ahead for causes of disunion, than we should look ahead for causes of separation from our wives, or for the murder of our mothers." Congress, he continued, had the undisputed power to tax slavery, but no member had ever even suggested it. Slave property was estimated at a billion dollars, and no other Government on earth left so much wealth untaxed. If Congress would not even tax slavery, why expect it "to commit flagrant violations of the Constitution, to harass or destroy slave property"? If the Senate could immediately vote on each question, "it would kill agitation so dead . . . that human power could not resuscitate it during this generation." The real preservation of the Union rested not in a committee room, the Senate chamber, nor the hands of politicians, but "in the hearts of the people . . . at home attending to their own affairs . . . who know that they themselves have enjoyed . . . more blessings under *THIS UNION* than ever fell to the lot of man upon earth; and who are determined that their children shall have the same right to the blessings of civil and religious liberty, and the same equal chance for the wealth and honors of the country which they themselves have had." [10]

Throughout the debates Foote did everything possible to provoke Benton into a physical attack or duel. On March 26 Benton appealed to the chair and pronounced the attacks false and cowardly. Foote answered with vicious insults and an open challenge. Certain "stains" had "most hideously blemished the character of the honorable Senator . . . since the days of his early manhood." A man of honor might well have no "obligation to recognize him as a fitting antagonist," but if Benton would "acknowledge himself responsible to the laws of honor," he could prove his prowess. If Benton wished "*to patch up* his reputation for courage, now greatly on the wane," he need only say so. Now he was "shielded by his age, his open disavowal of . . . the laws of honor, and his Senatorial privileges." Next day Benton continued to protest that insults in a situation where they could not be punished were the work of a coward. "Sir, let any person insult me where an appropriate chastisement can be employed . . . and he will find out whether I am not young enough . . . he will find out my age without consulting any calendar at all." Thomas Hart Benton did not intend to climax his career by shooting little Henry Foote, but even an elephant cannot endure hornet stings forever.

On April 17 Benton urged the Senate to pass his amendment forbidding the committee to discuss abolition. If Congress would thus proclaim its lack of power to touch slavery, it would "cut at the root of . . . agitation, and . . . cut up the whole address of the Southern members, by which the country was thrown into a flame." The votes would show there had been a cry of " 'wolf,' when there was no wolf," that the country was "alarmed without reason, and against reason," and that Congress did not intend "to aggress upon the South, nor to oppress them upon the subject of their institutions."

Southern senators wished no such assurances, and Henry Foote was ready for action. The Southern Address, he said, was written by "the late illustrious Senator from South Carolina," yet this "holy work" was being denounced in the very presence of his friends by "a gentleman who, on a late occasion—" Here Foote stopped, because Benton was advancing toward him.

Cocking a pistol, Foote retreated down the aisle. Senator Dodge momentarily halted Benton until Old Bullion saw the pistol. Breaking loose he again advanced upon Foote shouting, "I have no pistols! Let him fire! Stand out of the way! Let the assassin fire!" One witness remembered that when inviting the fire Benton stood like a statue and appeared the calmest man in the room. As pandemonium swept the chamber, Benton was led back to his seat, while Foote gave the pistol to Senator Dickinson. When order was restored, Benton insisted upon being searched and charged that a pistol had been brought there to assassinate him. Foote answered that he had carried the pistol because of his diminutive size and a fear that he might be assaulted. He had supposed that Benton also went armed.[11]

Benton and his friends spent several weeks trying to get Foote brought before the Senate for trial, but a committee of investigation refused to make suggestions beyond scolding the entire Senate for the use of personalities. It absolved Foote of any intent to assassinate Benton, but admitted that he had "without any sufficient provocation, indulged in personalities toward Mr. Benton of the most offensive character, such as were calculated to rouse the fiercest resentment in the human bosom. These were suffered by Mr. Benton for a long time with great forbearance." To Blair Benton insisted that he had not intended to assault Foote, "but to take a position near him—look him in the eye & only to appeal to the strong hand, in case Foote continued to abuse him & the Senate failed to take him under dealing." [12] Though Foote went unpunished, the adverse publicity, and perhaps the proof that Benton could be pushed too far, put a damper on his tongue, and formal exchanges between the two became relatively civil. Benton's only revenge, if such it could be called, was literary. When Foote later announced that he would write a little book in which Benton would play a major role, Benton sent word that he would write a very big book in which Foote would have no part whatever. Each kept his word.

On May 8 the compromise committee reported a single bill for admission of California without mention of slavery, territorial governments for New Mexico and Utah forbidden to legislate on slavery, and the adjustment of the Texas boundary. For an unspecified sum Texas should surrender part of its claim, but keep the southeastern quarter of present-day New Mexico. A fugitive slave act and the suppression of the slave trade in the District of Columbia were put into separate bills.

It was a reasonable settlement, but the so-called omnibus bill from the first had no chance for passage without amendments, and extremists on each side carried the balance of power against any amendments designed to appease their opponents. Clay, more than Benton, realized that to proud, suspicious, and sensitive Southern leaders the manner of reaching compromise might be as important as the decisions made, and his effect upon the hearts of men was the indispensable catalyst for the process of compromise. In concrete grasp of the actual issues, however, the angry Benton had the advantage. Old Bullion knew that satisfactory solutions for both California and Texas could not be passed in the same bill and was determined to end the dangerous delay by separating the questions.

After three weeks of furious and fruitless debate on the California and territorial provisions, Texas came to the front on June 7, and Clay's hopes for a quick settlement were quickly shattered. Southern radicals and the Texans would take nothing less than the entire disputed area, and a series of amendments all aimed at giving Texas a larger slice soon stirred up a bitter quarrel.

The Senate had reached Texas none too soon. General Taylor had developed an enormous distaste for Texas during his unhappy war days, and was determined to give New Mexico immediate statehood and let the Supreme Court settle the boundary. Under Presidential orders, Colonel Munroe, the military commandant of New Mexico, called a convention, and on May 25 a new state constitution placed the state's eastern boundary well within the bounds of ancient Texas. Texas reacted like a wounded bull. Governor Bell denounced Munroe's action as a vile outrage and called a special session of the legislature for August 12, as mass meetings all over the state demanded military action.

Benton watched the omnibus debate rage for a month, and then on June 10 attacked the bill in one of his few speeches on the subject of slavery. The suggested Texas boundary, he argued, took seventy thousand acres of New Mexico's best land. Parts of it were fertile and temperate and might support slavery, but the inhabitants did not want it, and he would not afflict them with it. His opposition to slavery extension, he said, went back to 1804 and the famous essay by the great Virginia jurist, St. George Tucker, and his principles had come from the school of Tucker, Jefferson, and Randolph:

The men of that day were not enthusiasts or fanatics: they were statesmen and philosophers. They knew that . . . emancipation . . . was not a . . . question of property merely—but a question . . . between races; and what was to be the consequence to each race. . . . The incurability of the evil is the greatest objection to the extension of slavery. It is wrong . . . to inflict an evil which can be cured: how much more to inflict one that is incurable, and against the will of the people who are to endure it forever! . . . It is a question of races, involving consequences which go to the destruction of one or the other: . . . It seems to be above human wisdom. But there is a wisdom above human! and to that we must look. In the mean time, not extend the evil.[13]

Thus, Senator Benton still stood with humility before the awesome magnitude of the problem of slavery. Here was no effort to rationalize a vicious evil into a positive good worth defending to the point of secession. Nor was it a call to put into practice the nearest available theory for eliminating the evil. The Senator knew the frightening possibilities of readjusting two races into a new situation of full equality after two centuries of a master-slave relationship, as well as the added handicaps which a solution by violence would bring.

The Senator would not spread an incurable disease, but he would defend the afflicted against any fatal cures. The rights of the slave states, he continued, were independent of the Federal Government and admitted in the Constitution—"a right to hold their slaves as *property,* a right to pursue and recover them as *property,* a right to it as a *political element . . .* by making five count three in the national representation." He would neither concede nor consent to purchase such rights in any compromise, and again called for separation and quick passage of the compromise issues.

The speech was a popular triumph in areas impressed by his opposition to slave extension, but made little impression on the section which needed his thinking and advice most. The deep South desperately needed the spirit of realism, but its spokesmen were asking no instruction from Thomas Hart Benton. Indeed, Benton County, Florida, would soon change its name because of his heresies.

On June 13 Henry Foote assured the Senate that if the United States shed one drop of Texas blood, every "heroic son of the South" would arm himself for the rescue. "Rivers of blood" would deluge the country, and "scenes of butchery [would] occur, more shocking than ever yet stained the pages of history." Tall, rugged Sam Houston followed with an equally stirring, if less gruesome, effort, but closed with a reminder that Texas was bound to "this Union, which we are ready to contribute the last drop of our blood to maintain— faithful to the Union, faithful to the Constitution, and faithful to Texas." The order of these loyalties was significant. The Texas senators had opposed the Southern Address, and while prepared to fill the air with awesome threats as long as hope remained for peaceful realization of their state's ambitions, neither would deliberately endanger the Union. Otherwise, the result might have been disastrous.[14]

Texas, meanwhile, had demanded a disavowal of the New Mexican constitution, angry editorials were filling the Southern press, volunteer companies for service in Texas were being formed, and the Governor of Mississippi formally offered an alliance. The *New York Journal of Commerce* reported that Texas was about to march with twenty-five hundred men, but Taylor was unmoved and threatened to assume personal command of the army against Texas.

Six days later Old Rough and Ready was dead, after a sequence of events beginning with a Fourth of July address by Henry Foote under a blazing sun and ending with the consumption of iced water, and cherries covered with ice-cold and possibly germ-laden milk. The power of the White House had passed into the hands of Millard Fillmore, a professional politician anxious to promote compromise. The slaveholding Taylor had stood rock-ribbed for the Northern position he considered right, but his death helped America avoid civil war in 1850.

Except for a brief personal exchange with Clay and the introduction of an amendment to draw the Texas boundary at 102°, Benton remained silent on the omnibus bill for thirty-five days more after his first speech. Useless oratory and recrimination, however, remained the chamber's sole accomplishment, as each day continued to prove Benton's arguments against combining the bills. A visitor recorded the scene on a blistering hot day when the salvation of the Union was at issue:

A Whig may be seen passing his [snuff] box to a Democrat, who passes it to a Southern ultraist, who passes it to a Northern "incendiary"—and all three forget their sectional differences in a delightful concert of sternutation. No business is too grave, no speaker too eloquent to be "sneezed at.". . .

Honorable Senators read newspapers, frank letters, receive their pay and write receipts at their desks; fans, snuff boxes, paragraphs, and caricatures go round; here are elevated a pair of slippered feet which may have done execution in an Alabama ball room; there is bowed a head, bald by the friction of many laurels; nods and winks . . . are on the increase, and yawns and stretchings grow frequent and contagious. Yet flows on, unceasing, the unheeded oratory—a drizzling stream of legal argument, or statistical statement, or a foaming current of patriotic statement, in a weak, wordy solution—bravado and balderdash for Buncombe.[15]

When the giants spoke, however, all was excitement both in the galleries and on the floor, and such occasions were July 15 and July 16, when Benton and Clay climaxed twenty-five years of parliamentary warfare with a furious debate over the proper road to the same destination. A young lady found Benton "the perfect embodiment of a great, inflexible will, the power of which one can only doubt when the eye is turned to the other side of the chamber, where sits his watchful, skilful, irresistible opponent, with the old fire of his wondrous intellect unquenched, and old strength of his Napoleonic will unbroken." Age had not destroyed the old Kentuckian's charm for the opposite sex.

Though Fillmore had sent an additional seven hundred and fifty troops to New Mexico Benton still feared the worst and defended brilliantly his version of a proper boundary. The line proposed in the omnibus bill, he said, would give Texas thirty towns and seventy-thousand New Mexicans who admitted no allegiance to Texas. The omnibus bill depended entirely upon satisfying the Texas senators, either with territory or money for Texas. The Texans held a four-vote margin—two votes for and two votes against either side—and so California and the territories must rise or fall on this stock-jobbing proposition. Thus the omnibus "was taken in the act—seized by the throat, and held up to the public view—(and here Mr. B. grappled a bill and held it up)—in the very act of auctioneering for votes to pass itself." As Benton wrestled with the bill, "a fire kindled in the wan cheek, and shot from the keen eye of Clay. Webster's sternest glances gleamed out from beneath the black ledge of his lowering brow; while the weighty countenance of Cass wore a shocked and mildly indignant expression."

On the following day a fierce exchange ensued between Benton and Clay over what Clay called "the boa constrictor struggle between the Senator and the bill," but Benton would not retreat. He assured the Senate that he had meant no insult to either the committee or the Texans, but insisted that the bill did make California and the territories dependent upon the price Texas would accept. Sitting in the galleries cheering his champion forward, little Francis P. Blair felt that Benton had silenced Clay "with an eloquence of which I thought him incapable & his manner was as much that of a master, as Clay wished his to be." The days when a Benton speech meant a national broadcast through the printing press of Blair were long past, but the little editor still found life's greatest interest in the struggles of his big friend.[16]

The issue finally came to a head on July 31. The Senate had already passed amendments to have the boundary settled by a Presidential commission and forbid any territorial government for New Mexico east of the river. Then Pearce of Maryland, an omnibus supporter throughout, suddenly pointed out that giving a government to New Mexico west of the Rio Grande and leaving the real territory ungoverned would be foolish. He would strike out everything related to New Mexico, reinsert everything but the restriction amendment, and replace it with one of his own.

Pearce had proposed a tricky parliamentary maneuver which could easily go astray. Benton eloquently defended Pearce, comparing the bill to the strolling players who performed *Hamlet* with the part of Hamlet left out because the ghost was sick. Challenging anyone to name a town west of the river, Old Bullion amid roars of laughter listed each tiny Indian village and pictured the astonishment of the braves at being asked to form a territorial government.

Benton was at the point of victory. New Mexico was stricken from the bill by 33-22. Then Pearce moved to re-instate the commission plan but delay territorial government for eastern New Mexico only until March 4, 1851. The radical Southerners were furious. Atchison immediately moved to strike out California, arguing that the Pearce amendment would give Texas territory to New Mexico unless the commission could

rule by April 4, and he would sooner vote for the Wilmot
Proviso. Yulee of Florida then dealt the fatal blow by moving
to strike out everything related to Texas. This would end the
omnibus, but the Texans had had enough. Abandoning Foote
and Clay, Rusk and Houston switched to Benton, and by the
margin of one vote Texas was cut loose from the bill. In quick
succession everything but Utah was eliminated, as the omnibus
opponents turned the Senate into a carnival of joy. Beaming,
bristling, and snorting with excitement, the old Missouri war
horse quickly denied any enmity toward the omnibus advocates and urged the immediate passage of Utah as a monument
to their work. The vote was 32-18.[17]

Benton was soon vindicated, as under the leadership of
Douglas the bills were considered separately and quickly
passed. New Mexico kept the southeast corner given Texas by
the omnibus, but Texas got the panhandle and ten million
dollars as a consolation prize. Stubborn to the end, Benton
voted against it as too generous to Texas, but it easily passed
by 30-20. California was admitted by 34-18, New Mexico followed by 27-10, and by mid-September the fugitive slave bill
and the suppression of the District slave trade were also law.
Always the realist, Benton abstained from voting on the fugitive slave law. Unwilling to oppose the principle, he found
the specific act filled with complex and unwise provisions likely
to cause trouble and cost the South more than their value.
Time soon vindicated this judgment.

When the struggle had ended, the old battler could not resist
offering a testimonial to his own judgment. For insisting that
the various measures could not pass together, he informed the
Senate, he had been severely censured, but the results had
proved him right. All four had passed by wide margins within
a few days, although only seventeen senators had supported all
four and only four members of the omnibus committee had
voted for all. He might have added that the sponsor of the
committee, Foote, had voted for but one. Clay peevishly
snapped that the compromise was a victory for the country and
no fit subject for individual triumph. But for opposition, the
combination might have passed four months earlier. Benton
angrily replied that the time had not yet come when opposition

could be stifled in the Senate as Louis XIV had suppressed opposition in France. The result proved that four months had been lost "about a matter which . . . failed, and the moment that it failed everything which was proposed was accomplished; at that moment the cats and dogs that had been tied together by their tails four months, scratching and biting, being loose again, every one of them ran off to his own hole and was quiet."

Appreciative senators laughed at the comparison, but frustrated little Henry Foote had the last word, because the Whig victory in Missouri was already known. If tyranny had been practiced in the Senate, shrilled Foote, "and if we have borne it with patience, yes, sir, for almost thirty years entire, thank God! we may exclaim at last, *'BEHOLD THE TYRANT PROSTRATE IN THE DUST, AND ROME AGAIN IS FREE.'* " [18]

Benton did not answer. He had labored to provide fellow slaveholders an unassailable constitutional position and had nothing further to say—for the moment. He had urged the South to avoid impossible demands and stand upon the constitutional protection of slavery where it existed—guarantees to be neither compromised nor conceded. He could do no more.

*   *   *   *   *   *   *   *

In Missouri the support of a few Whigs in the recently elected assembly might yet have re-elected Benton, but when Whig papers denounced him for deserting Clay, the Benton press defied them.

Knowing that a Whig would probably replace him, Benton assured a huge gathering in St. Louis on November 9 that he was completely satisfied. He had gone to Washington to attack Calhoun, he said, but the Carolinian's illness and death had brought compassion instead. America had awakened to the danger of disunion, and in Missouri all his objects had been accomplished. The people had crushed the Nullifiers, and no one had dared suggest Missouri delegates for the radical Southern convention at Nashville. The old Senator closed in the accents of a man who had selected a high road and would not be deterred by its hazards:

I have been a Senator thirty years—a continuance in service more honorable to the people, and to our republican institutions, than to me—answering, as it does, the monarchical accusation against the fickleness and ingratitude of republics. I have sometimes had to act against the preconceived opinions, and first impressions of my constituents; but always with full reliance upon their intelligence and equity—their intelligence to understand me and their equity to do me justice—and have never been disappointed. I value solid popularity—the esteem of good men, for good actions. I despise the bubble popularity that is won without merit and lost without crime. I have done some service to the State, but I put no claim on that account. I give up the past, and look only to the present, and want no change from the issue joined before the election.[19]

On January 22, 1851, after forty ballots, a Whig was chosen by a bare majority vote to replace Benton. Benton's fifty-five delegates stood firm throughout the balloting, but sixteen anti-Benton Democrats finally united for the Whig candidate. True to Benton's purpose, however, the assembly was overwhelmingly Unionist.

*   *   *   *   *   *   *

The roots of Thomas Hart Benton were deep in the old slaveholding agrarian South, and his economic principles remained those of the farmers' advocate, but he had long since bridged the gap to the future. His long life had been a process of steady growth, and he would never be out of place in a dynamic society. On November 14, 1850, he held a large meeting of the Mercantile Library Association of St. Louis spellbound with a stirring address on "The Progress of the Age."

In December, 1850, the Senator awaited January's final blow, but one last Senate session remained, in which slave arguments would be missing and the "real business of the country" could get on. He returned to Washington brimming with ideas, but faced a Senate in firm control of his enemies. Only a single minor place on one committee was available for the old veteran. Many Southerners were prepared to forgive Northern infidels, at least temporarily, but there was little mercy for the slaveholding heretic who with every opportunity to know bet-

ter had lent his mighty voice to those unwilling to recognize
the superior virtues of a society based upon slavery. Of the
Southerners only Sam Houston consistently stood by his side,
although the radical Jefferson Davis occasionally lent a helping
hand, probably as a means of opposing his hated colleague,
Henry Foote.

Benton had begun his senatorial career as the advocate of
French and Spanish land claimants in Louisiana, and now
finished with a mighty effort to help the older natives of California. In 1850 Frémont had lost the drawing for California's
long Senate term, ending his career before it had begun, but
Benton still considered California a personal responsibility.
Senator Gwin introduced a bill to settle land claims in California, but Benton for weeks attacked its lack of safeguards for
the original population. The son of Jesse Benton, who had
lost a small empire through inability to prove his claims, and
the frontier lawyer who had once brought the judicial system
of Tennessee tumbling down, pleaded mightily for amendments to reduce the hardships and costs of litigants. The
Senator believed in the lessons of history and wanted a bill containing "all the equitable and favorable provisions heretofore
allowed to land claimants in Upper and Lower Louisiana and
in Florida." He tried hard, but his amendments were defeated
one by one.[20]

The Senator also had a new railroad plan for Missouri. Most
Western states at their time of admission had relinquished the
right to tax public lands for five years after their sale, in exchange for five per cent of the proceeds. Ohio, Indiana, Illinois, and Missouri, however, had taken only three per cent,
accepting in lieu of the remaining two per cent the Government's pledge to build the Cumberland road to or through
their domains. The road had stopped forever in western Illinois, and Benton now introduced a bill to pay Missouri the
accrued two per cent for which it had never received a road
and the full five per cent in the future. The funds would be
used to finance railroads across Missouri, and as always Benton
defended the project as a great national purpose, not to be
confused with mere state interest.

A seashore vacation had breathed new life into Henry Clay,

and the great Kentuckian found a challenge in Benton's program. The two old men seemed to enjoy their final contest—no one else participated. Benton had spent thirty years opposing Clay's efforts to spend public funds for roads and other internal improvements and distribute land revenues and treasury surpluses to the states. In 1851, however, the economy-preaching Clay stood astride the national treasury denouncing Benton for attempting to raid it for the benefit of Missouri railroads. The project was buried by an overwhelming vote.[21]

Old Bullion again made a soaring plea for a great non-profit national highway and railroad, with free homesteads along the right of way. He was closing his Senate career as he had begun it—with ideas in step with the future but too advanced for his colleagues. All was different now, however. Thirty years before, his powerful mind and imagination had stood ready to ride the crest of the future to great power and influence. In 1851 the ideas could still ride, but the mighty Senator had been pulled from the saddle by the deadening weight of the slavery quarrel. Small wonder he could rarely distinguish America's troubles from his own.

On February 14 Benton made his last active Senate appearance. He asked permission to re-introduce his Missouri land rebate bill and began a speech to justify the request. Clay had been the only opponent, and his new ammunition consisted of past Clay speeches reversing the Kentuckian's recent arguments. Henry Foote, however, quickly rose to a point of order: the merits could not be discussed on a motion asking leave to introduce a bill. The Chair promptly agreed. No speech would be in order until the Senate had granted leave.

The old Senator stood his ground with an appeal to past glories: "The contrary has been decided heretofore. When I first commenced my movements against the Bank of the United States, I made as full . . . speeches as I could . . . asking leave to introduce the bills. The Senate and Presiding Officer will surely recollect it."

The Chair had no such recollection. "The Senator . . . must confine himself to stating the substance of the bill."

The Senator would not surrender. He would "do what he has done four or five times this session, and what other Senators

have done, or . . . nothing." He would "have the rights . . .
enjoyed here for thirty years . . . or . . . nothing."

For an hour the Senate debated the issue, until a motion
allowing him to proceed finally carried. The angry patriarch
finished with a bristling defense of Missouri's rights. The senatorial election was past, but there would be future contests.
Clay answered with his usual parrying skill, and leave to introduce the bill was denied.[22]

The thirty years had ended. The session continued into
March, but at sixty-nine even the physique of Thomas Hart
Benton was beginning to creak from his incredible exertions.
A sudden fever and doctor's orders brought his first rest in over
two years, and convalescence outlasted the session. The old
man's emotions when removing his belongings from the Senate
desk which had been home for three decades were not recorded,
but he showed no spirit of defeat to either friend or foe. New
challenges lay ahead, and he would take up the task of master-
ing them.

CHAPTER XX

RETURN OF THE BUFFALO

Francis P. Blair was crushed by Benton's defeat in Missouri, but agreed with many other former Jacksonian leaders that they must now "mount old Bullion & ride him into battle" for the 1852 Presidency. Again, however, Old Bullion would not be ridden. Sadly Blair wrote Van Buren that Benton remained "averse to offices—& especially . . . the Presidency." Instead Benton now planned to leave a memoir as "the basis of his fame and the best service to his country." Blair had "once thought that his abstinence of all invitations looking forward toward the presidential honor was a politic reserve to bring it within reach before he extended his hand to clutch it." Finally, however, Blair knew that his friend had "fixed his ambition to be great . . . without condescending to the peerage." [1]

Benton left his sickbed under a full head of steam. Forty years earlier he had informed Jackson that every young man should plan either to do something worth being written or write something worth doing. The doing was temporarily halted, and it was now time to write. He would produce the great work for the next two years and then seek election to the House of Representatives. Writing John Dix for help in approaching publishers, he outlined the project in simple terms. His own speeches had covered "all subjects, civil and military, legislative and diplomatic, for thirty years; and never . . . for

rhetorical, or clap-trap effect; but always to the business in hand."
His speeches were "enough to make them constitute . . . the
framework and scaffolding—the outline, and the salient points
—of all our history during the eventful period from 1820 to
1850.—they only want some filling up between, and some connecting by notes and illustrations, to become a complete history
of the working of our government during that time. . . ." He
would use the Jackson papers, having promised the General
"to take care of his administration in the eyes of posterity," as
well as the papers and memories of many others. He would
write "a popular work . . . for the masses," but in the largest
octavo and small type to get everything crammed in. The
Democrats of his day had served the people well, and it was
"due to them that their acts should neither be forgotten, nor
misrepresented nor the fruits of them lost to posterity." He
expected "the sale of millions of copies." Legend has it that
when the publisher asked how many copies should be printed
he answered by asking how many Americans could read. Place
a twinkle in the Senator's eye, and the legend becomes plausi-
ble.

Throughout the summer and fall of 1851 Blair found him
"big with his book—with President making—and the redemption of Missouri."

"I never felt better, not even at 30 years of age," he informed
Van Buren in a letter demanding recollections and rejecting
the excuse of "imperfection of memory." The book was growing in size, scope, and purpose, as the author scratched away
at his desk, with his beloved Elizabeth, by now able to walk
very little, sitting patiently by his side.[2]

For the Presidency Benton thought Supreme Court Justice
Levi Woodbury the candidate most likely to draw support from
both sections. There was nothing against Woodbury, he wrote,
and running Cass or Buchanan would be like "starting Methu-
salem." The true Democrats should ignore the convention
packers and go directly to the people with Woodbury. Old
Bullion was plowing ahead with plans to start a Woodbury
newspaper, to the disgust of Blair and others who thought the
Judge too friendly to the South, when somewhat to their relief
Woodbury suddenly died.[3]

Shorn of his candidate, the modest historian continued his scholarly concentration. By late October his interpretation of the sectional struggle was beginning to take shape. "A political disappointment & resentment in poor Calhoun for the loss of the presidency," he wrote Van Buren, "resting on the groundless assumption that you had robbed him of Jackson's favor and the succession, acting upon a real public grievance in the South (tariff & extravagant expenditures,) and pretexted by a slavery abolition alarm—is my view of the cause and means of this disaffection, which is deep and abiding, and only to be cured by returning the government to the simplicity and economy of its design." [4]

Slowly dying of tuberculosis in a Washington rooming-house, Henry Clay expected Benton's book to be an agglomeration of passions, but Blair assured him that Benton had already written a section fully exonerating Clay of the corrupt bargain charge of 1824. Benton, said Blair, had no malice toward Clay, regarding him as a great patriot against whom he was "proud of breaking a lance" and "carrying off the victory." Clay smiled with satisfaction, gratitude, and perhaps a trace of wise amusement at his own memories.[5]

In November, 1851, Benton returned to Missouri with his family, his manuscript, and a determination to win election to the House of Representatives in 1852. In January he returned briefly to Washington under conditions "which rivalled Napoleon's march from Moscow," as snow, ice, and rain froze up the steamboat machinery. He had come to sell Frémont's California land claim for a million dollars—$100,000 down and $30,000 annually. Delighted to hear of Clay's reaction to Blair's assurances, he would not go to Clay himself, but wrote asking Van Buren to write Clay that he would appear very favorably in the story of the Randolph duel and honorably in every case where the truth would permit. ". . . *there is a time when political animosities are to be obliterated under the great duties of historic truth.*" Van Buren acted with his usual tact, returning Benton's letter to Blair asking him to show it to Clay.[6]

Old Bullion remained in Washington long enough to upset Blair by taking a violent dislike to Kossuth, the famous Hungarian revolutionary. Benton feared that hotheads might get

America involved in European affairs, although Blair suspected also that Old Bullion resented having been kept waiting by Kossuth while he finished an interview with Douglas. Blair was certain Douglas had deliberately overstayed his visit to tax Benton's patience. The matter was more than academic because Kossuth was a great favorite with a host of new immigrants in St. Louis. Blair feared that Benton might start "a Hungarian Battle in the far West" and thereby lose votes in the coming race for the House. A letter from Van Buren finally reversed Benton's prejudice.[7]

Before the Congressional campaign began, personal tragedy struck hard. In May, 1851, the famous Catholic missionary, Father De Smet, had written Benton his reservations about the suggestion that he take young Randolph Benton on a projected voyage through Oregon and California, although the priest was anxious to help: "Nothing, Dear Colonel, shall do me more pleasure, than to be of service to your son, for your sake; I would do all in my power, to see him return to you, worthy of such a Father." Apparently Randolph did not go, although Catholicism became a strong influence in his life. On March 12, 1852, the young man suddenly became ill, possibly with a ruptured appendix and resulting peritonitis. For five days and nights his anxious father sat by the bedside. Father De Smet came, and on the night of March 16 received Randolph into the Catholic Church. Later in the evening Benton penned a note to Father De Smet:

> I went into the room. . . . He immediately said to me, *"are you pleased with what I have done?"* I said *"I am,"* and then urged him to yield to the opiates . . . and go to sleep. He said: *"Excitement and happiness have done for me* more *than sleep can do."* and immediately turning his eyes to heaven . . . he said in a clear, calm, modulated voice & radiant look, *"Thank God I am happy!"*. . . . *"I intended to do it long ago, but did not know whether you would like it."* I told him he made me happy. And truly it is the first feeling of relief I have had in these five terrible days and nights. . . . You are giving peace to me in giving it to him.

Early next morning the stricken youth died, and the father suffered the special tortures of loss compounded with regret.

As Blair saw it, Benton's "strong heart stood firm against his utter loss while he lived (for he was entirely a ruin) but his paternal instinct gives way under his death, which brings out grief for all his son suffered for years back." [8] Randolph's death at twenty-two was not Benton's fault, but Benton had been almost forty-eight when the boy was born. Elizabeth had collapsed when he was twelve, and during his crucial years of adolescence the Senator's fierce political struggles had left so little time for the doting attention earlier lavished upon the older daughters. Randolph's troubles remain a mystery, but may have been at least part of the massive personal price levied by the Senator's battle for the Union in the late 1840's.

Whether or not Benton thought in such terms, he found relief in a new onslaught on the same old enemies. As before he faced an anti-Benton Democrat and a Whig under circumstances which apparently made election of the Whig inevitable. Friends considered the cause hopeless, but the seventy-year-old giant mounted his horse and swept through the countryside with a vitriolic fury. His anti opponent, Lewis Bogy, fought also with bitter vindictiveness, denouncing Benton everywhere as an abolitionist and Free-Soiler, but was no match for Old Bullion. Calling for the expunging of the Jackson resolutions and the defeat of the little demagogues opposing the railroad and trying to "hitch Missouri to . . . nullification," Benton pledged continued work for a homestead for every family and the great national railroad. The antis, he roared, had no place in the Democratic Party, but should form a "grand sewer . . . to carry off all the filth from the democratic camp!"

The exchanges were vicious, but the old titan understood also the value of pathos and had a reservoir of genuine sorrow from which to draw. "What is a seat in Congress to me?" he asked a hushed crowd in St. Louis. "I have sat thirty years in the highest branch of Congress—have made a name to which I can expect to add nothing. . . . I have domestic afflictions, sorely lacerated . . . a wife . . . who needs my attention more than ever; children, some separated from me by the wide expanse of oceans and continents, others by the slender bounds which separate time from eternity. . . . What is my occupation? . . . gathering the bones of the dead—a mother—a sister—two sons—a grand child—planting the cypress over assembled graves, and marking the spot where I, and those who are dear to me, are soon to be laid; all on the sunset side of the Father of Floods, the towering city of St. Louis on one hand, the rolling stream of the Missouri on the other. . . ." [9]

On August 2, 1852, the people voted, and a distant newspaper analyzed the contest:

[Benton] is elected by a Democratic, slave-holding constituency . . . by a remarkably large popular vote, when his . . . opinions and . . . votes have notoriously made him obnoxious to the entire slave-holding section. . . . He is elected from a populous district against the opposition of a well-organized and enthusiastic body of Whigs, when his own party was split up into two irreconcilable factions, and when the Whigs knew that the whole of a long life had been devoted to the bitterest . . . warfare upon their cardinal principles and most eminent leaders. . . .

Before all this immense array of opposition he never faltered for a moment. The host of his enemies was fully and resolutely arrayed before him; the force of his own supporters . . . was scarcely visible to the far-off watcher of this singular battle. But one colossal figure, and that Benton, boldly confronting the array of his enemies and challenging them to the struggle, was to be seen. . . .

And strange to say, outraging every customary propriety of language, flaming in hot hate, towering and wrestling in fierce vindictiveness of passion, rushing forward, with blind fury, upon every obstacle like his type, the huge wild buffalo of the Missouri prairies—this strange, powerful, hateful, spiteful, remorseless man treads his enemies down under his feet in his angry rush, and comes out before the country victorious, defiantly challenging further opposition from Democrats, and finding an answer only in welcoming huzzas!

The Whig *Missouri Republican* blamed it all on the Germans, "Blucher and the Prussian forces." Other papers throughout the country, many of them ancient foes of the Senator, rejoiced at his vindication. The New York *Times,* while never expecting to support or approve any of his policies, celebrated the return of a *"real democrat,"* who "believes in the Declaration of Independence, and in the right of constitutional majorities to rule." The Boston *Daily Bee,* "Without favoring many of his political views," would "agree with the uniform American sentiment, in according to the great Western statesman a life-long devotion to the public interests, an ardent love for the prosperity of his country, and a very large share of the elements which go to make up that highest development of intellectual man—the *philosophical and practical statesman.*" [10]

After the election Benton returned to Washington in triumph, although not scheduled to take his seat until December, 1853. Victory was an exhilarating tonic, and Blair was delighted with his new "alacrity of look and carriage" and announced intention to play "the part of Dandolo, 'the octogenarian chief' celebrated by Byron."

"Dandolo" was soon busy. His book was moving ahead, and politics required constant attention. An American group had acquired a defunct concession originally granted by Mexico to one Don José Garay to build a railroad across the Isthmus of Tehuantepec. Mexico had invalidated the grant, causing a mild flurry of agitation for American intervention. In a blistering public letter, Benton reviewed the history of the grant, denounced the holders as "dupes of their own folly and greed," and continued on the general theme of Government mail subsidies to steamship lines instead of the Pacific railroad. One-tenth of the annual subsidies, he wrote, would open a wagon way from Missouri to California which a railroad would soon follow. The New York *Express* hotly defended the steamship lines, and the old warrior found himself embroiled in the kind of pen and ink battle he had always loved. In Missouri even Whig papers rallied to his side. The question was "above all party interests. The success of Col. Benton in arresting the downfall of Western interests by the moloch of ocean lines of steamships" was "to be desired by every man in the West, of every party." [11]

In December Blair found him hard at labor. "Thucidydes was not half so much in earnest in his immortal work." Even work, however, did not entirely quench the old man's loneliness. Elizabeth remained feeble in St. Louis with Susan, who was "unmarried, but not unsought"; Jessie was in Paris with Frémont, who had refused Benton's sale of the California land; the others were doing well. "I have reason for satisfaction with my children that live," he wrote Van Buren. "Still I have spells of depression which instead of being removed by time only seem to fall more heavily. . . ." And hearing of the death of the wife of an old friend, Benton offered poignant comfort:

> Truly you drew a great prize in the lottery of life; and tho half of it is just gone, yet you had it for a long time; and there is really a consolation in feeling that we are soon to follow. That is my own feeling with respect to my own good wife who has been spared to me for above thirty years, tho weak & feeble of late, and for whom myself & all the family that can be collected on the West bank of the Mississippi, I was employed when last in St. Louis in preparing the "narrow" bed which is to be our long home. You have consolations both in the past and the future, and we both have philosophy enough and christianity enough to be thankful for all the good we have had, and to be mindful of what is to happen to ourselves and to be prepared for it.[12]

There was little time for brooding, however, because enemies were already threatening from a new vantage point. The newly elected President, described by enemies as the "victor of many a well-fought bottle," was a handsome weakling whose chief fault was inability to resist any aggressive demand. The 1851-1852 elections had brought widespread triumphs to Unionist supporters of the Compromise of 1850, and many Southern extremists had been defeated. Pierce had been elected on a pledge to support the Compromise, but instead of using the White House patronage to strengthen Unionists he tried to avoid controversy and surrendered to the extremists. Jefferson Davis, defeated for the Mississippi governorship by Foote, received the powerful War Department and immediately began laying plans to use the office to promote a Southern route for the Pacific railroad. Douglas, still set on a route from Chicago rather than St. Louis, was anxious to undermine Benton, and he and Atchison were soon forcing their demands upon Pierce.

Blair and Benton had supported Pierce, and as a Missouri victor Benton expected consideration in the awarding of patronage. Pierce listened politely and affably, leading Benton to believe that agreement had been reached, and then gave every Federal appointment in Missouri to anti-Benton Democrats, despite the clear evidence that they were the minority faction.

The other two Democratic representatives from Missouri, Phelps and Lamb, elected as Benton Democrats, quickly caught the wind's direction and shifted to Atchison, and the anti faction, beaten to a pulp by Benton's 1852 campaign, suddenly sprang to life many times stronger. Opposition to Benton suddenly became the "title to federal office" in Missouri. The frustrated Old Bullion, too proud to complain and unwilling to denounce the President, could only assure friends that such acts would "have no effect on my *political* course . . . a point at which the vulgar herd of hack politicians cannot understand me." [13]

Secretary Davis, meanwhile, politely rejected Benton's suggestion that Edward Beale, newly appointed Indian Superintendent for California, take along a small force for official examination of railroad routes. Beale, a hard-bitten young plainsman who had served with Frémont, loved Benton as a man "for whom he was ready to lay down his life." [14] Instead, Davis sent an expedition to survey the southernmost route and was soon negotiating the Gadsden Treaty to get territory from Mexico for an easier right of way.

Thus rebuffed, Benton returned to Missouri, and April 30, 1853, found him seeing Beale's unofficial party off at the Kansas frontier. At the frontier towns of Kansas, Westport, and Independence he assured large crowds: "You stand on the brink of a mighty enterprise, and everyone should thank God that he lives in an age, and in a country, and under a form of government which enables him to act a part in the great undertaking, which is to unite two oceans and three continents, consolidate our Union, and make America the thoroughfare of Europe and of Asia." A major obstacle to the central route was the unorganized status of the great Kansas-Nebraska region, but Benton, facing an audience of land-hungry "boomers," offered a solution in the accents of the frontiersman. He would continue to work for immediate territorial government and the extinction of Indian titles, despite the intrigues of those trying to put the railroad on another route. Meanwhile, he declared, the territorial lands previously taken from the Western Indians for reassignment to Indians being moved from the East, but never actually reassigned, was already open for settlement by pre-emptioners. The invitation to defy existing interpretations of the law was clear, and listeners and supporters across Missouri were delighted. Again Benton had found a political gold mine consistent with his lifetime philosophy.[15]

Old Bullion had captured the imaginations of Americans from east to west. The Buffalo *Republic* was certain that in the House he would "furnish more relating to every part of that subject [the railroad], than can be obtained by the whole exploring commission now examining the different routes." Benton had "a mind capable of almost anything that a single human intellect can accomplish; and what he does not already know, his powerful penetration and his ceaseless energy, will certainly find out. . . . God speed 'Old Bullion'. . . . A great bereavement will it be to this country when that living encyclopedia and engine of national progress, shall be taken from us. . . ."

Returning to Washington, Benton spent the remainder of the summer and fall writing his book and keeping the press supplied with information on the railroad. Beale had reported the central route excellent, and a New Mexican public meeting had echoed his sentiments. There was also time for another Nebraska effort. Benton sent a map of the territory to the Commissioner of Indian Affairs, asking him to mark the assigned and unassigned lands. With this request filled, Old Bullion boldly published the map, proclaiming it an official designation of lands already open for settlement. The Commissioner denied any such meaning, but, headed by Benton, the pressure for territorial organization was building up to an irresistible point.

In August a reporter found Benton "the youngest man of seventy we have ever seen. . . . He wears his hat with a knowing expression a little on the left side, walks with a deliberate and measured tread, having something like a pride in its seeming—something that speaks a consciousness that he is Thomas Hart Benton. He feels his powers, and so does his country, and so will it ever." In November Blair found him still working from dawn to dark on his book, with Elizabeth still by his side, but "sinking daily." Blair had "never witnessed such an instance of conjugal tenderness, & attachment as his."[16]

On December 5, 1853, Thomas Hart Benton took his oath as

a Representative from Missouri in the Congress of the United States.

* * * * * * * *

In the House Benton found a happy relief from the animosities marking his last days in the Senate. The old veteran was immediately appointed chairman of the Committee on Military Affairs and the Library Committee. He wished to serve on the committees, but graciously asked to be excused from the chairmanships because of pressing personal commitments.

Much of the session dealt with the kind of issues for which the American machinery of government was best designed, and Benton played his usual prominent role. He worked hard but unsuccessfully for an additional $100,000 appropriation to complete a Federal customs house in St. Louis, stressing the long-range economy of a building large enough to hold all Federal offices in the city and constructed from fireproof stone materials which would neither burn nor rot down. He was more successful in getting a right of way granted to Missouri for the St. Louis and Iron Mountain Railroad. Always the plainsmen's advocate, he fought hard and successfully for reimbursement to the Jones and Russell Company for losses suffered in a snowstorm while transporting army supplies to New Mexico in 1850. The caravan had found safety in a canyon, but an army commander in Santa Fe had ordered an immediate advance, causing a loss in animals and supplies of almost thirty-nine thousand dollars. He also persuaded the House to authorize the sale of the St. Louis arsenal to the city for a public park, although the Senate rejected the proposition. On the other hand, his opposition to building six new warships and sarcastic remarks against appropriating twenty thousand dollars to build a West Point riding house were to no avail. His grandchildren, said the Colonel, had suggested "that the floor be carpeted, and mattresses be placed around the room, so that when the young men roll off their horses they may roll up against the mattresses so as not to endanger 'life and limb.' . . . The five-year-old boys of the Utah nation would be ashamed to have themselves put into a house to learn to ride." The House laughed heartily, but passed the appropriation.

Soon, however, the atmosphere of good-will disappeared, as personal and political ambitions revived the slave question from the anesthesia of 1850 and flung it again upon the Congressional stage.

Stephen A. Douglas was a brilliant, aggressive, ambitious, and reasonably responsible young statesman—and one of the coolest gamblers ever to deal in major affairs of men. In 1854 he was anxious to reunite the badly divided Democratic Party, join its warring factions behind his own Presidential efforts, open a western railroad route from Chicago and defeat the plans of Benton, and fulfill his duties as chairman of the Committee on Territories. All of these purposes called for the territorial organization of the Kansas-Nebraska region, which ordinarily would have caused no particular opposition. The area was entirely north of the Missouri Compromise line and thus by long-standing agreement destined to remain free of slavery. No evidence existed to indicate that the Southern people felt any particular concern with the matter, and a bill organizing the area without mention of slavery would probably have passed without significant opposition. In 1848 many Southerners had voted for extension of the Compromise line to the Pacific; there were no settlers already there to petition for anti-slave action; and the existing Compromise should have satisfied any anti-slave radicals in Congress.

Certain Southerners, however, led by Atchison, threatened Douglas with a new sectional quarrel if the attempt was made, and Atchison, who would "rather see the whole territory sunk into hell, than . . . organized as a free territory," had immense power as President *pro tem* of the Senate. Particularly important for Atchison, and perhaps also for Douglas, the territory must be organized under conditions which would pull the teeth of Benton before the Missouri Senate election of 1855.

Douglas was a realist. Certain that slavery could never go to Kansas, he saw no reason for any serious Northern objections to a bill permitting the settlers to decide the question of slavery for themselves. This, he apparently believed, would keep the Southerners quiet, accomplish his political and railroad objectives, and organize the area without difficulty. And when Atchison and others pointed out the inconsistency between this "popular sovereignty" position and the Missouri Compromise restriction, he was persuaded against his instinctive judgment to add a proviso repealing the Missouri Compromise. On January 23, 1854, the final version of the bill was presented to the Senate.[17]

A major flaw marred the logic of the Little Giant. He was not realistic enough to realize that most people were less realistic than himself. If Southern politicians could inflame their constituents on the question of slave rights in Oregon, there should have been little reason to doubt that Northerners could perform the same feat in saving Kansas for freedom. The Southern popular reaction to a Kansas territory under the ancient Compromise could not possibly have equaled the blazing fury of a North roused to defend the sacred barrier which had blocked the northward advance of slavery for thirty-three years.

Anti-slave radicals in Congress answered the bill with a shrewd, dishonest, and magnificently effective treatise, entitled "An Appeal of the Independent Democrats." In flaming prose it charged Douglas with betraying the Northwest into slavery for the sake of his own unholy ambitions. With a roar the North came to life from Maine to Iowa, denouncing the South and the "Slaveocracy" for its wicked designs. The Southern people, surprised, stunned, and bewildered at first, soon answered their attackers in coin, and overnight a new sectional quarrel was raging on all sides.

The administration promptly made adherence to the bill a test of Democratic orthodoxy for the dispensing of patronage—a test soon to rip large portions of the Northwest from the party they had supported since Jackson.

To Thomas Hart Benton the reopening of the quarrel was a crime beyond redemption. He had roused Missourians to a burning fever for the organization of Kansas-Nebraska, but was now ready to sacrifice every political advantage and fight against the emotions he had helped to create. "Is all Clay's labour to be buried with him?" he asked, and once more prepared for battle. On March 25 the House waited for the old patriarch's views.

Unlike the anti-slave radicals, Benton made no pretense that the bill would extend slavery anywhere. Instead he offered a long and involved constitutional defense of the Missouri Compromise and warned of the fearful impact the measure would have upon the public mind. As for administration pressures, he could only point out the fable of the ass which donned a lion's skin to scare his master. The master recognized his bray and rather than being frightened took a cudgel and almost beat him to death. The moral: "A caution to all asses to take care how they undertake to scare their masters. [*Great applause.*]" The Compromise, he said, had brought peace in 1820 when the Union had been divided like "enemies on the field of battle," yet Congress was now asked to destroy it—"Not by the inhabitants— not by any one human being living, or expecting to live on the territory . . . but upon a motion in Congress—a silent, secret, limping, halting, creeping, squinting, impish, motion, conceived in the dark—midwifed in a committee room, and sprung upon Congress and the country in the style in which Guy Fawkes intended to blow up the Parliament house. . . ." If as the bill stated, the Compromise of 1850 had nullified that of 1820, why do it again in 1854? If the bill intended neither to legislate slavery into nor out of the territories, then why legislate at all? Why all the disturbance if no effect were intended? All of this "untrue, contradictory, suicidal, and preposterous" reasoning was an effort to blame others for what the bill was doing—"destroying . . . all confidence between the North and the South, and arraying one-half the Union against the other in deadly hostility."

Old Bullion's words were biting hard. When his allotted hour ended, Long John Wentworth of Chicago promptly offered Benton as much of his own hour as would be needed to finish. This was a common custom, but objections quickly arose on all sides. Benton sat silently while Wentworth, "in the midst of much noise and confusion," made it clear "that the oldest man in the House, one who knows more than all the rest of us put together," would be heard to the end, "even though he [Mr. W.] kept the committee in session to the end of time."

Benton finally continued with precedent after precedent for Congressional control of the territories. Yet what was the excuse for "all this turmoil and mischief? To keep slavery out of Congress! Great God! it was out of Congress! completely, en-

tirely, and forever out of Congress, unless Congress dragged it
in by breaking down the sacred laws which settled it." Slaveholders would gain "nothing but an unequal and vexatious
contest" they could not win. Indeed, he concluded, the movement had begun "without a memorial, without a petition, without a request, from a human being." There had not yet been
a "word in its favor from the smallest public meeting or private
assemblage of any slave State." This was "the response of the
South to this boon tendered to it by northern members under a
northern President. . . . the response of silence—more em-
phatic than words. . . ." [18]

Some three weeks later Benton delivered his final word on
the bill. He still considered it "a deception and a cheat" to the
South, since no slaves would ever enter the region, but believed
he had discovered its purpose. James Gadsden in Mexico had
been authorized to spend up to fifty million dollars for a large
section of northern Mexico, while Pierre Soulé in Spain was
trying to purchase Cuba—"With a rumpus to be kicked up" if
the island was not obtained. Suspecting the Nebraska bill to be
"only an entering wedge to future enterprises," with northern
Mexico and Cuba the likely possibilities, Benton demanded explanations.[19]

The old titan had had his say. There was no direct connection between Kansas-Nebraska and the negotiations with Mexico and Spain, although some Southerners did hope to add
some slave territory. Gadsden did not get everything sought,
but did buy a strip of northern Mexican desert from Santa
Anna for a railroad right of way. After failing to buy Cuba,
Soulé and two fellow diplomats issued the famous Ostend Manifesto threating Spain with war, but American and world public
opinion soon throttled it. On the main question, however,
Benton had again looked ahead with clear vision. Congress accepted the assurances that slavery would not go to Kansas and
passed the Kansas-Nebraska bill, but the people refused to be
convinced, and the question opened a wound destined never to
heal. The Northwest in particular would not believe that the
Missouri Compromise would have been repealed if the South
actually were not conspiring to block western expansion with a
great slave belt from Texas to Canada. The "Appeal of the

Independent Democrats" was the work of false prophets—slavery never had a chance in Kansas—but the Northern fears, distrust, and hatred it generated were an indispensable part of the events which led America to civil war. Benton foresaw this and again chose to break a lance with the pro-slave sentiments of his own state.

And when Pierce summarily demanded that the House appropriate the necessary ten million dollars to complete the Gadsden Purchase, Benton posed an important constitutional question. Was the House obligated to pass without question any appropriation required by a treaty executed by the President and Senate? Benton insisted that in the acquisitions of Louisiana, Florida, and California, the House had been consulted in advance and was constitutionally entitled to this consideration. In this case, he said, the area had been bought for a railroad route, but how foolish to build a road along the outside border "through a country so utterly desolate, desert, and God forsaken, that Kit Carson says a wolf could not make his living upon it," when a splendid central route already existed. The land could best be evaluated by the story of the Virginian living surrounded by desolate land who assured a friend, "I am not so poor as you think for: I do not own all that poor land." [20] Again the old statesman had labored in vain. The Mexican dictator, Santa Anna, in power illegally anyhow, received the money and a few months later went into exile for the last time. The money contributed to the comfort of his declining years, while the worthless territory lay unused and unoccupied for many decades.

* * * * * * *

In the late spring of 1854 Congressmen began using and quoting from a new reference book. The first volume of the *Thirty Years' View* of Thomas Hart Benton was off the press. It covered some 739 pages of small print in double column, and through it moved an inside picture of the American Congress from 1820 through the reign of Andrew Jackson. If America's Congressional history was not entirely covered by the speeches of Benton, they made a reasonably fair substitute when mixed with appropriate lengthy quotations from his opponents. No major question was omitted, and the author rarely failed to allow his opponents to speak for themselves. "Justice to the men with whom I acted, and to the cause in which we were engaged," was the chief announced motive. "The hope of being useful to our republican form of government in after ages by showing its working through a long and eventful period . . . thereby justifying the hope of its permanent good operation in all time to come, if maintained in its purity and integrity," followed close behind. The author would "find far greater pleasure in bringing out the good and the great acts of those with whom I have differed, than in noting the points on which I deemed them wrong," and indeed the book was remarkably free from rancor. Clay and Webster emerged with honor, and even Calhoun was a dangerously mistaken genius rather than a deliberate criminal.

The author of course gave full treatment to his own efforts for western expansion, democratization of the electoral system, low tariffs, cheap or free land, hard money, economy in Government, destruction of the bank, and vindication of Jackson, but the book was more than a mere self-eulogy. It was a storehouse of information, containing many significant documents, letters, and speeches reprinted in full. Future historians would find much value in his treatment of the election of 1824 and vindication of Clay, his analysis of fact and fiction regarding Jackson's use of the spoils system, and his discussions of the great sectional debate of 1830, the nullification struggle and the tariff compromise of 1833, the personal conflict between Jackson and Calhoun, the Jackson side of the bank war, and the slave petition debates of the late 1830's.

Through it all ran a stirring faith in the wisdom and judgment of the people and a plea for more rather than less democracy. He was particularly concerned with the Frenchman, de Tocqueville, a "writer, whose book takes him out of that class of European travellers who requite the hospitality of Americans by disparagement of their institutions . . . whose general intelligence and candor entitle his errors to the honor of correction." De Tocqueville had written of Jackson's incapacity for governing a free people. Benton reviewed Jackson's achievements and answered that free people are governed by laws rather than men. The Frenchman had found the House of Representatives vulgar and undistinguished in contrast to the intelligent and eloquent Senate, and attributed the difference to the popular election of the representatives. Benton answered that most senators had previously been representatives, or had won prominence in other popular elections. Indeed, the House had actually contained some great men rejected by the Senate, such as John Randolph and John Quincy Adams—"I name no more, confining myself to instances of the illustrious dead." Popular elections were clearly "the safest and wisest mode of political election."

If Benton had hoped to leave a lasting memorial to Jackson and himself, his object was achieved, because generations of future historians would use the book for information, reinforcement, and pegs upon which to hang opposing arguments. Long after the monument had disappeared from public view, its stones and masonry were being reconstructed often and conspicuously.

Benton had hoped the book would provide a new rallying point and source of unity for the Democratic Party, and the old Jacksonian stalwarts did get much comfort from reliving their past glories, but the quarrels of 1848-1850 and Kansas-Nebraska had torn wounds in the old party which no book by Thomas Hart Benton could ease. The publisher did not require the latest census to keep account of sales, but for a book of its type the sale was excellent. The pre-publication subscription was the "greatest known in America, or in Europe," apparently in the neighborhood of sixty-five thousand copies, and the delighted author was already hard at work on his second volume.[21]

*   *   *   *   *   *   *

The long summer session of 1854 and Elizabeth's health prevented Benton from making the kind of march through Missouri which had carried him to victory in 1852. Faithful friends carried on his battle for re-election, but the odds were even greater than before, and again no holds were barred. In April he angrily announced that he would no longer receive mail through the St. Louis post office because of the Pierce-appointed postmaster. The aggrieved postmaster replied with an announcement that he would accept no Missouri bank notes bearing the picture of Benton.

In accepting nomination, Benton again emphasized his preference for Whigs over Nullifiers. The Whigs were "for the Union, and for the harmony and stability of the Union . . . a point of community between them and the democracy which enables them to act together on the questions . . . either too high or too low for party." The new nullification was "as much worse than that of Mr. Calhoun, as its champions" were "below him in talent, in purity of private life, and in decorum of behaviour," and its practitioners must be defeated regardless of the cost.[22]

A clear-cut, three-way choice among Benton, anti-Benton Trusten Polk, and Whig Luther Kennett might have gone for Benton, but a new element entered the picture. Large segments of America had been caught up in the anti-emigrant, anti-Catholic, Native American, Know-Nothing movement, which would nominate former President Fillmore for the Presidency in 1856. The organization had no platform other than emotional prejudices, but managed to mobilize these to an alarming degree in every section with a significant immigrant population. Such a region was eastern Missouri, and Benton, a true cosmopolite, had always been popular with immigrant groups since the days of his early friendships with the original French. The effort to turn nationality prejudices against Benton had begun in 1852, when the Whig press blamed his victory on the Germans. During the 1854 campaign the German *Anzeiger des Westens* praised Benton unstintedly, and the *Republican* promptly reprinted its editorials alongside criticisms of German beer-drinking and other customs. The *Jefferson Enquirer* later complained that Know-Nothingism forced hundreds of people into opposition who agreed with Benton on all the real issues, and on election day there was much rioting and minor bloodshed at the polls. The anti-Benton administration patronage, the emotional appeal of Kansas-Nebraska to Missouri slaveholders, the impact of Know-Nothingism, the personal popularity of Kennett, and the absence of Benton himself as a personal rallying force were too much. Whig Kennett won by more than a thousand votes, and Old Bullion had again been rejected.

The administration-supported Polk ran a poor third, while in the state-wide assembly elections, the three factions ran almost even. Some deals would be necessary if either Benton or Atchison were to gain the required majority for election to the Senate, but in January, 1855, state Representative Frank Blair held the Benton forces in line, and the Whigs and Atchison did not compromise. After forty-one ballots the Missouri General Assembly adjourned without electing any senator at all, and Atchison's seat was left vacant. For the next two years Missouri had only one senator.

In August, 1854, Benton had left for Missouri to help shape the coming senatorial contest. A few days later, Elizabeth Benton, by now unable to speak at all, took daughter Jessie by the hand, tottered into the living room, and pointed to her husband's empty chair. Jessie understood the message and sent an urgent dispatch for her father to return. On September 10, while he was still traveling, Elizabeth, aged sixty, died, and the long-dreaded blow had fallen. The family decided upon a Washington funeral and temporary interment to be followed by final burial in St. Louis in the following spring. It was a spectacular funeral, as a host of friends turned out to honor one who had lived long among them with charm, grace, and dignity. Watching her father's grief, Jessie was certain that "separation at his age" was "hardest upon the one who survives." [23]

* * * * * * *

As always, Benton again found solace in hard work. All efforts to push a non-profit national railroad program through Congress had failed, and he now decided the best hope lay in mobilizing the resources of "enlightened capitalists"—but not stock-jobbers—who should ask Congress only for a right of way through the public lands. He had invested nine thousand dollars in another Frémont expedition during the preceding winter and had the results ready to strengthen his arguments for the central route. Ideas always meant action for Benton, and in early December, 1854, he began a "Peter the Hermit" lec-

ture tour of Baltimore, Boston, Providence, Hartford, and Philadelphia. Thousands flocked to hear him, and everywhere he
found warm kindness and enthusiasm. His messages, soon published in pamphlet form, were long, colorful descriptions and
soaring prophecies of the world-shaking significance of the enterprise. Audiences listened breathlessly, although many probably shook their heads at his fantastic prediction that trains
might easily race along the prairie-level road at one hundred
miles an hour.

Along the way he conferred with leading businessmen, and his
addresses were clearly aimed at potential stockholders. Apparently he secured written commitments from at least twenty of
the most "solid men of Boston," promising money and influence when it could be put to practical use. Happily discussing
the venture with a reporter, Benton also had something to say
about the rival company headed by his old acquaintance, Robert J. Walker: "Their very names would damn any project,
however feasible and desirable. They have enough sin in them
to sink a fleet . . . to the bottom, sir. The Czar could not better
succeed in destroying the ships of the allies than by smuggling
the Walker Railroad Company on board of them; they would
go down at once, sir." [24]

The Colonel's railroading did not prevent attention to his
final session of Congress. The New England Emigrant Aid Society had financed and transported several hundred settlers to
Kansas already to win the area for freedom, while in recent
weeks western Missourians by the hundred had poured across
the Kansas line to vote in territorial elections. On December 13
Representative Mace of Indiana introduced a bill to forbid
slavery forever in the territories of Kansas and Nebraska, and
the debate raged around charges and counter-charges concerning events in Kansas. Benton was grasping for support in New
England, but with a consistency all his own fired an immediate
speech back to Washington to be read by his Missouri colleague, Representative Oliver. While commending Mace's
good intentions, Benton pronounced the bill impractical and
inadvisable. It could serve no useful purpose and would only
start a new agitation which would disquiet the settlers in Kansas, retard its population, and delay the railroad. Also, any bill

refusing to admit Kansas if it wished to be a slave state would be unconstitutional. And as for events in Kansas, he considered the sins evenly balanced. Missourians had crossed the line to vote illegally, but the Emigrant Society had sent men there to control the elections. He had warned Eastern men that artificial emigration would "rouse and exasperate the people of the Missouri frontier. . . . If any emigrants came from the free States in the usual way, they would be kindly and respectfully received, but sent by societies for the purpose of governing elections, and they would meet with ill-will and opposition." The Mace bill was defeated.[25]

In January Benton resumed his seat, embarking immediately on a one-man crusade against raids on the treasury and public domain by various groups anxious to lead America forward to progress on their own terms and at a price. On January 16 he delivered his railroad oration, again defending the central route and his program for private financing. He "would have preferred that Congress should have made the road, as a national work, on a scale commensurate to its grandeur, and let out the use of it to companies, who would fetch and carry on the best terms for the people and the Government," but this being impossible, a private road was now the preference. Above all, Old Bullion fiercely condemned "all plans for making private roads at national expense—of paying for the use of roads built with our land and money—of bargaining with corporators or individuals for the use of what we give them." Any such effort, said Benton, would result in the public being cheated like Moses Primrose in the *Vicar of Wakefield* when he sold the family horse for a gross of green spectacles. For once the future was slipping away from Benton. No one had done more to agitate and popularize the concept of transcontinental railroads, but the road would never be built by the solid, impeccably conservative businessmen on Benton's list. The Civil War would soon place America's technical and industrial progress squarely in the hands of a new race of adventurers, working in partnership with the Government to create, indeed, a new America of incomparable wealth and power, but at a sacrifice in public wealth, political morality, and democratic values greater even than Benton had feared.

The age of the Great Barbecue was coming closer, but the old order continued to speak through the voice of Benton. The Senate passed a bill offering extensive land grants and mail subsidies to any private corporation willing to undertake a railroad on any or all of three routes—West Texas to California, Missouri or Iowa to San Francisco, or Wisconsin to Oregon. The House engaged in other matters and perhaps fearful of a new deluge of Bentonian oratory, never brought the measure to a vote.

The Senate also passed a bill granting two million acres to a private firm as compensation for a projected subterranean telegraph line to California. Benton kept the House roaring with laughter at his discourse on the habits of the digger Indians, who would surely find this transcontinental "mole-track" and dig up the wire for use in spearing lizards. Even with guards straddling the line, the Indians would creep up at night and "cut it under them." This would all "be a God-send to the Indians, but destruction to the lizards." When proponents countered with a substitute surrendering the entire land grant, Old Bullion's indignation blazed forth. Yesterday they had fought all afternoon until he had "set the lizards upon them," insisting on two million acres; now, within twenty-four hours the entire demand had been dropped. This was "making a sport of legislation and of the property of the United States." How "disreputable to the American Congress to suffer such games of brag to be played upon it." The old man had done his work. The House passed the bill after striking out "subterranean" and eliminating the land grant, and the Senate accepted the amendments. The telegraph furrow was never plowed.[26]

Benton's last week in Congress began on Monday, February 26, and was as active and exhausting as any he had ever known. On Monday the House passed a resolution accepting the donation of Andrew Jackson's sword, and Benton rose proudly to deliver the major oration of the day. It was a splendid effort, concise but comprehensive, as Old Bullion vigorously retold the story of Jackson's early military exploits, not failing to recount his own role in Old Hickory's success. It was a non-partisan eulogy, but Benton took the occasion to praise a "member of a class now struck at," by lauding an Irish merchant at

Natchez who had sold shoes to Jackson's army on credit with no security. The House promptly moved to print one hundred thousand copies, and Old Bullion's brief return to past glory was shared throughout the country.[27]

Next day the old man was suffering from a bad cold, but could not stay out of the debate over a bill to give a one-hundred-and-sixty-acre land certificate to every man (or immediate heirs) who had served at least fourteen days in any warfare since 1790. To Benton the bill would be a godsend to speculators and defraud both the Government and the old soldiers. Armed with statistics from hours of research, he offered amendments, but was too hoarse to continue. His laryngitic frustrations were suddenly relieved, however, by far greater misfortune—the debate was interrupted by an announcement that Benton's house was on fire.

A defective chimney had ignited the inner walls, and the city water supply was frozen. The family was safe, but the old man could only stand helplessly in the bitter cold watching his books, papers, and personal possessions disappear in the flames. A host of people, including President Pierce, offered him lodging, but daughter Jessie lived only a few doors away, and there he settled until the house could be rebuilt. There was no insurance, but Benton's real grief was over the loss of such treasures as Elizabeth's personal effects and his precious books. There was but one consolation: "it makes dying easier; there is so much less to leave." [28]

Also lost were his manuscript and notes for the second volume of the *Thirty Years' View,* but the author unhesitatingly assured his publishers that the book would soon be rewritten.

It was all a dreadful shock, but next day the Colonel was in his usual place delivering a long speech against the land bounty bill. He had "arrived at that age, and at that state of feeling— particularly on *this* day—(alluding to the invaluable losses in his house, still smoking in view of the Capitol) which would render it impossible . . . to rise and speak . . . except under an inexorable sense of duty." The bill would rob the American people, and he must oppose it to the end. He presented a long, detailed review of the abuses resulting from past laws, minute in comparison to the one proposed, but all in vain. The bill

passed and ultimately fulfilled his worst predictions.[29] Its harm-
ful effects were alleviated only by America's limitless land resources and the final enactment of a homestead bill in 1862.
The homestead law was the final triumph for Benton's lifelong
philosophy of the earth as "the gift of God to man."

On March 1 Benton delivered his final judgment on the regular army and its western Indian policies. The Indian wars, he
said, were caused by removal of faithful and experienced Indian
agents in favor of "ignorant, unfit, mendicant politicians,"
and the sending of "school-house officers and pot-house soldiers
to treat the Indians as beasts and dogs." Lewis and Clark, Frémont, Carson, Beale, and the mountainmen had always moved
among the Indians in perfect safety, but the army with its foolish depredations was now forcing the Indians to fight back.
Repeating story after story from firsthand witnesses and semi-
official reports, Benton demonstrated conclusively, at least to
his own satisfaction, that American army misdeeds had caused
most of the recent troubles. His recommendations: send plains-
men who actually knew the Indians to make peace, and keep
the Indians in check with a version of his old Florida plan—
ranger companies to be rewarded with homesteads. It was the
only speech defending Indians Benton ever made, but was a
long and eloquent effort, ending with a plea for America to
examine its history and "try to settle, with all possible gentleness, these calamitous Indian wars, of which our own dreadful
misconduct has been too much the cause." [30]

The session ended on March 4 after running continuously
from Saturday morning until Sunday noon. Time and again
no quorum was present, and the sergeant-at-arms was sent out
to arrest absentees and bring them in. The usual custom of
requiring absentees to explain their absences and ask to be excused was waived, despite protests by some members. On Sunday morning Benton decided that the session had legally ended,
and in the midst of much confusion and a quorum-hunting fo-
ray appeared in the doorway to inform the Speaker *pro tem-
pore* in a loud voice that as an ex-member of Congress he
would sue anyone calling his name or seeking to arrest him.
The harassed Speaker, Orr of South Carolina, was no Benton
friend anyhow, and amid laughter and loud cries of "Good,"

answered: "If the gentleman from Missouri is not a member . . . the Doorkeeper will keep him outside the Hall." A great career had ended on a note of comic-opera tragedy.[31]

*   *   *   *   *   *   *

In late March Benton and Susan went to St. Louis for Elizabeth's final burial in the new and beautiful Bellefontaine Cemetery. The St. Louis funeral, like most such affairs, served mainly to renew the sufferings of the chief mourner. When the casket was carried into the church, Benton sat "convulsed with emotion," and tears of sympathy flowed freely among the observers. After a long and glowing tribute to the deceased, Elizabeth was laid to rest beside Nancy Benton and sons McDowell and Randolph. Another major chapter of Thomas Hart Benton's life had closed.

In June Susan was married to Gauldrée de Boileau, Secretary of the French Legation, and like her sisters was destined for a long and happy union. Benton was now alone, but work remained to be done, and the old man was not yet ready to retire into his memories. His beloved America was still in danger, and he would never be too old for battle in its defense.

CHAPTER XXI

———◦∞◦———

THE PEACEMAKER

FOR THE NEXT several months Benton labored from dawn till midnight rewriting his second volume, breaking the routine only with a daily hour or so on horseback. In May, 1856, the massive 788-page work was finished. The sale was less brisk than that of Volume I, but despite the author's handicaps and setbacks the book was the more profound volume of the two. His interpretation of the sectional struggle, beginning in the first and reaching its climax in the second work, contained many ideas and insights which historians would rediscover only after many decades of historical rationalization by sectional partisans. The South's relative economic decline after its early days of wealth, power, and baronial status; the resulting sensitivity and susceptibility to exaggerations of the abolition danger; the role of Calhoun in stirring up Southern fears; the unwise conduct of Southern extremists continuing through Calhoun's nullification, the petition struggle, the Texas and Mexican War questions, and the impractical and impossible Southern demands in the territories—these themes were all developed carefully. Step by step the author quoted his past arguments to prove that the South was in no real danger if it would turn away from the demands of pride and face reality. Northern support for slavery extensions such as removal of Southern Indians to make room for slaveholders, the addition of the

Platte region to Missouri, and the annexation of Texas; the collection of slave indemnities from Britain in 1827 by Northern commissioners; the complete absence of any Congressional pressure, or even taxation, against slavery; and the ever-rising slave prices—to Benton all these were proofs that slavery was safe if the South would accept Northern assurances at face value and stop needless agitations. The Southern demands, he wrote, could lead only to separation, a false remedy which would bring war and perpetual animosities. His treatment of the abolitionists, however, was equally harsh. "Truly," he wrote, "the abolitionists and the nullifiers were necessary to each other —the two halves of a pair of shears, neither of which could cut until joined together. Then the map of the Union was in danger. . . ."

In conclusion, the author had "seen the capacity of the people for self-government tried at many points, and always found equal to the occasion." Two questions, however, remained: whether Presidential elections should be "governed by the virtue and intelligence of the people, or . . . become the spoil of intrigue and corruption?" and whether nationalism should "remain co-extensive with the Union, leading to harmony and fraternity; or, divide into sectionalism, ending in hate, alienation, separation, and civil war." He hoped the book would help rouse the people to a resumption of their electoral privileges and the suppression of sectional contention, but if not, his consolation would be knowing that he had "labored in his day and generation, to preserve and perpetuate the blessings of that Union and self-government which wise and good men gave us."

In the spring of 1856 friends again begged him to be a Presidential candidate, but the old man answered that "no earthly consideration" could make him accept. He had spent thirty years "in a contest of great principles—of great measures—of great men," and could not "wear out the remainder of . . . [his] days in a slavery agitation, either on the one side or the other of it." The country must have a new candidate "unconnected with the agitation." [1]

The Old Roman instead had a new project in view. He would now abridge the debates of Congress from 1789 to 1850 into readable form for ordinary readers and then continue his history from 1850 to the day of his death. The excellent reviews and unusual sale of his books had convinced him that in this new calling he could be the most useful and, like his favorite, Burke, add the most luster to his future reputation.

As the self-appointed Thucydides labored at his *Abridgment,* his beloved party continued to crack apart at the seams. In Kansas, violence and political fraud not appreciably worse than that in most early frontier situations were being exaggerated and distorted by skilled reporters and eloquent politicians into "Bleeding Kansas," the battleground between slavery and freedom. Perhaps Benton's own analysis was indicated by his letter to Bryant at the New York *Post* urging editorials against the violence of recent elections in Kansas, St. Louis, and Louisville—clearly placing all in the same class.[2]

As the election of 1856 approached, such events began to hammer the scattered elements of older parties into a new one. Northwestern Democrats angry over Kansas, old-line Whigs seeking a political haven, abolitionists and Free-Soilers, and various remnants of the old Jacksonian Democracy, buried their obvious differences in the common ground of opposition to slave extension, and united to form the new Republican Party. Leading the parade was the old "pro," Francis P. Blair, who for the first time since 1844 found himself in a position for effective political action. The new party could not persuade Benton to be a candidate, but for the "new man" they selected the romantic knight of the plains, John C. Frémont. Blair was certain Frémont's father-in-law would exert the influence necessary to swing the election. Frémont, with an heroic legend and a genuinely honorable character, despite his occasional ineptitude, was a shrewd choice. He would not even be on the ballot in the South, however, and an ominous rumble of secession threats could soon be heard.

Benton had loved, helped, and defended Frémont for fourteen years. Frémont's election would mean the vindication of all of Benton's often-tested faith, and would undoubtedly make him the power behind the throne. Whether or not the old man was tempted, he did not hesitate. He could never support a sectional party which might divide the Union. For months before the nomination he sought to persuade Frémont to re-

fuse any such offer. Daughter Jessie, however, chose to agree
with "Father Blair," and the Frémont wing of the Benton family went its own way. Frémont was nominated, and Benton
found himself estranged from many of those he had loved most
—Jessie, Frémont, the Blairs, and many lifelong political
friends.

His own Presidential decision had already been made. In
early June, Benton for once stopped denouncing the wickedness
of the convention system and entrained for Cincinnati to play
his role in selecting the Democratic candidate. Above all he
went to work against Pierce and Douglas as candidates rousing
nothing but bad passions between the sections. His own choice
was James Buchanan, "never a leading man in any high sense,"
but "eminently a man of peace." Buchanan had been Minister
to England for the past four years, and was unconnected with
Kansas-Nebraska. In his hotel quarters Benton received a
steady stream of callers and lobbied hot and heavy for Buchanan. On the seventeenth ballot Old Buck was nominated as
Old Bullion sat rubbing his hands with happy satisfaction.[3]

When the Know-Nothings had nominated former President
Fillmore, the Presidential line-up was complete.

In Missouri, meanwhile, Frank Blair, though angry over
Benton's refusal to permit the launching of a full-scale Frémont
movement there, still hoped for a change of heart, and managed to get Benton nominated for the governorship by the still-
strong liberal faction in St. Louis.

The surprised Benton did not answer until after the nomination of Buchanan, but on June 7 announced his decision.
Led "by no paltry calculation of the chances of an election, but
wholly and entirely upon considerations of public good," he
would accept. The nomination of Buchanan had determined
his course, and he would be explicit: "I consider him the safest
chance for preserving the peace of the country . . . and . . .
hold it to be the duty of those who are in favor of that object
to assist in his election. . . ." Soon he announced a schedule of
twenty speeches at twenty-one towns in forty days. He was
seventy-four now, but he still rode a horse with the grace and
endurance of youth, and would end the campaign boasting that
while *"seventy-four* upon the calendar," he was *"only fifteen*

upon the turf." On one occasion his carriage sank in a stream, and the passengers were doused up to the neck, but he emerged no worse for wear. From beginning to end his message was the same: almost no mention of the governorship, a fierce denunciation of Pierce, Douglas, and the repeal of the Missouri Compromise, and an eloquent plea for Buchanan's election as America's best hope for peace. The Pierce administration "had done one thing which was thought to be impossible: made the Administration of John Tyler respectable." [4]

Family sacrifice won Benton no forgiveness from his old enemies. The Democratic Washington *Union* and Washington *Star* refused to believe their own eyes, and charged a secret intrigue whereby Benton was trying to throw Missouri to the Know-Nothings and cause a situation requiring an election in the House of Representatives. The Missouri anti-Benton Democrats, themselves pledged to Buchanan, could only spend their time also in manufacturing false plots by which Benton, by supporting Buchanan, was scheming to elect Frémont and become the power behind the throne.

It was Benton's last tour among his people, and it was a glorious effort. Everywhere he drew huge crowds, and listeners long remembered the white-haired old "Tribune of the People," in his final great performance. Back in St. Louis after the tour, he spoke outdoors to a throng measured in acres who responded with several minutes of deafening cheers.

On August 4 Missouri voted, and Benton ran well ahead in the St. Louis district. In the hinterland, however, Bleeding Kansas and his kinship with Frémont were too much. For the first time, the anti-Benton Democrats won a major election. State-wide, the old veteran ran last, but he had expected nothing else, and his real purpose had been accomplished. His audiences had included those most likely to vote for Frémont, and the possibility that Frémont might draw enough Missouri votes to throw Missouri to Fillmore had been crippled. His influence for Buchanan across the nation may also have been great—Blair feared it would be decisive.

Back in Washington the old man returned to his *Abridgment*. By the end of September, Blair, though still "in an exceedingly ill humor" with his old friend, happily reported to

Van Buren that Jessie had visited her father and that he had forgiven Blair to the point of coming out to dine with him.[5]

As the Frémont campaign continued to gather last-minute steam, Benton reached a spontaneous decision. On November 3 a slow-moving, uncomfortable train rattled up to the eastern side of the Mississippi across from St. Louis. Sitting muffled unobtrusively in a corner where he had been without sleep for two days and three nights was a tired but still-indomitable old man.[6] Forty-one years earlier he had stood eagerly on the prow of a boat watching a tiny frontier village take shape. True to his dream, it was now a great city stretching toward the one-hundred-fifty-thousand mark in population. Frank Blair had built a strong following for Frémont, and the city's vote might change the fate of America. Thomas Hart Benton knew this, and had come for a last persuasive effort.

Surprised friends hastily arranged for him to speak, and on a dark, stormy election eve, Thomas Hart Benton delivered his last message to the people of Missouri. One listener later described it as a speech "no other living man could make." To the Know-Nothings Benton recommended a reading of the early debates in his *Abridgment*—here they would find all there was to say about the naturalization laws. About Fillmore himself he would say nothing. "Next," said the old patriarch,

> is Mr. Frémont, standing near to me, in a relation dear as it could be to me not to be my own child. He has had an eventful life— great difficulties, great dangers, great trials to undergo. I stood by him in every one of them as a father would stand by a child. [*Long continued applause.*]
>
> . . . I spared nothing which I could raise and deliver him, in order to carry him through the eventful life in which he was engaged . . . knowing from the first that Mr. Frémont was to be the candidate of a sectional party, I told him from the beginning that it was impossible that I could support any such nomination. [*Cheers.*] No matter what came, he must be national, he must have a vision that could look over the Union. He must not be on a dividing line, he must be national, or I cannot [*sic*] only not support him but I must take ground against him.

The Missouri Compromise, he continued, was a measure of peace to keep the Union together and had been destroyed for wanton purposes. Once destroyed, however, he and Buchanan had opposed its revival because such an effort would only renew the agitation. Buchanan was now the best hope for peace. "I look to the peace of this land, the world's last hope for a free government on the earth." And once elected, Buchanan would need all possible aid. America was in grave danger, and there was but one remedy: "Do justice to all, administer the Constitution in its proper spirit," and "give to all its compromises full and free sway." Southern nullification and Northern abolition were the twin perils, but by abolitionist he meant no man opposed to extension of slavery where it did not already exist. Here Benton paid a tribute to a great lifelong opponent. Henry Clay, he said, "loomed colossally in the Senate . . . as he rose declaring that for no earthly purpose, no earthly object could he carry slavery into places where it did not exist before. [Cheers.] At the same time he would bare his breast against any infraction, against the rights of the slaveholder wherever it existed. . . . It was a great and proud day for Mr. Clay. . . . I could have wished that I had spoken the same words. I speak them now, telling you they were his, and adopting them as my own."

He had come, the old giant concluded, not to make arguments and seek to change minds at such a late date, "but to show myself among you, to look you in the face and let you see that I am one of you here in this last trial." [7]

Buchanan was elected, but runner-up Frémont did surprisingly well and he and Fillmore together had a solid majority. Benton's influence could not be measured, but as the results became known at Frémont's headquarters, Jessie could only admit that "Colonel Benton, I perceive, has the best of this family argument." Francis P. Blair in a voice choked with tears added, "Tom Benton's stubborn stand cost us many a vote outside Missouri." [8]

The outdoor air and exercise of the campaign appeared to renew Benton's strength, and after election he embarked on a lengthy lecture tour of New England, covering sixteen towns in a month and ending finally back in New York City. In the larger cities his fee was two hundred dollars, but with Benton money was "not the object of the lecture, tho not overlooked in the calculation. A great public object" required him to speak "in towns and villages as well as in large cities," and such a fee would not be expected where it could not be afforded. Everywhere his message was an eloquent appeal to national spirit, a dire warning of the fearful results of a separation, and a plea for the North to understand the South and stop all irritating agitation against the institution of slavery. The abolitionists, he charged, only played into the hands of Southern extremists trying to deceive the Southern people into thinking the North filled with aggressive intentions against slavery.

From January through March, 1857, the old peacemaker toured New England again and then swung through some twenty appearances in upstate New York. He enjoyed the income, prestige, and attention, but his purpose went far deeper and rested again on his prophetic vision. "Circumstances," he wrote Van Buren, "have enabled the disunion party to get control of public sentiment in the slave States, and to divide it in the free States. . . . If Mr. Buchanan continues the policy of the present administration, the Union will approach its last days, and to save it in 1860 will require all its friends, forgetting everything else, to stand together. The next presidential convention is to be held at Charleston, S. C., and a disunionist, or a tool, is intended to be nominated." Benton, however, would never give up. He had "an object in view, and a plan for its execution," and would "work at it for four years." [9]

In late February he received a shock from his Missouri friends. The Missouri General Assembly passed a resolution against emancipation over the opposition of Benton's younger friends like Gratz Brown and Frank Blair, who cited Benton in their arguments. The Old Roman immediately hurled a public letter denouncing this use of his name: "To add a State slavery agitation to the National agitation, at the very moment when we were opposing a National agitation, was an incredible thing. . . . For persons calling themselves my friends to attack the whole policy of my life . . . is the *Greatest outrage I have ever experienced.*" The St. Louis *Missouri Democrat* under Brown's editorship had been a staunch supporter for years, but soon Benton was urging more conservative friends to get control of the paper and change its name and character because it was agitating for state emancipation against his own well-known views.[10]

In March Grandfather Benton enjoyed a happy family reunion among daughters, sons-in-law, and grandchildren, when the entire tribe gathered at the Frémont home in New York for a farewell to Susan, whose husband had been appointed French Consul General in Calcutta, India. In April he took his last trip west, visiting daughter Sarah en route and continuing on to St. Louis for a brief stay with friends. His lecture schedule was again full, however, and he was soon swinging back through the Northwest for lectures in Chicago, Cleveland, and Pittsburgh.

En route to Pittsburgh, the train jumped the track, flinging Benton's car on its side. Many people were badly injured, and Benton suffered a badly cut head and painfully bruised back. With his usual determination and sense of the dramatic, however, the old man insisted upon walking and delivering his speech, although compelled to lean on a chair while speaking. Three weeks later he was still in pain and could not sit a horse. His travels were over.[11]

There was still plenty to do in Washington. His massive *Abridgment* was running a race with time, but the volumes were beginning to roll off the press—five by the end of 1857, and eventually a total of sixteen. In stripping the debates of extraneous material and rendering them accessible to libraries and colleges unable to afford the original volumes, Benton was performing a notable service. In this work every side spoke for itself, and Benton hoped only that enough people would read the debates and judge for themselves.

And the politics of crisis still swirled and eddied. In March, 1857, the Supreme Court reached a momentous ruling. Slave Dred Scott had been taken from Missouri to free territory by his army-doctor master and then returned to Missouri, apparently without protest. His master had then died, and the widow had married an abolitionist. All parties agreed that Scott was in fact to be set free, but to get a judicial ruling on the principle involved Scott was financed in a suit for freedom on the grounds of his residence in free territory. On previous occasions the High Court had ruled such questions beyond its jurisdiction, and this was the actual ruling in the Scott case. When two justices dissented, however, the Court's majority, led by Benton's old friend Taney, issued a long, unnecessary, unwise, and constitutionally fallacious statement of principle on the merits of the case. In effect the Court ruled that the Constitution automatically covered all United States territories, that slaves as property were protected by the Constitution in all territories, and that the already-repealed Missouri Compromise had been unconstitutional from the beginning.

The Dred Scott decision could not impose slavery upon a single western territory. As in the case of Kansas-Nebraska, however, this fact was not at all clear to the Northern public. Again a roar of indignant fury resounded throughout the North, and the Republican Party had another issue to go with Bleeding Kansas.

To Benton the decision was the height of constitutional sophistry, and duty required the exposure of its errors. Writing with incredible speed he soon produced a 192-page book devoted to an *Historical and Legal Examination* of the case. The first hundred and thirty pages comprised one of the most meticulous, thoroughly documented, and closely reasoned pieces of historical research ever done on a single subject of constitutional law. The decision's worst crime—instead of settling the question, the opinion itself had "become a new question, more virulent than the former." The citizens of each state, he reasoned, were equal in capacity to carry property into the territories, but every such citizen must accept the property laws of his new territorial residence. Otherwise, the differing and conflicting property laws of the various former homes of a territory's citizens would create a mad babel of confusion. Thus, slavery had been carried into the Missouri, Arkansas, and Florida territories, not by the Constitution, but because the people in those areas wanted it. Precedent after precedent Benton cited to show that Congress had always ruled the territories. The Northwest Ordinance, written by Jefferson and supported by Southerners, had been enacted by the Congress under the old Articles of Confederation and re-enacted by the Federal Congress, with no pretense that the Constitution was involved. North Carolina and Georgia had ceded their western lands to the Federal Government, asking that the anti-slave restriction be lifted, which indicated clearly their acceptance of the right of Congress to make the decision. The Louisiana Territory had been ruled for several years by the President and Congress simply assuming the functions of the Spanish officials under a system wholly incompatible with the American Constitution. Jackson had been sustained when he had refused to grant habeas corpus in Florida on the grounds that the Constitution did not apply there. An anti-slavery restriction for the Arkansas Territory had been defeated in a fierce debate, but no constitutional objections had been offered. The Missouri Compromise had been supported by most Southerners, and of the forty-two dissenters in the House, not one offered a constitutional objection. Calhoun himself had supported the Missouri Compromise and had written its principle into the joint resolution which annexed Texas in 1845. The South had voted overwhelmingly for extension of the Compromise line to the Pacific in 1847 and 1848. And in 1850 an amendment to the same effect had received twenty-four Senate votes—all Southern. The superior reasoning of the Founding Fathers and the practices of two generations of American statesmen acting in calmer times, he concluded, clearly deserved more weight than the views of six judges moving in an atmosphere of bitter partisanship.

The final sixty pages reviewed his attacks against repeal of the Compromise in 1854 and his usual analysis of the sectional conflict. To include as abolitionists all those defending the Missouri Compromise, he said, was "to libel ninety-five per centum of the population of the free States." The conflict resulted "exclusively from the nullifiers and the abolitionists playing into each other's hand . . . as indispensable to each other as the two halves of a pair of shears, neither of which can cut without being joined to the other."

Benton informed friends that he had written his *Examination* for mass distribution to overthrow the politicians who made such decisions, and that the volume must get "into the hands of the masses, & become a household book." [12] Perhaps this comment revealed a major key to Benton's political misfortunes. Thomas Hart Benton really did believe that ordinary

Americans would read, understand, and appreciate his book of dull and unemotional, even if soundly reasoned, arguments. His idol, Jefferson, had believed the people to be the safest repository of power. Benton had gone a step further, becoming dedicated to the proposition that the people were also somehow gifted with an inherent wisdom in all matters related to their welfare. This faith had been shaken somewhat by the election of Harrison in 1840, but he had explained all such mistakes since in terms of the corrupt convention system thwarting the popular will, and never ceased to believe that the people would follow the right voices if the voices could be heard. Benton's greatest victory, the bank struggle, had been won because his interminable speeches had coincided with popular emotions toward both the bank and Jackson personally. His twenty-four years of invincibility in Missouri had rested largely upon his devotion to land policies which stimulated not wisdom, but the simplest of selfish motivations. He would never have admitted these facts, however, and had learned few political lessons from them.

Despite the vigorous personal quality of his Missouri campaigning since 1843, the essence of his efforts had been a complex and involved appeal to reason on issues loaded with emotional dynamite. He had made no effort to conciliate, cajole, flatter, or win converts among either neutrals or enemies, trusting implicitly in the capacity of his people to recognize the wisdom of his ideas. True, the emotional weapons had been in the hands of his foes, but a skilled conciliator might have fared much better. Benton was to a degree the victim of the weaknesses of an immature democracy which he himself had helped create but never did fully understand. Jacksonian Democracy was created by, and in turn helped develop, an America in which the successful political leader would need more than devotion to a righteous cause and a capacity for profound reasoning. Benton had helped teach this painful fact to President John Quincy Adams in 1828, but had never fully learned it for himself. With politics offering ever greater rewards, the party system inevitably led to an exaggeration of differences, a stress upon emotional issues, and fierce contests for the support of an electorate entirely too ill-informed and personally involved for the impersonal, objective, wise reasoning expected by Benton. This did not mean that Benton's faith in democracy was misplaced. America would prove many times that a mass electorate can produce, choose, and follow wise decisions and leadership, but successful leadership in a democracy would more and more require an understanding and acceptance of human weaknesses and willingness and ability to deal with them at their own level. Abraham Lincoln answered the Dred Scott decision with "A house divided against itself cannot stand." The statement was not necessarily true, and his following implied warning that America might become all slave was absurd, but Lincoln's words had more effect than all of Benton's 192 pages.

* * * * * * *

America desperately needed its elder statesmen, but even Thomas Hart Benton could not last forever. Advanced age and the exertions of a dynamo had scarcely slowed his headlong pace, but in September, 1857, an advanced intestinal cancer struck an almost fatal blow. For two weeks he lay at the point of death, fretting all the while over the delay in the writing of his Dred Scott *Examination*. His doctor was certain the end was at hand, but Benton, like Jackson before him, would not die with a task unfinished. Soon he was back at his desk and again able to take short walks and occasional rides on horseback. At the end of the *Examination* the author had to apologize for two topics left undeveloped because of his illness.

Through the winter he slaved over the *Abridgment*. In March, 1858, Volume VI, carrying the debates through 1821, was published. The author was far ahead of the publishers, but running neck and neck in the race with his disease. By the end of March he found relief from pain only when lying down, but converted his bedroom into a study and kept on working.

The Frémonts had returned from Europe after his September attack, but in February the old man persuaded Jessie that his recovery was well-advanced, and she and Frémont departed for California. Susan by now was in Paris, but daughters Eliza and Sarah, with their husbands, came to Washington to take charge of their dying father. The faithful William Carey Jones,

husband of Eliza, served as secretary, gathering materials and
taking dictation as Benton lay with his bed covered with books
and papers. Bearing his pain "with a stoicism almost super-
human," the invalid continued to assure Blair daily that he was
better. Blair kept Van Buren, also seventy-six, informed of the
condition of "Our friend Col. Benton"—"His patience & tenderness to attendants is amazing & love for his friends in-
creases as his vitality decreases." [13]

Even at the point of death, Benton had to borrow a thousand
dollars to meet expenses. The scattered estates in Virginia,
Kentucky, and Missouri which had supported his long career
were gone, the rebuilding of his house had required a ten-
thousand-dollar mortgage, and expected funds from publishers
were his only resource. His elaborate will would be negated by
a provision that all debts be paid first.

On April 4 Lewis Cass called, remembering later that Benton had had nothing but kind words for the Buchanan administration. On April 6 Blair found his beloved old friend too
weak to move and barely able to whisper, but later recalled a
long Bentonian denunciation of Buchanan for supporting the
pro-slave Kansas Lecompton Constitution. Three evenings
later President Buchanan himself came. Sarah Jacob heard her
father whisper to Buchanan that they were friends, even though
they had "differed on many points." The President must "look
to a higher power" for support and guidance. The dying man's
last thoughts would later be the subject of a bitter public controversy, but in all likelihood Cass, Blair, and Buchanan themselves did most of the talking, and their host for once did not
choose to argue. All remembered his concern for his beloved
Union and its future trials.[14]

On April 8, following the example of his long-dead friend,
Randolph, Benton penned a note to another lifelong friend,
Sam Houston, requesting that Congress take no formal notice
of his death.

He had resolved to abridge the debates through 1850, and
was especially anxious to get the great Compromise speeches of
Clay and Webster again before the public. Death, therefore,
would have to wait until the task was finished. On April 9 the
last word of Volume XVI was dictated, and the great work was

done. He had already had a final consultation with the clergy
and could now die in peace. In the evening he assured his
children that the concern of old comrades had made him happy
and that he was *"comfortable and content."* A few hours later
he beckoned Kitty, his faithful black nurse, to the bedside and
whispered. "I shall not trouble you much longer—Do you
hear that?" She laid her ear against his chest. "Kitty that is
the death rattle." At seven-thirty, Saturday morning, April 10,
1858, he was dead. A giant had passed.[15]

*   *   *   *   *   *   *   *

Two days later the family suffered a second tragedy. Eliza's
little son, McDowell, suddenly fell ill and followed his grandfather in death.

On a stormy, rainy April 12, a large and distinguished
throng, including the President, braved the elements to attend the double funeral at the Benton home. Grandfather and
grandson, "the gray haired and the sunny haired," lay side by
side. After an eloquent Presbyterian sermon, the funeral procession moved slowly through the rain-swept streets to the rail-
way station. The towering form of Sam Houston stood head
and shoulders above most of the mourners.

In St. Louis the people of a stunned and silent city measured
their loss and awaited the fallen giant with black-draped buildings and tear-stained faces. Steamboat flags flew at half-mast,
and all business stopped. On a store front near the courthouse
hung a large crepe-bordered lithograph of Benton and an in-
scription on canvas:

> Among the foremost men in all this land,
> The great Missourian stood pre-eminent;
> A man whom gold could neither buy nor bribe,
> Nor smooth-faced flattery, with soft tongues reduce,
> Nor domineering clans nor cliques control.
> "Old Bullion" was no disrespectful name;
> His words were gold, coined in the mint of mind;
> In council wise, in battle always brave—
> A statesman—scholar—hero—gentleman!

For more than twenty-four hours the body lay in state on a
platform in the black-draped but brilliantly lighted Mercantile

Library Hall, and thousands upon thousands filed by for a last look. The funeral day dawned inauspiciously—heavy rain had fallen all night and the streets were wet and muddy—but before time for the services the sun "shone resplendently, and dispelled every trace in the heavens of storm and cloud. . . . Immense multitudes of people . . . of every age and condition, thronged the streets. Balconies and windows, and even roofs of the houses along the line of march arranged for the solemn cortege to pass, were throbbing with life. The thoroughfares were so densely packed, that it was with difficulty any could move." [16]

The two caskets were carried to the altar together, and after another long Presbyterian sermon, the endless procession of tearful mourners began the slow march to Bellefontaine Cemetery. At the grave there was music by the German Singing Associations and a final brief service.

The long struggle of Benton had ended. The tragedy from which he had labored to save America still lay ahead. The democracy in which he had believed would stand firm, however, and the nation he had called "the world's last hope for a free government on the earth" would survive. Perhaps the contentment of his final hours rested in part upon the instinctive faith that this would be so.

NOTES

Documentation of facts clearly established by earlier writers has been minimized. After combing the originals in the Library of Congress I have cited for the reader's benefit the highly accessible printed Jackson collection edited by John Spencer Bassett. I have also footnoted by theme rather than by paragraph, and thus various notes may serve as documentation for several preceding paragraphs. The following abbreviations and designations are used:

Annals	*Annals of Congress.*
CG	*Congressional Globe.*
Debates	*Register of the Debates in Congress.*
AHA, 1899	J. Franklin Jameson (ed.), "Correspondence of John C. Calhoun," *Annual Report of the American Historical Association,* 1899, II.
AHA, 1929	Robert P. Brooks and Chauncey S. Boucher (eds.), "Correspondence Addressed to John C. Calhoun, 1837-1849," *Annual Report of the American Historical Association,* 1929.
Benton MSS	Benton Collection, Missouri Historical Society, St. Louis, Mo.
VB MSS	Martin Van Buren Papers, Library of Congress.
Duke	Duke University Library.
LC	Library of Congress.
MHS	Missouri Historical Society, St. Louis.
N.C.	University of North Carolina Library.
Va.	Alderman Library, University of Virginia.

I. THE CRADLE

1. William N. Saunders (ed.), *The Colonial Records of North Carolina,* V, 591, VI, 342, 343, 399, 405, 824, 910, 1157-1158; William K. Boyd, "Some North Carolina Tracts of the Eighteenth Century," *North*

Carolina Historical Review, III, 54-55; 61-64; Nannie M. Tillie, "Political Disturbances in Colonial Granville County," *loc. cit.,* XVIII, 339-358; cf. William N. Chambers, "As the Twig Is Bent: The Family and North Carolina Years of Thomas Hart Benton," *loc. cit.,* XXVI, 387 ff.

2. Walter Clark (ed.), *The State Records of North Carolina,* XVII, 823, 833, 883, 886-887, 947, XIX, 392.
3. Jesse's many letters to Thomas Hart, 1780-1790, *Thomas J. Clay Papers,* LC; cf. Thomas H. Benton, "Autobiographical Sketch," in *Thirty Years' View,* I (1854), i. (Hereafter cited as Benton.)
4. Clark, *op. cit.,* XXVI, 1312; list of Jesse Benton's taxable property, 1788, *Orange County Records, 1788-1793,* State Department of Archives and History, Raleigh, N.C.
5. Jessie Benton Frémont, "Biographical Sketch of Senator Benton," in John Charles Frémont, *Memoirs of My Life* (1887), I, 3-4.
6. John Umstead to Thomas Hart, Oct. 24, 1791, Nancy Benton to Thomas Hart, April 25, 1792, Sept. 25, 1792, bonds of Nancy Benton to Hart, Oct. 26, 1791, Aug., 1792, *Thomas J. Clay Papers,* LC.
7. Frémont, *op. cit.,* I, 4; Benton, I, i; Benton speech, in *National Intelligencer,* Dec. 25, 1856.
8. *Faculty Records,* 1799-1814, University of North Carolina; H——, "About Thomas Hart Benton," *Charlotte Democrat,* Oct. 1, 1880, clipping in N. C.
9. *Minutes of the Philanthropic Society,* Jan., 1797-March, 1799, N. C.
10. *Faculty Records,* March 19, 1799.
11. H——, *op. cit.*
12. *Minutes of the Philanthropic Society,* 1821-1832, entry for May 9, 1827; R. D. W. Connor, *A Documentary History of the University of North Carolina* (1953), II, 405.

II. THE LAWYER

1. Benton, I, i-ii.
2. Benton to John and Nicholas P. Hardeman, Dec. 10, 1804, Benton to Captain Thomas Hardeman, Nov. 22, 1829, copies in *Benton MSS.*
3. *Williams County Minute Book* (typewritten copies in Tennessee Historical Society, Nashville), I (1800-1812), 86, 303, 399; *Impartial Review and Cumberland Repository* (Nashville), Nov. 20, 1807; Benton to Thomas Hart, March 14, 1807, *Benton MSS.*
4. *Impartial Review,* quotations from issues of Feb. 25, March 31, April 28, Sept. 29, 1808.
5. *Ibid.,* June 23, 30, July 7, July 14, 21, 28, 1808.

6. Tennessee General Assembly, 1809, *Senate Journal*, pp. 11, 21, 54-56, 64-65, 87, 150, 158-161, 165-166, 189-190, 199; Benton, I, 105-106; *Acts of Tennessee*, 1809, pp. 65-74, 809.
7. Frémont, *Memoirs*, I, 6.

III. THE SOLDIER

1. John S. Bassett (ed.), *Correspondence of Andrew Jackson*, I, 213-214. (Hereafter cited as Bassett.)
2. Benton, I, 737; "Autobiographical Sketch," p. iii.
3. Bassett, I, 220-222.
4. *Democratic Clarion and Tennessee Gazette* (Nashville), July 8, 1812. (Hereafter cited as *Clarion*.)
5. *Ibid.*, April 28, June 23, 1812. Identification of Benton as "Americus" rests entirely upon a comparison of ideas and literary style. Benton used almost identical language in later years in repeating ideas unique at the time.
6. Bassett, I, 241-242; Benton, "Autobiographical Sketch," p. iii.
7. *Clarion*, Nov. 28, Dec. 15, 22, May 19, 1812.
8. *Ibid.*
9. The following account entirely from Benton's journal, *Clarion*, Feb. 9, 16, March 9, 1813.
10. Entire quarrel traced letter by letter, *Clarion*, Feb. 23, March 2, March 9, May 5, 1813.
11. Bassett, I, 307.
12. *Ibid.*, I, 311.
13. Statement of Carroll, Oct. 24, 1824; Bassett, I, 311-312.
14. Bassett, I, 309-310.
15. *Ibid.*, I, 310-315.
16. The actual battle has been described many times and requires no documentation. The somewhat unique rules of the Carroll-Benton duel have usually been ignored.
17. William N. Chambers, "Thwarted Warrior," *The East Tennessee Historical Society's Publications*, No. 22, pp. 38-39.
18. Bassett, II, 23, 47-49.
19. Oct. 25, 1814, *Jackson MS*, LC; Bassett, II, 65-66.

IV. THE MISSOURIAN

1. Benton to Governor James Preston, May 17, 1817, Nov. 14, 1819, copies in *Benton MSS;* Timothy Flint, *Recollections of the Last Ten Years* (1826), pp. 107-120; J. Thomas Scharf, *History of St. Louis City*

and County (1883), I, 192-193, 195, 277, 359, 1014-1015. The Scharf *History* is poorly organized, but it is an invaluable collection of documents, early contemporary accounts, newspaper clippings, and other original sources quoted in detail. (Hereafter cited as Scharf.)

2. Frémont, *Memoirs,* I, 9-10.
3. Flint, *op. cit.,* p. 179.
4. Frémont, *Memoirs,* I, 7-9; Scharf, I, 153, 200; various letters of and related to Benton's nephews and nieces of St. Louis in *Benton MSS.*
5. Scharf, I, 823-826, 829-830.
6. Benton to Governor Preston, May 20, 1818, photostat in *Benton MSS.*
7. Benton to Preston, Nov. 14, 1819, *Benton MSS.*
8. John F. Darby, *Personal Recollections* (1880), pp. 90-92, 97, 174; Scharf, I, 331-334.
9. Scharf, I, 560.
10. Documents in Duels Envelope, MHS; Scharf, II, 1854.
11. Benton statement, Aug. 13, 1816, *Benton MSS.*
12. Original documents and various pamphlets in MHS; contemporary accounts by Thomas C. Gannt, Judge Lucas, and others quoted in Scharf, I, 589-591, II, 1850-1853; E. B. Washburne, *Historical Sketch of Charles S. Hempstead* (1875), pp. 6, 8; cf. William M. Meigs, *The Life of Thomas Hart Benton* (1904), pp. 105-116.
13. *Missouri Gazette* Supplement, July 25, 1819.
14. *Missouri Gazette,* Feb. 20, March 6, 13, April 24, Sept. 4, 11, 18, 1818; John Ray Cable, *The Bank of the State of Missouri* (1823), pp. 58, 62-63, 67, 69; *American State Papers, Finance,* IV, 758.
15. Frémont, *Memoirs,* I, 9-10; Benton's many later speeches on the subject.
16. Scharf, I, 902, 907.
17. Scattered issues of *St. Louis Enquirer,* 1819-1820; cf. Perry McCandless, "The Rise of Thomas H. Benton in Missouri Politics," *Missouri Historical Review,* L, 18-19.
18. "Selections from Editorial Articles from the *St. Louis Enquirer* on Oregon and Texas, as Originally Published in that Paper, 1818-1819," MHS; Benton, I, 15-18, 109-110; Meigs, *op. cit.,* 91-95.
19. Darby, *op. cit.,* pp. 25-33.
20. Benton, I, 5-6.
21. Benton to Nancy Benton, Dec. 13, 1820, to Robert Wash, March 24, 1821, to General John Preston, Aug. 4, Nov. 21, Dec. 1, 1821, *Benton MSS;* Benton to James McDowell, April 21, 1821, *McDowell MSS,* Va.; Benton to James P. Preston, Dec. 20, 1820, March 20, 1821, to General John Preston, Dec. 16, 1821, photostats in *Benton MSS.*

V. THE SENATOR

1. Cited by Ernest Sutherland Bates, *The Story of Congress, 1789-1935* (1936), p. 111.
2. E. D. Keyes, *Fifty Years' Observation of Men and Events* (1884), pp. 117, 147, 403; Oliver Dyer, *Great Senators of the United States Forty Years Ago* (1889), pp. 196-217; Grace Greenwood (Sarah J. Lippincott), *Greenwood Leaves* (1851), pp. 322-323; Darby, *op. cit.,* p. 188; Ben Perley Poore, *Perley's Reminiscences, or Sixty Years in the National Metropolis* (1886), I, 65-68; William C. Kennerly, *Persimmon Hill, A Narrative of Old St. Louis and the Far West* (1948), p. 77, to mention only a few sources.
3. Benton, I, 45, 57-58, 114, 473-475; Poore, *op. cit.,* I, 66-68.
4. Benton, I, 58.

VI. THE WESTERNER

1. *Annals,* XXXVIII (17 cong., 1 sess., 1821-22), 180-181, 229-234, XL (17 cong., 2 sess., 1822-23), 200, 255, XLII (18 cong., 1 sess., 1823-24), 2617, 3256 ff.; *Debates,* I (18 cong., 2 sess., 1824-25), 637, V (20 cong., 2 sess., 1828-29), 44.
2. Benton, I, 13; Hiram M. Chittenden, *The American Fur Trade of the Far West,* I, 382, 315.
3. Chittenden, *op. cit.,* I, 12-16, defends the system ardently.
4. *Annals,* XXXVIII, 317-331.
5. *Ibid.,* 339-343, 357; Crooks to Benton, April 1, 1822, photostat in *American Fur Company Letter Book,* II, Part 2, 1822-1825, Wisconsin Historical Society.
6. Stuart to Crooks, Nov. 22, 1822, Crooks to Benton, Dec. 31, 1822, *Letter Book,* II, Part 2, pp. 437, 381-382; Kenneth W. Porter, *John Jacob Astor* (1931), II, 705.
7. Nancy Benton to Samuel Benton, Jan. 12, 1823, copy in *Benton MSS.* William Kinney to James McDowell, Dec. 15, 1843, *McDowell MSS,* Va.
8. *Annals,* XXXVIII, 415-423.
9. *Ibid.,* XL, 431-439.
10. *Debates,* I, 689-695, 699-713, quotations, 691-692, 712-713.
11. Benton, I, 48; *Debates,* I, 109-110, 341-347, quotations, 345.
12. Examples: *Annals,* XLI, 534-541, 568, *Debates,* I, 676-677, 686, III (19 cong., 2 sess., 1826-27), 55-56, 174, 338, IV (20 cong., 1 sess., 1827-28), 109-110, 629-631, 715-719. Cf. letter to Chicago Rivers and Harbors

Convention, June 8, 1847, *Niles' Weekly Register,* LXXII (1847), 266. (Hereafter cited as *Niles.*)

13. *Annals,* XXXVIII, 465-467, XL, 238-243, quotation, 240; *Debates,* II (19 cong., 1 sess., 1825-26), 408-409, III, 52-55; U.S. vs Gear, 44 U.S., 120-132; *Statutes at Large,* IX (1845-51), 37, 146.
14. *Annals,* XLI, 582-583, *Debates,* II, 720-748, quotations, 742, 748, XIII (24 cong., 2 sess., 1836-37), 733.
15. Benton, I, 58-64, 107-108, 163-166 for basic attitudes; *Annals,* XXXVIII, 229 ff., *Debates,* I, 640-649, quotation, 641, II, 707, 766-781, III, 267-269, 498.

VII. DEMOCRATS AND POLITICIANS

1. *Annals,* XLI, 167-203, quotation, 185.
2. Meigs, *op. cit.,* pp. 141-142; Bassett, III, 159-162, 165, 176, 217.
3. *Niles,* XXXIII (1828), 376.
4. *Ibid.,* p. 51.
5. *Debates,* II, 304-341.
6. Benton, I, 70-77, 473-475; William C. Bruce, *John Randolph of Roanoke, 1773-1833* (1922), II, 356; James Parton, *Life of Andrew Jackson* (1860), III, 554.
7. *Debates,* IV, 736-786, quotations, 765-768.
8. *Ibid.,* II, 672, 707, appendix, 120-138; Benton, I, 80-87.
9. *Debates,* II, 749-753, quotation, 753, III, 40-47, IV, 483-497, quotation, 490.
10. Curtius, *Torchlight—An Examination of the Origin, Policy and Principles of the Opposition to the Administration and an Exposition of the Official Conduct of THOMAS H. BENTON, One of the Senators from Missouri (Missouri Republican* Office, 1826), MHS; David Barton to Rufus Easton, April 29, 1826, *Rufus Easton Papers,* MHS; Scharf, I, 1460-1461; Roy V. Magers, "An Early Missouri Political Feud," *Missouri Historical Review,* XXIII, 261-264.

VIII. THE SECTIONALIST

1. For contrasting viewpoints on Jackson and Jacksonian Democracy, see the works of James Parton, William McDonald, Frederick Jackson Turner, Claude Bowers, Theodore Roosevelt, Avery Craven, Marquis James, Gerald Johnson, Richard Hofstadter, Arthur Schlesinger, Jr., and others. Mr. Schlesinger's brilliantly written *Age of Jackson* clearly

exaggerates the Northeastern radical influence on the Jackson movement and divides the competing class and interest factions along lines much sharper and more distinguishable than actually existed.

2. *Debates,* V, 18-22.

3. *Ibid.,* VI (21 cong., 1 sess., 1829-30), 3-6, 22-26, quotation, 24.

4. *Ibid.,* pp. 35-41, 95-119, 418-419, 435-452, quotations, 96, 111-112.

5. *Ibid.,* pp. 106-108; cf. *Congressional Globe,* XIX (31 cong., 1 sess., 1849-50), appendix, 681. (Hereafter cited as *CG.*)

6. Benton, I, 142.

7. *Debates,* VI, 8, 9, 11.

8. *Ibid.,* pp. 172-179.

9. Benton, I, 148.

10. Benton's Americanus and LaSalle articles, *St. Louis Beacon,* July-October, 1829, copies in *Benton MSS;* Benton to Thomas H. Williams, Aug. 11, 1829, copy in *ibid.*

11. *Senate Journal* (21 cong., 1 sess., 1829-30), p. 307; *Debates,* VI, 456.

IX. THE DRAGON SLAYER

1. Ralph C. H. Catterall, *The Second Bank of the United States* (1903), pp. 29-30, 32-50, 68-113, 132-137, 145-163. This classic study is essentially pro-bank, but clearly shows the institution's weaknesses.

2. *Debates,* VII (21 cong., 2 sess., 1830-31), 46-78, quotations, 51-52, 54.

3. Cited by Schlesinger, *op. cit.,* p. 82.

4. Benton to Finis Ewing, Oct. 7, Nov. 12, Nov. 21, 1831, to Lt. Gov. Dunklin, March 26, 1832, *Benton MSS.*

5. *Debates,* VIII (22 cong., 1 sess., 1831-32), 133-134.

6. *Ibid.,* p. 972.

7. *Ibid.,* p. 1005.

8. *Ibid.,* pp. 1073, 3852.

9. *Ibid.,* pp. 1240, 1274, 1293-1296.

10. *Ibid.,* pp. 665-666.

11. *Ibid.,* pp. 566-590, quotations, 573-574, 585.

12. *Ibid.,* pp. 1096-1118, quotations, 1102, 1107, 1146; cf. Claude Bowers, *Party Battles of the Jackson Period* (1922), pp. 195-200.

13. *Historical Statistics of the United States, 1789-1945,* p. 293. Sixty representatives and eight senators classified themselves as belonging to neither major party.

X. HOUSE LAMB–STREET LION

1. Frémont, *Memoirs,* p. 7; Poore, *op. cit.,* 66-68; Charles F. Adams (ed.), *Memoirs of John Quincy Adams,* X, 257; Meigs, *op. cit.,* pp. 435-440.
2. Jessie Benton Frémont, *Souvenirs of My Time* (1887), pp. 130-141.
3. Benton to Col. James Preston, Dec. 22, 1822, photostat in *Benton MSS;* Frémont, *Souvenirs,* pp. 121-122.
4. Undated note in *Benton MSS;* Sally's letters and other family correspondence in *McDowell MSS,* Va. and Duke; cf. Frémont, *Souvenirs,* pp. 130-174; Catherine C. Phillips, *Jesse Benton Frémont* (1935), 31, 33-39.

XI. OLD BULLION

1. Benton to Van Buren, Dec. 16, 1832, Feb. 16, 1833, *VB MSS,* LC; Van Buren to Jackson, Feb. 20, 1833, Bassett, V, 20; Benton, I, 303-360; *Debates,* IX (22 cong., 2 sess., 1832-33), p. 688.
2. *Debates,* IX, 713-716, 720-725, 809; cf. *CG,* VII (26 cong., 1 sess., 1838-39), 172-173, for Clay version of the events.
3. Linn to Henry Dodge, Feb. 15, 1833, photostat in *Linn MSS,* MHS; Linn to Van Buren, April 8, 1837, *VB MSS,* XXVII.
4. Benton to Finis Ewing, July 20, 1833, *Benton MSS.*
5. *Debates,* X (23 cong., 1 sess., 1833-34), 59, 94, 58-94.
6. *Ibid.,* pp. 97-139.
7. *Ibid.,* pp. 206-223.
8. Bowers, *op. cit.,* pp. 336-337.
9. *Debates,* X, 1317-1336, 1346-1365.
10. *Ibid.,* pp. 2007-2019; Carl B. Swisher, *Roger B. Taney* (1935), 284-285. Swisher covers the deposit story thoroughly.
11. Swisher, *op. cit.,* pp. 290-292; Benton to Jackson, June 11, 1834, *Donelson MSS,* LC.
12. Pamphlet in *VB MSS,* XIX.
13. *Debates,* XI (23 cong., 2 sess., 1834-35), 367-392, 418-439; Nathan Sargent, *Public Men and Events* (1875), I, 282-287; Bayard Tuckerson (ed.), *Diary of Philip Hone,* I, 133.
14. Parton, *op. cit.,* III, 580-582.
15. Richard E. Parker to Van Buren, Feb. 22, 1835, Taney to Van Buren, May 12, 1835, Benton to Van Buren, June 7, 1835, *VB MSS,* XXI; *Niles,* XLVIII (1835), 200.
16. *Niles,* XLVIII, 462-463.

17. Memorandum by Abel R. Corbin, *Corbin Papers*, MHS; MS copies of Strother challenge and reply of Strother's second, *VB MSS*, XXII; Thomas Hart Benton, Jr., to Nathaniel Benton, June 25, 1835, copy in *Benton MSS*.

18. *Debates*, XII (24 cong., 1 sess., 1835-36), 1064; Henry A. Wise, *Seven Decades of the Union* (1872), pp. 137, 141-142, 145.

19. *Debates*, XII, 106-111, 566-577, 592, 613, 1385-1396, 1512-1525, 1582.

20. *Ibid.*, pp. 1744-1745, 1763-1769, 1793-1846.

21. *Ibid.*, p. 1155.

22. *Ibid.*, pp. 85-87, 485, 487-488, 495-496, 499-531, 656-721, 726-788, 803-810. No one in the debate defended abolition.

23. *Ibid.*, pp. 1286-1287, 1414-1424, 1525-1537, 1759-1763, 1846-1848, 1915-1928.

XII. THE VINDICATOR

1. *Debates*, XIII (24 cong., 2 sess., 1836-37), 21-68, 578-617, 619-644, quotations, 610, 621.

2. *Ibid.*, pp. 872-892, 894-981.

3. *Ibid.*, pp. 382-416.

4. *Ibid.*, pp. 429-506, 564; Benton, I, 727-731; Bowers, *op. cit.*, pp. 465-466.

5. Bassett, V, 450.

6. Benton, I, 735-739.

XIII. THE DEFENDER

1. Public letter in *Niles*, LII (1837), 268; Benton to Ewing, Aug. 18, 1837, *Benton MSS*.

2. *Debates*, XIV (25 cong., 1 sess., 1837), 15-45.

3. *Ibid.*, pp. 105-269, 311-383, 496-511, 1685.

4. Blair to Jackson, Oct. 1, 1837, Bassett, V, 514.

5. *CG*, VI (25 cong., 2 sess., 1837-38), 416, appendix, 347-353.

6. *Ibid.*, pp. 55, 74, 80, 81, 96-99.

7. *Ibid.*, VII (26 cong., 1 sess., 1838-39), 40-44.

8. *Ibid.*, appendix, pp. 162-165; pp. 194, 235.

9. *Ibid.*, pp. 198, 212, 224-226, appendix, pp. 308-316.

10. Public letters in *Niles*, LVI (1839), 334-335, LVII (1840), 207.

11. *CG*, VIII (26 cong., 2 sess., 1839-1840), 96-98, 202-203.

12. *Ibid.*, appendix, pp. 116-124, 378-382, 425.

13. *Ibid.*, pp. 71-74, 164, 183, 203-204.

14. *Niles*, LIX (1841), 310.

XIV. THE DEMOCRAT

1. *CG*, IX (26 cong., 2 sess., 1840-41), 14, 90-91, appendix, 34-88.
2. *CG*, X (27 cong., 1 sess., 1841), 27-35, appendix, 129-130, 133.
3. *Ibid.*, pp. 337-340.
4. *Ibid.*, p. 379.
5. *Ibid.*, pp. 324-330, 342, 355-361, 364-366, 370-373, 387-388.
6. *Ibid.*, p. 129.
7. *Ibid.*, p. 515; Benton, II, 499-502.
8. Benton to Van Buren, April 14, June 3, June 8, 1842, *VB MSS;* Benton to Jackson, March 10, 1842, Blair to Jackson, March 31, Nov. 13, 1842, *Jackson MSS;* Benton, II, 399-403.
9. James McDowell, Jr., to his father, Dec. 18, 1841; cf. Phillips, *op. cit.;* Allan Nevins, *Frémont, Pathmarker of the West* (1939).
10. Family letters in *McDowell MSS,* Va. and Duke; press clippings, trial documents, and absurd Thomas pamphlet, Va.
11. *Ibid.*
12. Benton to James McDowell, Oct. 16, 1842 (P.S. by Elizabeth), Dec. 2, 1844, *McDowell MSS,* Duke.
13. Rockbridge County (Va.) Deed Book "Z," p. 446, cited in William N. Chambers Benton collection, MHS; numerous Benton letters to McDowell, 1842-46, *McDowell MSS,* Duke; Robert Taylor to James McDowell, Feb. 2, 1844, *ibid.*
14. *CG*, X, 104.

XV. THE PROPHET

1. In 1861 Lincoln, receiving only 39% of the popular vote, took office, pledged in his platform, campaign addresses, and inaugural, to defend slavery where it already existed and to enforce the fugitive slave laws. Until the secession, Congress and the Supreme Court rested firmly in conservative hands.
2. Numerous letters, 1842-43, in *VB* and *Jackson MSS; Niles,* LXIII (1842-43), 202, 214, 247, LXV (1843-44), 203; Levi Woodbury to Samuel Treat, May 12, 1843, *Judge Samuel Treat Papers,* MHS.
3. Official and private correspondence leading to the first Texas treaty in House Executive Document, 271, *Cong. Doc.,* no. 444 (28 cong., 1 sess., 1843-44, VI); detailed accounts in Jesse H. Reeves, *American Diplomacy Under Tyler and Polk* (1907), pp. 114-137, and Justin H. Smith, *The Annexation of Texas* (1911), pp. 76-99; cf. Marquis James, *The Raven* (1930), pp. 338-357; Donald Day and Harry H. Ullom

(eds.), *The Autobiography of Sam Houston* (1954), pp. 183, 186-187, 196, 200-202, 210-211.

4. Chauncey S. Boucher and Robert P. Brooks (eds.), "Correspondence Addressed to John C. Calhoun, 1837-1849," *Annual Report of the American Historical Association*, 1929, pp. 188, 191-192 (hereafter cited as *AHA*, 1929); J. Franklin Jameson (ed.), "Correspondence of John C. Calhoun," *ibid.* (1899), II, 555, 846-849, 871 (hereafter cited as *AHA*, 1899).

5. *AHA*, 1899, pp. 588-592, 935, 954-955; *AHA*, 1929, pp. 191-193, 237; Calhoun to J. R. Matthews, May 9, July 2, 1844, *Miscellaneous Calhoun MSS*, LC; cf. *The Globe*, Aug. 28, 1844; Smith, *Annexation*, pp. 204-213.

6. Benton, II, 581-596; George L. Rives, *The United States and Mexico* (1913), I, 467-476; Charles H. Ambler, *Thomas Ritchie* (1913), p. 244; the bonds were still an enormous source of pressure in 1850, Holman Hamilton, "Texas Bonds and Northern Profits: A Study in Compromise, Investment, and Lobby Influence,' *Mississippi Valley Historical Review*, XLIII (1957), 579-594.

7. Bassett, VI, 230, 255, 260, 264, 283-285.

8. Reeves, *op. cit.*, pp. 142-155; *Cong. Doc.*, No. 444, pp. 48-49; Calhoun to J. R. Matthews, July 2, May 9, 1844, *Misc. Calhoun MSS*, LC; Calhoun to Andrew J. Donelson, Jan. 9, 1845, *Donelson MSS*, LC; on Dec. 20, 1844, Duff Green assured Donelson there was "nothing to fear in Texas by deferring the question until next year."

9. *The Globe*, April 29, 1844; Bassett, VI, 293-294.

10. Clarence H. McClure, "Early Opposition to Thomas Hart Benton," *Missouri Historical Review*, X, 151-196.

11. *CG*, XIII (28 cong., 1 sess., 1843-44), appendix, 474-486, quotations, 485, 486.

12. McClure, *op. cit.*, p. 181; Bassett, VI, 296; Benton, II, 591-596.

13. *CG*, XIII, 653-657, 673, appendix, 568-576, 588-590, 607-611, quotation, 610; *National Intelligencer*, July 11, 1844; press reprints in *Niles*, LXVI (1844), 272, 295; Blair to Jackson, July 7, 1844, Bassett, VI, 299-302.

14. *Missouri Reporter*, Feb. 8, 1844; *National Intelligencer*, June 15, 22, 1844.

15. Clarence H. McClure, *Opposition in Missouri to Thomas Hart Benton* (1927), pp. 83-89; Shadrach Penn, *Letters to Thomas Hart Benton* (1843), MHS; Penn to Van Buren, Jan. 4, 1842, *VB MSS;* David Atchison to Governor Thomas Reynolds, April 6, 1843, Benton to Reynolds, Nov. 10, 1843, *Reynolds MSS*, MHS; Montgomery Blair to Andrew Jackson, Nov. 20, 1843, March 16, 1844, *Jackson MSS;* letters

of March 19, 20, May 23, June 12, 1844, to M. M. Marmaduke, in *Dr. John S. Sappington MSS*, MHS; Thos. Dunn English, *Aurora* Office, New York, to Emmanuel Fisher, editor of the *Republican* (Cleveland), July 22, 1844, MS copy of original sent by Blair to Jackson, *Jackson MSS;* Blair to Van Buren, April 9, 1847, *VB MSS.*

16. *Jefferson Enquirer,* Aug. 1, Nov. 7, 1844; David Atchison to M. M. Marmaduke, Oct. 5, 1844, *Sappington MSS;* McClure, *Opposition in Missouri,* pp. 85-96.

17. Bassett, VI, 299, 304-305, 309, 313-314, 319-320, 377; Blair to Van Buren, May 30, Sept. 13, 1844, *VB MSS; AHA,* 1899, pp. 613, 629, 630, 968.

18. Bassett, VI, 325, 331-332, 338, 342, 345-351, 354-355; 366; Benton to Donelson, Jan. 10, 1845, *Donelson MSS; AHA,* 1899, pp. 1011-1012.

19. *CG,* XIV (28 cong., 2 sess., 1844-45), 154-155; *Missouri Reporter,* Feb. 3, 6, 1845.

20. *CG,* XIV, 16-17, 192-194, 244-245, 343-345, 358-363; Benton to McDowell, Feb. 13, 1845, *McDowell MSS,* Duke; Smith, *Annexation,* pp. 343-345; Bassett, VI, 374, 378-379.

21. Benton, II, 634-638; Smith, *Annexation,* pp. 348-350 (footnotes); Eugene I. McCormac, *James K. Polk: A Political Biography* (1922), pp. 315-317; Benjamin Tappan to the *New York Evening Post,* July 28, 1848; John A. Dix to Van Buren, Feb. 18, 1845, William Haywood, Jr., to Van Buren, May 30, 1849, *VB MSS.*

XVI. THE STATESMAN

1. Feb. 14, 1845, *Polk MSS,* LC.

2. Jackson to Polk, Dec. 16, 1844, *Polk MSS; AHA,* 1899, pp. 1039, 1054.

3. Milo M. Quaife (ed.), *The Diary of James K. Polk During His Presidency, 1845 to 1849* (1910), I, 55-56, 68-72. (Hereafter cited as *Polk Diary.)*

4. *Ibid.,* pp. 116-118.

5. *Niles,* LXIX (1845-46), 166-169; *Polk Diary,* I, 140-141; Benton to Van Buren, Dec. 15, 1845, Blair to Van Buren, Jan. 18, 1846, *VB MSS;* Benton to McDowell, Feb. 1, 1846, *McDowell MSS,* Duke.

6. *CG,* XV (29 cong., 1 sess., 1845-46), 253-255, 388-394, 401-405; *Niles,* LXIX, 341; *Polk Diary,* I, 246, 250, 254-255, 278-279, 345.

7. *CG,* XV, 581-583, 587-591.

8. *Polk Diary,* I, 326.

9. *Ibid.,* pp. 375, 390.

10. *CG,* XV, 784-785, 787-804; *Polk Diary,* I, 392.

11. *CG,* XV, 851-855, 857-862, 913-920, quotation, 895.

12. *Ibid.*, pp. 866, 1015-1016, 1025-1026.

13. *Polk Diary,* I, 408-409, 411, II, 189.

14. *Ibid.,* I, 472; Sister Mary Loyola, "American Occupation of New Mexico," *New Mexico Historical Review,* XIV, 162; cf. Bernard DeVoto, *The Year of Decision* (1943), pp. 250-251, 263-264, 269-271.

15. *Polk Diary,* I, 437-440, 481; Nevins, *op. cit.,* pp. 239-250; DeVoto, *op. cit.,* pp. 197-201; Justin H. Smith, *The War with Mexico* (1919), I, 331-346; Frémont, *Memoirs,* I, 489.

16. *Polk Diary,* II, 5, 16; original MS in Benton's handwriting, with Polk's handwritten comments, additions, and endorsement, *Polk MSS.*

17. Nevins, *op. cit.,* p. 199.

18. *CG,* XV, 1056, 1142, 1150, 1158, 1219-1220, appendix, 698-702; Gideon Welles to Van Buren, July 28, 1846, *VB MSS; Polk Diary,* II, 68-69.

19. *Polk Diary,* II, 221-223, 227-228.

20. *Ibid.,* pp. 236-240, 243, 259.

21. *Ibid.,* pp. 262, 268-269; Blair to Van Buren, Dec. 26, 1846, *VB MSS.*

22. *Polk Diary,* II, 224-230; Benton, II, 678-679; *CG,* XVI (29 cong., 2 sess., 1846-47), 246-247; parts of Benton speech in *Niles,* LXXII (1847), 222-223.

23. *AHA,* 1899, pp. 714, 717.

24. *Polk Diary,* II, 308-310.

25. *CG,* XVI, 160, 175-177, 187, 246-247.

26. *Ibid.,* pp. 356-359, 453-455, 494-501, quotation, 498.

27. *Polk Diary,* II, 353-356; *CG,* XVI, 527, 573; *Cong. Doc.,* No. 492, pp. 265, 270, 277, 279, 287; *The Daily Union,* March 11, 1847.

28. *Polk Diary,* II, 406, 408-418.

29. *National Intelligencer,* March 9, 13, 1847; *Polk Diary,* II, 419-420, 424, 444-445.

30. *Niles,* LXXII (1847), 222-223, 225.

31. *Polk Diary,* III, 52, 61-62, 120-121, 197-198, 228-230, 327-338; Benton, II, 715-719; Nevins, *op. cit.,* pp. 305-342; *CG,* XVII (30 cong., 1 sess., 1847-48), appendix, 977-1040; Blair to Van Buren, Jan. 23, 1847, *VB MSS.*

32. Reeves, *op. cit.,* pp. 312-326; McCormac, *op. cit.,* pp. 487-537; Smith, *War with Mexico,* II, 127-139; Winfield Scott, *Memoirs of Lieut.-General Scott, LL.D.* (1864), pp. 576-580.

33. Jan. 26, 1847, *VB MSS.*

34. Blair to Van Buren, April 13, 1852, *VB MSS;* Father P. J. De Smet to Benton, May 11, 1851, copy in *Benton MSS;* family letters in *McDowell MSS,* Duke.

35. Benton to Frémont, Oct. 14, 1847, *California Historical Quarterly,* XIII, 154.

XVII. THE REALIST

1. Benton letter, *Niles,* LXXII (1847), 148; *CG,* XVII, 804-805, appendix, 684-686, quotation, 686.
2. *CG,* XVII, 1074.
3. *Ibid.,* pp. 1075, 1074-1078.
4. *Ibid.,* p. 1078.
5. Blair to Van Buren, Aug. 13, 14, 1848, *VB MSS.*
6. *Niles,* LXXIII (1848), 402-406; Benton to Van Buren, May 29, 1848, *VB MSS; New York Daily Tribune,* May 27, June 5, 1848; *Daily Union,* June 3, 8, 1848.
7. Gideon Welles to Van Buren, June 5, 1848, Azariah Flagg to Van Buren, June 19, 1848, *VB MSS.*
8. Reports from newspapers along the route reprinted in *Daily Union,* June 9, 10, 11, 13, 15, 1848; *New York Daily Tribune,* June 9, 13, 1848.
9. Samuel Treat notation on letter from Cass, July 3, 1848, *Treat MSS;* insinuations in *Missouri Republican* denied in *St. Louis Union,* June 30, 1848; Benton, II, 10-11; Benton to David L. Lagre, Oct. 6, 1848, microfilm copy in Chambers collection, MHS; Blair to Van Buren, Nov. 16, 1848, *VB MSS;* cf. Benton to Cass, June (?), 1848, July 10, 1848, photostats in Chambers collection, MHS.

XVIII. PROPHET REJECTED

1. McClure, *Opposition in Missouri;* P. O. Ray, "The Retirement of Thomas H. Benton from the Senate and Its Significance," *Missouri Historical Review,* II, 1-14; *St. Louis Union,* Aug. 17, 1848; *CG,* XIX (31 cong., 1 sess., 1849-50), 97-98.
2. Blair to Van Buren, Dec. 30, 1848, Jan. 6, 1849, *VB MSS.*
3. Benton to Buchanan, Aug. 20, 1848, *Buchanan MSS,* Pennsylvania Historical Society; Benton to people of California and New Mexico, Aug. 27, 1848, *Niles,* LXXIV (1848), 244-245.
4. *CG,* XVIII (30 cong., 2 sess., 1848-49), 34-37; Dyer, *op. cit.,* pp. 204-205.
5. *CG,* XVIII, 438, 448-454, 494-502; Senate Executive Doc. 1, *Cong. Doc.,* No. 549, 69-89; *Polk Diary,* IV, 320-330; Buchanan to Nathan Clifford, March 2, 1849, John B. Moore (ed.), *The Works of James Buchanan* (1909), VIII, 350-354.
6. *CG,* XVIII, 470-474; *Liberty* (Mo.) *Weekly Tribune,* May, 18, 1849.
7. *Niles,* LXXV (1849), 332.
8. *Ibid.,* pp. 390-393, 397-399; *Liberty Weekly Tribune,* June 8, 1849; *National Intelligencer,* June 21, 1849.

9. *Niles,* LXXV, 375; Blair to Van Buren, June 11, 1849, Azariah Flagg to Van Buren, July 9, 1849, *VB MSS; National Intelligencer,* June 28, July 21 (Calhoun Address), 1849; *AHA,* 1929, pp. 511-512, 517-518, 524-525.

10. *Republican* reprint in *Fredericksburg* (Va.) *News,* Oct. 12, 1849; *St. Louis Daily New Era,* July 21, 1849; *National Intelligencer,* June 23, 1849, lists pro- and anti-Benton papers.

11. Lowrey to M. M. Marmaduke, May 13, 1849, *Sappington MSS; Palmyra Whig* reprint in *Lexington* (Ky.) *Observer and Reporter,* July 14, 1849.

12. *Liberty Weekly Tribune,* June 29, Aug. 17, 24, 31, Nov. 10, 1849; *Lexington Observer and Reporter,* June 9, July 14, 1849; *Fredericksburg News,* Oct. 19, 1849; *Missouri Republican,* May 31, 1849; *Speech of the Hon. James H. Birch in Reply to Those of the Hon. Thomas H. Benton.* . . . (Jefferson City: 1849); *The* (Jefferson City, Mo.) *Metropolitan,* Nov. 6, Dec. 18, 1849; Flora Caldwell to Mrs. Mayer, Nov. 16, 1849, *Mayer MSS,* MHS.

13. Blair to Van Buren, Aug. 8, 1859, *VB MSS; Liberty Weekly Tribune,* June 29, July 6, Aug. 17, Sept. 14, 1849; *St. Louis Daily New Era,* July 19, 1849; *Lexington Observer and Reporter,* Sept. 12, 1849; *Fredericksburg News,* Oct. 12, 1849; Meigs, *op. cit.,* p. 456 (Meigs corresponded with many contemporaries) .

14. Pamphlet copy in *VB MSS;* Darby, *op. cit.,* pp. 182-183.

15. *AHA,* 1899, pp. 770, 1204-1205; *National Intelligencer,* Nov. 1, 1849; Calhoun to Samuel Treat, undated, *Treat MSS.*

16. Robert R. Russell, *Improvement of Communication with the Pacific Coast as an Issue in American Politics* (1948), pp. 47-48; Darby, *op. cit.,* p. 183.

17. *National Intelligencer,* Oct. 20, Nov. 3, 1849; Samuel Treat, a Benton enemy, was carried away by the speech and complained years later that the pose on the Benton statue in St. Louis failed to do justice to either speaker or occasion, description in *Treat MSS.*

18. *Jefferson Enquirer,* April 6, May 4, 1850; McClure, *Opposition in Missouri,* pp. 201-202.

19. Oct. 12, 1849.

20. *National Intelligencer,* June 23, 1849; *Liberty Weekly Tribune,* June 1, 1849 (reprint from *N. Y. Tribune*), July 27, 1849.

XIX. VALEDICTORY FOR GIANTS

1. *The Republic,* reprinted in *Lexington Observer and Reporter,* Aug. 4, 1849.

2. Dyer, *op. cit.*, pp. 128, 139, 278; Henry S. Foote, *Casket of Reminiscences* (1880), pp. 78-82, 187-188; Greenwood, *op. cit.*, pp. 302-303, 316; *AHA*, 1899, pp. 1204-1205.

3. *CG*, XIX, 97-98.

4. W. C. Binkley, "The Question of Texas Jurisdiction in New Mexico Under the United States, 1848-1850," *The Southwestern Historical Quarterly*, XXVI, 1-38; F. S. Donnell, "When Texas Owned New Mexico to the Rio Grande," *New Mexico Historical Review*, VIII, 65-75; Loomis M. Ganaway, "New Mexico and the Sectional Controversy, 1846-1861," *ibid.*, XVIII, 113-147; *Santa Fe Republican*, April 7, 1849, reprint in *National Intelligencer*, May 31, 1849.

5. *CG*, XIX, 355-356, 712.

6. *Ibid.*, pp. 365-368, 371-373, 395-398, 400-401, quotation, 395.

7. *The Republic*, Feb. 26, March 12, 22, 1850.

8. *CG*, XIX, pp. 451-455.

9. *Ibid.*, pp. 463-464; *The Republic*, March 12, 1850; *Jefferson Enquirer*, April 6, 1850; John Wentworth, *Congressional Reminiscences* (1882), pp. 23-24.

10. *CG*, XIX, 656-662.

11. *Ibid.*, pp. 602-604, 609, 610, 762-764.

12. *Ibid.*, pp. 1480-1481; Blair to Van Buren, April 27, 1850, *VB MSS*.

13. *Ibid.*, appendix, pp. 676-684, quotation, 681.

14. *Ibid.*, appendix, pp. 859-863, 865-866.

15. Greenwood, *op. cit.*, pp. 314-315.

16. *Ibid.*, pp. 304, 323; Blair to Van Buren, July 15, 16, 1850, *VB MSS;* *CG*, XIX, 1380-1383, appendix, 1261-1266.

17. *CG*, XIX, appendix, 1420-1485; cf. Allan Nevins, *Ordeal of the Union* (1947), p. 340.

18. *CG*, XIX, appendix, pp. 1555, 1560-1565, 1573, 1589, 1660, 1829.

19. *Jefferson Enquirer*, Oct. 2, Nov. 16, 1850; McClure, *Opposition in Missouri*, pp. 210-213.

20. *CG*, XXIII (31 cong., 2 sess., 1850-51), 123, 158-160, 165, 317, 349-351, 360-364, 373-378, 387-391, 407-408, 451, appendix, 48-66.

21. *Ibid.*, pp. 19, 345, 451, appendix, 138-143.

22. *Ibid.*, pp. 541-544, appendix, 173-179.

XX. RETURN OF THE BUFFALO

1. Blair to Van Buren, Jan. 26, Feb. 6, May 14, 1851, Preston King to John Van Buren, Feb. 25, 1851, *VB MSS*.

2. Benton to Dix, May 15, 1851, to Van Buren, June 16, 1851, Blair to Van Buren, June 17, 1851, *VB MSS*.

3. Blair to Van Buren, March 10, June 17, Sept. 14, 1851, John Van Buren to Martin Van Buren, March 4, 1851, *VB MSS;* R. E. to Woodbury, June 23, 1851, Benton to Montgomery Blair, Aug. 29, 1851, *Blair MSS,* LC.
4. Benton to Van Buren, Oct. 22, 1851, *VB MSS.*
5. Blair to Van Buren, Dec. 21, 1851, *VB MSS.*
6. Blair to Van Buren, Jan. 11, 1852, Benton to Van Buren, Jan. 11, 1852, Van Buren to Blair, Jan. 16, 1852, *VB MSS.*
7. Blair to Van Buren, Feb. 4, 22, 1852, *VB MSS.*
8. Father P. J. De Smet to Benton, May 11, April 1, 1852, Benton to Father De Smet, April 1, 1852, copies in *Benton MSS;* Blair to Van Buren, April 3, 1852, *VB MSS.*
9. Pamphlet of Bogy speech, MHS; *Liberty Weekly Tribune,* Oct. 1, 1852.
10. *New Orleans Crescent,* Aug. 13, 1852, reprint in *Liberty Weekly Tribune,* Sept. 3, 1852; *Missouri Republican,* Aug. 5, 1852.
11. Blair to Van Buren, Sept. 30, 1852, *VB MSS;* letters and reprints in *Jefferson Enquirer,* Oct. 9, 16, 1852; *Liberty Weekly Tribune,* Oct. 15, 1852.
12. Blair to Van Buren, Dec. 18, 1852, Benton to Van Buren, Jan. 16, 1853, *VB MSS;* Benton to ?, Feb. 3, 1853, *Benton MSS.*
13. Thomas L. Price to M. M. Marmaduke, Oct. 17, 1853, *Sappington MSS;* Blair to Van Buren, April 1, 1853, *VB MSS;* Benton to Montgomery Blair, April 30, 1853, *Blair MSS.*
14. Benton-Davis letters, *Liberty Weekly Tribune,* April 22, 1853; Montgomery Blair to his wife, May 3, 1854, *Blair MSS.*
15. *Jefferson Enquirer,* May 28, 1853; James C. Malin, *The Nebraska Question, 1852-1854* (1953), pp. 126-134.
16. Malin, *op. cit.,* pp. 132-134; *Liberty Weekly Tribune,* Aug. 5, 1853; *Jefferson Enquirer,* June 30, July 7, July 16, Aug. 13, Aug. 30, Oct. 15, Oct. 29, 1853; Blair to Van Buren, Nov. 27, 1853, *VB MSS.*
17. Roy F. Nichols, "The Nebraska Act: A Century of Historiography," *Mississippi Valley Historical Review,* XLIII (1956), 187-212; Malin, *op. cit.,* pp. 300-308; Malin, "The Motives of Stephen A. Douglas in the Organization of Nebraska Territory . . . ," *Kansas Historical Quarterly,* XIX, 321-353.
18. Benton to Bedford Brown, Jan. 30, 1854, *Brown MSS,* Duke; *CG,* XXVIII (33 cong., 1 sess., 1853-54), 986-989, appendix, 557-561.
19. *CG,* XXVIII, 1232.
20. *Ibid.,* appendix, pp. 1031-1037.
21. Benton to ?, May 29, 1854, microfilm in Chambers collection, MHS.
22. *Liberty Weekly Tribune,* May 5, May 26, 1854; *Jefferson Enquirer,* July 22, 1854.

23. Jessie to Dr. Robertson, March 3, 1856, *Benton MSS.*
24. *New York Herald,* Dec. 26, 1854.
25. *CG,* XXX (33 cong., 2 sess., 1854-55), 79-80; *Liberty Weekly Tribune,* Jan. 12, 1855.
26. *CG,* XXX, 335, 475-478, 483, appendix, 73-82; cf. Benton to Augustus C. Dodge, "Tuesday Night, 1853," photostat in *Benton MSS.*
27. *CG,* XXX, 947-948.
28. *Ibid.,* p. 974; Frémont, *Souvenirs,* pp. 104-106.
29. *CG,* XXX, 996-998.
30. *Ibid.,* appendix, 334-341.
31. *Ibid.,* p. 1190.

XXI. THE PEACEMAKER

1. *Liberty Weekly Tribune,* April 3, 1856.
2. Sept. 16, 1855, copy in Chambers collection, MHS.
3. *Jefferson Enquirer,* June 3, 1856; *Liberty Weekly Tribune,* June 13, 1856.
4. *Liberty Weekly Tribune,* May 30, June 13, 20, 27, July 4, 1856; *Jefferson Enquirer,* June 18, 21, 28, 30, July 4, 1856; Henry D. Gilpin to Van Buren, July 17, 1856, *VB MSS; Missouri Historical Review,* XXXIII, 497-498.
5. Blair to Van Buren, Sept. 22, 1856, *VB MSS.*
6. *Jefferson Enquirer,* Nov. 8, 1856.
7. *Ibid.;* cf. Samuel Simmons to Montgomery Blair, Nov. 18, 1856, *Blair MSS.*
8. Phillips, *op. cit.,* p. 214.
9. Benton to Lyman Draper, Sept. 1, 1856, *Draper Correspondence,* Wisconsin Historical Society; Benton to Jared Sparks, Jan. 1, 1857, to Mr. Calef (undated), copies in Chamber collection, MHS; Benton to Van Buren, Feb. 17, 1857, *VB MSS.*
10. Benton public letter, Feb. 23, 1857, copy in *Benton MSS; Liberty Weekly Tribune,* Feb. 4, 1859; *Jefferson Enquirer,* May 16, 23, 1857.
11. *Jefferson Enquirer,* June 27, 1857.
12. Benton to ?, Jan. 3, 1858, photostat, MHS.
13. Blair to Van Buren, April 2, 1858, *VB MSS.*
14. Blair to Van Buren, April 12, 1857, *VB MSS;* Lewis Cass memorandum, photostat, MHS; Blair letters in *New York Daily Tribune,* May 25, 1858; William Carey Jones, *Col. Benton and His Contemporaries,* pamphlet, (May 17, 1858), *VB MSS.*
15. Blair to Van Buren, April 12, 1858, *VB MSS.*
16. *Liberty Weekly Tribune,* April 23, 1858; *Jefferson Enquirer,* April 24, 1858.

INDEX

98; opposes Gadsden Purchase, 299; 1854 defeat, 302-03; opposes New England Emigrant Aid Society, 304-05; opposes railroad and telegraph subsidies, 305-06; Jackson sword oration, 306-07; home burns, 307; opposes military land certificates, 307-08; *Abridgment of Debates,* 311-12, 318, 323-24; opposes Frémont, 312-16; defeated for governorship, 313-14; last Missouri speech, 315-16; opposes use of name in emancipation resolution debate, 317; New England tour, 317; train wreck, 318; *Examination* of Dred Scott decision, 319-21; final illness and death, 322-25

Biddle, Nicholas, 117-18, 126-27; panic of 1834, 147-51

Biddle-Pettis duel, 59, 124

Birch, James H., 243; libel suit vs Benton, 251

Birney, James G., 202

Bissell, W. H., 266

Blair, Francis Preston, 126, 132, 147, 149, 169, 202, 204, 218, 238, 277, 284, 286, 323-24; friendship for Benton, 122-23; wager on 1844 election, 201; peacemaker between Jackson and Benton, 201; loses editorship, 207; a founder of Republican Party, 312

Blair, Francis Preston, Jr. (Frank), 259, 313, 317

Blair, Montgomery, 171

"Bleeding Kansas," 312

Bloody Island, 59

Boileau, Gauldrée de, marries Susan Benton, 309

Boston *Daily Bee,* 289

Brant, Henry, 182

Brown, Gratz, 317

Bryant, William Cullen, 312

Buchanan, James, 161, 171, 208, 215, 219, 244, 313-14, 316, 323

Buckner, Alexander, 124, 146

Buffalo *Republic,* 293

Burr, Aaron, 36

Butler, Andrew P., 236-37, 265

Butler, Benjamin F. (New York), 239

Butler, William, 223

Cabanné, John P., 56, 66, 70

Calhoun, John C., 13, 121, 148-50, 164, 177, 181, 207, 216, 219, 231, 245; personal characteristics, 112-13; break with Jackson, 113-14; nullification, 142-46; 1835 quarrel with Benton, 152-54; opposes petitions and incendiary publications, 158-59; Texas (1836), 160; rejoins Democrats, 168; quarrel with Clay, 173; role in Texas issue, 189-91, 193-97; British letter, 193-94; debates with Benton, 221-22; Oregon debate, 233-36; Southern Address, 245; answers Benton, 249-50; debates of 1850, 261-63, 267-69; death, 269

California, U.S. conquest, 213-14

Campbell, George, 25

Campbell, Patrick, 25-26

Carr, William C., 56

Carroll, William, 44-45, 48

Carson, Kit, 182, 226

Cass, Lewis, 239-41, 276, 323

Catholic chaplains in Mexican War, 213

Chambers, Talbot, 82

Chapultepec, Battle of, 228

Charless, Joseph, 67

Cherokee Indians, 142

Cherry Grove Plantation, 135-37

Cherry, William, 21

Cholera epidemic (1833), 146

Chouteau, Auguste, 53, 56, 66, **70**

Chouteau, Auguste Pierre, 66

Chouteau, Jean Pierre, 66

Chouteau, Pierre, 70

Chouteau, Pierre, Jr., 66, 185

Clark, William, 54, 56, 66

Clay, Henry, 13, 101, 104, 164, **168,** 177, 202, 254, 266, 281-83; election of 1824, 94-95; Randolph duel, 96; political ideas, 106-07; distribution policy, 108; bank advocate, 126, 128, 148-50; nullification crisis, 144-46; quarrel with Calhoun, 173; resigns from Senate, 180; Texas position, 194; son killed in war, 215; compromise of 1850, 261-62, 264-66, 272-73, 275-78; reaction to *Thirty Years' View,* 286

Clayton, A. S., 125

Clayton, John, 234

Clemens, Jeremiah, 266

Clemson, Colonel Eli, 63

Coffee, John, 37, 47